RENEWALS 458-4574.

DATE DUE

GAYLORD			PRINTED IN U.S.A.

The Way That Lives in the Heart

Chinese Popular Religion and
Spirit Mediums in Penang, Malaysia

JEAN DeBERNARDI

The Way That Lives in the Heart

Chinese Popular Religion and

Spirit Mediums in Penang, Malaysia

STANFORD UNIVERSITY PRESS

Stanford, California   2006

Stanford University Press
Stanford, California
© 2006 by the Board of Trustees of the
Leland Stanford Junior University

Library of Congress Cataloging-in-Publication Data

DeBernardi, Jean Elizabeth.
  The way that lives in the heart : Chinese popular religion and
spirit mediums in Penang, Malaysia / [Jean DeBernardi].
     p.   cm.
  Includes bibliographical references and index.
  ISBN 0-8047-5292-3 (alk. paper)
  1. Pinang—Religious life and customs.   2. Chinese—Pinang—
Rites and ceremonies.   3. Chinese—Malaysia—Rites and
ceremonies.   I. Title.
BL2080.D43 2006
299.5′1095951—dc22

                                        2005031346

Printed in the United States of America
Original Printing 2006
Last figure below indicates year of this printing:
15   14   13   12   11   10   09   08   07   06

Typeset at TechBooks, New Delhi, in 10/12.5 Minion

Contents

Maps, Figures, and Table

Maps

Figures

Table

Preface

WHEN I BEGAN to study Chinese popular religious culture in Penang, I did not intend to make spirit mediums a particular focus, nor was I drawn to them. I could not, however, avoid them. My friends took me to see spirit mediums who performed in an abandoned garden, to family séances in their homes, to out-of-the way temples in remote villages, and to urban temples that celebrated enormous festivals. In the afternoon or evening, a short walk from my house would bring me to small temples where I could visit with the Monkey God, the Third Prince, the Vagabond Buddha, the Crippled Immortal, and the Wealth God as they possessed their spirit mediums, and again to roadside shrines that invoked local spirits residing in trees and rocks.

Spirit mediums in trance perform impressive self-mortifying feats during temple festivals, and use language poetically in their day-to-day healing consultations – lures for an anthropologist trained in symbolic and interpretive traditions. Claude Lévi-Strauss explained the shaman-healer's performance as a form of folk psychoanalysis, but as a novice researcher I questioned how tissue paper charms, talismans, and luck-changing rituals could possibly ameliorate a client's hardships. And when I sought explanations for their practices, spirit mediums often answered my questions evasively, further dampening my interest. Asked, for example, about a ritual in which seven burning oil lamps stood in front of a temple, a spirit medium responded offhandedly: "Oh, that's just something that I learned in Taiwan." Asked about the deities, more than one person answered with a faint smile: "That's something that you should ask someone old, really old, like two hundred years old!" But Chinese often said, "If you ask [the gods], there will be a reply," and one day a committee member for a major downtown temple took me to meet a spirit medium whom he claimed could help me in my work.

As usual, I stood to the side and listened while the possessed medium counseled a client. This time, however, the committee member urged me to ask the god-in-his-medium a question. I moved to the side of the altar and asked, "Right now I am doing research on Chinese religion. Will I be able to write a book?" He not only predicted success, but to my surprise began to lecture me on self-cultivation and the Dao. I realized that I had been mistaken in seeking to interview the spirit mediums when it was their gods who were the experts in spiritual matters. With the temple as backdrop, in the personality of a Chinese god, and with the authority and dignity conferred by that status, the spirit medium could lecture effectively on these arcane matters. So enlightened, I transformed my approach to my research, and became the student to several spirit mediums/gods.

I have formally interviewed twenty-two practicing spirit mediums at eighteen Penang temples – three women and nineteen men. Most of these spirit mediums were Hokkien speakers, but that number includes two Cantonese, three Hakka (a father and his two sons), and one Teochiu. I interviewed most of these people in the front room of private homes, asking about how they came to become spirit mediums, about the experience of trance, and about their patron deity's story. I also have interviewed six possessed spirit mediums – of course from their perspective, I interviewed the gods themselves.

But I also have talked to many other people in both Penang and more recently Singapore – temple committee members, spirit mediums' clients, research assistants, the families whose homes I shared, friends and neighbors – and listened to their stories and interpretations. In my study of Christianity in Singapore and Malaysia, I have gained valuable insight into popular religious culture from Christian converts who maintain critical but also analytical perspectives on those practices.

Most of these individuals discussed popular religious culture with me in response to my questions and evident curiosity, often in the context of quasiformal interviews that I both taped and recorded in a notebook. Bourdieu has critiqued the anthropologist's use of "instruments of objectification" such as genealogies, maps, diagrams, and even mere transcription into writing as constructs that destroy the logic of practice in the process of seeking to understand it (Bourdieu 1990 [1980]: 11). Too often (he further concludes) the anthropologist confuses the interviewees' overly coherent synoptic accounts – which after all they produced to teach the struggling anthropologist – with a rule book local people use to guide their everyday practices.

Undoubtedly many of the stories, symbolic exegeses, and moral teachings that I discuss in this monograph were the product of the dialog of fieldwork. But the stories that I elicited in interviews were very like those that my landlady and her friends exchanged in the kitchen on an almost daily basis. Although my questioning about the meaning of ritual symbols undoubtedly prompted some people to greater self-consciousness, often I simply entered into an ongoing conversation. Spirit mediums in particular often spoke fluently and at length on occult matters, clearly enjoying the opportunity to share stories that had been retold many times, and they deflected the topic away from subjects that did not interest them, including the histories of the gods that I sought with such enthusiasm.

I had studied Mandarin Chinese with Professor George Chao at the University of Chicago prior to beginning research in Penang, and decided on my arrival to study Hokkien, which is the *lingua franca* spoken by most Chinese. With the help of Ch'ng Oon Hooi and my second landlady, Tan Gaik Suan, I developed a good passive understanding of Hokkien, and a basic speaking ability. I also developed a file-card lexicon of Penang Hokkien vocabulary with around 2,800 entries, a time-consuming but useful undertaking. Whenever possible I conducted interviews in Hokkien, and I usually transcribed those interviews with the assistance of research assistants. I translated many of the written texts that I collected in Penang (invocations, scriptures, divination charms, and poems) with the assistance of Dr. Wu Xu. The final responsibility for any errors of transcription or translation is mine.

In 1991, I embarked on archival research with the intention of returning to my ethnographic research materials – including much that I did not incorporate in my doctoral thesis – with greater depth of insight. That research resulted in a very long monograph that I finally divided in two. *Rites of Belonging: Memory, Modernity, and Identity in a Malaysian Chinese Community* (2004) examines Chinese popular religious culture under colonial rule and in the contemporary period, focusing on the role of religion in reinforcing power, claiming social honor, and strengthening ethnic solidarity. This monograph continues that project with an in-depth study of the everyday practices of popular religious culture and spirit mediums.

I published an earlier version of Chapter Five in 1996 as "Teachings of a Spirit Medium" in *Religions of China in Practice* (Lopez 1996), and it was reprinted in *Religions of Asia in Practice: An Anthology* (Lopez 2002). The description of my experience while meditating in Master Lim's temple has been published as a poem in *Reflections: The Anthropological Muse* (DeBernardi 1985). I thank Penguin Press for permission to use excerpts from several chapters from D. C. Lau's translation of the *Tao Te Ching*, published by Penguin Classics (Lao Tzu 1963).

A grant from the East Asian Studies Program at the University of Chicago supported a pilot study for a project on Penang Chinese folk religion in 1978, and a Fulbright-Hays Doctoral Dissertation Abroad Fellowship and a Training Grant from the National Institute of Mental Health funded a two-year period of research on "Ritual and Change in a Malaysian Chinese Community" in Penang, Malaysia, from 1979 to 1981. For funding for library and archival research on Chinese popular religious culture in Penang, I thank the Center for Southeast Asian Studies at Cornell University, the American Philosophical Society, and the Southeast Asian Council of the Association for Asian Studies. I have taken advantage of periods of ethnographic and archival research on Chinese Christian syncretism and pilgrimage to continue my investigation of popular religion and spirit mediumship, and I also thank the Social Science and Humanities Research Council of Canada (1997–2000), the Wenner-Gren Foundation for Anthropological Research (1997–1999), the Chiang Ching-kuo Foundation (2003–2005), and the University of Alberta's Faculty of Graduate Studies and Research, Faculty of Arts, and Department of Anthropology for research support.

The Social Science Faculty at Universiti Sains Malaysia in Penang (1979–1981), the Institute of Southeast Asian Studies in Singapore (1995, 1997, 1999), the Centre for Advanced Studies at the National University of Singapore (1999), and the Asia Research Institute (2004) extended the favor of institutional support during periods of research in Malaysia and Singapore. I would also like to thank the staffs at the National University of Singapore, the Institute of Southeast Asian Studies (ISEAS), the Singapore National Archive, the Singapore High Court, and the Brethren missionary agency Echoes of Service in Bath, England, for allowing me access to their library and archival collections.

I owe much to friends and contacts in Malaysia and Singapore who have assisted me in my research efforts over the years. In particular, I would like to thank Ch'ng Oon Hooi, Mr. and Mrs. Chuang Keng Hee and family, Robert Goh, Lee Say Lee, Lim Peng Eok, Low Boo Pheng, Low Boo Jin, Low Jiu Liat, Ong Seng Huat, Poh Eng Lip, Tan Gaik Suan, Wong Suchen, Victor Yue, and the many individuals who were willing to interrupt their busy lives to answer my questions about their society and culture, and to share materials with me. For their collegial support I owe special thanks to Lawrence B. Breitborde, Sharon Carstens, Janet Carsten, Paul Kratoska, Stephen Kent, Jeffrey Snodgrass, and Geoffrey Wade. Maire Anderson-McLean, Bernard Faure, D. J. Hatfield, Stephen Kent, Daniel Overmyer, Gary Seaman, Donald Sutton, and Yeoh Seng Guan read earlier versions of this manuscript, and their comments have been invaluable. For research assistance in Canada, I thank Carol Forster, Maire Anderson-McLean, and Wu Xu. Finally, I would like to offer special thanks to Mariel Bell, Kirsten Oster and John Feneron at Stanford University Press, and to Abby Ford, Darren Shaw, and Vageesh Sharma for their work in bringing this project to completion.

Although all those who participated in this study were fully informed of my intentions to publish my research findings in the form of a book, nonetheless I have followed the convention of changing the names of almost all of the individuals I interviewed. I also have altered or omitted the names and obscured the locations of most temples.

A Note on Romanization

L INGUISTS AT Xiamen University (PRC) have developed a new romanization of Hokkien using pinyin, the details of which I provide here for comparison (Xiamen Daxue 1982). Because this system has not been adopted in Southeast Asia, I use a more widely known standardized missionary romanization system in my transcriptions of Hokkien terms (Embree 1973, Chiang n.d.). In my citation of Hokkien terms and names, I provide both a romanized transcription and a standard Chinese (*putonghua*) equivalent in pinyin. In the reference matter appearing at the end of this book, I also append a glossary of Chinese characters arranged according to their pronunciation in standard Chinese.

Hokkien romanization (missionary and pinyin) and International Phonetic Alphabet (IPA) equivalents

Consonants			Vowels		
Missionary romanization	Pinyin	International Phonetic Alphabet	Missionary romanization	Pinyin	International Phonetic Alphabet
p	b	p	i	i	i
ph	p	p^h	i^n	ni	ī
b	bb	b	e	e	e
m	bb	m	e^n	ne	ē
t	d	t	a	a	a
th	t	t^h	a^n	na	ā
l	l	l	o·	oo	ɔ
n	l	n	o^n	noo	ɔ̄
k	g	k	o	o	o
kh	k	k^h	u	u	u
g	gg	g			
ng	gg	η			
h	h	h (initial)			
h	h	ʔ (final)			
s	s	s			
ch	z	ts (ʦ)			
chh	c	ts^h (č)			
j		dz			

Illusion, Temperament, Succession, Surface, Surprise, Reality, Subjectiveness – these are threads on the loom of time, these are the lords of life.

Ralph Waldo Emerson

Introduction

PENANG CHINESE SPIRIT mediums practice a deeply traditional art in a modern, capitalist economy and a nationalist state. Their temples – grandly deemed palaces or pavilions, but usually set in the front rooms of modest homes or apartments – overflow with the symbols of popular religious practice. On the altar stand statues of the temple's pantheon, facing a long red table on which worshippers place brass incense urns filled with fragrant sandalwood joss sticks, plates heaped with flowers and fruits, small triangular silk flags, and a carved wooden temple seal, vermilion ink, and a writing brush – three symbols of civil order. If warrior gods possesses the spirit mediums in this temple, then the altar also holds the five generals – five daggers, their handles miniature heads, set upright in a row – and a coiled hemp whip wound around its erect carved handle, a hooded cobra poised to strike. Spears, halberds, swords, and pikes – the divine warriors' exorcizing weapons – line the wall, together with a large black flag emblazoned in gold with a *yin-yang* symbol encircled by the eight trigrams symbol and a ring of constellations. These sacred objects translate Chinese cosmology into visual symbols replicated at hundreds of temples, and they immediately identify those temples as sites at which individuals may seek help from the gods in their combat with life's uncertainties and misfortunes.

Anthropologists conventionally note that Chinese who practice popular religious culture believe in gods, ghosts, and ancestors. But Chinese often describe their religious practices by saying that they worship deities (*angkong*), saints (*sin, shen*), or Buddhas (*hut or put, fo*).[1] In this eclectic pantheon we also find Daoist immortals (*sian, xian*) who cultivated themselves in order to escape the cycle of death and rebirth, the divine spirits of the founders of sectarian groups (*cho·su, zushi*), and Bodhisattvas (*pho·sat, pusa*) who turned back from nirvana

F I G . 1. Possessed by the spirit of the Emperor of the Dark Heavens, a spirit medium falls into trance at a major Nine Emperor Gods festival during the ninth lunar month. His assistants dress him in the god's stomacher and leggings, George Town, 1980. Photo: Jean DeBernardi in order to save humans from suffering. People hold that the gods, saints, and Bodhisattvas are immanent in their images, which Daoist priests or spirit mediums infuse with spirit in a ceremony to 'open the eyes' (*khui bakchiu, kai muzhu*) of the image. When people worship, they offer ritualized acts of respect, which may include a symbolic kowtow made with the hands, the burning of incense or candles, or the offering of food or drink. Gods, saints, and bodhisattvas also live in their stories: People know them through legend and works of popular fiction, but also through local miracle stories about events whose outcomes are ascribed to the intervention of the deity.

But traditional Penangites claim to know some gods far more intimately. Believers invite the gods, sometimes enticing them with expensive brandy and fine food, to descend to the human world and enter the spirit medium's body. The gods-in-their-mediums[2] feast on the offerings but also engage in dialog with their followers, who may seek their advice and wisdom. Each trance performance is both stereotyped and novel, allowing people to experience many of the gods of the Chinese pantheon as embodied individuals and to add new, deeply personal stories of their interactions with their saving deities to the gods' centuries-long biographies.

Chinese Spirit Mediums

Many scholars acknowledge the importance of spirit mediumship as the foundation of Chinese religious practice, but scholarship on this topic remains marginal by comparison with the study of Daoist liturgy or Confucian ideology. Although informed by China's literary tradition, the trance performance is oral, improvisational, and evanescent. However powerful a performance experience may have been, its only lingering trace may be stories that circulate in local neighborhoods for a few weeks and a growing or declining reputation for spiritual efficacy.

Like any dramatic display, the trance performance appeals to the audience along multiple channels: the melody of the invocation, the rhythm of the drums and gongs that call the god to descend, the poetic diction of the god's speech, the vivid reds and gold of the altar, and the scent of the sandalwood incense that burns throughout the performance, accompanying all but the most unexpected trance displays. Using the scholar's toolkit of textual exegesis and historical analysis, the sensorial experience of the trance performance is not easily captured. Indeed, we might conclude that ethnographic film has greater potential than the written word in conveying its meaning for participants. By contrast, the recitation of a Daoist scripture or Buddhist sutra is literary and fixed, and the scholar may easily view and study the written text apart from its performance.

Despite its relative neglect as a topic for scholarly analysis, the trance performance is a widespread and enduring performance frame. In the Southern Min-speaking communities of Fujian Province, Taiwan, and the Southeast Asian diaspora, we find local communities, sectarian movements, and entrepreneurial small temples employing spirit mediums who claim to have the ability to embody the spirits of divine beings. The beings imagined to possess spirit mediums are many, but they include ancestors, local protectors, the founders of religious sectarian groups, and military heroes.

As a prolegomena to a more in-depth consideration of the history, habitus, and ideology of the Chinese trance performance, allow me to delineate some of the common assumptions that inform the practice of spirit mediumship in contemporary Malaysia and Singapore. First and most basic, people assume that there are invisible spiritual entities that can be tempted to inhabit human bodies and supplicated for help. Whether people identify these spiritual entities as Chinese saints or local spirits imagined as having Malay or Indonesian ethnicity, they are considered to have similar powers to give health, prosperity, and protection to those who invite and host them. Chinese sometimes describe these spirits in light of a tripartite cosmos spatially ordered into upper, middle, and lower worlds. People inhabit the central world, and spirits the upper and lower worlds – heaven and hell. Hell – the 'earth-prison' (*diyu*) – and its ghostly population are very near the human life world: one spirit medium compared the relationship to the two sides of a sheet of paper. The trance performance enacts this tripartite cosmology as a drama of human-mediated control over gods and ghosts: the devotees sing invocations to invite the gods to descend from heaven, and the descended gods-in-their-mediums whip the ground to drive off ghosts.[3]

While the spirit medium waits to go into trance, those tending him (or her, more rarely) invite the spirits to descend. People first prepare the altar with offerings – flowers, food, and drink – then offer the ascending scented smoke of sandalwood for Chinese saints, or camphor incense for Malay *datuk* spirits. Typically, two men each beat a drum and a gong rhythmically while another sings an invocation to the god, inviting him or her to descend. Meanwhile, the spirit medium, often barefoot and bare-chested and wearing only yellow cotton drawstring pants, waits seated on an eight-trigram stool. Some speculate that the rhythmic drumming and gonging and fragrant incense smoke not only please the god but also assist the spirit medium to enter the trance state, sometimes with the further aid of wine or opium. The highly charged atmosphere also affects the clients and the audience, drawing them into a trance-like involvement with the performance.

FIG. 2. Taking his flag and incense, the god-in-his medium cracks his snake-handled whip in Doumu's temple to exorcize 'dirt' (ghosts) from the premises, George Town, 1980. Photo: Jean DeBernardi

When the god possesses the spirit medium, the spirit medium's personality or manner is transformed. This personal transformation includes speech habits, including the use of a 'deep' or archaic form of language that identifies the god as being from another time and place, and the use of verbal skills like writing poetry or teaching philosophy. The god also has unique preferences for foods and intoxicants, and often openly enjoys having the opportunity to drink wine or brandy, or to smoke a cigarette while he inhabits a human body. The gods' movements are distinctive, and military gods demonstrate their physical skills through public displays of martial arts. Their social position is supreme, and the gods enact that superiority by taking a central physical position in the space of the temple facing the main altar.

In exchange for their gifts, the god's followers request the amelioration of their condition and ask for remedies for a variety of life's problems. These problems may include any illness that does not respond to normal treatment; mental disturbances, including anxiety; the desire to check and mend luck before undertaking a risky venture, such as gambling, investment, or opening a new business; and the desire for prosperity. People ask the gods-in-their-mediums

FIG. 3. In a ceremony in which he may also 'wash' in boiling oil, the god-in-his medium blows liquid onto heated oil, George Town, 1980. Photo: Jean DeBernardi

FIG. 4. Before offering advice, the god-in-his-medium calculates a client's fate on his hands, Ayer Itam, 1980. Photo: Jean DeBernardi

to diagnose whether or not their afflictions are the result of a so-called spiritual collision with vindictive spirits and to prescribe ritual remedies.

Possessed spirit mediums also perform extraordinary (indeed, superhuman) feats that seem to transcend human endurance, either at periodic festivals or special processions organized in response to a community crisis like an epidemic or an economic downturn. At these 'hot and exciting' (*laujoah*, *renau*) events, people invoke their spiritually powerful (*sia*, *ling*), demon-expelling gods to banish calamity from their midst. When these heroic martial artist deities possess the spirit medium, the gods-in-their-mediums engage in a range of self-mortifying acts, including piercing the body with swords or spears, "washing" in boiling oil, walking across hot coals, beating the body with a sword or with a ball of nails, and crossing a sword bridge or climbing a sword ladder. (See DeBernardi 2004: 182–215.)[4]

Because it conjoins past and present, the dead and the living, trance is a vehicle for the transmission and construction of tradition, historical myth, social memory, and the embodiment of a traditional habitus in movement, gesture, and expression.[5] Penang Chinese popular religious culture transmits the memory of the Chinese origins of this immigrant community by representing a pure Chinese tradition in the enactment of Chinese gods. At the same time,

FIG. 5. Possessed by the Red Datuk, a Malay spirit, a Chinese spirit medium distributes fruit and blessings to children, Ayer Itam, 1981. Photo: Jean DeBernardi

when Chinese spirit mediums are possessed by local spirits, the spirit-in-the-medium speaks Malay, has different food preferences and taboos, and employs the *kris* rather than the seven-star sword as his magical exorcizing weapon. Consequently, the trance performance reminds them both of the boundaries that separate Chinese from ethnic others and of their immigrant roots in Malaysia.[6]

Exorcizing Polytheism: A Speculative Prehistory

As many have observed, the practices of Chinese popular religious culture are eclectic and locally diverse. Indeed, the four case studies that I present in Part II of this work demonstrate that Chinese spirit mediums are *bricoleurs* who propose unique doctrinal syntheses and who innovate in their ritual performances. Nonetheless, I seek to demonstrate in Part One of this study that these innovative practices are founded upon a widely shared cosmology and theodicy that Chinese transmit through ritual performance, but also through written and oral literature, including scriptures, invocations, divination charms, popular novels, folklore, opera, and puppet performances. This written and oral literature deeply connects spirit mediums to the literary traditions of Daoism, Buddhism, and Confucianism, and to the Chinese cultural world. At the same time, the embodied practice of spirit possession links spirit mediums to non-Chinese shamans throughout Southeast Asia, who share a logic of practice with Hokkien spirit mediums.

Dutch colonial translator and sinologist Jan Jakob Maria de Groot proposed that the *wu* exorcists mentioned in Zhou and Han dynasty texts were the ancient precursors of the spirit mediums and Daoist priests of late nineteenth-century Amoy, a city in Fujian province that was the embarkation point for many Chinese immigrants to Southeast Asia, including Penang. He also considered them to be members of the "general priesthood of Asian paganism":

[The ritual dances] suggest indeed that the wu were nothing else than what we might call the Chinese ramification of a large class of priests of both sexes which is distributed over several parts of Asia under a variety of names, such as shaman in Siberian lands, faquir or dervish in the Persian, bazir and balian, respectively of the male and the female sex, among the aborigines of Borneo; wewalen in Bali, bissoo in south-west Celebes, etc. (de Groot 1964 [1892–1910] Vol. 6: 1190).

Indeed, the practice of "exorcizing polytheism," as de Groot termed it, is pan-Asian. Many tribal peoples practice traditional forms of shamanism, including the hill tribes of northern mainland Southeast Asia, the 'original people' (*Orang Asli*) of the central Malay peninsula, and the interior and upland Austronesian groups of island Southeast Asia, in particular Sumatra, Sulawesi, and Borneo. But the practice of spirit possession (which some term shamanism) also is widespread in mainland, state-controlled societies adhering to major world religions like Islam and Buddhism (Winzeler 2004b: 834–7). Consequently, we might add to de Groot's list of *wu*-like priests the Malay *bomoh*, the *tau kawalia* of the Wana of Sulawesi, the *guru perdéwal-déwal* of Sumatra's Karo Batak, the Iban of Borneo's *manang*, the *maa khii* (literally, 'rider's horse') of northern Thailand, and the *tiam* of northeast Thailand, among many others.[7]

Many scholars describe these diverse Asian ritual practitioners as shamans, a term now widely used both in anthropological literature and in popular culture (Stutley 2003; Walter and Fridman 2004). Mircea Eliade broadly defined shamanism as an archaic technique of ecstasy involving certain magical specialties, including the ability to communicate with spirits. But Eliade distinguished between shamans, whose ritual practice typically involves the claim that the shaman's spirit has made an ascent to heaven or descended to the underworld, and spirit mediums, who invite the spirits to enter their bodies (Eliade 1964 [1951]: 4–7). In this study I use the term spirit medium rather than shaman, but I concur with Marcel Mauss, who observed "From both the individual's and society's point of view, sending out a soul or receiving one are two ways of looking at the same phenomenon" (Mauss 1972 [1950]: 39).

As a social practice and an improvisational art, Chinese spirit mediumship is a performance frame based on assumptions that Chinese share with many Southeast Asians and South Asians, including the notion that humans can invite spirits to share with them, and that in exchange the spirits will offer them comfort, assistance, and protection from a potentially malicious spirit world. Chinese living in the Malay Peninsula share this performance frame with many non-Chinese, including Malays, Hindus, and tribal peoples like the *orang asli*.[8] Indeed, throughout Southeast Asia we find ritual healing and the rescue of afflicted souls performed as a battle between invisible opponents and possessed spirit mediums, who aggressively wield weapons to drive off malevolent spirits (Appell and Appell 1993: 78; Winzeler 1993b: xvi).

The practice of Penang Chinese spirit mediumship is deeply inculturated into Hokkien Chinese religious culture, and some of its elements even may be unique to Southern Min peoples. We find, for example, that the leaders of diverse sectarian movements have taken up the practice of spirit mediumship as a strategy to divinize their authority structures and ethical codes, and that spirit mediums become the vehicle for sacred teachings derived from textual sources – some canonical, others deemed heterodox. Nonetheless, the similarities between these diverse forms of shamanic practice are so striking that I cannot refrain from commenting on these resemblances, which I speculate are the result both of a shared ancient prehistory and contact and intermarriage in recent centuries.

Contemporary Hokkien populations speak varieties of the Min language, which has two major dialects, Northern and Southern Min. The deepest substratum of the Min language derives from the Austroasiatic-speaking peoples known as the Yue or the Bai Yue, who lived in southeastern China in the pre-Han period. But over the course of 2,000 years, wave after wave of immigration from north China sinicized these populations (Norman 1988: 210). The process of sinicization had linguistic, cultural, social, and economic dimensions.

Chinese immigrants introduced the written language and China's prestigious literary traditions to the south, and Min speakers studied characters using the literary or 'deep' (*shen*) pronunciation of their topolect. Mastery of the Chinese writing system was a prerequisite for entry into the prestigious Chinese bureaucracy and the scholar-elite class; aspiring bureaucrats committed to memory the classics of Chinese culture and deeply internalized its Confucian ideology. Literacy and printing also allowed the popular didactic texts of Buddhism and Daoism to spread widely in southern China, and the practice of writing and distributing moral books (*shanshu*) was a way for the pious to make merit and improve their chance for a good rebirth. Popular books included moral texts like *Taishang's Treatise on Action and Retribution* (*Taishang Ganying Pian* N.d.), but also vernacular novels like the *Canonization of Deities* (*Fengshen Yanyi* N.d.)[9] and *Journey to the West* (Yu 1977–1983) that taught moral lessons and introduced the gods of the popular pantheon.

Although these literary sources have had enormous influence on the practice of spirit mediumship, nonetheless the religious culture of Fujian, the homeland of Penang's Hokkien-speaking community, is founded upon a syncretism of Chinese culture with autochthonous local cultures that have left persistent traces in contemporary Hokkien language and culture. The Min language retained an Austroasiatic substratum, as linguist Jerry Norman has demonstrated by identifying cognates in Austroasiatic languages in Southeast Asia and South Asia (Norman 1988: 18). Serendipitously for this study, he points specifically to the Min word for shaman, pronounced *taŋ* (*tong* or *kitong, jitong*) in the Xiamen dialect of Southern Min. These cognate terms include the Vietnamese *ʔdoŋ²*, which means "to shamanize, to communicate with spirits," the written Mon [Burma] *doŋ*, meaning 'to dance (as if) under daemonic possession,' a Santali [North India, Bangladesh, Nepal and Bhutan] word *dōŋ* meaning 'a dance connected with marriage,' and the Sora [India, Bangladesh, and Nepal] word *toŋ-*, meaning 'to dance' (Norman 1988: 19).

As archaeologists reconstruct it, two major waves of migration passed through the Fujian area in prehistoric times. These ancient populations spoke languages that are ancestral to two contemporary language families, Austroasiatic and Austronesian, and some linguists have hypothesized that these two language families further belong to a single phylum that German anthropologist Wilhelm Schmidt (1868–1954) named Austric.[10] Linguists and archaeologists propose that Austroasiatic languages may have originated in the Yangzi river valley and that the contemporary distribution of Austroasiatic languages in China, mainland Southeast Asia, and north India "reflects the diaspora of agricultural societies that began over 8,000 years ago" (Higham 2004: 51).

Peter Bellwood proposes that south China also was the ancestral homeland of Austronesian languages. According to Bellwood, the ancestors of contemporary

Austronesian speakers were seafaring peoples who migrated from south China to Taiwan, and from Taiwan to locations throughout Island Southeast Asia and the Pacific starting around 3,000 BC, reaching Madagascar in the mid-first-millennium AD (Bellwood and Glover 2004: 11; Bellwood 2004: 31).[11] As the Austronesian seafarers migrated throughout Southeast Asia and the Pacific Islands, these agricultural peoples encountered and colonized many long-resident hunting and gathering populations (Bellwood 2004: 35).

Genetic and linguistic evidence demonstrates that contemporary Austronesian populations are far more closely related to the Austronesian-speaking aboriginal tribes of Taiwan, whose ancestors probably inhabited Taiwan as early as 6,000–4,000 BC, than they are to Southern Min speakers, whose language and culture have an Austroasiatic substrate, and who speak a sinitic language.[12] Although Southern Min may not be linguistically related to Austronesian, nonetheless, southern Chinese spirit mediumship bears a strong family resemblance to some forms of shamanic practice found in the Austronesian-speaking world, which encompasses "half the world's circumference in tropical latitudes."

Based on a broad comparative study, Bellwood concludes that spirit animism and ancestor cults are so widespread and deeply rooted in Austronesian societies that they must be practices of great antiquity. In particular, he notes that "inspirational priests or mediums who are able to converse with spirits through trances," the dualism of male-sky and female-earth deities, concepts of supernatural and mystical power, and taboo are "virtually pan-Austronesian" (Bellwood 1997 [1985]: 153). In Hokkien popular religious culture we also find the practice of spirit mediumship, the concept of spirituous power (*sia*, which is not cognate with the equivalent Mandarin word, *ling*), the dualism of male-sky and female-earth deities, and the strict observance of ritual and social taboos, prohibitions that speakers of Penang Hokkien call *pantang*, using a term apparently borrowed from Malay.[13] The broad similarities between southern Chinese spirit possession and forms of shamanic practice in Southeast Asia are so striking, and their geographical extent so vast, that they undoubtedly are the consequence of a very ancient shared prehistory.

These similarities exist despite the historical influence of literate, universal religions in both China and Southeast Asia. Some authors write as if shamanism were an archaic survival from prehistorical times, its purest forms found in hunting and gathering societies. But shamanic practices are just as historical as any other human practice, even if the materials available to write a history of shamanism are few. Just as Daoism and Buddhism have influenced Chinese spirit possession, we must consider Southeast Asia's "long and complicated history of involvement with other major zones of Asian civilization," including the literate and ritual traditions of Hindu-Buddhism, Vietnam's sinicized Confucian culture, Islam, Theravada Buddhism, and Christianity (Winzeler 2004a: 799). Diverse forms of shamanism persist throughout the region among tribal peoples and in small villages remote from centers of political and religious authority (Winzeler 2004b).[14] But throughout South Asia, Southeast Asia, and Southeastern China, the practice of spirit possession also coexists (perhaps not always comfortably) with more highly institutionalized forms of religion, including Buddhism, Daoism, Hinduism, and Islam.

Although the deep resemblances between Chinese spirit mediumship and the diverse forms of shamanism found in Southeast Asia point to shared roots in prehistory, I propose that contact and intermarriage in recent centuries between Hokkien Chinese and Southeast Asian peoples renewed and reinforced resemblances between southern Chinese and Southeast Asian forms of shamanic practice. Allow me to offer a few speculative examples. Although the practice of climbing a sword ladder as a ritual of symbolic ascent may be found in many forms of shamanic practice both north and south (Eliade 1964 [1951]: 455), southern Chinese share with Indonesians, Malaysians, and Melanesians the practices of battling with invisible spirits to protect the well-being of human souls, and exorcising demonic spirits in a boat that people set to sea to send off the source of their misfortune (Eliade 1964 [1951]: 356).

In Kelantan ritual healing, for example, the *bomoh* sometimes prescribes the building of a 'royal audience hall' (*balai*), which Clive Kessler terms a 'ritual scapeboat.'[15] The ritual *balai* is a multi-tiered structure made of bamboo and decorated with pennants whose highest level is modeled on a royal palace, and whose lower levels are decorated with miniature humans and animals. At the conclusion of the ceremony, the ritual officiants place offerings upon the structure to attract the spirits, then take the *balai* to a remote place and abandon it, or set it adrift on a stream or on the sea (Kessler 1977: 300).

The practice of using a ritual scapeboat here and elsewhere in Southeast Asia resembles the southern Chinese ritual of expelling spirits to sea in what some call the 'king's boat' *(wangkang, wangchuan)*. Like the *balai,* the king's boat connotes royalty and royal authority, but Chinese use it not in individual healing rituals but rather in mass ceremonies of community exorcism designed to rid communities of epidemics. At the conclusion of the Nine Emperor Gods festival on the ninth day of the ninth lunar month, as many as 10,000 participants – including many possessed spirit mediums and their assistants – escort a small boat laden with offerings to the sea, sending the gods back to heaven to ensure harmony and long life for all (DeBernardi 2004: 200–203; see also Katz 1992, 1995).

We find intriguing traces of mutual influence in Chinese and Southeast Asian festival displays. The energetic Chinese lion dance, for example, bears a strong family resemblance to the Barong figure in the Rangda and Barong dance drama that Margaret Mead made famous in the film "Dance and Trance in Bali," and which Clifford Geertz used to exemplify the ritual performance that fuses ethos and worldview, a model both for and of religious belief (Geertz 1973: 114–18). The Balinese Baris dance, a trance-like performance in which warriors present their weapons in the temple, and dance a military display, is remarkably like the trance performance of Chinese martial deities, each of whom takes his typical weapon and performs on the temple grounds. Indeed, Renon Village in Bali performs a *Baris China* – the dance of a warrior who takes a Chinese sword and dances to monotonous Chinese-style music (*gong beri*). The warrior's black and white costume and sword are preserved in a temple dedicated to *Tuan*, or Lord, which also means 'foreigner,' and a Balinese author speculates that *Tuan* might be the deified spirit of a Chinese trader who introduced this distinctive Chinese performance to local residents (Anon. 2001).

Chinese immigrants also had extensive contact with the autochthonous peoples living in more remote areas of the Malay Peninsula and Borneo, where Chinese migrated to work in tin-mining ventures. In Borneo, some Chinese intermarried with tribal peoples, and Robert L. Winzeler speculates that the "competitive and innovative" character of spirit mediumship encouraged and promoted the "mutual exchange of ritual belief and practice" between Chinese and the tribal spirit mediums of Borneo (Winzeler 1993b: xviii–xix). These exchanges have left little documentary trace, and the web of influence is difficult to disentangle.

Trance performers commonly expand their repertoire to include the spirits of ethnic others whom members of their own in-group encounter in their everyday lives, amusing their audiences with mimetic interpretations of self and other.[16] Spirit mediums also commonly expand their repertoires to encompass the new. For example, the Temiars, nomadic hunter-horticulturalists who live in central Malaysia and who speak an Austroasiatic language, often compose healing songs whose words and melodies come to healers in their dreams. But their forest habitat is under attack from development, and their nomadic way of life is increasingly restricted. Their shamans now receive songs from the Chinese Lumber Camp Cave Spirit, whose dream image is a mini-skirted young Chinese woman, the Spirit of the Woman of the Marketplace, and the Canned Sardine Spirit, who calls for market goods (Roseman 2001). Far from being a living fossil from the archaic past, spirit mediumship and shamanism world-wide are engaged in an ongoing dialog with modernity.[17]

Southern Min Communities in Southeast Asia

Although much of the early history of contact between Chinese and Southeast Asian peoples was unrecorded, some early travel records exist, including

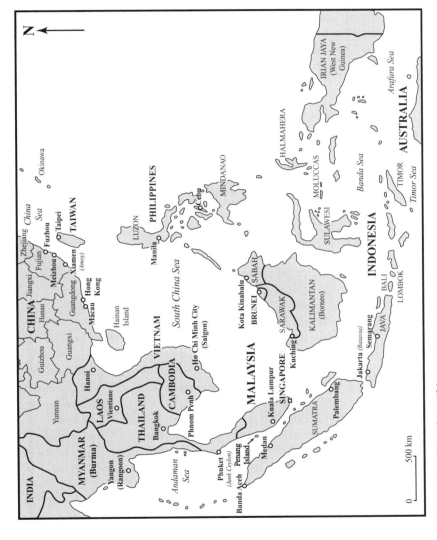

MAP 1. Southeast Asia and Southern China.

an account that the Buddhist monk Fa Xian (334–420) wrote of the journey he and his companions took to India, recording an unplanned stopover in *Java-dvipa* (possibly Sumatra). Admiral Zheng He (1371–1433), the Chinese Muslim eunuch, commanded Ming expeditionary fleets that sailed to Southeast Asia in the early fifteenth century. Although the documentary record is fragmentary, contact with the early Ming dynasty left many traces in Southeast Asia, including engraved multilingual pillars, but also stories in fifteenth-century annals written in Brunei, Malacca, and Java claiming that Chinese princesses had married local rulers and heroes (Reid 1996: 25).

Chinese in port cities throughout the region, including Malacca and Penang, offer incense and prayer to the sainted spirit of Zheng He, whom they call Sam Po (*San Bao*). In Penang, people claim that Sam Po left his numinous footprints on a stone boulder in a small fishing village, Batu Maung, and a sacred well at his temple at the foot of Bukit China in Malacca provides water believed to have special qualities (*The Star* 1981a). Chinese in Java also perpetuate the memory of Zheng He in temples in Jakarta, Cirebon, Surabaya, and Semarang, where devotees claim to preserve an anchor and fragments of his wooden junk, but also conjoin his worship to Sino-Muslim sacred (*keramat*) sites (Salmon 1991: 10; see also Suryadinata 2005; Widodo 2004).

The Portugese took control of the wealthy port of Malacca in 1511; in the seventeenth century the British East India Company began to develop a trading empire based in India, and the Dutch VOC (Vereenigde Oost-Indische Compagnie, or United East India Company), established a competing empire based in Batavia [Jakarta] on the island of Java. The British and Dutch sought to gain control over an already thriving regional trade that linked India to China in order to profit from the trade of Asian and European goods.

But even before the era of European mercantile empires, Chinese migrants had established small communities in many major cities in mainland Southeast Asia, including royal capitals throughout the region, from Ayuddhaya (whose ruins lie near contemporary Bangkok) to Mandalay and the courts of Aceh. Chinese also had settled in many coastal cities throughout island Southeast Asia, where some intermarried with local peoples and developing local blended intercultures and creolized languages – including the *peranakan* Chinese of Batavia (now Jakarta), the Nonya-Baba of Malacca and Penang, who spoke languages that creolized Malay and Hokkien, and the *Mestizo de Sangley* of Manila and Cebu.

With colonialism came the developments in transportation and communication that linked the region into an increasingly efficient global mercantile network. Chinese became established in colonial entrepôts like Penang and Singapore, where they formed spatially segregated and ethnically distinct social groups (Aasen 2004: 3). Throughout the far-flung network of port cities in the region, Chinese built temples facing the harbor where they prayed for safe journey, including Malacca's Cheng Hoon Teng (c. 1645), Penang's Kong Hock Keong (1800), and Singapore's Thian Hock Keng (1820; rebuilt c. 1840).

Many of these community temples were dedicated to Mazu – the Queen of the Sea, enfeoffed by the Ming Emperor as the Queen of Heaven (*Tianhou*), although some like Kong Hock Keong are now regarded as Buddhist temples dedicated to Guanyin. The origin of Mazu worship can be traced to Meizhou Island in Fujian Province, which is said to be the site where a young woman named Lin Moniang (960–987) ascended to heaven from a mountaintop on the ninth day of the ninth lunar month. Worship of the goddess, who was believed to offer miraculous protection to sailors and fisherman, spread throughout the region. Consequently, Mazu temples linked a network of port cities extending from Fujian Province and Taiwan throughout mainland and island Southeast Asia, including Macao, Nangang (Taiwan), Palembang (Sumatra), and Semarang (Java [Widodo 2004]).[18] In Penang, Malacca, and Batavia (present-day Jakarta), these community temples further served as the headquarters for the Chinese *kapitans*, leaders whom colonial authorities invested with responsibility for governing their communities, and who also served as the temple's directors, the keepers of the incense urn (*lo·chu, luzhu*).[19]

The British established Penang as an entrepôt for the China trade in 1786, and the new settlement quickly attracted Chinese sojourners and merchants already resident in the region. Although Singapore soon overtook Penang as a major hub on the sea highway between India and China, nonetheless throughout the nineteenth and early twentieth centuries Penang continued to attract settlers and sojourners from Europe and Asia, including Chinese from Fujian Province, Guangdong Province, and Hainan Island in southeastern China. Immigration produced a highly diverse Chinese population that spoke dialects of three Chinese languages, Southern Min (Fujianese, Chaozhou, and Hainanese), Cantonese, and Hakka. Chinese merchants built Penang's Kong Hock Palace, dedicated to Mazu and Guanyin and facing the harbor, in 1800 as an offshoot not of a temple in China, but of Malacca's Cheng Hoon Teng. (See DeBernardi 2004: 27–28.)

In Penang as elsewhere in Southeast Asia, the Chinese immigrants claimed a separate identity through the construction of temples, lineage associations, and guildhalls. But as the consequence of long residence in Penang, several intercultures had developed, including the fusion of Southeast Asian and Chinese culture known as Nonya-Baba culture. Members of this settled community often sent their children to be educated in British schools, and in the late nineteenth and early twentieth centuries the anglicized Straits Chinese keenly adopted

FIG. 6. Bowing before entering to show respect to Guanyin, a spirit medium possessed by Nazha leads his disciples in procession from his temple to the Kong Hok Palace, George Town, 1980. Photo: Jean DeBernardi

modern technology and programs of social reform. The English-educated Straits Chinese also took the lead in promoting social movements designed to preserve and defend Chinese identity and culture, including the Confucian renaissance of the early twentieth century.[20]

The developments of early modernity resulted in intensified contact between the diverse peoples of Asia in multiethnic colonial port cities like Penang. Although their high textual traditions may have differed, members of diverse Asian cultures who migrated to cosmopolitan, multiethnic port cities like Penang shared a common fund of knowledge concerning the placation of ghosts and animist spirits. Mutual recognition of the congruency between different forms of spirit mediumship practiced by immigrant workers – Thai, Burmese, Chinese, and Hindu – and local peoples promoted borrowing and syncretism.

As I discuss in Chapter Four, Chinese in Southeast Asia not only performed their traditional rituals, they also adapted their ritual formats to the placation of potentially vindictive local spirits. In Penang, for example, the practice of placation includes a prohibition on offering the local spirits pork, because the early settlers imagined them to have Malay ethnicity and to practice Islam. This syncretic and profoundly local form of worship implicitly recognizes congruencies between the Chinese and Southeast Asian forms of animist worship, as does local Chinese devotion to a local God of Prosperity (*Tua Pek Kong, Dabo Gong*)

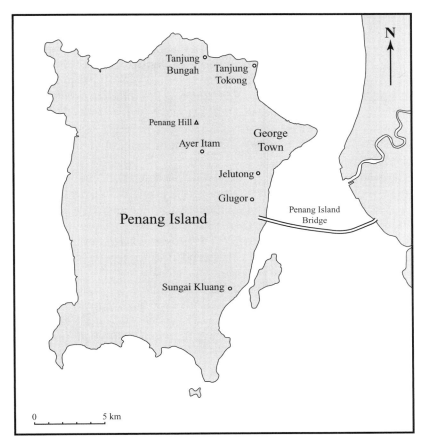

MAP 2. Penang Island circa 2004.

whose history suggests a convergence between the local worship of community founders and the Chinese tradition of sworn brotherhood (DeBernardi 2004: 149–54).

Remaking Chinese Religion in a Field of Religious Practice

The ethnic, linguistic, and religious landscape of the Straits Settlements and colonial Malaya was extraordinarily diverse, and as early as 1836 the curious on-looker could observe "the rites of most of the religions of Asia" in cosmopolitan Penang and Singapore (Low 1972 [1836]: 298–99). In multicultural Penang, some of these religions were universal, salvific, and evangelical, and others were eth-nically defined. By the mid-nineteenth century, Christian evangelists also were a force in the region, circulating tracts and religious books in an extraordinary range of languages as they sought to create diverse, multiethnic communities of like-minded believers. Their tracting is testimony to the diversity of peoples flowing through the port cities of Penang and Singapore: to sailors they distributed tracts in English, French, German, Italian, Swedish, Danish, Dutch, Greek, Spanish, Portuguese, and Russian; to local people they offered tracts in Chinese, Malay, Tamil, English, Urdu, Gurmuki, Persian, Arabic, Portugese, and Thai. In Brethren Assemblies in Singapore and Penang, English sailors and Chinese converts together underwent baptism by immersion in the sea (see DeBernardi N.d.b.).

By contrast with Christian missionaries' aspirations of universal brotherhood, in nineteenth-century Southeast Asia, many Asian religions defined boundaries for ethnically defined communities. For the internally diverse population of Chinese immigrants, the incense urn represented a point of contact with the gods but also a collective identity. People gathered to worship deities brought from their ancestral homelands, and collective acts of worship joined the members of lineages, surname groups, regional associations, and guilds.[21] But the immigrants also collaborated to form community temples and joined together in sworn brotherhoods, worshiping universal savior gods like the Goddess of Mercy and the Emperor of the Dark Heavens. Just as the immigrants formed new associations, so too did their gods, whom they sometimes grouped together on a temple altar and imagined as a divine brotherhood. These forms of worship united wider groups on the basis of a perceived shared need for leadership, supernatural protection, and moral guidance. During most of the nineteenth century, community leaders who took the role of keeper of the incense urn at major temples also served as intermediaries with the British authorities.[22]

Although religious organizations often were formed on a basis of sub-ethnic identity, we also find in these diasporic communities new forms of interethnic collaboration. To give but one example, in the nineteenth century, Shia Muslims commemorated the tragic death of their founder Hussain during the sacred month of Muharram with public displays of collective mourning. But the organizers of the event also invited multiethnic groups of dancers to join them in a carnivalesque and competitive public event. In 1859 and 1862 the registered participants included teams of Bengali, Malay, Hindu, Kling [Tamil], Chinese, Burmese, and Portugese (no doubt Eurasian) dancers. The Chinese contributed two *singha* or lion dance teams of fifteen to twenty performers.[23]

During the colonial period, local elites gained access to new technologies and ideologies that promoted both cosmopolitanism and ethnic nationalism. Although some became secular "free thinkers," others participated in the reform and revival of Asian religions – most notably Buddhism, Hinduism, and Confucianism – as an expression of their aspirations to social honor and autonomy.[24] In the early twentieth century, for example, Penang's elite supported the Confucian revival, a nationalistic social movement that proposed that Chinese should adopt scientific rationality and modernity from the West, but maintain Chinese identity through the practice of Confucianism.

Reformer-in-exile Kang Youwei promoted the Confucian renaissance in Chinese communities outside China, including Singapore and Penang, where English-educated Straits Chinese Dr. Lim Boon Keng and his brother-in-law Dr. Wu Lien-teh became its advocates. Lim, for example, viewed the Confucian cult of memory (that is, ancestor worship) as a form of racial pride. He observed that Confucianism "teaches that every man must remember the tradition of his country just as he is to revere the memory of his ancestors," adding that, "The Anglo-Saxon pride of race is justified on Confucian principles" (Lim 1905: 76).[25] Lim further argued that although Christianity and science conflicted, Confucianism was compatible with modern scientific thought.

At the same time that some Straits Chinese promoted the reform of Confucianism, others promoted the modernization of Buddhism and Daoism, a modernization promoted in part through the influence of the Theosophical movement. This movement, which blended Hinduism, Buddhism, and Western esoteric philosophy, had widespread influence in India and Southeast Asia, an influence largely transmitted through English rather than Asian languages. In India and Sri Lanka, the movement lent support to the revival of Hinduism and Buddhism in the late nineteenth and early twentieth centuries. The influence of the theosophical movement spread to Penang through the formation of a local branch of their society, but also through their publication industry, which produced magazines and widely popular books like Edwin Arnolds' *Light of Asia* (1995 [1879]), an epic-length poem comparing the lives of Buddha and Jesus.

In 1880, two founders of the Theosophical movement, Madame Helena Petrovna Blavatsky and Colonel Henry Steel Olcott, publicly converted to Buddhism under the guidance of the high priest of the temple of Adam's Peak. In Ceylon [Sri Lanka], Colonel Olcott further promoted the development of modernist Buddhist practices, including the use of a Buddhist flag, the movement to have Wesak Day (Buddha's birthday) declared a public holiday, and the establishment of Buddhist schools modeled on mission schools, and he researched and wrote a widely used Buddhist catechism. He is credited with fostering the development of anticolonial Buddhist nationalism, and Sri Lankans still celebrate the day of his first arrival in Ceylon as Olcott Day "in memory of the man who encouraged them to assert their own religion against the pressure of their colonizers and missionaries."[26] In the same period, King Mongkut also worked to reform Theravada Buddhist institutions in Thailand, using the organization of Western churches as an administrative model for centralization and control, and proposing to rationalize Buddhist doctrine to conform to modern scientific rationality.

In the late nineteenth and early twentieth centuries, modernist Thai and Sri Lankan Theravada Buddhist monks came to Malaysia, and English-educated Sri Lankan monks influenced both Chinese Mahayana Buddhists and spirit mediums through their public dharma teachings. The Sri Lankan monks further engaged in missionary outreach, promoting reformed Buddhist practices first to Ceylonese immigrants, and later to Chinese. Concurrently, the practice of Mahayana Buddhism underwent significant reforms as Penang Chinese constructed the monumental Temple of Paradise (*Kek Lok Si, Jile Si*), which on its completion in 1904 replaced the Kong Hok Palace as Penang's preeminent temple. In the twentieth century, Penang's Chinese Buddhists also founded a number of modernist Buddhist associations, including the Penang Buddhist Association (1925) and the Malaysian Buddhist Association (1955), which offered dharma instruction and organized youth activities.

After World War II, Penang's Theravada and Mahayana Buddhist leaders worked together to have Wesak Day declared a public holiday, a proposal first made by a Sri Lankan monk, K. Gunaratana Nayaka Maha Thera (1919–), the

FIG. 7. Monks from Kek Lok Si preside over a ceremony at a modern Buddhist association, Hui Yin Se, on the occasion of Wesak Day, Ayer Itam, 1980. Photo: Jean DeBernardi

second chief abbot of the Mahindarama Buddhist Temple (Ong 2002). Penang's Buddhists achieved this goal in 1949, and in 1962 the government declared Wesak Day a federation-wide holiday (Lim Teong Aik N.d.). Today, the event is celebrated as a public holiday in Malaysia and Singapore, and Penang's Theravada and Mahayana Buddhist temples and associations collaborate to organize a spectacular float parade to honor the event on a date fixed by Theravada tradition.

The reform of religious Daoism has been more fragmentary than that of Buddhism, which is no doubt due to developments in China. Sri Lankan and Thai leaders who promoted the reform of Theravada Buddhism viewed the religion as a vehicle for identity maintenance. By contrast, modernist Chinese promoted Confucianism, secular modernism, or Marxism as ideological frameworks for their programs of social reform. Indeed, after 1949 the Chinese government condemned Daoism and spirit possession as superstitious and anti-modern, outlawing many sectarian groups that are still influential in Taiwan, Southeast Asia, and North America. These modernist forms of Daoism include the syncretic Religion of One Unity (*Yi Guan Dao*, sometimes written *I Kuan Tao*), which is now worldwide in its scope (but prohibited in China), and various moral uplifting associations, including the Red Swastika Society, the philanthropic branch of the Daoyuan sect of the Great Way of Former Heaven (*Xiantian Dadao*). The *Daoyuan* sect was established in China in 1922, but suppressed after 1949, although it still exists in Hong Kong, Taiwan, Malaysia, Singapore, and North America. I discuss a Penang offshoot in Chapter Three, the True Heavenly Dao.

Although modernized forms of Daoism have not received the same level of official support as has Buddhism, nonetheless some of Penang's self-identified Daoists also remade their practices in the conjuncture with modernity. Daoist priests perform exquisite rituals that appeal to eye and ear. But they do not systematically teach their occult knowledge to lay people, and in Southern China and Southeast Asia lay Daoist groups are much more rare than are lay Buddhist ones. Although a number of modernist Daoist organizations have been established in Penang, let me discuss the one that I believe to be Penang's oldest.

In 1882, a Chinese miner founded Penang's Taishang Laojun Temple, a syncretic temple dedicated to teaching Laozi's philosophy and the practice of meditation to lay Daoists, and to promoting filial behavior through moral acts. In 1914, the resident Daoist priest translated into Hokkien romanization a poetically written Daoist scripture, *Old Ancestor Taishang's Ethical Scripture* (*Taishang Laozu Daojing* [Chun 1914]), which we might regard as a Daoist catechism. The text is bilingual, with Chinese characters side-by-side with Hokkien romanization, a form of writing that Christian missionaries introduced to Penang

Hokkien speakers in the early nineteenth century. Meanwhile, the physical format of the scripture is compact and portable, resembling nothing so much as a Christian tract.

Old Ancestor Taishang's Ethical Scripture describes Taishang's powers and history, and also lays out a doctrine of moral cause and effect that I consider to be basic to the practical logic of Chinese popular religious culture as I discuss it in Part I of this monograph. The scripture emphasizes that self-cultivation (*siuheng, xiuxing*) is the means to happiness and immortality, but also teaches a doctrine of moral cause and effect:

Saints, immortals, Buddhas, and humans all practice the Dao, their reward is that they ascend to heaven and stand on a cloud. . . . The proverb says that to achieve goodness and to cultivate oneself well it is better for one to improve his character. If a person cultivates himself well, then heaven will not treat him unfairly . . . If you achieve success in moral cultivation, you will enjoy a thousand years of happiness. (Chun 1914: 1–2)

The message is identical to that of the important Daoist text, *Taishang's Treatise on Action and Retribution*: If people do good deeds and cultivate their character, then they will be rewarded with every kind of happiness, from health and longevity to wealth, high status, and immortality. The temple still distributes this tract to visitors, although since World War II spirit mediums or self-identified masters rather than Daoist priests have been the resident religious specialists.[27]

I agree with Kenneth Dean that the "acts and utterances" of spirit mediums are "too diverse and specific to local circumstances to take the form of a doctrine or a set of particular beliefs" (Dean 2003: 33). Nonetheless, I heard echoes of *Taishang's Treatise on Action and Retribution* and *Old Ancestor Taishang's Ethical Scripture* in the teachings of many spirit mediums. This doctrine of moral cause and effect teaches that the gods will help humans, but only if humans first demonstrate their moral worthiness through their actions. I propose in Chapter One that we might consider this rather than Confucianism to be the ethos that informs the spirit of Chinese capitalism.

In Penang, spirit mediums reformed and modernized their practices in the conjuncture with modernity, including the emergence of Asian forms of nationalist ideology, globalization, and pressures toward the rationalization of religious doctrine. We find the traces of those reforms in the teachings of spirit mediums that I present in Part II, but their development is not well documented. Unlike the Chinese secret sworn brotherhoods (which fascinated the British and Dutch colonials, prompting them to write many speculative articles and books), spirit mediumship repelled the colonials, and no one sought to deeply probe the history and inner meanings of their practices. Although the topic has not been richly documented, nonetheless in the discussion below I glean what I can from the publications of colonial administrators and missionaries.

Colonial Perspectives on Chinese Spirit Mediums

Although Indians, Malays, and Chinese all practiced forms of spirit possession, nonetheless colonial observers found these practices to be weird, uncanny, curious, and ghastly looking. European rationalists found spirit mediumship to be superstitious and distasteful, and Christian missionaries publicly decried mediums as demon worshipers and charlatans. Nonetheless, the practice of spiritual curing through the expulsion of demons was commonplace, and persisted in the face of British rationalism and skepticism.

In the latter part of the nineteenth century, Chinese exorcist spirit mediums in Thailand, colonial Malaya, and the Straits Settlements publicly performed community exorcisms with violent, self-mortifying acts that drew European attention and distaste. De Groot described similar acts of self-mortification performed in early twentieth-century Fujian, including fire-walking on red-hot coals, use of the spike ball, and piercing the body with daggers attached to the heads of the five generals (de Groot 1964 [1892–1910] Vol. 6: 1276–78).[28] De Groot further described in excruciating detail the palanquins, nail beds, and sword litters on which bloody spirit mediums were carried around the town (de Groot 1964 [1892–1910] Vol. 6: 984).

De Groot found historical precedents in Chinese textual sources for many of the exorcizing practices he described, including the driving out of pestilence and ghosts with noise, fire, the authority of the written word, swords, and other weapons. He further speculated that the dramatically staged masked exorcistic *no* processions that were part of the state religion until after the Tang Dynasty, might have inspired similar popular events in southern China where, he guessed, they continued to be celebrated even in the absence of official sponsorship (de Groot 1964 [1892–1910] Vol. 6: 980–81). Nonetheless, he found no precedent in Chinese antiquity for many of the mediumistic practices that he described for late-nineteenth-century Fujian, including fire-walking and self-mortification.[29]

Some of these practices have no analogue in contemporary China or are only found in Taiwan and China's southeastern coastal provinces. They do resemble, however, Hindu devotional practices, including both fire-walking and the body piercing that is so conspicuous a part of the Thaipusam festival as performed by Indian communities in Malaysia and Singapore (see also Kapferer 1983). This similarity to Hindu practices prompts some to speculate that Chinese who observed these practices in South or Southeast Asia borrowed them and syncretized them with their own mediumistic practices, possibly transmitting them back to south China and Taiwan.[30]

In the Straits Settlements, colonial Malaya, and southern Thailand, Europeans sometimes observed with horror public processions at which possessed spirit mediums engaged in violent self-mortifying acts with swords and spike balls, and whose disciples carried them through city and town in sedan chairs whose arms and seats were formed of sharp sword blades. These exorcist processions were especially prominent in worship of the Nine Emperor Gods, deities whose veneration spread from Phuket in Southern Thailand throughout the Malay Peninsula in the 1880s, and are still widely popular in the region. Although we find elements of the Nine Emperor Gods tradition in Daoism, including veneration of the Emperor of the Dark Heavens and the ritual of ascent of a mountain on the ninth day of the ninth lunar month, nonetheless this ritual tradition appears to have no exact analogue in China, and many have concluded that it had its origins among nineteenth-century Chinese immigrants in Phuket, Southern Thailand, who performed these ceremonies in response to devastating epidemics.

Although local memory dates the start of the Nine Emperor Gods tradition in Phuket to 1825, Brethren missionary W. D. Ashdown reported that Chinese only began observing the annual Nine Emperor Gods festival in the decade before he observed it. As he described the event in 1894, Phuket's Chinese spirit mediums displayed their extraordinary self-mortifying skill with the iron spike

FIG. 8. Celebrating the birthday of Tua Pek Kong, the local God of Prosperity, men ceremoniously carry antique flags and a spike ball from a temple in the hills above Ayer Itam to a temporary altar in the marketplace at an open site where the festival is held, 1979. Photo: Jean DeBernardi

FIG. 9. The Lord of the Dark Heavens, possessing his spirit medium, mortifies himself with two spike balls on the occasion of the Nine Emperor Gods festival. Tall posts of dragon incense line the road behind him, George Town, 1980. Photo: Jean DeBernardi

ball, the two-bladed sword, and the knife-edged sedan chair:

A big item in the procession is the sorcerers. These profess to have become possessed after some incantations ere the idol [*Kao Ong Ia, Jiu Wangye*, the Ninth Divine King] issues forth. One or two may be seen carrying an iron ball, set all over with spikes. Each proceeds with a strange, uncertain sort of gait, and disheveled hair, and now and then he will stop and dance round in a half dazed way, all the while swinging round this heavy ball of spikes, which he brings down on his back or other part of the body lacerating the flesh each time, while one or two attendants with sticks seek to break the force of the blows. Further on another man will be acting in a similar way, only wielding with two hands a short, broad two-edged sword, and with blood streaming from his wounds, present a ghastly sight. Some uncovered sedan chairs are carried, the foot-rest, seat and back of one being set with knives with upturned edges, and another similarly with spikes. Upon these these [*sic*] men leap up sometimes and stand or sit for awhile. So the procession goes and returns. (Ashdown 1894: 21)

A few years later, Alfred Green, also a Brethren missionary, encountered a similar procession in Kuala Lumpur, at which believers carried a spirit medium through the streets in a chair whose seat and footrest were made of "sword blades edge upwards!" The spirit medium had pierced his cheek with a dagger, and also beat his back with "a large ball with long thorny spikes," which he swung over his shoulders by a rope (Green 1899: 346).

This spirit medium also engaged in regular healing consultations, charging individuals two dollars for a consultation. Thus we know that by the turn of the century the spirit medium's divinatory and exorcistic powers were commodities with a known economic value in a marketplace of remedies. Indeed, the procession may have been designed to instill fear and stimulate business, since the god-in-the-medium had predicted that during the next month 4,000 or 5,000 people would die of plague in Kuala Lumpur, and people were collecting subscriptions for offerings to appease the gods (Green 1899: 346).

In the early twentieth-century accounts, the practice persisted of organizing exorcizing processions "on account of drought, sickness or general distress" (Stirling 1924: 41). In 1924, Chinese Protector William G. Stirling described the wildly disheveled appearance of the entranced spirit medium as he was carried in procession on a palanquin:

From the look of his eyes and his deathly pallor, he appears to be in a state of delirium or trance. He is naked to the waist and his hair hangs disheveled down his back. . . . With a two-edged sword he cleaves the air, assaulting the evil spirits which he alone has the power to see. Suddenly the palanquin halts, and the medium leaps down and makes an onslaught on some invisible being. Having cut the spirit into a thousand pieces he runs back to the palanquin and resumes his place behind the God. (Stirling 1924: 42)

Ashdown described the blood produced in ghastly acts of self-mortification, but Stirling explained that Chinese used the possessed spirit mediums' blood as a prophylactic against spiritual disturbance:

> Other mediums have a thin dagger thrust through their tongue whence the blood drips onto sheets of paper, which are eagerly fought for by the crowd. What more potent charm against evil could there be, than this blood which contains the power of the Devil-dispelling God? So these paper charms are highly prized and are worn on the person or pasted over the door of the house. (Stirling 1924: 42)

Stirling does not discuss how ordinary lay people participated in these ritual exorcisms, which today sometimes involve individual acts of self-purification through the following of moral precepts, including abstinence from eating meat, and deep repentance of sins.[31]

Although colonial authors commonly witnessed mass exorcistic performances staged on public streets, they offer far fewer accounts of ordinary healing trance performances, even though these undoubtedly were commonplace. In his 1879 study of Chinese in the Straits Settlements, for example, police superintendent and amateur sinologist Jonas D. Vaughan observed that even educated and wealthy Straits Chinese sought out spirit mediums for magical cures. Vaughan recounted secondhand the story of a wealthy Baba man who became ill with dysentery and visited a spirit medium, who "began to shake all over as if moved by some spirit," then directed him "to do a lot of nonsensical things which he said would cure him." When the Baba tried the remedies without success, he turned to an English doctor and recovered. Vaughan noted that although the Baba's confidence in spirit mediums had been undermined, he continued to believe that the spirits of the dead returned to earth during the third and seventh lunar months, and that if the living neglected them, the spirits would retaliate against them (Vaughan 1879 [1971]: 94–95).

Brethren missionaries sometimes glimpsed spirit mediums at work when they entered Chinese temples to preach their Christian message. In the late nineteenth century, for example, Mary B. Langlands, whose mission involved work with women, noted that Chinese women often met in the front room of a house fitted as a temple on one of Kuala Lumpur's main streets. She and her fellow missionaries attempted to enter this storefront temple to speak with the women, but discovered to their disappointment that none of them could understand Malay.

The missionaries later returned to the brilliantly lit temple, and there witnessed an event that a man at the door explained to them as "demon worship" (Langlands 1894: 233). A crowd of women thronged the small temple, and the altar overflowed with offerings of fruit, food, and flowers. At the offering-laden table sat a woman dressed in maroon garments, her hair wreathed in flowers. She used her fingers to eat from a basin of food, sometime speaking, sometimes "uttering inarticulate sounds." The woman's position, hair, distinctive costume, and speech, together with her peculiar habit of tearing at her food with her hands, suggested the enactment of a god who, so embodied, could savor the offerings of flowers, food, and fruit, and could also interact with her disciples.[32]

Stirling, who could speak Hokkien well, offered a rare description of a healing exorcism performed in the sick person's home. Because the sick individual was too ill to come to the temple, devotees carried the god's image to the ailing person's house and placed it on the family altar, then invited the god's spirit to descend into the medium:

Armed with the two-edged spirit sword, the medium dances and hops around the room, uttering cries and shrieks. He whirls the sword about his head, over the sick man, under the bed; touches the bed, door posts windows and furniture; throws aside the sword, seizes the spirit whip with its carved dragon stock and lashes the air; again he seizes the ball of spikes and slashes his back till the blood flows; finally he runs a large needle through his tongue, and the blood is collected on sheets of paper which are pasted on the sick mans's bed and over the windows, and doors of the house. If his ecstasy carries him further, the medium thrusts a devil-dispelling dagger through his cheek. (Stirling 1924: 46)

Finally, the spirit medium's interpreter announced that the offending spirits had been discovered, and indicated the correct ritual remedies, in this case the placing of candles and offerings at the base of a tree, which is one typical abode for the local animist spirits known as Datuk Kong (see Chapter Four). Stirling reported that "China-born Hokkiens of the vegetarian sect" performed this kind of exorcistic ritual, but his description fails to report any details concerning the sect's teachings (Stirling 1924: 41).

A Modernist Straits Chinese Spirit Medium: The Shancai Boy

Because missionaries and colonial observers lacked curiosity about the teachings of spirit mediums, they failed to document the impact of sectarian religious teachings and practices on Penang religious culture, and few records or scholarly studies exist. But the insider view of the development of a Penang spirit medium cult provides a very different perspective on that cult's practices than the descriptions offered by these observers, who eagerly wrote about shockingly dramatic mediumistic performances but provided little more than snapshot descriptions. My sources are few and slim – two procession souvenir volumes published in 1952 and 1955 – but they document the development of one spirit medium cult from the spirit medium's first practice of ritual healing in the 1930s to the establishment of a small temple in 1957. The essays in these slim pamphlets suggest that the spirit medium was influenced by one or more popular Chinese sectarian form of Buddhism but also by the teachings of Thai Theravada Buddhism, which he studied in Penang.

In 1937, Mr. Khoo Guan Seong (b. 1914) – a young, English-educated Penangite – founded the Shancai Hall (*Sianchai Tong, Shancai Tong*), a small temple devoted to the worship of the Virtuous Boy and the Mother of the Earth. Photographs taken of Mr. Khoo reveal a serious, frail young man whose spectacles overpower a slim face, wearing either a suit and tie or Buddhist robes with long, heavy strands of prayer beads around his neck. Groomed for a job in business in colonial schools, he attended the prestigious Penang Free School, a school that the British had established in 1816, which was 'free' insofar as it admitted students irrespective of their race or religious beliefs. He obtained a certificate from the Government Commercial Day School and went to Singapore, but arrived in the region's commercial center just as the world slipped into an economic depression. Although Mr. Khoo had some success in making paper flowers, a skill for which he won a prize at a Trade and Livestock Exhibition in Singapore, and for a short time worked in a Japanese department store, he failed to find secure employment.

Meanwhile, after an episode of illness in 1932, he determined to devote his life to "do good and became a medium," and clients began regularly to seek him out at his flat at Serangoon Road. Although he was poor, he claimed that his popularity as a medium ensured that he had friends of all "castes, creeds, or nationalities," and his needs were always fulfilled. As in any case he could not settle accounts with his debtors for a business venture that he had undertaken with his brother, he closed the business and returned to Penang to continue his practice as a spirit medium.

When Mr. Khoo returned to Penang in 1937, he brought with him two incense urns filled with the ashes of his possessing deity, the Shancai Boy (*Sianchai Tongchu, Shancai Tongzi*), a so-called Baby God whom the spirit medium identified as one of the chief disciples of Guanyin Pusa, the Goddess of Mercy, and whom devotees addressed as Sir Crown Prince (*Thaichu Ia, Taizi Ye*).[33] The cover of the 1937 pamphlet depicts the young Crown Prince standing on a lotus flower and hovering over the Malay Peninsula, watchfully facing Penang Island, his hands together in a prayerful stance. An English poem printed in both souvenir volumes praises this Baby God for curing illness, helping devotees, conferring the blessings of longevity, prosperity, matrimonial harmony, and luck in the lottery – a list of concerns and desires that remains largely unchanged for believers (Shancai Tong [Sian Chye Tong] 1952: 15). Although a photograph of a statue of the Virtuous Boy suggests that he is wearing the stomacher and paneled

SIAN CHYE TONG
20. Nanning Street,
PENANG.

"FLAT LUX"

Lead a righteous life by joining us in our monthly praying services on the 14th day and the last day of the Chinese Moon at 8 p.m. sharp.

Manager
Khoo Guan Seong.

— 18 —

FIG. 10. Photograph of the Shancai Boy's Buddhist medium, published in a temple anniversary volume, Penang, 1952.

skirt of a martial artist deity, nothing in the two pamphlets suggests that this spirit medium performed the self-mortifying exorcistic rituals that so horrified and fascinated European onlookers.

The spirit medium reported that after he introduced worship of Sian Chai (*Shancai*) to Penang in 1937, the Baby God soon became well known, and was even popular among Malays, who called him *Datuk Kecik*, Malay for 'Little God.' For a time, Mr. Khoo lamented, jealous people spread false rumors about him, and many turned away, but when World War II broke out, his temple's fame once again spread. The young crown prince, possessing Mr. Khoo, predicted the outbreak of the Greater East Asia War in 1941, and his devotees held a *chingay* (*zhuangyi*) procession that year – a grand-scale procession with decorated floats that is something of a Straits Chinese invention and specialty – praying that the god would intercede to avert this "great holocaust" and protect the peace. Despite the procession and the prayers, the Japanese bombed Penang – but none of the god's worshippers were harmed in the bombing. They ascribed their survival and safety to their continued belief in the god.

Meanwhile, Mr. Khoo's small house temple began to venerate the Mother of the Earth (*Tebu Neoneo, Dimu Niangniang*). The Mother of the Earth predicted the Allied victory in World War II, and her Penang devotees vowed to honor her with an annual procession on her birthday – the eighteenth day of the tenth lunar month – should her prophecy prove correct. A few months after liberation her devotees honored their vow with a "gorgeous Chingay Procession," carrying the god's images throughout the city on a decorated chariot.

In 1951, the spirit medium entered a new phase of his spiritual career, becoming vegetarian on Shakyamuni Buddha's birthday on the eighth day of the twelfth lunar month. He also set his sights on building a temple for his two possessing deities in order to peacefully practice "the doctrines of our deity, such as Loving Kindness, Compassion, Sympathetic Joy and Equanimity, and finally helping our fellow worshippers in time of need." He set about raising funds from his devotees, and reached an agreement to build the new temple on the grounds of a Guanyin Temple in Ayer Itam. Among his supporters were a head nun at a Guanyin temple in Kuala Lumpur and one of her devout disciples, Mrs. Aw Boon Haw, the wealthy wife of a famous Hakka entrepreneur who made his fortune selling Tiger Balm, a soothing salve.[34]

The small new temple opened in December 1956 amid a flurry of press coverage, and with the participation of the nuns from Guanyin temples in Kuala Lumpur, Klang, Singapore, and Penang. The temple invited the President of the Penang Buddhist Association to make an address, and the Thai Consul presided over the opening ceremony. The formal, posed photographs of participants at the opening ceremony show a gathering of Straits Chinese, the men wearing

FIG. 11. The Cover of a Sian Chye Tong anniversary volume shows the god hovering protectively over Penang, 1957.

crisp white shirts and ties – like the spirit medium, they probably were educated in the English school system – and the women in their elegant *sarong kebayas*, the formal dress of the locally born Straits Chinese woman. Not only the five participating nuns but also the spirit medium donned Buddhist robes for the celebration.

By 1957, the spirit medium had formed a friendship with a monk at Penang's grand Thai Temple of the Reclining Buddha, Wat Chaya Mangkalaram, who practiced a modernist form of Theravada Buddhism that included lay instruction and missionary outreach, and who sometimes visited the Sian Chye Hall to lecture. At the opening of the new temple, the spirit medium proclaimed the small temple's goals, which included the propagation of Buddhism, "the practice of Metta – loving kindness, and to foster fraternity among all Buddhists and to practice Dana – charity." Also mentioned were plans to build branch temples in Kuala Lumpur and Singapore for the group's 'healing mission,' and the building of two additional rooms for individuals suffering from mental breakdowns (*Straits Echo and Times of Malaya* 1956). In this small pamphlet, the spirit medium further proposed a devoutly Buddhist morality:

> Sian Chye Phor Sat our deity being one of the chief disciples of Kuan Say Im Phor Sat [Guanyin], we therefore firmly believe and uphold that to be a good Buddhist one has to live along with the Dhamma [dharma]. We must believe that the various suffering we are facing now especially in this present atomic world are due to our Karma, so we have to lead a noble life and cleanse ourselves of all sins by living a good and righteous life in order to aim at the precious goal of Nibbana [nirvana]. Be not deceived by selfishness and think of selves alone, for what is gained in this world is of short duration only. Nothing in this world is permanent and everything is transient. There is no resting place in the universal turmoil where our troubled hearts can find peace and cessation of anxiety.
>
> The burning desires of ours can never be extinguished and our minds can never become peaceful and composed if we do not see and understand the vanity of worldly pleasures. . . . The world is not a permanent place for us and what matters most is after death and life eternal. Our good thoughts produce good actions and bad thoughts produce bad actions for what we sow, the same we must reap. The path of immortality is to be in good earnest, and thoughtlessness is the leading way towards death and misery. Cease to do evil, purify the mind, then peace and happiness will surely reign throughout the world. . . . Follow the Dhamma seriously and aim for Nibbana (Shancai Tong [Sian Chye Tong] 1957).

One of his enthusiastic followers added that the god's main objectives included not only healing the sick in body and soul, but also giving advice on religious matters and "last but not least to give discourses on the Buddhistic way of life." This the deity did every Sunday, at least when there was a "fair turn-up."

Regrettably, no anthropologist documented the Buddhist teachings that Mr. Khoo offered while the Shancai Boy possessed him. Nonetheless, these pamphlets at least allow us to know something of the trance performance in Penang from the perspective of participants rather than outsiders.[35] Most striking is the degree to which this spirit medium's devotional practices to the Shancai Boy and the Mother of the Earth developed in the encounter with modernity: with European colonialism (which offered him an English education and the promise of a well-paying job in commerce), with the cycles of global capitalism (which left those promises unrealized), and with warfare and Japanese colonialism – a period of "great stress and constant terror," according to Mr. Khoo, in which many continually prayed to their gods for protection. And perhaps it is more than coincidental that the spirit medium strove to establish a more permanent temple amid the insecurities of the post-war world. The threat of further nuclear warfare terrified many, and the return of British colonialism sparked years of guerilla warfare and horrifying violence. This temple's establishment in 1956 only slightly preceded Malaysian independence and the end of the colonial era in 1957, in a period in which some Asians, including Sri Lankans and Thais, already had turned to Theravada Buddhism as a support for projects of nationalist identity construction. Throughout these disturbing changes, the god reassured his disciples that "nothing in this world is permanent and everything is transient," and that the only answer to their 'troubled hearts' in a period of universal turmoil was charity and the quest for a utopian life eternal through good deeds.

Spirit Mediums and Sworn Brotherhoods

Curious Brethren missionaries in the Malay Peninsula and Southern Thailand sometimes described their spiritual competitors, albeit with a low level of comprehension of their practices, but no scholarly accounts exist of prewar spirit medium temples like Mr. Khoo's Sian Chye Tong. But in 1950, a British-trained anthropologist did conduct anthropological research on Chinese spirit mediums in Singapore. Alan Elliott (1955) focused on a spirit medium cult whose chief spirit medium was possessed by the Great Saint, or Monkey God, providing for comparison a Buddhist cult whose female spirit medium was possessed by Buddhas and Bodhisattvas, a sino-Malay cult devoted to a Muslim saint, and a scattering of urban, rural, and suburban temples. Elliott documents the theory and practice of Chinese spirit mediumship in a compactly written monograph that many continue to cite as the most authoritative source on this topic.

Elliott conducted a meticulous content analysis of 100 consultations of clients with spirit mediums in Singapore. He provided the useful information that the 168 topics about which clients consulted fell into the following categories: 53 cases involved miscellaneous illness; 32 cases involved bad luck; 13 cases involved possession by evil spirits; 12 cases involved childbirth; 6 cases involved investment advice; 6 cases involved news of relatives in distant parts; 6 cases involved the choice of auspicious dates; 5 cases involved gambling advice; and 5 cases involved wayward children. The remaining cases involved accidents (4), advice concerning partnerships (4), insanity (3), protection in courts (3), communication with the dead (2), and trouble with an employer (1) (Elliott 1955: 161).

As befit his training in the British functionalist tradition, Elliott also paid close attention to the social structural dimensions of the spirit medium cult. He observed, for example, that supporters of the Great Saint cults that he studied were, like the supporters of the Sian Chai Boy, English-educated, Straits-born Hokkien Chinese, whereas supporters of the sino-Malay cult were Baba Chinese whose primary language was Malay but who were not inclined to become Muslim (Elliott 1955: 80; 113). He also noted that in Singapore a number of spirit medium cults of "the rather less reputable type" maintained a clique-like affiliation (Elliott 1955: 72–73). In her review of this study, Marjorie Topley, who herself had done extensive research on Chinese religion in Singapore, amplified this point, suggesting that these spirit medium cults were connected with secret societies, and that "this latter type of organization is superimposed on some of the cults." She concluded that if this were so, then this would "tend to make closer investigation extremely difficult if not impossible" (Topley 1956: 219).[36]

In his encyclopedic study of the *Religious System of China* , which combined his knowledge of Chinese practices in Fujian Province with citation of classical sources, de Groot also observed that spirit mediums were associated with sworn brotherhoods:

In several cases also, a *ki tông* [spirit medium] god is the patron deity of a small club or association of so-called *bîng hia^{ng} -ti* [*beng hia^n ti, meng xiongdi*] or "sworn brethren", such as is formed very often among the lower classes for mutual help and protection, especially in time of need. (de Groot 1964 [1892–1910] Vol. 6: 1272)

He added that the sworn brothers call the god their "oath Buddha" (*beng Put, meng Fo*) because they swore their oath of mutual allegiance before his image. Indeed, a god or founding patriarch (*Cho·su, Zushi*) may become the focus for group identity formation for unrelated individuals on the model of ancestor worship. According to de Groot, in Fujian the spirit medium sometimes became a source of both income and oracles for these small sworn brotherhoods, and sometimes the god was raised to the status of a local god with a temple.

In nineteenth-century Penang, a diversity of sworn brotherhoods existed, including the Ghee Hin, Ho Seng, Hai San, Chun Sim, and Kian Tek (or Tua Pek Kong) Societies.[37] Before the British criminalized them, the ritual performers at the groups' lengthy initiation rites took on the names and identities of the groups' founders in what appears to be a form of spirit possession, recreating the chrono-tope of the Ming Dynasty (see DeBernardi 2004: 79–108). Although the topic is not readily investigated, at least some contemporary Penang Chinese spirit medium temples appear to have inherited elements of their ritual traditions.

This brief historical overview of Penang Chinese spirit mediumship sug-gests that spirit mediums perform three distinct roles. First, on behalf of the wider community spirit mediums perform rituals of collective exorcism, taking on the community's sins and purifying its members of all evil through their self-mortifying performances at large-scale festival events. Second, vis-à-vis in-dividual clients, the god possessing his spirit medium is a healer, counselor, and moral guide. Finally, for the small group of insiders who sponsor worship of the god, the spirit medium in trance is both their patron deity and their charismatic leader.

I closely analyze rituals of collective exorcism in *Rites of Belonging: Memory, Modernity, and Identity in a Malaysian Chinese Community* (2004) when I discuss the ritual practices and allegorical narratives associated with the Nine Emperor Gods festival and its enormous processions. Consequently, in this monograph I focus on the spirit medium in the role of folk healer, moral guide, inventive performer, and charismatic leader. I do, however, describe the smaller-scale festival events that spirit mediums celebrated at their individual temples, which like the Nine Emperor Gods festival often involved the collaboration of teams of spirit mediums in the performance of self-mortifying rituals for eager crowds, and processions through neighborhood streets.

Overview

In this monograph, I combine an analysis of the theodicy, morality, and poetics of Chinese popular religious culture in Part One with four case stud-ies exploring the teachings and practice of individual Malaysian Chinese spirit mediums. In adopting a strategy of ethnographic representation that joins to-gether a generalizing analysis of the practice of Chinese popular religious cul-ture and spirit mediumship with dialogic case studies, I concur with Pierre Bourdieu's insight that the analytical task for anthropologists is not to abandon either objectivist models that focus on those structures and rules that constrain the individual, or subjectivist models that focus on the ongoing construction of social life in interaction, but rather to reconcile the two approaches to social analysis (Bourdieu 1990 [1980]).

As one step in this theoretical reconciliation, Bourdieu proposed using the term habitus to describe people's practical orientation toward the contingencies of everyday life, which he regarded as "embodied history, internalized as second nature and so forgotten as history" (1990 [1980]: 56). Whereas anthropologists often seek to learn about a society not their own by seeking exegesis and explanation, members of these social groups acquire a feel for the game through experience, on the basis of which they develop both a commonsense understanding of action and a pragmatic faith in their own social order (1990 [1980]: 69). Bourdieu concluded that people's belief in witchcraft or divination, for example, is not a matter of representations, dogmas, or the intellectualist's logic, but rather is instilled by a gradual process of learning that "treats the body as a living memory pad" (1990 [1980]: 70). In a useful extension of Bourdieu's concept of habitus to the analysis of charismatic healing, Thomas Csordas further proposes a phenomenological approach to religious imagery that reconciles "language and experience, representation and being in the world" (Csordas 1994: 82). To accomplish this, we must both analyze the abstracted image as a sign and examine the embodied image in the consciousness of real persons, at least insofar as we can know them based on people's stories about their habitual practices and extraordinary experiences.

In this study, I seek to convey both an understanding of shared practices and orientations and a sense of how individuals imagine, represent, and transform the popular religious habitus in the time and space of their own lives. After a vignette of a festival celebrating the birthday of a healing deity, Chapter One investigates the everyday habits of interpretation and action that motivate people to seek answers to problems through divination or spirit mediums. This analysis abstracts the key terms and symbols with which people explain events in their lives and in the larger cosmos, and the cultural logic of the remedies offered by the gods possessing spirit mediums. In particular, I focus on Penang Chinese concepts of the good life and its vicissitudes, as represented in people's personal narratives, in rituals performed by spirit mediums, and in the visual and narrative representations of the gods. I base a theodicy of Chinese popular religious culture on these diverse practices, but also view it from the perspective of contemporary philosophical discussions about moral luck.

Chapter Two explores the everyday ritual practices and narratives that contribute to people's imagining of the powers and dangers of occult, invisible worlds. As Robert J. Barrett observes, the analysis of ritual performance must include not only a close consideration of the dynamic, transformative effects of the ritual performance, but also people's metacommentary on ritual and the "talk that takes place in and around ritual action" (Barrett 1993: 235). People seek to communicate with the numinous along many channels, including divination and interaction with the gods as they possess their spirit mediums. Narratives — occult gossip and local urban legends — magnify the magical powers of spirit mediums and their opponents, including out-group magicians and afflicting ghosts and spirits. I focus on spirit mediums and their salvation work, and explore how people imagine the relationship between human and otherworldly realms, each with its own powers and vulnerabilities, in their narratives and ritual acts.

Chapter Three investigates the practice of spirit mediums. In their performance of Chinese deities, Penang's spirit mediums perform the chronotope of invisible spiritual worlds. In this chapter, I explore the use of costume, movement, and language in the performance of military and literary gods, but also the stories that inform people's images of the gods and their powers, allegorical narratives that people know through popular novels, traditional opera, and (more recently) film. The authors of these didactic allegories taught abstract religious truths through the embodied adventures of engaging characters like the Great Saint, who is known more familiarly as the Monkey God, Nazha, and the Vagabond Buddha. When they possess spirit mediums, these characters join the human life world, and people come to know them as individuals with personality and passion.

In Part Two of this study, I present the ritual practice and teachings of four spirit mediums. Many authors have written about Chinese spirit mediumship, but most focus on their practice as folk healers; few have documented the role of spirit mediums as teachers, masters, and moral guides, or their role as the charismatic leaders of small groups. Although these case studies are not as minimalist as a collection of Boasian texts, nonetheless in Part Two I seek to present a detailed ethnographic record of a time and place rich enough to allow the reader the possibility of reinterpretation and comparison.

I present these case studies in part as dialogs that include my research assistants' and my questions, describing the contexts in which I interacted with these spirit mediums or their possessing gods. In representing their findings dialogically, anthropologists seek to convey the processes through which the ethnographer obtained experience and knowledge of another culture, but also to present the voices of those who responded to the ethnographer's request for cultural knowledge and exegesis. Some object to this method of representation, arguing that a polyphonic approach stressing individuality and process over social facts and structures reduces sociological representation to the microscopic and personal. The strength of this approach, however, is its potential to capture the intersection of structure and process, history and event, through the words and lives of individuals.

I begin Part Two with the teachings of the Datuk Aunt, a female spirit medium who specialized in the placation of Malay animist spirits. The Datuk Aunt provided magical remedies for persons troubled by these local spirits, which spirit mediums commonly diagnose as a source of spiritual disturbances. But she also was an energetic and gifted storyteller who offered us a wealth of narratives about gods and ghosts at the same time that she promoted herself as an expert who could provide antidotes to disturbances from the invisible world of ghosts and spirits.

Chapters Five and Six present the teachings of two spirit mediums, Master Poh and Master Lim, each of whom taught a doctrine of self-cultivation that synthesized China's three religions. Master Poh's discourse was filled with exegesis of classificatory and ethical terms deriving from Daoism, Buddhism, and Confucianism, and he advised my research assistant and me how to escape from the cycle of death and rebirth by following a path of self-cultivation, including meditation and moral action. He further taught people how to behave morally and to 'be human,' using stories to explicate basic moral and cosmological concepts like filiality and the Dao.

Whereas Master Poh taught in deep Hokkien, Master Lim translated and commented on foundational Daoist texts for an English-educated, Hokkien-speaking elite. An integrative cosmopolitan, he drew upon a variety of sources, including the *Bible*, Theosophy, and Theravada Buddhism, to develop a unique interpretation of Chinese tradition. He convened a weekly class for a small number of disciples, and his healing and teaching practices addressed modern, well-educated, literate urban Chinese's desire to know their own traditions. In his class, he often commented on classical texts like the *Daodejing* and *Yijing* by telling stories based on his life experiences, localizing an understanding of metaphoric images and abstract principles in the real time and space of his life in Penang and Singapore.

In Chapter Seven, I examine a Chinese spirit medium cult that also was a sworn brotherhood whose members were involved with Penang's underground economy. I closely explore the ritual practice at one temple, and provide a dialogic account of my encounters with that temple's chief spirit medium, especially while he was possessed by the Vagabond Buddha, whom he performed as a trickster god. I conclude that this spirit medium borrowed the sanctity and authority of a religious framework of meanings to validate an alternative moral code.

However extraordinary their self-mortifying performances or eloquent their teachings, undoubtedly most spirit mediums occupy a marginal and ambivalent position within Penang society. Although some poets and artists now appreciate its popular aesthetic, many educated Chinese – often practitioners of modernist forms of Buddhism or Daoism – regard the trance performance as a superstitious, irrational form of practice designed to exploit the ignorant. Sceptics argue that spirit mediums set up temples not to save the world but rather to seek financial gain, and they observe that the medium's claim to speak and to act as a god is a potentially powerful and even dangerous means of social control. The Conclusion investigates contemporary challenges to the authority and efficacy of spirit mediums, including the mystification of the gift and mystification of charismatic power.

Let me begin, though, as anthropologists often do, with my own tale of entry into the field.

PART I

Heaven on Earth

I CAME to the Dragon God's temple entirely by chance. Still new to Penang, my quest for a room to rent with a Chinese family had yielded few prospects, and I remained at the university guesthouse, far from the bustle of urban George Town. I often lined up at the campus post office to buy stamps, and the postmaster inquired who I was and what I was doing. When I explained my plans to study Chinese religion, he was astonished, then pleased, observing that because Western culture was chaotic and immoral, Penang was the right place to study spiritual matters. He told me about a spirit medium, a poor man who wore tattered clothes and lived in the hills but who had extraordinary powers: he could magically transport himself from the Botanical Gardens to town; if he drew a circle around an insect, that insect could not move.

The postmaster offered to help, and invited six of his friends to meet with me a few days later at the Government Office Worker's Association in George Town. I asked them question after question, including where I might find this extraordinary spirit medium. Such spirit mediums no longer exist, they lamented, except maybe one, and they promised to take me to meet him – a promise never fulfilled. But by meeting's end, I had agreed to employ a Chinese sundry shopkeeper's daughter as my research assistant, and to rent a room from one of their friends, a long-distance truck driver who lived with his family in a modest housing development. My new research assistant's father was involved in the establishment of a new temple, and a few weeks later he and his daughter took me to meet the temple's Master of Ceremonies (*Sinse^n*, *Xiansheng*), Master Khoo, in an abandoned garden filled with enormous trees and a naturalistically designed shrine-grotto.

When we arrived that night, the Master, the spirit medium, and a few friends were having tea in the starlit garden. They sat near the main shrine room, a grotto fitted with Chinese-style brilliant red and gold-embroidered satin hangings. The main altar held two god images – the Dragon Great Official and a Thai-style Buddha. Not far away was another small shrine whose altar was overflowing with small bronze Buddha images, but which also held the modest possessions of its caretaker. The saffron robed monk – a local Chinese who they claimed had lived in the abandoned garden for several years – sat nearby in the darkness on a low-arched bridge spanning what once had been a pond but now was only a hollow depression. The architect of this sacred site also had built an elevated meditation altar in one of the garden's enormous trees, and its roots now entwined themselves around the archway framing the steps to this tropical aerie.

Soon, the trance performance began. Standing by the altar, the Master took a school lesson book in which the Chinese text had been handwritten, and repeatedly chanted a Hokkien invocation to invite the god. Finally the spirit medium, now shirtless and wearing yellow drawstring pants, approached. As the Master chanted the god's name, calling him to descend into the medium, the medium slowly began to rock forward and back. Finally, he assumed a martial pose and slapped the ground. The spirit of the Dragon Great Official (*Long Daguan*) had arrived.[1]

A client, a young man complaining of ill health, was waiting and approached the god. The god-in-his medium felt the man's wrist and his back, and advised him to sleep well and not to worry so much. He also prescribed an herbal tonic (dictating a long list of ingredients that the monk wrote down), together with the advice that the herbs should be stewed together with a whole chicken with the head still on. Chicken soup, I thought, unimpressed and not especially curious to know the contents of this folk remedy. Next the Master's daughter consulted with the god about a problem with her niece that my research assistant could not find words in English to explain to me, and the medium again dictated a prescription. There were no more clients, and the god's assistants manipulated a board on the altar and studied the results of this spirit writing. They next placed before the god a short red bamboo stick with the character for 'command' (*ling*) written on it, and began to read out the list of donors so that the god could chose a name. But the god refused to make his selection, and demanded that they return on the following Sunday, the ninth day of the lunar month, which he deemed a more auspicious day. He then seemed to fall out of his divine persona, giving the men detailed instructions on how to sing the trance invocation in what appeared to me to be more of a dress rehearsal than a performance.

Although I had studied Mandarin well enough to pose a few questions to the Master before the trance performance began, I could not yet conduct an interview in Hokkien, and relied on my newly hired young research assistant to interpret. The Master answered my questions at some length, but my research assistant proved to be a diffident interpreter, offering monosyllabic translations. I resolved to find a new research assistant and to learn Hokkien. When I returned again the next month for the celebration of the god's birthday on the sixth day of the sixth lunar month, I invited a Hokkien-speaking friend who was a reporter for a local newspaper. Together we interviewed the spirit medium before the event started, and she published an article about this extraordinary garden shrine in one of Malaysia's main English newspapers (Low 1979).

This time I learned much more. According to Master Khoo, a monk who had meditated there had discovered that the gods favored the spot, and in 1939 had constructed the garden and its shrine, whose entrance was framed by three archways constructed to resemble natural stone outcroppings. The monk may have been Fa Kong, "Empty Dharma," a locally famous Chan Buddhist monk who had used lottery winnings to build himself a private zoo in Ayer Itam on a street very near this remarkable meditation garden (Khoo 1993: 56). Flanked by new homes and a construction site, the lush tree-filled garden with its decaying shrine was scheduled for demolition, its trees and shrines to be flattened to make way for a road.

FIG. 12. The shrine-grotto in Ayer Itam. Tree roots have twisted around the entryways to small shrine rooms. Recorded on the hanging strips of paper are the names of donors and the amounts of their contributions, 1979. Photo: Jean DeBernardi

Since my earlier visit, the worshippers had repainted the carved inscriptions on the archways, and enlivened the area with red tables heaped with offerings. They piled the altar facing this spirituous grotto with bowls of fruit and other sweet offerings, and attached to its two sides tall stalks of sugarcane festooned with yellow paper, which Hokkien always offer to the Lord of Heaven as thanksgiving for a miraculous rescue from imperial troops. On another table facing the small puppet theater stage, they placed porcelain statues of the Monkey God, Guanyin, and other deities whose eyes were covered with red paper, awaiting a ceremony in which the entranced spirit medium would open their eyes and infuse them with consciousness.[2]

Master Khoo explained that the temple's principle deities were three gods from China who were brothers, adding that there were thirty-six brothers altogether scattered throughout the world. The number thirty-six is an auspicious number that suggests the thirty-six generals guarding the gates of heaven, or the thirty-six benevolent stars thought to govern human fate. At the same time, the sum of three plus six is nine – a *yang* number associated with imperial power and masculine strength.[3]

According to Master Khoo, the main deity of these three was Chu Kong, a learned official who had been a judge in his lifetime and who went to heaven because of his good deeds. He now had responsibility to keep track of the conduct of the living. When people died, Chu Kong reviewed their lives to mete out judgment, sending sinners to hell to be punished and sending the pure of heart to be reincarnated or else to live in paradise. Hell, he added, was very much like earth, with gangsters, police, and a judge to keep the peace. Chu Kong's two brothers were a heavenly god and a keeper in hell. The three gods together thus appear to have bureaucratic responsibilities over the living and the dead within the three major divisions of the cosmos: the Celestial, the Terrestrial, and the Human Realms. This tripartite alliance of gods also corresponds to the division of the soul into spiritual, material, and moral components. Thus these three gods may simultaneously represent three souls or aspects of a single deity, and serve as a model of the tripartite elements of both the cosmos and the human spirit.[4]

The medium claimed that Chu Kong was a healing god who had the power to cure minor illnesses, like light bruises from gongfu, or internal injuries. The god could also cure people who had been troubled by black magic or had fallen ill because they had offended a certain god or local animist spirit, although he cautioned that the god's powers did not extend to curing serious illnesses like paralysis. He emphasized that this god did not give lottery numbers, adding that money was of little consequence to the god, and that people should only donate if they could afford to do so.[5]

According to Master Khoo, many local spirits also lived in this garden's enormous trees, including Datuk Ali, who was in charge of the site, and the Black and Yellow Datuks. Penangites call these local spirits *Datuk Kong* (often pronouncing *Datuk* as *Natu* or *Latu*), a hybrid term that combines Malay and Chinese honorific titles for elders, and they often reside in trees or extraordinary rock formations that people regard as eruptions of the numinous into the landscape. Many Penangites believe these spirits to be a potential cause of illness or even death, and they attend spirit mediums' trance performances in order to find ways to placate them. Master Khoo claimed that the garden had once been 'dirty' (*lasam*), that is, haunted by these spirits and dangerous for humans, but that since the gods had taken up residence all had been peaceful. The pending development, Master Khoo claimed, deeply disturbed Datuk Ali, and the spirit advised him that he wanted to be left in peace as he had very little time before he had to vacate his home. The spirit medium added that these spirits were very touchy and fierce, and my reporter friend entitled her article "Shrine to Go: Will Evil Befall Poser?" (Low 1979).

At the conclusion of our tour around the garden, Master Khoo urged us to return in the evening when Chu Kong would invite minor gods to enjoy the celebration with him: "His bodyguards will bring him in, and he will preside over the court." He added that there would be a puppet show for his entertainment. I returned in the evening with my reporter friend, her brother, his girlfriend, and another young man, all recent high school graduates who had free time while they waited for their college entrance examination test results. The girlfriend's Catholic mother, Mrs. Hwang, also joined us, and to my surprise I found that she knew a great deal about popular religious culture.[6]

When we arrived, the puppet show already was in progress. Ten or so teenagers from the Penang Buddhist Association lined up at the altar to sing a prayer, and the Malaysian Buddhist Dhamma Society already had visited, leaving their banner by the altar, perhaps to show respect to the shrine's Chan Buddhist founder. Soon the Master sang to invoke the gods, accompanied by hypnotically rhythmic gonging and drumming. One spirit medium took off his shirt, and waited seated on a stool in front of the small temple's main altar. As we observed the first trance session, Mrs. Huang explained to me that the flag and the suit of clothes were very important for the spirit medium, adding that the music and sometimes opium assisted the spirit mediums when they went into trance.

His assistant beat a rhythmic tattoo with a drum and gong, and the tempo and intensity of the music increased as the spirit medium rocked his body with increasing force. Finally, the spirit medium struck a martial pose to show that the spirit of the Great Saint had entered his body. His friends covered his torso with a green silk garment with yellow trim that covered his chest and left his back bare; then they tied green petaled garments around his waist and shoulders. They also placed a green silk crown on his head. Scratching his body and pretending to pick lice, he leapt acrobatically, startling and entertaining the small crowd. The Great Saint is, of course, Monkey, a riotous trickster figure whom Guanyin tamed to protect Tripitaka when he made the perilous journey to India to obtain the Buddhist scriptures, and he is the hero of the vernacular novel *Journey to the West* (Yu 1977-1983).

Next came a god whom Mrs. Hwang identified as a very lucky god; a man wrote down his name for me – the Third Prince (*Sam Thaichu, San Taizi*). After he fell into trance, the prince took praying beads and a spear. Then his brother arrived. His helpers dressed him in the yellow bib-like garment and leggings, and tied a yellow sash across his forehead. He hopped energetically to indicate that he traveled on a fire wheel and carried a long, braided snake-handled whip. The god bathed his body in burning joss sticks in a self-mortifying display that became so violent that his helpers first threw rice on him then blew water in his face to calm him.[7]

The final deity to enter was an intimidating figure dressed in green stomacher and leggings and wearing a yellow headband. He carried in his teeth a double-bladed sword and cracked a long, snake-handled exorcizing whip, weapons that spirit mediums use to intimidate ghosts. One of the men identified him as a bodyguard in the temple.[8] This temple guardian enacted the role of a demon-expelling god, whipping the ghosts with his long braided whip. Each of the gods, possessing their mediums, then placed incense on the altar as an offering to Chu Kong. Their assistants followed them, burning wads of paper money to placate dangerous wandering spirits that might be nearby. Then the four spirit mediums fell out of trance, and a short lull followed.

At 11:00 p.m., Master Khoo finally appeared, wearing yellow drawstring pants and a yellow singlet, and prayed at the altar. The drumming and gonging started up again, and all five spirit mediums quickly fell into trance. Chu Kong was dignified and slow in his movements, and one of the young men whispered to me that the god looked very prestigious. The god-in-his-medium wrote a message on the altar table with lit joss sticks, then strafed the lit ends over his back, while the other possessed spirit mediums performed acts of self-mortification, hitting their backs with swords or spiked balls. At this point, Mrs. Hwang dramatically exclaimed, "We are witnessing heaven on earth!" The god-in-his-medium and the men tending him then charged off through the dark construction site to 'open the road,' perhaps seeking to drive out the dark forces of urban development. On their return a few minutes later, the five spirit mediums fell out of trance, concluding the night's performance.

On the second day of the festival – the seventh day of the sixth lunar month, a date on which heaven's gate is opened – three Daoist priests chanted in the morning, and in the afternoon the gods collaborated to perform a ritual to 'change the luck' (*ke-un, guoyun*) of participants, including one man who hoped to be cured of blindness. The two young Princes and Chu Kong fell into trance. The younger prince, who hopped to suggest that he rode a flaming wheel, performed the luck-changing ritual to the accompaniment of drumming and gongs. Each person undergoing the ritual stepped forward holding three lit joss sticks, then the assistant held up the person's replacement body (*thoesin, tishen*), a small human effigy wrapped first in paper money, and then in a sheet of red paper on which was written the person's name, their age, and the date, passing the small effigy in front of and behind the person's body. The god then stepped forward and touched the person on both shoulders and the back with the snake handle of the whip. The assistant handed him the temple seal, and he stamped the person's back with red ink.

In the meantime, the Third Prince placed an offering of peanuts (which represented a wish for long life) on a nearby altar for the gods, then took a pink pacifier and popped it into his mouth. The puppet show that the temple committee sponsored for the gods' entertainment was in progress, its musicians cacophonously competing with the gongs and drums of the trance performance, and the Prince sat on a stool in front of the stage, making a great show of being entertained by the puppets. The festival concluded, and I left this hidden, magical shrine-garden. Penangites tell stories about demolition and earth-moving equipment that, faced with a sacred site, mysteriously and irreparably breaks down.[9] Master Khoo and his followers may have hoped for similar supernatural assistance from their gods, but their attempt at revival proved ephemeral in the face of a road construction project.

Conclusion

In his classic and still influential study of *The Religion of China*, Max Weber observed that historically, both orthodox and heterodox Chinese tolerated a magical image of the world founded on archaic empirical knowledge whose forms of practice included the imperial cult, ancestor worship, Daoist magical therapies, chronomancy, geomancy, and the demonic expulsions performed by spirit mediums. But he claimed that concurrent with Western-assisted modernization, Chinese increasingly regarded experts in this magical religion – the Daoist priest, astrologer, fortune-teller, and spirit medium – as mere swindlers for whom profit interests predominated (Weber 1968 [1951]: 199, 229).

But in the early modern period, China's geomancers used their craft to demand alterations in construction projects, leading the builders of canals, roads, or bridges to make costly detours of many miles in order to avoid potential demonological disturbances. Geomancers also opposed mining, which could potentially incense the spirits, and deemed railroad and coal-burning factory installations that produced smoke to have "magically infested" areas. Weber concluded that with their "magical stereotyping of technology and economics," China's geomancers created obstacles to the development of "indigenous modern enterprises" that Chinese elite investors were able to overcome only when Western high capitalism sat in the saddle (Weber 1968 [1951]: 199). We must at least consider, however, whether some of these so-called swindlers made use of the magical stereotype of spiritual revenge to interpret local conflicts with the developers on the transposed plane of unseen forces. Recall Master Khoo's dark hints that in destroying the verdant shrine grotto he and his friends so prized, the people building the new road would provoke retaliation from dangerous spirits.[10]

In establishing this temple in the face of plans for demolition, participants sought to sacralize the space of this grotto-shrine, hoping to rescue its architectural beauty and its enormous jungle trees. There, they performed rituals that disclosed their vision of seen and unseen worlds, "making place" and recalling the past until forced to disperse by a "straight-line project of modernity" (Feuchtwang 2004: 178). The garden's tree-wrapped shrines evoked the monk who realized his vision on this site, but also the jungle that human expansion has pushed back again and again, claiming not only vines and trees but also entire hillsides, blown up to make space for roads and high-rise apartment buildings.

Although modest in scale, at this temple festival we find the trance performance of Chinese gods who take on imperial roles based on a political order long since overthrown. But these performances took place in the here-and-now of a settled community of Penangites, most of whom held Malaysian citizenship, and most of whom had never seen China.[11] And although he performed the role of a magistrate who epitomizes a Chinese model of political authority, Master Khoo also acknowledged the prior territorial claims of invisible Malay spirits. Indeed, he claimed that these long-resident autochthonous spirits, whose jungle home had been repeatedly disturbed by humans, posed an immediate danger to the developers who planned to demolish the site. Apparently, though, Datuk Ali and his companions shared their territory amicably enough with Chinese gods and Thai Buddhas.

In this sacred garden, the spirit mediums performed images of an ordered cosmos. As a divine, just magistrate, Chu Kong weighed human merits and demerits, rewarding virtue and punishing vice. At the event, spirit mediums, possessed by the spirits of omniscient, saving gods, offered ordinary people rituals to help them pass over a period of bad luck, assisting them in mastering their fate in the face of life's uncertainties. To this ordered cosmology and the risks of life I next turn in my analysis of the performance of spiritual healing and the theodicy of popular religious culture.

CHAPTER ONE

Mending Luck

When millionaire Chinese with great influence in their community
regulate their investments by the throw of the bamboo slips in the
temple of Toh Pek Kong [the God of Prosperity], it is impossible to
expect the Chinese community as a whole to alter at a great rate.
                                    Purcell (1967 [1948]): 128

... Of the honored and highly placed, there is none greater that he
who possesses wealth and rank ....
                                    I Ching [*Yijing*] (1950): 321

R ECENTLY, SCHOLARS have widely debated the question of whether
the Confucian ethic has contributed to the "rise of industrial East Asia"
(Tu 1996: ix). Ambrose King notes that contemporary writings on Confucianism
and development are simultaneously Weberian and anti-Weberian, as these
studies emphasize examination of China's ethos, but do so in order to explain
China's success at modern capitalism rather than its failure (King 1996: 266).
Some authors are skeptical, seeing the promotion of Confucianism in Singapore,
for example, as a politically motivated and unsuccessful revitalization movement
(Kuo 1996). Others have concluded (contrary to Weber's arguments) that a social
structure based on Confucian ideals of authority and cooperation is basic to
the development of a distinctively Asian form of modern capitalism (see, for
example, Redding 1996).

Many of these discussions focus on the impact of Confucianism on patterns
of governance and social organization, to the neglect of Max Weber's arguments
regarding the implications of Chinese religiosity for the life orientation of the
individual. Weber was concerned with the force of morality in the practical
life of believers, and in his analysis of Protestantism he argued that the Puritan
concept of the calling and the Puritan practice of asceticism in everyday lives had
directly influenced the development of the capitalist way of life (Weber 1946a
[1906]; 1958 [1920].

Weber found these elements lacking in Chinese religion, and also noted that the Chinese "would simply refuse to be continually burdened with 'sin'" (Weber 1968 [1951]: 228). Weber argued that because god raised no ethical demands, the inner personality was never reformed by the demands of a religious ethos (Weber 1968 [1951]: 230). He also concluded that Confucian rationalism led Chinese to adapt to the world, whereas Puritan rationalism "means rational mastery of the world," an orientation that promoted the emergence of modern capitalism (Weber 1968 [1951]: 248).

In *The Religion of China*, Weber treated Confucianism, Daoism, and Buddhism as three coexisting traditions, each with its own ethos and theodicy. Contemporary scholars follow his lead by exploring implications of the Confucian ethic, with its emphasis on education, family values, and autocratic government, for modernization and capitalist development (Tu 1996). Although a useful starting point, this focus on the Confucian ethic tends to lead scholars to neglect popular religious culture. This is a significant oversight, for one finds the most convincing base for a Chinese capitalist ethos not in Confucianism, but rather in the syncretic blend of Confucianism, Buddhism, and Daoism that informs popular religious practice.

As many have observed, the capitalists of China's south coast who migrated to Southeast Asia were not Mandarins, nor were they steeped in the Confucian classics. Rather, they were persons who "knew how to handle money, and organize men in relation to money" (Freedman 1979 [1959]: 26). Their pragmatic ethos found expression in popular religious culture, with its temples, festivals, secret societies, and spirit mediums. Confucian ethics were one important element in that culture, but Buddhism, Daoism, and local forms of worship were also blended into the syncretic mix.

This pragmatic ethos persists in the Penang Chinese community. One of Penang's community leaders, a member of a centralized steering committee that coordinated the street-level committees celebrating the Hungry Ghosts Festival to raise funds to support collective projects like private Chinese schools and the rebuilding of the Chinese Town Hall, summed up Penang Chinese values in these terms:

Penang people have the mentality (*sixiang*) to pray, to earn money, to support Chinese culture and Chinese education. You don't see this strength anywhere else in Malaysia. Penang people have strong feelings (*ganqing*).

He concluded that in coordinating the month-long, Penang-wide celebrations of this festival, the centralized committee used worship of the gods to collect the power of Penang's Chinese community. His statement points to a convergence of religion, business, and Chinese culture in defining community. (See also DeBernardi 2004: 156–81).

In this chapter, I examine the popular religious ethos rather than the Confucian ethic alone to see what it might reveal about the Chinese orientation to economic action and aspirations. In particular, I investigate the everyday habits of interpretation and action that motivate people to seek answers to problems through divination or consultation with spirit mediums. I focus on Penang Chinese concepts of the good life and its vicissitudes, as represented in people's personal narratives, in rituals performed by spirit mediums, and in the visual and narrative representations of the gods. I also explicate Hokkien terms like luck (*un, yun*) and fate (*mia, ming*), benefactors (*kuijin, guiren*) and opponents (*siaujin, xiaoren*), concepts that people draw upon to explain events in their lives. Undoubtedly, scholars who take a culturalist approach have overestimated the power of a reified Chinese culture to explain Chinese business success in Southeast Asia.[1] Nonetheless, economic and material values and desires permeate the symbols, stories, and ritual practices of popular religious culture, and I consider it worthwhile to explore that ethos as one foundation for an understanding of Chinese popular religious culture.

Chinese popular religious symbols repeatedly and insistently celebrate the good things of life: prosperity, joy, luck, wealth, good health, long life, success, high social status, peace, and family harmony. In short, people pray for happiness. Graphic artists and storytellers interpret these achievements through the symbolic idioms of visual symbols and narrative exemplifications. But even the sharing of food may symbolize hoped-for successes through punning correspondences. At Chinese New Years, hosts offer their guests special foods so that they can 'eat meaning' (*chiah isu, chi yisi*). The word for 'eat' also means 'to participate,' so a Chinese who is invited to 'eat' a particular meaning is also being invited to participate in the good fortune represented by the festive food.

For example, because the Cantonese word for mandarin orange puns with the word for gold, Penang Chinese offer their guests at Chinese New Year oranges as a wish for wealth. They also offer cakes made with baking powder (*hoat koe, fagao*). Because the cakes rise, they are a symbol of growth and development, and by extension prosperity. The name for peanut rhymes with 'old age,' thus in offering guests peanuts they also wish them a long life. (See also Wong 1967: 73–74.) People also pray to their gods with meaning-laden foods, including pineapple (*onglai, huangli*), the Hokkien name for which puns with the phrase 'luck comes,' and this offering communicates the person's desire for good things to come. Hokkien do not offer watermelon (*sikoe, xigua*), because *si* puns with a word meaning 'to dismiss or resign' (*si, ci*) which suggests losing your job.

Since their earliest contact with Chinese, first Western missionaries, and later some scholars, characterized Chinese religion as materialistic, magical, and more focused on placating local demons than on submitting to transcendent gods. As Jan Jakob Maria de Groot described it:

The great thing which strikes us in the Confucian religion and its popular outgrowth is its thorough materialistic selfishness. Promotion of the material happiness of the world is its aim and end. As a religion of the *Tao*, it is practiced by the emperor and his government for no other purpose but to insure a good and regular working order of the *Tao*, so that the throne may stand firm and safe. And by the people it is diligently observed in order that their ancestors and gods may give them protection and bestow material blessings. There is in Confucianism not a trace of a higher religious aim, and I think that this fact suffices to define it as a religion of a lower order (de Groot 1912: 130–31).

Max Weber joined his voice to this chorus when he concluded that asceticism was lacking in Chinese religion, noting that the Confucian sought only "long life, health, and wealth in this world and beyond death the retention of his good name" (1968 [1951]: 228). Peasants and merchants exalted the God of Wealth, whom the creators of paper gods depict accompanied by a coin dragon and a treasure horse, in scenes filled with images of fine jewels and coral, coins, gold and silver ingots, and money trees. Artists also depict Wealth Gods in association

FIG. 13. A gilded cart loaded with 'gold ingots' for sale at a ritual goods shop in Singapore. Temple committees raffle items like these at banquets to raise money for their temples or for a charitable cause, 1997. Photo: Jean DeBernardi

with other forms of good luck, including having male descendants, longevity, "merit, fame, wealth, and glory" (Alexeiev 1989 [1928]: 43). Nothing could be further from the austere, self-abnegating Protestant ethic so exalted by Weber.[2]

Fulushou and the Habitus of Penang Chinese Popular Religious Culture

A Hokkien proverb has it that "writing 'person' (*lang, ren*) – two strokes – is easy, being a person is hard." For many Penang Chinese, 'being a person' or 'being human' (*choelang, zuoren*) means aspiring to a good life in which social relations are properly ordered and harmonious, and in which the individual has obtained wealth, social status, and family. Chinese commonly display representations of three values, either as characters written on scrolls, or in the embroidered, painted, or porcelain representations of three star gods. The first representation of Chinese "great expectations" carries a child and represents good fortune and prosperity (*hok, fu*); the next wears the robes of the magistrate, and represents high social status (*lok, lu*). The last has a tall bald forehead and, holding the peach of immortality in one hand and a medicine gourd in the other, represents long life (*siu, shou*).[3]

In colloquial Hokkien, the term *hok* (*fu*) is compounded in expressions relating to happiness (*hoklok, fulu*) and good fortune (*hokkhi, fuqi*) a term that Hokkien Christians use to translate the English word 'blessings.' Penang Chinese sometimes explained that this star god represented descendants, thus also equating human fertility with good fortune or blessing. Penang Chinese further associated good fortune with eating well, linking blessings with the fecundity of the earth. For example, friends often observed that because temple committees frequently invited me to be a guest at their lavish ten-course temple banquets, I undoubtedly had eating luck (*chiah hok, chi fu*). A local lay Buddhist nun called the Golden Aunt (*Kimko, Jingu*), a widow who was caretaker for a small Guanyin temple and a well-known fortune-teller, confirmed this assessment, interpreting the painted illustrations in her book in this way when she told me:

Your eating luck is very good! Five bottles of wine, rice, fifteen sorts of dishes to eat. Lots of money! You have 90 katis of fish and meat. Food, clothing, you have no worries. You have food and clothing. So many things for you to eat!

My abundance of eating luck further meant that I had money and freedom from worry.

As sociologists and anthropologists often remind us, people aspire not only to wealth, but also to achieve a high social status and public recognition (Weber 1946b). These values are exemplified by the second star god, *lok (lu)*, representing

FIG. 14. Statues of star gods representing long life, success, and prosperity, Singapore, 2005. Photo: Jean Debernardi

both happiness and official pay. In the Confucian frame of reference, a position in the official bureaucracy was a path both to financial success and reputation (*miasia^n*, *ming*) or face (*bin*, *mian*). Although the official bureaucracy has long been ended, the desire for social visibility and respectability remains highly valued, and still is represented by the image of a man wearing the Mandarin's robes.

Although this star god represents social status in the dress of the Chinese Mandarin, Penang's status system depends upon wealth rather than the cultivated distinction of the Confucian superior man. As Chan Kwok Bun and Claire Chiang have noted, entrepreneurs used their wealth to gain elite status, and "the masses would accord merchants their desired status in return for the latter's readiness to channel their wealth back to society" (Chan and Chiang 1994: 303–4). Wealth indicates that a person has moral merit, but it also enables individuals to perform acts of charity that further confirm their moral merit.[4] Georg Simmel notes that this social distinction is an "unearned increment" of the ownership of wealth that is unavailable to those who lack the means to demonstrate public benevolence (Simmel 1978 [1907]: 220). As Weber aptly put it, Chinese believe in "the value of wealth as a universal means of moral perfection" (Weber 1968 [1951]: 242).

Persons with social distinction are said to have face, and they command respect. Others recognize and greet them, and invite them to be honored guests at temple banquets and fund raisers. At temple banquets the guests of honor are active and visible: they make speeches, lead others in song, award prizes in the lucky draw, give or receive awards that recognize distinguished citizens, events that reporters for the Chinese press record with photographs and articles. A person with face sits at the head table at the banquet, and the hosts insist that he (or more rarely, she) takes first from the shared dishes brought out course by course, and they keep drinks flowing. Chinese highly esteem acts of charity, and in Penang the guest of honor often further builds face at these events by announcing a contribution to a public cause, such as a construction fund for a Chinese school or an emergency relief fund.

For example, fund-raising was a major goal of the cycle of banquets coordinated by the Universal Ferry (Central Primordial) Committee formed in Penang in 1974 to coordinate fund-raising at community banquets during the month-long Hungry Ghosts Festival. The organizers invited prominent Penangites to attend the banquets as guests of honor, and to donate to community causes. When one prominent English-educated politician arranged to be out of town during the seventh lunar month, during which time there were probably over 130 fund-raising banquets, many took note of his absence. When he next ran for public office, he lost the election to a candidate who was widely rumored to have the support of the temples because he had promised them generous donations were he elected.

FIG. 15. Calligraphic representation of the characters meaning prosperity, status, and long life (*fulushou*) in a decorative arts store in Singapore, 1997. Photo: Jean DeBernardi

The achievement of face in the community through public participation, including acts of charity, has another potentially pragmatic function in a community enmeshed in network capitalism. If a person is recognized in the community and has face, then their social network will continue to grow to include the friends of friends. A large network is an important element of a person's symbolic capital, and the larger the social network, the more likely the person is to run into 'valuable people' (*kuijin, guiren*), who are benefactors or persons who will bring them luck.

Finally, Chinese traditionalists also pray for long life and health, symbolized by the third star god, who holds a peach and a gourd and has the high forehead of the Daoist immortal. As I will discuss, some spirit mediums taught that the goal of self-cultivation through fasting and meditation was immortality: escape from the cycle of death and rebirth. Most humans, however, face a finite, predetermined life span. Still, as Richard Smith points out:

Although the Confucian classics and a number of popular proverbs emphasized that health and longevity were predestined, few individuals in Ch'ing [*Qing*] China accepted their fate passively. Most people believed that they could modify their fate, either by moral or magical means. In fact, the two sources of power were closely related. (Smith 1993: 163)

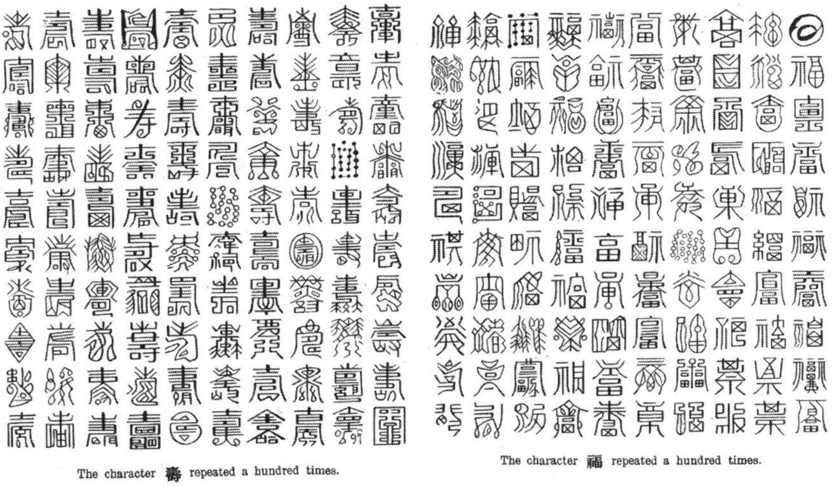

The character 壽 repeated a hundred times.

The character 福 repeated a hundred times.

FIG. 16. Two charm papers, one repeating the character for 'long life' and the other repeating 'prosperity' a hundred times each. From J.J.M. De Groot 1964 [1892–1910] Vol. 6: Plate 14.

At temple fairs, spirit mediums often perform simple rituals that involve prayers for long life, just as the Third Prince did at the shrine-grotto on Choo Kong's birthday, using tiny replacement bodies to change the luck of participants.

People prize good fortune, high status, and longevity, but do not always attain them. As one Hainanese teacher explained to me, it is difficult for any individual to have all three ingredients of the good life. One of Penang's most prominent millionaires had great wealth, was over eighty years old, and in good health – but he had no son, and adopted three nephews to take over his businesses. A Hokkien Christian friend observed that she had her children and her health, but did not have the "luck to get money." She pointed out, however, that money could not buy health.

Chinese Popular Religious Theodicy: Threats to Good Fortune, Wealth, and Long Life

Chinese popular religious culture is permeated with images of the good life. But commonly, people lack the luck to achieve their goals, even when their behavior is moral and their intentions are excellent. People cannot control their constitutive luck, in other words "the factors that set up our personalities" (Luper 1996: 9), nor do they choose their gender or their parents. This comment from a Buddhist fortune-teller known as the 'Golden Aunt' directly addresses her view of my constitutive luck and its limitations: "You are a girl who is like a man. You have a man's way of thinking. If you were a man, you could be a president...."

Constitutive luck not only imposes limits, but also "acting on our plans is fraught with luck; acting as we plan is not something we can guarantee" (Luper 1996: 11). A person may mean well, but events still may go awry; a person may act in ways that affront morality, but still do good, and philosopher Bernard Williams captures the uncertainty of these outcomes in the notion of moral luck (1981: 32). He describes the term moral luck as radically incoherent from the perspective of a Kantian concept of morality, but the term nicely captures the limitations to the notion that good behavior will lead to a good outcome.

Williams explains the limits to our ability to achieve a successful moral life through rational choice in these terms:

One's history as an agent is a web in which anything that is the product of the will is surrounded and held up and partly formed by things that are not, in such a way that reflection can go only in one of two directions: either in the direction of saying that responsible agency is a fairly superficial concept, which has a limited use in harmonizing what happens, or else that it is not a superficial concept, but that it cannot ultimately be purified – if one attaches importance to the sense of what one is in terms of what one has done and what in the world one is responsible for, one must accept much that makes its claim on that sense solely in virtue of its being actual. (Williams 1981: 29–30)

The ethos of Chinese popular religious culture captures these limitations both in the concept of predetermined limits to life, happiness, and life span, and in the notions of karma and luck.

Fate

People commonly say that heaven controls how many children and how much money a person will have in life, as well as how long he or she will live. People describe these aspects of life as 'determined' (*chutia^n*, *zhuding*) by fate or heaven.[5] Master Poh offered these comments on money and the human life span:

In a life, you are given just so much money. Money – so much is yours, you speak of money as yours, and if you have lots it's better. These things are borrowed to use, lent to you to use, if you have money you can eat. We come to earth for a few decades, only a few decades. It's not to say that you have eternal life.

He continued with a story of Ancestor Pi, an old woman who lived until 803 years old, who only died after ghosts sent by hell's bureaucrats tricked her into telling them her age (see Chapter Five).

The year, month, day, and even hour of a person's birth profoundly determines a person's fate, which Daoists call *benming*. We may translate the term *benming* as a person's astrologically determined constitutive fate, created in the intersection of the rotation of the heavens with the temporality of a unique human life.[6] Like the rotation of stars in the heavens, an individual's constitutive fate is both orderly and dynamic, and the dynamics of fate influence life's successes and failures.

One Singaporean entrepreneur observed:

I think I am the optimistic sort. It did not bother me how much I had lost (in my film business). I felt that since I did not bring any money to this world, the fact that I am making money now must be attributed to fate. In fact what I had lost in my business was not because I was not capable or lacking in good judgment. I attributed my failure to fate as well and that made me feel at peace with myself.... (Chan and Chiang 1994: 264).

And a friend commented that she consoled herself after a business failure with this Hokkien proverb: "Fate (*mia, ming*) is like waves, sometimes low, but then rising so high." She also cited another proverb: "Money has four legs, people have two legs," which she explained to mean, "You cannot chase money, money must find you."

The gods-in-their-mediums frequently urged people to have sympathy for those who were poor or unfortunate, explaining that they were fated to be so.[7] For example, at a temple festival celebrating the ascension day of Laozi, a spirit medium possessed by his deified spirit – Taishang Laojun, the Very High Old Lord – gathered his temple committee members together and lectured them. Later, a temple committee member summarized his teachings for me:

Do not look down on the poor. You must put yourself in the other's place.... Human beings tend to discriminate. You should do good deeds. That will benefit your descendants. Some men are rich, some are poor, some are disabled, some are old, that is your fate. You must do good, do charity, help the poor.

Although people cannot undo their fate, nonetheless he exhorted his disciples to shape the future by doing good deeds.

To learn more about their constitutive fate, people visit fortune-tellers who can interpret their eight-character horoscope, a horoscope based on the year, month, date, and time of birth. The Golden Aunt, for example, used a richly illustrated, hand-written book as her guide to prognostication, although the book's pictures appeared to guide her interpretations more than the text itself. At the consultations that I observed, she told friends the star of their birth, predicted when in their lives they would have good or bad fortune; when they would encounter benefactors or enemies; when they would meet their husband or wife; and how many children they would have. As a Buddhist fortune-teller, she also advised them about the impact of their grandparents' karma on their lives, and about their identity and behavior in previous lives.

For example, after translating my birth date into the lunar calendar system, and identifying me as a dragon, she offered this prognostication:

Your luck is bad (*soe, shuai*). You are not yet flying high. Your dragon is inside a well [referring to an illustration]. To be a person, you must wait until you have passed over this luck. After this, you can definitely fly very high. Then only will you have benefactors....Your grandparents did good deeds. Now you, the child, get the benefit.... In your former life you were named Chu. In your former life you were a good person. In this life you were born to be a good person. But now don't be vegetarian. When you are old, give to charity....

She also read my palm and advised me that when I reached twenty-nine and thirty years old I would encounter many enemies ('small people'), but starting at thirty-two I would walk into great luck, and that when I reached thirty-five, I would have everything I wanted. She predicted, however, that this period of fulfillment would end when I reached thirty-eight, and that at thirty-nine I should pray a lot.

The Chinese astrological cycle associates every year in the twelve-year cycle of Earthly Branches with an animal, and Malaysian Chinese conventionally hold that those born in certain animal years are incompatible with others. Persons born in the Ox year, for example, are deemed incapable of getting along with those born in the Sheep year. As the Datuk Aunt explained it, "In the old days, if you wanted to marry you must first look at the couple's horoscope, and you would face a quick death if the years were not suited." More recently, she concluded, people paid less attention to their astrological fate, and paid for their neglect with shorter life-spans.

A child's horoscope also must be harmonious (*hapho, hehe*) with those of their parents; otherwise, misfortune may result. For example, a Christian friend married to a Buddhist was indifferent to traditional Chinese beliefs about astrological compatibilities. Despite a warning from her husband's aunt, the Christian woman became pregnant and gave birth to a daughter whose animal year was incompatible with her husband's. When their business failed, leaving them overwhelmingly indebted to their creditors, some members of her husband's family attributed the failure to this astrological incompatibility.[8] By contrast, when her cousin's wife struck the lottery just after she gave birth, gambling on her uncle's car license number when he came to visit, the family attributed this lucky event to the harmony between the parents and child.

My friend overheard women on the bus discuss an even more dire case of astrological incompatibility: a child was born in the tiger year, in the tiger month, at the tiger hour. The mother died when he was born, his father died when he began to speak, and when he shot his third arrow he missed and hurt himself, becoming lame. In cases where astrological disharmony exists, people commonly arrange a fictitious adoption of the incompatible child to another couple who are astrologically better suited, praying to the man's ancestors that the child be recognized as an adopted son or daughter (*khoe, qi*), and teaching the child to address their new fictitious parents as 'mama' and 'bapa.'[9]

Karma and Moral Merit

From the perspective of the popular religious theodicy, people are individuated by their relation to time, most significantly defined by the time of birth, which determines their constitutive fate. But Penang Chinese also commonly interpret worldly success and high social status as a reward for actions done in a past life that determine the individual's fate in this life, and a lack of luck as evidence of misdeeds in a former life. The notion of karma is a particularly powerful way to explain misfortune. Indeed, Weber concluded that karma provided the "most complete formal solution of the problem of theodicy" (Weber 1968 [1951]: 145).

The relationship of karmic cause and effect is stated very baldly in the *Cause and Effect Sutra*, which despite its name is likely to be a contemporary text written by planchette divination. A number of pious sponsors paid for the publication of a bilingual illustrated edition of this short text in English and Mandarin, together with eight stories about karmic retribution, which they distributed as a means of accruing merit. According to the *Cause and Effect Sutra*:

> Buddha Shakyamuni told Ananda and the rest of the disciples to listen carefully. He said, "Well, well, I shall explain things with the truth: in the present world, you may see that some are suffering poverty but some are enjoying wealth. All these have been soundly ordained with causes depending on what they did in their previous lives. Firstly, parents must be loved. Secondly, Buddha must be respected. Thirdly, there must not be killing or fighting and all living things should be well taken care of. Fourthly, eat only vegetables and give alms for public welfare. These are the good causes that, when carried out, will bring a man wealth and happiness." He continued to reveal the truth of causes and effects as follows: "Wealth in this life is conditioned by the things one did in the previous life. It is the Cause. If one fulfilled the Cause faithfully, one's life would be ensured with wealth, peace, safety, and happiness." (*Cause and Effect Sutra* 1980: 2)

The Sutra continues with questions and answers. Why is a man a powerful official? He must have richly clothed the Buddha in gold leaf in a previous life. Why is another man a millionaire who lives in a big house? He no doubt donated generously for the building of temples and other public facilities. Why is a man single and lonesome? He raped another man's wife in his previous life. Why is a man born deaf and dumb? He despised and scolded his parents in a previous life. What were the previous lives of cows and horses? They are humans who failed to pay their debts (*Cause and Effect Sutra* 1980: 2–5). Finally, anyone who insults the *Cause and Effect Sutra* will be reborn as an animal in the next life, whereas anyone who has it printed and distributed will have "honourable or royal status in the next life," and may even be "born blessed in the Happy Kingdom of Buddha Amitabha" (*Cause and Effect Sutra* 1980: 8–9).

People may seek to learn the sources of karmic bad luck through divination, and may compensate for misdeeds in a past life through acts of merit-making. For example, the Buddhist fortune-teller, the Golden Aunt, advised one friend that in a previous life she had stolen an old lady's dress, and that she should repay this debt. The Golden Aunt warned another that he had owed rice and money to monks in a former life, and advised him to pray and make merit in order to atone for these sins. People also invoke karma to explain an inharmonious family life in light of karmic retribution. For example, a young Buddhist nun explained her decision not to marry in light of the fact that if you had children, it was possible that they would be people you had wronged in a former existence who came into life to seek their revenge, and they might beat you or kill you.

Popular religious practice encourages people to improve future karma through moral actions, which alleviates a stark predestination with the suggestion that through good deeds, the individual can improve their fate. The deities possessing spirit mediums frequently urged their followers to do good deeds in order to get luck, suggesting that moral behavior would generate worldly success and good fortune for one's descendants. A spirit medium possessed by the Holy Mother put the ethos succinctly: "If you do good, you can be fortunate (*hokkhi*)." And Master Lim taught that, "Whether something is your fate or not is the result of your own actions."

Although the notion of karma is originally Buddhist, Daoists also adopted it and incorporated it into their moral code. Several spirit medium temples distributed morality books that taught this law of moral cause and effect, including a pamphlet-length version of *Taishang's Treatise on Action and Retribution* (*Taishang Ganying Pian* N.d), whose opening passage teaches:

> Taishang said: misery and happiness have no door. Just as shadow follows form, humans themselves cause their own happiness and misfortune. This is because in Heaven and Earth there exists a God who takes charge of human faults. According to the seriousness of the offence, this God will take away from the human's allotment [reckoning]. When a person's lot is reduced, he will become poor, and often meet with distress and worry, and everyone will loathe him. Penalty and misery will follow him, luck will avoid him, and the evil-star will bring him disaster. When the reckoning is complete, he will die.

Taishang's Treatise on Action and Retribution also notes that if people behave morally, gods and other celestial spirits will assist them. But they must first qualify for this assistance by their moral actions: "People who ask for help from a heavenly god must do 1300 good deeds, people who ask for help from an earthly celestial being must do 300 good deeds." Moreover, if a person seeks longevity, they must avoid any misdeeds. The moral is: "If the path is correct, then go forward; if not, then retreat" (*shidao zejin, feidao zetui*). Penang Chinese sum up this doctrine with an optimistic proverb: "If you have a good heart, you will get repaid." The law of moral cause and effect has its limits as an explanatory tool, however, and there is also a commonly used parody of this proverb which goes: "If you have a good heart, you'll get a thunder kiss."

Good and Bad Lives

Georg Simmel observed that:

Wealth, indeed, is often regarded as a kind of moral merit, as is indicated by the term 'respectability' and by popular references to the well-to-do as 'upright citizens' or 'the better-class public.' The same phenomenon is shown from the other side by the fact that the poor are treated as if they were guilty, that beggars are angrily driven away, and that even good natured people consider themselves naturally superior to the poor. (Simmel 1978 [1907]: 217–18)

The interrelation of morality and social status find clear expression in the Chinese ranking of deities, whose identities and passions, or transcendence of passion, express their moral being.

Take, for example, a spirit medium known as the Datuk Aunt's explanation of good and bad local spirits. The good ones were the spirits of good people, and had houses. The bad ones were "trishaw pullers, cart pullers, people who haven't studied, who don't know how to read." The bad spirits lived by the roadside and in trees and swore at people, and although they might help humans, if they felt slighted by the repayment they wanted the person's life back in exchange. The contrast between good and bad spirits parallels a division of people into good and bad. Good Datuk Kong have houses; the bad ones are homeless and illiterate. Those without moral merit might help people, but they are also more likely to follow an amoral path if provoked. Popular images of rebirth confirm the identification between moral merit and wealth. One committee member at a spirit medium temple, who was also a member of the Red Swastika Society, a well-known moral uplifting association observed:

God, Buddha, Mohammed, all teach us to do good things. If you do good, next time your soul will return to a good person – a wealthy person. This is karma, the idea that suffering is a result of past life. We must do good to clear our debts, so that in the next life we will not suffer. There are three stages of life. The first is simple – animals. The second is self-conscious – human beings. The third is cosmic consciousness – saints, Buddhas, and Bodhisattvas. The aim is to reach the third stage.

As if to confirm their original lack of moral merit, people with a bad fate (*pai mia, dai ming*) are the most likely to "do bad" (*choe phai^n*, *zuo dai*), that is, to throw in their lot with the dark side of society in order to enjoy some of life's goods (see DeBernardi 1987). At the same time, "a 'good' person is a moral person; and a moral person, a successful person" (Chan and Chiang 1994: 304). Thus morality and social status are mutually confirming.

Although possessed spirit mediums sometimes offer their followers winning lottery numbers (or so they claim), more often they console individuals who have been disappointed in their quest for the good things of life. At one well-attended family trance session, for example, most of those present asked the god possessing the spirit medium for improved prosperity and winning lottery numbers. The god did not hold out high hopes for most: he told one woman that her luck was not strong, and that this was why she was not wealthy. Another man, tense and agitated, told the god that he wanted money and success. The god advised him that he worried too much about money, and that he should pray more instead. In these two cases, the popular religious framework of meaning rather than promoting optimism rather served to alleviate anxiety over a lack of worldly success. As Taishang Laojun advised his temple committee: "It is better to have peace than to get money. It is better for things to be smooth."

Cycles of Luck and Divination

In a study of Malacca's Cheng Hoon Teng Temple, Datuk Tan Cheng Lock, an English-educated Straits Chinese leader, emphasized the prominence of divination and fortune-telling in the temple, including use of the bamboo sticks to divine hexagrams from the *Yijing*. He concluded that, "The science of the *I Ching* [*Yijing*] is not based on the causality principle of western science, but on the assumption that things or events can be connected by another sequence, which Jung has tentatively called synchronism, according to which whatever is born or done this moment of time has the qualities or basic conditions of this moment of time" (Tan 1949: 11). The notion of 'synchronism' or 'synchronicity,' which Jung defined as 'meaningful coincidence' (Jung 1960: 428) has important consequences for the popular religious theodicy.

Penangites commonly interpret as meaningful unexpected events in their everyday lives. When I left a gate unlatched while paying a Chinese New Year visit to my neighbor, for example, a white cow followed me into the yard. I was apologetic, expecting my host to be annoyed, but instead she eagerly sought for her God of Prosperity dream book to translate 'white cow' into a lottery number. And when I phoned my landlady to tell her that my car had broken down, she exclaimed that she had known that something had happened because my license plate number had been the winning number in the four-digit lottery, and she reproached me for not phoning her sooner so that she could have bought a ticket. By contrast, when my landlord lost MR1,500 at the racetrack, he commented that he should have known that it would be an unlucky day when his pen would not write in the morning.

People also commonly ascribe misfortune to spiritual collisions (*chhiongtioh*, *chongde*), which are especially likely to occur when an individual's luck is low. As one temple committee member observed, "when a bride's luck is low and she meets a funeral, she can *chhiongtioh*. If it's high, there's no problem." Similarly, people whose luck is low are considered to be at risk for disturbance from the unseen world of spirits that might result in a lingering illness, disharmony in their social relations, or problems like infertility. He added that Chinese commonly visited spirit mediums to check to see if their misfortunes were the result of a spiritual collision. (Of this, more in Chapter Two.)

Many consult spirit mediums or oracles to ascertain whether their luck is high or low before deciding whether or not to take a risk, including the economic risks of investing money or gambling. Members of one temple committee observed that many Chinese men prayed in the early morning at the Guanyin temple on Pitt Street, observing that one Chinese millionaire, Yeap Chor Ee, visited the Pitt Street temple before speculating on sugar futures. They unanimously attributed his investment success to Guanyin's assistance.[10]

The practice relates to a more general trust in the principals of what de Groot has termed chronomancy, the science of selecting auspicious times for important activities. As he notes, the almanac was everyman's guide to this ebb and flow of auspicious times, and guided the selection of favorable moments to perform important events like weddings and rituals (de Groot 1912: 52–53). Those observant of Chinese taboos, for example, would not schedule 'red events' (*angsu*, *hongshi*) like weddings during the seventh lunar month, when the ghosts are roaming the earth on vacation from hell, because the cosmic forces of these joyful and mournful events do not agree, and their intersection might lead to a spiritual collision.

People commonly divine auspicious times for events. At the start of a Hungry Ghosts festival, for example, the committee consulted a medium whose possessing deity told them to have the opening ceremonies at noon rather than at 9:00 a.m. as planned in order to ensure good fortune. The god also advised that those born in the dragon, tiger, and rabbit years could not watch the ceremony because they risked a spiritual collision with the King of Hell, and he wished everyone peace and prosperity (*pengan hoatchai*, *pingan facai*). Although some committee members grumbled that rescheduling the ceremonies would be highly inconvenient and considered adhering to their original schedule, they reluctantly decided that they had no choice but to follow the god's command.

FIG. 17. A temple committee member throws divining crescents to ask the god to select the new keeper of the incense urn, George Town, 1980. Photo: Jean DeBernardi

Divination to make personal decisions is common practice, and people often consult the gods in their temples for advice using a pair of divining crescents that give three responses. The crescents are curved on one side and flat on the other. If they both fall with their flat sides down, the answer to the question put to the god is no. If they fall with their flat sides up, the god is 'laughing,' but if they fall with one side up and one side down, then the response is yes.

Another form of divination also entails kneeling before the altar to ask a question of the gods, but instead of throwing the divining crescents, people shake a tube filled with sixty or sixty-four bamboo sticks (*chhiamsi, jianshi*) until one falls out. This bamboo stick will have a number. Sometimes the divining crescents are used to confirm that this is indeed the correct number. Then the stick is taken to the temple attendant who gives back a corresponding charm. The charm is a small slip of paper on which is written a poem and an interpretation, which the supplicant then interprets in light of the question he or she has asked.

A ritual store near Penang's main Guanyin Temple, the Kong Hock Palace (*Kong Hock Kiong, Guangfu Gong*), sold a book that included reprints of the temple's sixty charm poems, each of which is four lines long, each line seven characters in length. The first of these poems, number one, is entitled "Baogong Invites the Thunder God to Surprise the Renzong Emperor." Baogong is a famous judge who represents the ideal, incorruptible official, and the title alludes to an incident in which this highly principled official rebuked the emperor for an unspecified misdeed:

> When the sun comes out, you see that the wind and clouds have scattered,
> Bright and pure it shines on the world,
> The path in front passes through the Big Dao,
> The myriad things and pure luck protect peace.

The poem is followed by a detailed explication that expands on the image of the sun coming out and dispersing the clouds, creating brightness and a 'pure great peace.' The prophecy exhorts the asker to energetically face the future, because "all roads will lead to Rome" for that individual. Moreover, the gods will protect the person in everything he or she undertakes, ensuring bright fortune and peace.

This short poem is followed by a more specific interpretation that assesses the answer to twenty-six potential questions, including: shipping, raising fish and seedlings, making money, farming, trade, pregnancy, marriage, family matters, lost items, missing people, letters from afar, livestock, building a house, the location of tombs, travel, sailing, miscellaneous concerns, healing illness, doing things, examinations, lawsuits, domestic matters, and getting a son. The judgments in this very auspicious fortune include such descriptors as: 'no wor-ries,' 'very lucky,' 'harmonious,' 'peaceful,' and 'will win the advantage.' Other less auspicious poems assess the situation to be just the reverse: difficult, unlucky, inharmonious, or impossible (*Guanyin Pusa Lingqian Jieshuo* N.d.).

At many temples, divination specialists interpret the poems in light of the supplicant's question. For example, when I visited the Mountain-top Earth Mother Temple (*Shanding Dimu Miao*), a temple managed by Cantonese nuns whose temple belonged to the Great Way of Former Heaven tradition, I threw the bamboo sticks and drew charm number two, with this text:

> The whale has not yet grown up [changed] to protect the rivers and streams
> If you cannot yet ascend to the heights, you can still look towards them.
> Another day a majestic body will develop.
> Then very likely the Lord will reach the dragon gate with one leap.

The interpretation on the charm prosaically added, "You must content yourself to be patient. Honor will be yours in the future."

Although I told the vegetarian nun who fetched the charm for me that I was simply checking my luck, she knew that I was in Malaysia with no apparent worries about money or health, and guessed that it was an unhappy relationship that troubled me. She comforted me that my luck would be better in the future:

> This year, when you speak, you say the words, but in your heart it's not true. You are like a fish that has just been born. You are going to be set down in the big sea. Your heart is big, when you think of things, you think big.
>
> Now, if you have an affinity [*ianhun, yuanfen*, a boyfriend or girlfriend], he is not the real affinity. Next year he will come, the one who comes next year is good. Now your heart is confused. You mustn't worry [literally, 'think east, think west']. If you're confused, you can't eat or sleep. Then your temper is bad, it's not good. . . . You shouldn't put things in your heart. You're clever at worrying. You think and think. Don't think this and that.

By contrast, a fortune that I drew at the Prosperity Palace (or Snake Temple), whose main deity is the healing Pure Water Patriarch, locally called the Snake God, specifically addressed the healing of illness:

Luokun Falls Ill (number four) [11]
> Seek assistance from the gods and tell Buddha that you think this [illness] will be difficult to heal.
> Illness has wrapped the body for some time.
> Happiness arrives and peace; you will recover in a short time.
> In the spring wind the plum and peach again grow new branches.

This is an inauspicious charm, but even so it predicts that recovery will come soon, just as in spring flowering trees put out new branches. Although much briefer than *Guanyin's Numinous Charms*, the explication adds four specific predictions: that business will be good in the winter; that the asker will give birth to a boy; that if a person is sick, the illness will linger; and that there will be no marriage.[12]

Indeed, these poems and their interpretations are a catalog of people's aspirations and fears, but also offer hope that whatever a person's current condition might be, in the future there will be change: the sun will come out from behind the clouds, the person will grow stronger just like the small fish that transforms into a whale, or be reborn like the fruit tree that puts out new leaves and branches in the spring.

Mending Luck

Penangites often comment that individuals have personal cycles of high or low luck, and that these may determine the success or failure of their undertakings. Take, for example, this story, which describes the divergent fates of two sisters:

My aunt spent thirty years in an asylum. She saw a flower on the way back from Bukit Mertajam. My mother's luck was high, it was bright, so she didn't pick the flower. My aunt picked it, and she went mad. She sang instead of sleeping, she refused to bathe. The magic (*kongtau*) was not intended for her, but since she picked up the flower, she went mad. There's no way to send it back since you can't hypnotize your enemies. You have no idea as to its origin.

My friend's explanation of why one sister went mad, while the other stayed healthy in their chance encounter with a black magic charm evokes Jung's notion of meaningful coincidence, and also recalls E. E. Evans-Pritchard's explanation of Azande belief in magic (see Evans-Pritchard 1937).

Evans-Pritchard (1937) noted that Azande understood the chain of cause and effect that led to the collapse of a granary, but asked why particular persons happened to be injured when it fell, and found the answer in witchcraft. Chinese popular religious theodicy explains misfortune in light of magic, but it goes one step further and proposes that one person was injured while the other remained uninjured, because one's luck was low while the other's was high, a notion not unlike the idea of resistance to disease. Whereas the Azande diviner employs a system of divination that eventually would lead to a witchcraft accusation, the Chinese system allows for a greater degree of randomness, in this case the intersection between a random encounter with black magic and an individual's cycles of high and low luck. Because the magic was encountered through chance and not sent to this individual deliberately, however, it cannot be undone: to a certain extent, this coincidence is *not* meaningful. Had the black magic been directed to her by an enemy, a spirit medium could have fought a spiritual match with the enemy, invoking a higher spiritual power to undo the magic.

The gods-in-their-mediums sometimes instruct individual clients to perform rituals to change their luck (*kai-un, gaiyun*). For example, after a business failure, a spirit medium told a friend's husband to wash his face in water in which seven colors of flowers had been placed in order to "change your bad luck" (*kai lu-e phai^n un, gai nide daiyun*). Spirit mediums also perform collective rituals to 'mend' or 'nourish' luck' (*po· un, bu yun*) at temple festivals.

On the occasion of a festival celebrating Taishang Laojun's birthday, for example, the god's spirit medium performed a luck-mending ceremony. The worshippers set up a table in front of the altar to the Lord of Heaven, and placed on it eight bundles of five to seven replacement bodies, together with offerings of food and gold paper. The spirit medium, possessed by Taishang Laojun, stood behind the kneeling person and cracked his exorcizing whip, first to the left of the person, then to the right. He waved the scepter of longevity over the client's head, or around clothing brought in proxy for the person, and said "Eat [participate in] old age!" (*chiah laulau, chi laolao*), then stamped the client's clothing with the temple seal. A small paper and bamboo replacement body (*thoesin, tishen*) on which the person's name and date and time of birth had been written was then thrown under the table. A temple committee member explained to me that the replacement body was "like the holy ghost," and drove off evil. At the end of the day, the medium burned all the tiny paper replacement bodies together with hell money and yellow paper charms at the side of the road.

Compare this ritual with an Amoy ritual reported by de Groot, in which a Daoist priest recites a "spell . . . of the following tenor" while moving the replacement body over the body of the afflicted person:

This contact with the front of the body brings purity and prosperity, and the contact with the back gives power to eat (i.e. to live) till an old, old, old age; the contact with the left side establishes well-being for years and years, and the contact with the right side bestows longevity; happy fate, come! ill fate, be transferred to the substitute! (de Groot 1964 [1892–1910] Vol. 6: 1103)

Thus this ritual both invites good luck and exorcizes bad.

At another temple dedicated to Taishang Laojun, Daoist priests performed an even more elaborate and well-attended ceremony to 'pass over' a period of bad luck (*ke phai^n un, guo daiyun*) on the occasion of Taishang Laojun's Ascension day. At this ritual performance, the committee members each took a paper replacement body (*thoesin, tishen*) and three joss sticks, entered the temple, and faced the altar. While the Daoist priests chanted, the chief priest

F I G . 1 8 . Daoist priests perform a luck-changing ritual for members of the temple committee, Ayer Itam, 1981. Photo: Jean DeBernardi

called each individual to stand in front of the temple facing in, and announced his or her name and address. He then passed the replacement body over the front of the person's body. He faced out of the temple, towards the Lord of Heaven's altar, then faced in again, and passed the effigy over the back, then over the head of the person. He slid the replacement body down a cloth slide formed from three unfurled bolts of cloth – red, yellow, and flowered, which one committee member explained represented good, average, and bad luck. During the ceremony, the flowered cloth was on top, and he noted that the ceremony reversed that position in order to mend the participants' luck (*po· un, buyun*).[13] Finally, the person was given a pink tortoise-bread (*miku, miangui*), which represented longevity, and the priest moved on to the next person whose luck was to be mended.[14] Although having a long life may be the result of predestination, the person still must take steps to treat invisible spiritual forces with proper respect in order to avoid bad luck that might cut that life-span short.[15]

Benefactors and Enemies

Constitutive fate and cycles of luck are not the only explanation of good and bad fortune. Penang Chinese also regard a person's network and chance encounters as a source of luck or misfortune. Arthur Schopenhauer discusses this dimension of luck:

All events in a man's life would accordingly stand in two fundamentally different kinds of connection: firstly, in the objective, causal connection of the natural process; secondly, in a subjective connection which exists only in relation to the individual who experiences it, and which is thus as subjective as his own dreams. . . . That both kinds of connection exist simultaneously, and the selfsame event, although a link in two totally different chains, nevertheless falls into place in both, so that the fate of one individual invariably fits the fate of the other, and each is the hero of his own drama while simultaneously figuring in a drama foreign to him – this is something that surpasses our powers of comprehension, and can only be conceived as possible by virtue of the most wonderful pre-established harmony. (Schopenhauer 1913: 49, cited in Jung 1960: 428)

The theodicy of Chinese popular religious culture also explores this dimension of synchronicity, the impact that others have on an individual's fate. Consequently, people pray to encounter benefactors (*kuijin, guiren*; 'honourable' or 'valuable people'), and to avoid enemies (*siaujin, xiaoren*; 'small people'), since even chance encounters may be sources of new opportunity or misfortune.[16]

According to one friend, for example, some worship the Tiger God (*Ho· Ia, Hu Ye*) both for longevity and for protection against human threats to one's well-being and success:

The day of worship is the 2nd and 16th of every lunar month. He is worshiped with eggs, preferably duck eggs, and lard: you put the lard into the tiger's mouth. You throw peas at the statue to attain longevity. People say "If you throw to the tiger, you will 'eat' a long life" (*tim Ho · Ia, chiah dngmia,* tim *Hu Ye, chi changming*). We spit on a piece of paper with figures depicting small-minded people (*siau jin, xiaoren*), and step on it with our shoes. People worship the tiger god to keep bad hats from harming us. It is believed that by worshiping the tiger god it will eat up all the bad hats and they will not be bold to harm us.

People not only pray for protection against 'bad hats,' they also sometimes paste a charm on their door to represent a prayer for a helpful benefactor. Thus people seek human and spiritual benefactors who can help them but also protect them against their enemies.

Perhaps, then, it is not so surprising that a military god, the God of War (*Kuan Kong, Guangong*) is the patron of business success.[17] According to my landlady, she worshipped the God of War on her family altar because he helped with business, adding that, "If you worship him, you can kill people, but other people can't kill you." When I registered surprise at her answer she laughed, and added: "You can get money, and others won't get your money."

My landlord demonstrated Guangong's protective power with a story, claiming that Guangong had saved his father, who worked for the colonial civil service but ran illegal numbers on the side:

> Each week he took in 4,000 to 5,000 dollars, and he could earn 400 to 500 dollars. A friend turned informant to the police, and on a Friday, the day before the race, the police raided. My mother hid the chits in a tin sunk in the rice bin. They opened the safe and found 20,000 dollars, but they wanted the chits as evidence. The sergeant put his cane in the rice bin, and moved it around, but he couldn't find the tin. In the meantime, my grandmother was praying to Guangong. He saved them. Otherwise, eight children and the mother and grandmother would have had no breadwinner.

In the popular religious theodicy, protective deities like the God of War assist people in life's struggles by helping them in the unending battle for victory over spiritual and human opponents.

Household deities also have a role in protecting those who live in their domain. When a friend was beset by misfortune and ill health, her neighbor speculated that this was because she had married into a Buddhist family. As a consequence of this interfaith match, the Buddha blocked the entry of the Christian god into the house, and she and her children had lost their spiritual protection. Indeed, Penang Chinese often comment that everyone has to worship a god, implying that it was not necessarily important which god, so long as one had spiritual protection.

Moral Lessons

Classicist Martha Nussbaum has observed that Greek tragedies are ethical reflections, worthy of study in their own right:

> Tragic poems . . . are likely to confront and explore problems about human beings and luck that a philosophical text might be able to omit or avoid. Dealing, as they do, with the stories through which an entire culture has reflected about the situation of human beings and dealing, too, with the experiences of complex characters in these stories, they are unlikely to conceal from view the vulnerability of human lives to fortune, the mutability of our circumstances and our passions, the existence of conflicts among our commitments. (Nussbaum 1986:13)

Although they may not equal Greek tragedies in their narrative development, Chinese popular religious culture also offers stories that are reflections on the combination of ethical behavior, fate, and personal connections that shape a human life.

As I illustrate at much greater length in the four case studies Part Two, Chinese religious experts often explain Chinese theodicy through narratives that also offer ethical lessons to their audience. Take, for example, the following story, entitled "The Prince was Unfilial to his Father," in which the Datuk Aunt identified a particular kind of bad luck related to one's stage in life:

> A prince imprisoned his father in jail. He married, and when his wife was nine months pregnant, he invited the people to see where the Emperor was. When he went to see his father, his father was chanting. The son grew angry, and had his father's feet skinned so that he couldn't circumambulate the room as he chanted. The father sat and chanted prayers.
>
> If our luck comes to this, it's very unfortunate (*soe, shuai*) indeed. The title of this story, "The Prince Was Unfilial to his Father," represents this kind of bad luck, if people are very bad to you, for example, if someone succeeds in undercutting your business. You can know if you're going to have this sort of luck by calculating on your fingers.
>
> The son later realized that he had wronged the heavens by capturing his father and imprisoning him. His sin was very heavy, and he wanted to free the father. But his father had died.
>
> There are definite ages that are not good; people try to take away your good job. For women, 40, 25, and 28 are bad years. People cheat you of money, bother you, you have to mourn. At least one of these things will happen. If you mend your luck, you won't meet with the rest. For men, the bad years are 3-6-9, 36 and 39. People will gossip about you, you will have many troubles, people will borrow money from you and won't return it.

The Datuk Aunt dramatically presented the image of the son taking the kingdom away from his father, and then denying him the comfort of his religion, emphasizing the weight of his sin and the futility of his repenting after his father has died. But she equated this with the problems faced in a larger sphere of relationships with people who would undercut your business or take away your good job. These problems emerge in the human life cycle, and she proposed times that are particularly dangerous for men and women. She concluded, however, by advising us that everyone should perform rituals to mend their luck in order to prevent these troubles from arising.

Conclusion

The quest for prosperity, improved luck, and a good fate are central to the habits of interpretation and practice of Malaysian Chinese popular religious culture. People celebrate good fortune and seek to defend themselves against negative forces, be they black magic, or a police search for gambling chits, or a collision with a territorial spirit. While these celebrations of success have a moral dimension, the concepts of luck and fate acknowledge the randomness of human success or failure measured in terms of one's prosperity, status, and health.

In the Chinese popular religious ethos, money or its lack gives symbolic expression to the ebbs and flows of a person's life, representing an accumulation of merit from a past life or good fortune rewarded in the present life. It should come as no surprise, then, that the Chinese turn to their gods to pray for wealth and blessings, and that those who are less well off visit spirit mediums for lottery numbers, hoping that divine regard will be translated into a lucky turn of fate.

Simmel observed that "money is simply a means, a material or an example for the presentation of relations that exist between the most superficial, 'realistic' and fortuitous phenomena and the most idealized powers of existence, the most profound currents of individual life and history" (Simmel 1978 [1907]: 55). He also noted that money represents a potentiality that stores up future possibilities. But possibility has two very different aspects. A future event may be possible because a person has the necessary skills and tools to accomplish some act, like playing the piano. But even a person with the necessary ability to accomplish an act will only achieve that goal if certain conditions are met "whose occurrence we are unable to predict." Thus money crystallizes two elements of capability – skill and chance. The ethos of Chinese popular religious culture also emphasizes the dual nature of human potential: people can be instrumental in performing meritorious acts to secure future happiness for themselves and their descendants, but still must depend on their moral luck if they are to have the best possible outcomes.[18]

I have considered the habitus of popular religious culture, in particular focusing on the practical meaning of luck, fate, and wealth. In the practices of Chinese popular religion, symbolic images, rituals, and narratives celebrate many dimensions of human happiness. Means to happiness include good deeds (including charitable acts in the service of the larger community) and alliances with human and spiritual benefactors who may offer the individual protection and opportunities. The emphasis on wealth, community merit-making, and networking are compatible with a modern capitalist work ethic in which the individual strives for material symbols of success, community recognition of that success, and an ever-enlarging sphere of social relationships. Although these dimensions of the popular religious habitus are community and network oriented, the popular religious theodicy also leads the individual to confront a unique destiny. That theodicy explains the randomness of a person's success or failure in light of the combined operation of fate and cycles of luck, karma, moral merit, and synchronism.

Weber concluded that, "In the magic garden of heterodox doctrine (Taoism), a rational economy and technology of modern occidental character was simply out of the question." In particular, he singled out the absence of natural scientific knowledge, the power of chronomancers, and Daoism's "crude, abstruse, universist conception of the world" (Weber 1968 [1951]: 227). We may question, as many theorists have done, whether natural scientific knowledge is in fact incompatible with Daoism's magic garden. Bronislaw Malinowski demonstrated, for example, that Trobriand fishers invoked magic when deep-sea fishing (where the risks were high), but not in the lagoon. But they also built strong boats (Malinowski 1948: 30–31).

With a similar logic, Evans-Pritchard demonstrated that the Azande understood natural causality, but invoked witchcraft to explain coincidence. Similarly, a Penang Chinese investor or gambler employs skill, but recognizes limits to his or her ability to control outcomes. If the popular religious theodicy does shape a method of life, as a Weberian would argue, we might conclude that ascribing responsibility for success or failure to the impersonal operation of cycles of fate, rather than holding the individual responsible, will lead to greater peace of mind for the entrepreneur, and a greater willingness to take risks.

A Chinese Singaporean businessman observed that the worship of gods for protection instilled a confidence in him that contributed to his success:

When you believe a thing spiritually, you worship it. If you keep worshipping it even after your prayers have been answered, it is *sin* [*shen*, a deity]. Once a person has prayed to the deity, he receives the urge and the confidence to set about his objective. When one's confidence is strengthened, one is likely to succeed. It is not for one to worship *sin* [*shen*] and simply sit and wait for its protection. (Chan and Chiang 1994: 124)

When individuals invoke fate, luck, spiritual collisions, and coincidence as explanations for events in their lives over which they have little control, this may serve to build confidence, allay anxiety, and exonerate the individual from a personal sense of guilt in the face of failure. At the same time, however, the popular religious theodicy teaches that good deeds result in a longer life and greater success, thereby mitigating a fatalistic determinism with the message that a person can make his or her own luck through moral deeds.[19] The habitus of popular religious culture may well provide a useful life orientation for dealing with the risks and rewards of contemporary life in a capitalist society.

Let me now explore the practice of worshipping gods and placating ghosts as remedies for life's difficulties.

CHAPTER TWO

Spiritual Collisions

Choo-tzu says, "The spiritousness (ling) *of* Shên *is the result of the accumulated earnestness of the people – there is really no* Shên. *When one turns his back upon it, the spiritousness is immediately dispersed. Therefore, when the people honor it the* Shên *keeps its place, but you may scatter it with a kick."*

N. B. Dennys (1876): 91

WHEN THE MAGISTRATE CHOO KONG held court in the verdant meditation garden with his four bodyguards, Mrs. Huang exclaimed, "We are witnessing heaven on earth!" For believers, the trance performance of Chinese gods makes the workings of invisible worlds visible, and allows the gods to bring their numinous powers to influence human lives.

In this chapter, I examine the ways in which people, including spirit mediums, talk about, communicate with, imagine, and control gods and ghosts. I concur with Thomas Csordas that the anthropological analysis of religious imagery should reconcile "language and experience, representation and being in the world" (Csordas 1994: 81). Although formalized religious ideologies and ritual practices are crucial to the formation of the popular religious imagination, we must also examine the ways that people – including spirit mediums – imagine and construct the numinous in image, story, action, and experience.

Penangites know the gods through standardized cultural images, including the god images sold in religious shops, and also through books, films, and television serials.[1] People also construct the deities' immortality through ritualized acts of reverence or veneration. But as we have seen, people also feel the impact of invisible forces in their everyday lives in the experience of luck and misfortune. They tell stories about ghosts, magicians, and spirit mediums, and much occult gossip about spiritual collisions and black magic circulates in kitchens and coffee shops.[2] Chinese judge deities to be efficacious (*sia, lingyan*) if they have helped their worshippers, often through the spirit medium, in bettering their lives. A god will gain this reputation for a few years, only to lose it to another god who has done more for humans.

People often interpreted extraordinary events as intrusions of unseen forces into the world of the living. In one of his classes, Master Lim recalled that unexplained bad luck first led him to worship:

Sometimes you have a spate of bad luck. You don't know where it comes from, or what it is. One time, there were six of us in a house on Hutton Lane, and we called for a round of sweet bean drinks. I stirred mine, and went to eat it, and as I picked up the glass the bottom of the glass falls out! Everything was haywire. That was right as I went to Singapore to teach. I worshipped from the day I left Penang.

And another man, a temple committee member at the Taishang Laojun temple in Ayer Itam, explained to me that he prayed to the gods because he sought spiritual protection:

Religion is faith. When you have children, you realize how many pitfalls there are, possible accidents, but you cannot protect them twenty-four hours a day. To ask for protection you have to believe in a higher being. That's what I believe is religion. Ceremonies are different, but all religions are essentially the same.

Indeed, many people seek the assistance of spirit mediums precisely because they suspect that they or someone they know is suffering the effects of unexplained disturbances from the spiritual world.

Several spirit mediums observed that although the gods are invisible, nonetheless they protect or defend (*poho·, baohu*) people from a range of misfortunes. A former spirit medium observed:

Mr. Lim: You need faith. If you have faith, the god, the general, will send his subordinates to guard your house, and you will have no trouble. You won't see anything, this is a belief. But if you are a non-believer, then something may manifest itself. Don't joke about this!

Master Poh also asserted that invisible things came to protect people:

You fall down, have an accident, whatever, a close call, but there's no real trouble. How does this thing protect us? Pure things come and protect us, dirty things [ghosts] don't, must not come near us. . . . You say he doesn't exist, he takes care of you, you say he takes care of you, but you cannot see him, you cannot see him. He cannot let you see, it's like that. This is very deep, these are the deepest matters.

Visual images often represent these protective deities as military gods, fierce generals who subdue their spiritual inferiors.

In *The Religious System of China*, Jan Jakob Maria de Groot based his analysis of Chinese cosmology on the tension and opposition between gods (*sin, shen*) and ghosts (*kui, gui*). He viewed popular religious practice as fundamentally shaped by the belief that these two existed in tension, but also that the demonic spirits were empowered to harm humans. He puts his analysis elegantly:

The oldest and holiest books of the empire teach that the universe consists of two souls or breaths, called *Yang* and *Yin*, the *Yang* representing light, warmth, productivity, and life, also the heavens from which all these good things emanate; and the *Yin* being associated with darkness, cold, death, and the earth. The *Yang* is subdivided into an indefinite number of good souls or spirits, called *shen*, the *Yin* into particles or evil spirits, called *kwei* [*kui, gui*] specters; it is these *shen* and *kwei* which animate every being and every thing. It is they which constitute the soul of man. His *shen*, also called *hwun* [*hun*], immaterial, ethereal, like heaven itself from which it emanates, constitutes his intellect and the fine parts of his character, his virtues, while his *kwei* or *poh* [*pek, po*], is thought to represent his less refined qualities, his passions, vices, they being borrowed from material earth. Birth consists in an infusion of these souls; death in their departure, the *shen* returning to the *Yang* or heaven, the *kwei* to the *Yin* or earth (de Groot 1912: 3–4).

Spirit mediumship enacts the war between these two eternally opposed yet interdependent forces.

But de Groot further noted that this dualism is both internal and external since the human self and the cosmos both unite *yang* and *yin*, the spiritual and the material, and the human being is a microcosm of the macrocosm. Like the cosmos, the Chinese soul is divided into two parts, one spiritual and potentially divine, the other material and passion driven. Consequently, we sometimes find slippage between the cosmology of gods and ghosts and tensions within the human psyche between the material soul, with its egoistic desire for life's pleasures and rewards, and the spiritual soul, which is a socially oriented, moral superego prompted to acts of altruistic self-sacrifice and generosity to others. Indeed, gods and ghosts represent complementary aspects of the self that are dissolved only in death.[3]

For example, one spirit medium concluded that heaven and hell both 'live in the heart':

Taishang Laojun's spirit medium: The deities are on different planes. Heaven and hell have no gates. You are welcome in both places. It is up to you to choose, to choose good or bad habits. Heaven and hell by the right definition actually live in the heart. When the heart stops, you will know where you will be.

The planets have altitudes. Heaven and hell are not visible to human eyes, but are very near to us, we are on a very close plane to heaven and hell, like two mountains coming down to a plain. This is why some people can see ghosts and demons, why they want to communicate with deities and god.

And the former spirit medium who acted as his assistant observed:

Mr. Lim: In mediumship, if you have faith in the spirit it will come, or another spirit will come to cure. The important thing is that the medium must be sincere. Money should be far from his mind. The other planes are closer than you think, once you know. Once you believe you will find spirits who come and claim to be this deity.

The Monkey God is legendary, not factual. A priest went [to India] in fact for the Buddhist Scriptures, not the Monkey. So how is it that the Monkey possesses the medium? Humans have faith in the deity, so a god appears and the man assumes it is the Monkey. It is not really the Monkey, but a god come to earth to do good. He claims to be the Monkey, but his purpose in coming is to help these humans.

Thus faith and belief determine the identity chosen by the god, whom this spirit medium frankly identified as a god who adopts the persona of a fictional character.

Becoming a God

The Chinese popular religious pantheon is not systematized, but people discuss a rich array of supernatural beings, including saints (*sin, shen*), who are humans who achieved sainthood by means of virtuous behavior, deities (*angkong*), immortals (*sian, xian*), Buddhas (*Hut, Fo*), Bodhisattvas (*Pho·sat, Pusa*), and Lohans. The colloquial Hokkien term for deities, *angkong* refers precisely to the gods, whereas the term *shen* refers to a god, divinity, or spirit, but also the supernatural or magical, and may even refer to mind, intelligence, and the look in a person's eyes.[4] In the context of religious practice, however, the term finds a reasonable equivalent in the English term saint, because *shen* typically are humans who were invested (*hong, feng*) with rank after death by either a human or a divine emperor.

Master Lim further distinguished between saints (*shen*) and immortal ancestors (*siancho·, xianzu*) who were divine beings born of the "light of god," who came to earth to save humans. Although they may have been divine in origin, immortal ancestors like the Daoist immortal Lü Dongbin and the Emperor of the Dark Heavens in other respects are very like ordinary saints, since they often are born to a human life and achieve new levels of spiritual attainment and reentry to heaven through a life of self-cultivation and spiritual achievements. Unlike ordinary saints, however, people often worship these immortal ancestors as the founders of a school of teaching and a sect, and sometimes assume them to be extrahuman. In this respect, immortal ancestors are precisely like Christianity's Jesus Christ, who was both god and human. (See also Faure 1986.)

Spirit mediums sometimes taught that if people transformed themselves through religious cultivation (*siuheng, xiuxing*), they could become gods and return to heaven, escaping the cycle of death and rebirth. According to Master Poh:

These gods, immortals, Buddhas are transformed human beings, living men who transformed. They are not dead men, they achieved the way and became immortals. This is *Daoli* [the organizing patterns of the Way]. You are born, you come, but to return – you don't definitely return. If you want to return, in fifty years you can return.

Historically, of course, Daoist priests practiced self-cultivation and sometimes alchemy in order to achieve immortality. But even today some spirit mediums teach that these practices were a path to escape from the cycles of death and rebirth to "ascend to heaven and stand on a cloud," as a vernacular Daoist scripture distributed in Penang puts it (Chun 1914). Master Poh and other spirit mediums observed, however, that people in the modern world rarely sought to achieve this level of self-cultivation.

Although people might not seek immortality, some humans – especially those who have died violent deaths – do become gods. My landlady, for example, told me the story of a young girl who died in a tragic accident during the seventh lunar month, a dangerous period when the ghosts are believed to be roaming the earth, on vacation from purgatory, the 'prisons of earth' (*tegek, diyu*). The girl's family enshrined her as a goddess after a spirit medium advised them that the King of Hell had taken her as his bride (see also DeBernardi 2004: 164). Such tales abound. For example, a school teacher who was also well known for his expertise in numerology told me:

In Perak, there is a deity known as the White Horse General. He was one of twins, and he worked as a bus conductor. One day he was helping someone board the bus, and he fell and died. He came to his brother in a dream and said that the Jade Emperor had appointed him as a stable boy. So, the brother had a temple built.

As many anthropologists studying Taiwanese popular religion also have noted, in order to placate and contain them, Chinese commonly treat dangerous ghosts who have died violent, untimely deaths with the deference and offerings due to gods.[5]

Extending this insight to China, Barend ter Haar concludes that the worship of many widely popular deities in Fujian Province developed from the propitiation of ghosts. Ter Haar studied the origin and spread of veneration of eight popular deities – including Mazu, Holy King Kuo, and the Pure Water Patriarch (the so-called Snake God), documenting that the temple cults associated with these deities overwhelmingly originated from the veneration of individuals who had died unnatural or mysterious deaths before reaching maturity. Because their life-energy remained unspent, they were doomed to stay on earth as a threat to the living. Unlike some Chinese saints, none of them had achieved extraordinary distinction in their lives, and they owed their deification to the fact that people ascribed miracles to them after their death (ter Haar 1990).

Spiritual Power

Chinese represent and experience spirits in the habitus of everyday worship. Chinese describe the gods as big or small (*toa, da*; or *se, xiao*), and their powers as high or low (*koan, gao*; or *ke, di*), and order them according to their status on family altars. The Chinese pantheon is diverse and eclectic, and people sometimes are unsure of and even argue over the gods' ranks relative to one another. When, for example, my landlady's son asked his aunt whether the Third Prince or the God of Prosperity was bigger, she reflected for a long moment, finally responding, "The Goddess of Mercy is bigger."

Although these orderings may express personal devotions and values, some aspects are fixed, including most importantly the ordering of above and below, Heaven and Earth. The altar to the Lord of Heaven or his delegate always is elevated at the front entrance of the house, or placed in front of a temple as a free-standing structure. People place deities, Buddhas, and Bodhisattvas on the main altar, facing the entrance of the house or temple, and they locate the shrine to the gods of the earth and sometimes one of hell's rulers, the Inconstant Uncle, on the ground beneath the altar.

Some deities like the Lord of Heaven are so high and pure that they often have little to do directly with the lives of ordinary humans. As one spirit medium explained it, self-control and self-transcendence are marks of high spiritual status, whereas passion marks lower deities:

Taishang Laojun's spirit medium: But stages of enlightenment determine respect in the upper realm. Taishang [Laozi] has reached the stage where he has overcome all passions or emotions. Guanyin [The Goddess of Mercy] also has no passions or emotions. Her assistants do have passions.

High deities are not only controlled in their passions, they are also exceptionally pure. The sky itself honors the distinction, according to Taishang's spirit medium, who claimed that it always rained on the eve or the day of an important deity's birthday to cleanse the place.

Master Lim explained that you could also discern the contrast between 'high' and 'low' gods from the form the trance performance takes:

When the god returns, the medium slumps and the people are called to look after him. If it is a real, large god (*toasin, dashen*) then there is no slump: the medium simply returns to himself. The more simple it is, the greater the spiritual power. Power is high if it is like this. The lower gods are more violent.

Although people sometimes claim that higher gods, even the Buddha himself, can possess spirit mediums, those deities who assist humans usually are passionate lower gods like the chaotic Third Prince, the acrobatic Great Saint ("Monkey"), or the antinomian Vagabond Buddha. People describe these lower deities as being closer to humans, and more approachable and willing to help them. Most were once human themselves, and desire the opportunity to inhabit a human body again to enjoy life's pleasures. Thus people tempt these lower gods to descend by bringing offerings, and repay them for their help with steamboat feasts, Chinese wine or Martell brandy, opium, Guinness Stout, or tobacco. Like the Third Prince who joined the temple festival at the shrine-grotto to celebrate Magistrate Choo Kong's birthday, they enjoy the puppet theater or opera staged for their pleasure and amusement.[6]

By contrast with gods, ghosts are 'below,' on earth, or in the prisons of hell. When I asked one spirit medium to explain the difference between *sin* and *angkong*, he said that they were the same, but that Buddhas were different: the gods lived in the Southern Heaven, and Buddhas in the Western Heaven (*Sethian, Xitian*). I asked him, "What about the ghosts?" He laughed, incredulous at my ignorance:

Ghosts? Ghosts live in that *yin* space (*imkan, yinjian*)! The *yin* space is invisible. They live in the prisons of earth (*tekek, diyu*). These ghosts are like spirits (*hun*). Now some can be seen, some are invisible. If someone's luck is not good, then they can see these things. You can see these things, but very rarely.

Arthur Wolf suggests that ghosts represent the social category of 'stranger,' and that Taiwanese only rarely recognize that one person's ancestor may be another person's ghost (1974: 172–73).[7] Recalling his arguments on this point, I asked the spirit medium, "Are ancestors ghosts?" He responded decisively:

The same, they are also souls (*hun*), this is part of the soul. We're talking about the soul, the divine soul (*linghun*). What we are speaking is Mandarin, in Hokkien what we call it is ghosts (*kui, gui*), that is to say, the ghosts are part of the soul (*hun*). That sort of ancestor, that is to say, when they're dead, people must serve (*hoksai, fushi*) them. Like that. Like, the first and the fifteenth you pray (*pai, bai*). . . and when his death day arrives, you pray, once a year, like that. Like within the seventh lunar month, you pray, on the fifteenth you pray, until the twenty-ninth, you can pray. This is called 'worship' (*chongpai, chongbai*).

His answer was clear: ancestors are the souls of individuals served and worshipped by their descendants. After death, their spirits are imagined in text and ritual performance as passing through judgment and tortuous ordeals in the courts of hell. But filial offspring may sponsor Daoist rituals or Buddhist masses for the dead to transfer merit to their ancestors, seeking to release them from hell and its torments (see DeBernardi 2004: 164–66). As the Datuk Aunt explained it, people with good hearts had nothing to fear upon death, but people who had wronged others would be judged and locked up in hell's jail, where a horse-faced demon would beat the dead unless a person's descendants were filial and prayed to improve their parent's treatment.

During the seventh lunar month, when the ghosts are said to be 'on vacation' from hell for the entire month, people offer ancestors a feast of fine dishes in front of their family altar. At the same time, they make offerings to placate

FIG. 19. A spirit medium possessed by Nazha, also known as the Commander of the Central Altar, performs with a prick-ball in front of the altar to the Lord of Heaven at a temple festival, George Town, 1980. Photo: Jean DeBernardi

wandering ghosts who have no descendants to care for their spiritual needs, offering them simple buns, incense, and candles on the ground by the roadside, as befits their low status. Like lower-status gods, people consider ghosts to still have human desires, and many of the offerings made to them are intended to fill needs very like those of human beings: at the community celebration of this festival, people offer the ghosts food and wine on a long banquet table, provide days and nights of Chinese opera or other entertainment, place cigarettes and playing cards on the altar to the King of Hell and his assistants, and also burn paper clothing and hell money for their use.

Indeed, the King of Hell sometimes enters a spirit medium to select entertainment for the event. At the 2003 Victoria Street celebration of the festival, five spirits – the King of Hell, the Inconstant Ghost and his partner, Nazha, and Hao Chu, a god epitomizing filiality – possessed their spirit mediums, blessing the event, but also enjoying the Chinese opera performances. The gods also planned the following year's entertainment; in 2002, for example, the King of Hell decided that the Singaporean opera company hired for the event should perform the story of Mulian, a filial son who entered hell to rescue his mother's soul. The residents of Victoria Street know with great certainty that the King of Hell prefers Chinese cultural opera but does not object to puppet shows or the projection of *gongfu* moves by Jackie Chan on the side of a building; but they also know that he dislikes modern concerts. Indeed, residents recall that when a committee member proposed booking a modern concert in order to attract a larger crowd, he was knocked down by a car as he left the meeting and died soon after (Dielenberg 2003).

People regard ghosts as potentially dangerous. Penangites often say, for example, that if a person dies before his or her predestined life-span is complete, then the person's soul will stay in the place of death, seeking to capture the soul of another in order to find release. Although ghosts may threaten human well-being, people can take steps to control and contain them: they note that ghosts fear the paper charms that possessed spirit mediums dispense and also fear images of a tiger's head. To repel ghosts from their homes, people commonly place a mirror over their front door, either encased in an eight-sided wooden frame on which is painted the Daoist eight trigrams, or draped in a strip of red cloth. They say that when a demon seeks to enter a house, he sees his own hideous face in the mirror, is terrified, and flees instead: "Ghosts are ugly, and if they see their faces above the door they'll be disgusted and leave." People also place fans above the door to block the ghosts.

Because the world of ghosts is so very close to the human life-world, people say that humans sometimes can see ghosts, but only if their luck is low (*un ke, yun di*); a person whose luck is high (*koan, gao*) sees nothing, avoiding a potentially hazardous encounter. The relationships between earth and hell, the living and the dead, is so intimate that the Datuk Aunt compared it to the two sides of a sheet of paper: "Hell and earth, one sheet of paper. Hell and humans here, one sheet of paper. They can see humans, humans cannot see them. In the bright light of day, don't criticize humans; in the darkness, don't criticize ghosts."

She also claimed that people could visit hell in their dreams, or even visit there as long as seven days and still return to the world of the living.[8] She told us a story that resembled that of Mulian, the filial son who visits hell to rescue his mother, a charter for Buddhist masses for the dead:

A woman died. Her daughter was very pure, and she went to save her mother; immortals gave the daughter something to eat so that her body would not decay. She rapped on hell's door, and found the King of Hell so that she could get her mother out. Her mother had a bad heart, but she herself did good, so she was able to save her mother. She did good deeds for her mother, and since her mother's body was not yet bad, she snatched her mother to return. She saw her mother live again. Her mother returned to worship Buddha.

But her brother was bad, and the Thunder God killed him. Her brother killed a dog, he had a bad heart, his sin was very heavy. He fed dog meat to the Buddhist [monks], and threw the dog's bones into a waterlily pond [a symbol of purity]. While he was standing next to the bones, lightning struck him. If you teach people to be bad-hearted, your crime is very heavy. When you teach people to fight, it is like this.

Like the moral doctrine of *Taishang's Treatise on Action and Retribution*, the Datuk Aunt taught a straightforward moral lesson that good actions were rewarded, and evil ones punished by the Thunder God.

Gods, Ghosts, and Spiritual Status

Representations of gods and ghosts divide these spatially in a relation of above to below, cosmologically in the relationship of Heaven to Earth, and socially as a relationship of cultivated upper class to illiterate lower class. People often represent deities as imperial bureaucrats, generals, and kings – all persons of high social status – whereas they sometimes compared ghosts to beggars and thieves. They also imagine the difference between gods and ghosts as a contrast between the purity of the gods and the impurity of ghosts, whom they also call 'dirt' (*lasam*).

As I discuss in Chapter One, the doctrine of karma reiterates the relationship between morality and privilege, teaching that the reward for a moral life is to be reborn as a higher-status person in the next life, and the punishment for immorality is a lower rebirth. As Master Poh taught my research assistant and myself:

> You must have good deeds, good morals (*totek, daode*). A good rebirth is the reward for your good deeds. Then only can you combine with a human womb and be reborn. If you're not good, you will go and join with animals of the Heavens, Earth, and Water.

Following a similar logic, people often explain that the gods were rewarded with their high postings in the celestial bureaucracy as a result of their good deeds, and attest to their good hearts (*hosim, haoxin*). Although they sometimes offer ghosts similar honorific titles, they also quietly explain that these are more dangerous beings, and their worship is in fact placation.

Communicating with Gods and Ghosts

The media of communication with gods and ghosts, however imagined, are many: incense, candles, flowers, gold and silver paper money, food, wine, tea, and brandy and other intoxicants appropriate to the taste of the spirit to whom they are made in offering. One spirit medium explained that incense represented the mortality of human life, as the incense smoke escaped and was gone, and that flowers, too, represented life's evanescence but also the hope of renewal: "We will fade like the flower, but the plant we hope will grow again, will blossom again, all these things happen in a circle."

No act of worship is more fundamental than the offering of incense. The burning of incense is a simple act of worship that represents the opening of a channel of communication between the human and invisible worlds. People typically light a small bundle of incense sticks, and at each location where they pray they make offerings with three incense sticks, moving from higher-status to lower-status gods. One spirit medium explained that the incense represents the human body and human mortality:

> We offer the joss stick. This signifies our life. We need to offer our sincerity to our teacher who is in a different plane, who advises us to lead a good life. The joss stick represents human beings. As it burns, it gets shorter and shorter, just as our own life gets shorter and shorter, it burns to the end to the wooden stick, just as life limits our body....

Master Lim explained the significance of the three incense sticks:

> *Master Lim*: Three sticks of incense, three sticks. The trinity is important in all religions. Three is the number of Heaven; two is the number of Earth, but still you pray to the Lord of the Earth with three; one cannot stand.

Incense represents those praying, and it connects them with the gods to whom they pray. For example, members of the Heavenly Dao Association, a moral uplifting association, sung this invocation on the occasion of the Vagabond Buddha's birthday:

> Every sort of pure incense revolves in the sacred emptiness,
> Incense revolves in the sacred emptiness.
> Gods and people are connected,
> Gods and people are connected just through their heart's feelings.
> The heart's feelings believe,
> Incense transforms into the azure sky.
> At the Nanwei Heaven's cloud-sea you can meet every immortal and perfected one.

Sung three times, this invocation resembled the one sung to invite gods to descend and enter their spirit mediums, but in this case it was a prelude not to a trance performance but rather to further chanting and offertory prayer (see Chapter Three).

People also commonly burn paper money (gold for the gods, silver for the ghosts), and use a variety of paper goods to pray to the gods and make offerings to ancestors. One commonly used charm paper, for example, is a woodcut showing six well-dressed men riding horses (symbolic of worldly success), representing the supplicant's desire for benefactors (*kuijin, guiren*). People also offer words, in the form of prayers, invocations, and sutras.

Just as people host friends, family, and political patrons at feasts, they offer the inhabitants of the invisible world of spirits foods appropriate to their taste and identity. Fruit or vegetarian foods are offered to Buddhas and Bodhisattvas, as Buddhists are vegetarian. By contrast, Chinese offer pork to the gods and ghosts on major Daoist holidays: on the ninth day of the first lunar month, households and businesses offer thanksgiving to Heaven with whole roasted pigs; during the Hungry Ghosts Festival of the seventh lunar month, local communities offer whole pigs, both raw and roasted, to placate the King of Hell, his bureaucratic assistants, and the ghosts. Penangites never offer pork to local animist spirits, who are assumed to have Malay ethnicity and to be Muslim, offering instead chicken curry and the accoutrements of betel nut chewing. When I asked one man at a Hungry Ghosts Festival celebration about the long, heaping tables of food offerings laid out for the ghosts, he commented that it was the same as offering food to a business associate "to be on the safe side." Thus, generosity with gifts is designed to keep the spirits benign.

Penang Chinese traditionalists like to say that if you ask, you will get a response (*u-kiu pit-eng, youqiu biying*). But they also recognize that this incurs being in debt to the god or spirit from whom they have asked the favor. For example, when Daoist priests performed a sacrificial ritual on the occasion of Taishang Laojun's birthday, they chanted a memorial entitled "Limitless Longevity" (*Wanshou Wuliang* 1981). This memorial was a prayer thanking Taishang Laojun for his blessings, but it also requested continued peace, safety, and happiness for the forty-two persons whose names the priests announced to the god:

Emperor, please listen! We respectfully and sincerely present our wishes for your blessings. Please listen! [We] share the wish to unite the crowd to pray for safety, and pray that all will increase their fortune and happiness. We prostrate ourselves on the ground! The longevity star is shining brightly; we gladly greet the auspicious brilliant morning sunlight of [your] birthday; we humbly follow the exalted invocation ritual (*Song Huzhi Li*). Consider the crowd speaking their thanks quietly and worshipping silently. We have not yet reciprocated your blessings.

Offerings of food, incense, paper money, flowers, and prayer are channels of communication with the gods, but also ways to repay them for their favors.

People make thanksgiving offerings to the gods and seek to placate spirits, but they also seek to communicate with them. As I discuss in Chapter One, they commonly receive answers to their questions by throwing divining crescents (*poah poe, bu bei*), a pair of cashew-shaped blocks of wood. These gives only three responses: yes (*siu^n poe, shun bei*, one flat side and one curved side up); no (*im poe, yin bei*, both curved sides up); or the gods are laughing (*chhio poe, xiao bei*, both flat sides up). When people make ancestor offerings in their homes during the seventh lunar month, the divining crescents are thrown to ask the spirits if they have eaten their fill before the dishes can be shared among the living. Temple committee members make similar use of the divining crescents to communicate with their gods during festivals, for example to find out whether a god is willing to allow his or her image to be taken to another god's altar, where he or she will be a guest during the celebration of that god's birthday. At many temples people kneel in front of the altar, shake out from a special holder a numbered bamboo stick (*chhiamsi, jianshi*), use the divining crescents to confirm the correctness of the number, then draw out a corresponding numbered oracular charm.

People also may communicate with invisible worlds through dreams and visions. For example, Master Lim grew aware of his own religious calling as a consequence of his vivid dreams, from which he invariably awoke at 3:00 a.m. Another spirit medium observed that he had dreams while meditating:

I sometimes have dreams in which I'm taken to places that are very beautiful. I don't know if it's real travel or imagination, but these places are really not of this world. There are flowers of extraordinary beauty, and spirits, sentinels. When you meditate it appears you can travel and see lovely things.

People also pray for hints in dreams that would allow them to select winning lottery numbers. A female spirit medium, the Datuk Aunt, invoked the spirits of ordinary household objects – a stolen mortar and pestle – to ask for lottery numbers in her dreams. She noted, however, that bookies invoked the spirit of a sieve to prevent the person from correctly deciphering these dreams (see Chapter Four). And at the Seven Sisters Festival, young Cantonese girls offer rice powder and cosmetics to the stars known as the Seven Sisters, praying for dreams that will reveal to them the identity of their future husbands.

Although people may communicate with invisible worlds through incense and divining crescents, dreams and visions, spirit mediums open up an unparalleled channel of communication with the invisible world of spirits, and remedies for spirit threats to an individual's peace and happiness. I will discuss the trance performance in Chapter Three, but its foundation is simple: powerful spirits enter the bodies of their spirit mediums and engage with the human life world again, entering into relationships of commensality and exchange with their followers. Whereas they may have lofty identities as warriors, scholars, or kings, people compare spirits to their parents, elder brothers, or elder sisters. The gods have the social capital and interactional powers of elders: they can scold, they can label clients filial or unfilial, good or bad, and they can teach and guide their juniors. Take, for example, this interaction between a possessed spirit medium and a small boy who was the first to pray with Taishang's scepter at a temple festival:

Taishang Laojun (the spirit of Laozi): "You had better study, or the Holy Mother will spank you!"

Or this one, when the Vagabond Buddha scolded a committee member for not attending the temple festival for all four days:

The Vagabond Buddha: "You say you're not free, heh!" He struck him on the head with his fan. "Next time you come, bring me three cartons of Guinness Stout!"

The spirit medium plays a variety of complementary roles vis-à-vis the client, roles that involve the enactment of authority.

Familiarity and Respect

In her 1981 study of *Chinese Ritual and Politics*, Emily Martin Ahern concludes that "the acts intended to control Chinese spirits often parallel whatever acts are believed most effectively to control other people in everyday life." She concludes, however, that "interaction with spirits will often be modeled on political processes" (Ahern 1981: 5). Ahern argues that because the spiritual hierarchy was modeled on the human bureaucracy, it performed a useful function in a peasant society by teaching people "the principles underlying the operation of their powerful central government" (Ahern 1981: 97).

She admits, however, that her informants denied that there were parallels between their interactions with contemporary bureaucrats and their interactions with their gods:

I asked a sample of Ch'inan villagers which human relationship most resembles that between man and god: student-teacher; child-parent; citizen-official; patient-doctor; upper-lower generations; or sister's son-mother's brother. Half expecting them to chose 'citizen-official', I was startled to find that the choice was almost invariably 'child-parent'.

Her informants explained to her:

"Parents teach their children to do good and the gods do the same. If you were sick your parents would want to help you. The gods are the same. As long as you do good deeds and respect them, they will exert their strength to the utmost to help. Parents will do likewise, if you are obedient and good. Neither gods nor parents want anything to do with delinquents and gangsters or useless, directionless people." (Ahern 1981: 99)

Although the bureaucratic metaphor powerfully informs people's images of the hell justice system, in Penang as well as in Taiwan, people discuss and enact their relationship with the gods on the model of family relations and relations with respected community elders and teachers.

As we have seen, Chinese traditionalists distinguish between large and small gods as a way of ordering their complex pantheon. We also find, however, that one of the most basic social categories for the Penang Chinese is that which separates large from small, elder from junior, within the family. Traditionally at least, parents teach juniors to defer to their elders and to recognize status differences through modes of linguistic interaction and visible expressions of respect.[9] Forms of worshipping Chinese gods and acts of respect made to those gods are analogous to the rules for deference paid by junior to seniors.

For example, in the family, adults teach children to greet persons with the appropriate terms of address, and in turn they greet the child with a name or nickname. Thus the junior 'gives face' (*ho· bin, gei mianzi*) to the elder by addressing him first with a respectful title, and the elder condescends to the junior with the more informal name.[10] Parents also commonly teach children to offer food to their elders. When my research assistant's young son would buy an afternoon snack from a passing food hawker, for example, he always ceremoniously offered it me before enjoying it himself. Similarly, when banquet organizers invite honored guests (*kuipin, guibin*) to the event, they treat them with special acts of respect, even taking the choicest pieces of food from the shared platters and placing them on the guest's plate. In turn, favors are expected from the guests of honor, including donations of money to community fund-raising projects or, in the case of elected politicians, an effort to address local needs for new storm drains or roads.

In the context of the family, the asymmetry between elders and juniors is underlined in the visiting that accompanies the celebration of the Chinese New Year. In the Hainanese family that I celebrated one New Year with, for example, male household heads took turns in order of birth, eldest-to-youngest, in hosting the rest on the first day of the festival. The elder siblings first stayed home and waited for visits from their younger siblings, after which they re-paid the visits. The hosts offered their guests special foods, many of which involved 'eating meaning' (*chiah isu, chi yisi*). They also delighted the children of their guests (at least those who were unmarried and living at home) with red packets (*angbao, hongbao*) – small red envelopes, brightly decorated with gold foil, containing a gift of money. In this way, brothers and their families reen-act the order of age-stratification, both within the sibling group and between generations.

The tea ceremony that ritually incorporates a bride into her husband's kin group also displays the system of age-stratification. At a Chinese Christian wed-ding that I attended, for example, after fetching the bride from her home the groom ceremoniously invited her across the threshold of her new home. Partic-ipants set up a pair of chairs in front of the family altar in the front room of the house, and called the groom's patrilineal elders, husband and wife together, to sit there, two by two. The newlyweds stood together facing their seated elders and offered them cups of tea. As she offered tea to her husband's family elders, the bride addressed them for the first time with the appropriate terms of ad-dress, prompted when necessary by the master of ceremonies. The husband or wife then returned the teacup to the newlyweds, with a red packet containing a gift of money. Next the couple received red packets from their peers in the family, some of whom refused to sit, reluctant to claim themselves senior to the couple. Finally the bride and groom themselves turned and sat. Their juniors in the family came one by one to greet the new relative with the proper term of address and to receive a red packet from the couple. Often the adults prompted the children with the correct terms of address, since many did not know the precise Chinese terms that distinguish siblings in terms of birth order and that separate maternal and paternal kin.

Thus these two ceremonial observances highlight the pervasive stratification into elders and juniors. The ritual performance reveals the network of social relations, confirming social asymmetry through the offering of refreshments by juniors to seniors, and the return gift of money from seniors to juniors. The ceremonial enactment of junior–senior ranking and the interdependence of generations, acted out both in the order of visiting and in the nonreciprocal offering of gifts, expresses a more general set of social expectations. Juniors should defer to elders, and elders should take care of their juniors. Elder siblings often contribute, for example, to the support or education of a younger brother or sister, or help their juniors get started on business ventures with loans that are often ultimately regarded as gifts. This sense of obligation between elder and junior continues throughout life. For example, I went to dinner at a costly seafood restaurant with a friend and her business partner. He discovered on entering the restaurant that one of his younger sisters was finishing a meal there with several friends, and promptly settled their bill. My friend later commented that even though brother and sister had encountered each other only by chance, still the elder should treat.

Family elders nurture their juniors, but they also teach them proper norms for behavior. Often this teaching takes the form of scolding, an expression of anger that may be faked by elders who are as amused as they are annoyed at a child's behavior. Parents sometimes described their children as *loan* (*luan*), a bit chaotic and confused, unable to sort out truth from fancy, fearless when the situation calls for caution. Chinese do not consider children to be able to take total responsibility for their actions. Consequently, their elders have the responsibility to control them. Most often this task falls to the mother or grandmother, who have the authority to remind the child of his or her place in the social order fiercely and directly. So when, for example, my research assistant's young son called to an elder with the Hokkien equivalent of, "Hey, you!" instead of using the appropriate term of address, or if he reprimanded someone older than himself, my assistant or her mother-in-law would scold, "You don't distinguish big from small! Don't act like that!" The expression of anger is, however, one-sided. Social norms dictate that even if a child believes that he or she has been falsely accused of an infraction, the scolding must be endured (*lun*, *ren*) without comment. At best the child can complain to a third party, who may or may not intercede.

Similarly, when the gods possess their spirit mediums, they become enmeshed in personal social relationships with humans. People respect their gods by addressing them with highly honorific titles, inviting them to descend to the altar to interact with their younger brothers (*siuti*, *xiaodi*), just as speakers at banquets politely refer to themselves as the younger brother to the audience.[11] Although people usually address a god with lofty titles, the god, speaking through the spirit medium, sometimes uses familiar nicknames for temple committee members, addressing one as Old Tan, another as Fatso, and a third as Little Duck. At the same time, the spirit medium may have an especially intimate relationship with his or her possessing deity. For example, a Cantonese woman

FIG. 20. A spirit medium dots the image of his god on a plaque to bring consciousness into it before it is placed on a family altar, Ayer Itam, 1980. Photo: Jean DeBernardi

spirit medium explained that the Goddess of Mercy, who possessed her on the first and fifteenth of every lunar month, was her elder sister, adding that they were sworn kin (*kiatpai, jiebai*).[12]

The gods themselves live within networks of kin and fictive kin. For example, the family that I lived with invited a spirit medium possessed by the Third Prince (*Nazha*) to consecrate their new family altar. In paintings and statues, artists represent Tua Pek Kong (the God of Prosperity) as a white-haired, smiling old man. When the god-in-his-medium dotted his image with red ink to bring life into it, he addressing the god in a tiny, childlike voice as 'Uncle' (*Ah Pek, A Bo*), inviting him to enter his image. After the ritual the eldest son, a teenager, laughed as he recalled this detail: "He called Tua Pek Kong 'Uncle.' That's correct!" And when the members of a small temple performed a ceremony to send the gods to heaven before the Chinese New Year, the Third Prince invited the Holy King (*Seng Ong, Sheng Wang*) to possess his spirit medium in a plaintive, childish voice, "Dad, I'm calling you!" then later addressed the Li Tieguai, the so-called Crippled Immortal, as his "Great Uncle" (*Kukong, Jiugong*).

When the gods possess their spirit mediums, people offer them their favorite food and drink, just as they would an honored guest. The Vagabond Buddha, for example, drank Guinness Stout and demanded that I bring him some as a mark of respect, whereas the Third Prince – as befit his identity as a 'Baby God' – sometimes drank milk from a bottle or sucked on a plastic pacifier. The Holy Mother demanded cooling tea and scolded her temple's caretaker for not providing it, even though it was the Holy Mother's first visit to this temple. Her spirit medium commented: "The Holy Mother insists on drinking cooling Chinese tea. I myself don't drink tea, I prefer coffee...." Sometimes the gods even attend feasts with their followers. At a special anniversary celebration at one small house temple, the Inconstant Uncle and his younger brother joined the temple's inside members, many of them family, for a steamboat reunion dinner, and enjoyed Chinese wine and cigarettes afterwards (see DeBernardi 1994b). In return, people hope that the gods will draw on their omniscient knowledge to aid humans.

When the deities possess their spirit mediums, the way in which people offer up food, drink, and other objects reflects the god's status. At one temple fair, for example, while the spirit medium was possessed by the God of War his parents knelt and his mother dramatically offered him first the god's scepter (*lu-i, ruyi*) and then a cup of tea. Later Laozi, possessing his spirit medium, commented to me that this proved the trance was genuine. Otherwise, if the spirit medium's elders made such deferential offerings to their son, kneeling and asking for a favor (Laozi argued), the medium would not be able to tolerate this gross inversion of the normal social order and would raise the elders up immediately; he would be unable to continue and would break off the trance performance.

Although people regard the gods as their elders and superiors, nonetheless when they speak of putting the spirit medium into trance, they use a term meaning 'control' or 'force' (*koan, guan*). As one research assistant explained:

Koan means to put into trance by singing the prayers, and burning paper money. In other contexts it means "force." For example, you may say to a difficult child, "I force you to drink water."

The spirit medium's assistants control the god with words (the invocation) and with the compelling power of the gift.

"If you ask, there will be a response . . . ."

People's images of the numinous are informed by ritual practice, and the god's status is constructed through people's interactions with him (or, more rarely, her). People also come to understand the god's powers through their experience of consultations with spirit medium possessed by their gods. They may first glimpse the god's prodigious powers at a temple festival where the spirit mediums are displaying their self-mortifying powers, but they also meet with the gods more intimately at the spirit medium's temple, where the gods meet with clients on a regular basis. At Master Ooi's temple, for example, the medium went into trance three nights a week, possessed either by the Vagabond Buddha or the Crippled Immortal. Clients usually arrived early and waited for the spirit medium to enter a trance state; the temple committee sometimes gave out numbered plastic discs to organize the queue. Although no fee was charged, most clients brought along a red packet with an offering of money.

People sometimes visit spirit mediums because they suspect that black magic or a spiritual collision has caused their misfortunes. Usually the client or the person representing them describes the well-known symptoms of anxiety and depression: insomnia, pessimism, physical aches and pains with no apparent cause, lack of energy and motivation. The spirit medium counsels that they are worrying too much, sometimes diagnosing a spiritual conflict and prescribing simple ritual acts to resolve their problem.[13]

Scholars agree that spirit mediums usually treat mental disturbance in a culturally appropriate way. The god may explain the business failure that undoubtedly precipitated a client's depression, for example, as the result of bad luck due to a disturbance from the spirit world. This diagnosis both absolves the individual of personal responsibility for the failure and treats his bad fate with a simple ritual, thereby reinforcing an optimistic outlook for the future. Arthur Kleinman concludes that the Taiwanese clients he observed often left the temple much happier than when they arrived (1980: 220). Kleinman also recognized, however, that in some cases the possessed spirit medium gave an individual advice that, from a medical perspective, the psychiatrist regarded as unsound, as when the god advised a stressed woman with a large family to remove her birth control device and have another child (1980: 230).

In Malaysia also, the spirit medium's healing practice ranges from beneficial (or at least benign) to ineffective or inappropriate. Indeed, people often visit temple after temple seeking help for an intractable problem, which suggests that the last remedy, however hope inspiring it might have been, had not had lasting benefit. I prefer to analyze the spirit medium's healing practice, however, not by asking about its medical efficacy (an efficacy that even a highly trained medical anthropologist like Dr. Kleinman found difficult to evaluate with any precision), but rather by investigating it as a form of magical practice with powerful psychological dimensions. When they consult with the god, people receive an authoritative response that gives them a specific diagnosis and a concrete remedy, from a being they believe has the power to know the workings of the invisible, dangerous world of spirits, and who also knows their heart.

James McClenon, a sociologist who has studied spirit healers in Japan, Korea, the Philippines, Taiwan, China, Sri Lanka, and Thailand, observes that the anthropological explanations of spiritual healing tend to focus on the healer's ability to render apparently chaotic experiences sensible through ritual process, which has several stages. Diagnosis, or the labeling of the affliction, comes first, followed by the performance of a ritual manipulation that promotes the patient's attachment of emotion to culturally ordered symbols. Then the healer applies new labels to the afflicted person (declaring their demons to have been successfully expelled, for example), and the individual healed.

McClenon critically notes, however, that these models fail to specify how ritual healing actually works, observing that healing entails far more than "labeling sicknesses, manipulating labels, and applying new labels" (McClenon 2002: 78). He recommends that these models be reformulated to include hypnotic response, inferring that the healer uses magic and ritual performance to compel attention and raise patient expectations, persuading them that their problems can be understood in terms of mythic structures. Client responses, he argues, are "equivalent to responses produced by hypnosis," and a successful response to shamanic treatment is very likely to be correlated with patient hypnotizability (McLenon 2002: 78–79). This highly plausible hypothesis promotes a very different research agenda than anthropologists have pursued to date, but nonetheless it raises the interesting and important question of the way that spirit mediums' clients make a deep emotional connection with the symbols of popular religious culture, symbols that undoubtedly infiltrate their dreams and imagination. Although many scholars have observed that hypnotic drumming and singing induces trance in the spirit medium, they have not so often taken note of the fact that the insistent percussive rhythms that call the gods to enter their spirit mediums also may induce a trance-like state in clients.

Consulting the Gods

At the eighteen temples where I attended trance performances, Penangites consulted on a range of topics: illness that did not respond to conventional treatments, including anxiety and sometimes mental illness; children who cried excessively because they had 'taken a fear'; the suspicion that an individual had 'collided' (*chhiong, chong*) with invisible forces or had been the victim of black magic; the desire for advice before undertaking a risky venture, especially gambling, investment, and the opening of a new business, and the desire for remedies for bad luck. The god's magical remedies easily adapt to new situations and anxieties: the Vagabond Buddha offered a charm to a man who feared that the motor vehicle department would condemn his taxi, advising him to pour charm water on the car's hood so that his old taxi would pass inspection: "The inspector's eyes will be hypnotized, and he will think that he is seeing a new car!" he confidently predicted. As we have seen, people invite the gods to possess spirit mediums and then honor them. In return they seek some kind of benefit.

Although they sometimes are seeking help in resolving a spiritual collision or black magic, just as often they are seeking a lottery number, information about when their luck will improve, or help with upcoming school examinations. Indeed, sometimes people simply wish to check the state of their luck and to reassure themselves that they are making sound life decisions. For example, at an ordinary trance session, a temple committee member persuaded me to consult with the spirit medium. I had no pressing issues, so he suggested that I simply check my luck in coming months (*chha unto, cha yundao*) to see what stage things were in for my life cycle, and to ask about my career. The Vagabond Buddha used his prescient powers to advise me that I had chosen the right career, and that an academic calling suited me. He foresaw no problems. He also identified several lines on my palm without looking – two were there, one I'm very sure was not – and concluded that all would go well for me in the future.[14]

Penangites often seek to tap into the god's omniscient powers to gain tips for gambling, in particular in illegal lotteries that base their winning numbers on racing results. Take, for example, this interaction between committee members and the Third Prince. After a long late-night trance session after regular clients had left the small temple, the Third Prince sat at the offering table, facing the altar. Those present spread out paper before the god, whom they implored for lottery numbers:

"New Year is coming, we'll repay our gratitude! You must whip the horse!" Then after the god wrote meaningless squiggles, the discontented committee member asked the child god, "No meaning la! Do you know how to write?" A visitor from another town took another tactic: "Prince, we ask you to help us, people are suffering!"

But the next round of writing proved equally impenetrable, and finally the Third Prince departed from his spirit medium.

Despite the opacity of many predictions, one of the most impressive powers claimed for the gods is omniscience. The medium for the Third Prince described the planchette divination, for example, that sometimes occurred at his temple:

Tok tok tok, ka ka ka, he [the god] writes, and they can read it! This also is an Amoy thing. It's also like he's talking. He writes on the table, so if you are ill, or have offended a god (*hoantioh, fande*), or something, he talks with you. Where you collided with a spirit, where you have a problem, he can tell you all. Like we [spirit mediums] speak, but he sees, he writes characters to talk, he writes characters to let you see. People can interpret them, he tells you what problems this man has.

FIG. 21. A planchette divination rod is displayed on an altar between two cobra-handled whips, one black, one white. Temple seals and the five generals are at the back of the altar table, Tanjung Bungah, 1999. Photo: Jean DeBernardi

The interpreter translates the god's deep speech or writing into ordinary language for those present, and often more than one interpreter is available to translate the god's words into different dialects, typically Hokkien and Cantonese.[15]

In regular trance sessions, the gods often comment on a person's situation without being told, based no doubt on what they have heard about the individual's life through rumor networks. Enthusiastic committee members who had attached themselves to a particular temple often claimed that the first time they came to the temple, the god had discerned their problems without them having to be described, and offered a cure:

Committee member for the Vagabond Buddha, and member of the Heavenly Dao: Even if you ask about the illness of others, the god will know about your own sickness. This happened to me. The god said to me, "Why haven't you asked about the trouble with your ear?"

And my landlady offered this comment on the Vagabond Buddha:

Mrs. Low: If you go to see the god, you will tell him your name, address, and age. Then you ask if he can help. Before you can speak and tell him your problem, he will tell you why you have come, what sort of problems you have. He then gives you a talisman (*hu, fu*) that you burn and drink in water, or put in water and bathe, or keep in your pocket. If you tease this god, he will draw a circle around you and you won't be able to move, you must use a knife to free yourself....

These reports of their extraordinary magical powers fortified people's conviction that the gods were spiritually efficacious.

The gods are even able to diagnose individuals they have never met. One woman came to ask about her nineteen-year-old son, whom she reported was running a fever. The god, possessing his spirit medium, offered a diagnosis:

The Imperial Jade Prince: He is the eldest son. Since he was born, he has had a bad fate (*phaiⁿ mia, dai ming*). His heart is troubled (*sim loan, xin luan*). Because his luck is not good (*un boho, yun buhao*), he is sorrowful (literally, has a 'stabbed heart,' *kek sim, zha sin*). Is this true or not? The reason for his bad luck is that he has offended [a spirit] (*tioh hoan, de fan*). When the person is weak, they encounter trouble. There is no black magic (*kongtau*) involved. Give him nourishing foods [a Chinese medicinal tonic prepared with herbs]. He should eat a charm so that he will have strength (*lat, li*).

Thus the possessed spirit medium offered a diagnosis and dispensed charms for the boy without ever seeing or interviewing him.

In another case, a Cantonese female spirit medium gave a young man suffering from headache and fatigue a charm to influence a girl he liked. The young man claimed to have seen his father's ghost, but he also asked about the young woman, who was planning to go to Singapore to seek work. His father had recently died, and the young man followed contemporary Hokkien practice by wearing black mourning dress.[16] Unspoken was the fact that on the death of a parent, those who follow tradition must marry within 100 days or wait until the three-year mourning period is over, and the young man may have feared that this prohibition would hinder his courtship of the young woman. The god-in-his-medium advised the anxious young man that he should not wear black mourning dress for the full three years, but rather should change to blue after 100 days. Then the god gave him six charms to burn and one to wear. The possessed spirit medium also gave him three charms to burn to influence the young woman, saying, "If you burn this, the girl cannot think immoral (*loan*) thoughts."

Possessed by their gods, spirit mediums scold people just as family elders do, make direct observations about the person's situation that people ordinarily would not state, and give them advice. But when diagnoses are incorrect, the client may find it difficult to correct the god, because the interactional setting is designed to enhance the spirit medium's authority, an authority usually supported by temple committee members. One Indian man whose mother took him to see a spirit medium possessed by the Great Saint when he was young, vividly recalled that the god had accused him of being a very wicked child, a stinging charge that he was powerless to refute as a child, and that he continued to resent as an adult.

Take, for example, the prediction offered me by the Vagabond Buddha possessing Master Ooi (also see Chapter Seven). The god-in-his-medium predicted that after three years, I would go to Hong Kong, and when I agreed that I intended to go there, he patted my head with his fan, saying, "I know your heart, what you think in your heart I don't know?" But when I added that I was also thinking of going to Beijing, he contradicted me, saying, "No, Hong Kong."

For Master Ooi, these alleged powers of omniscience persisted even when he was out of trance. After a lengthy trance session at this temple, Master Ooi offered to tell my fortune, and his temple committee members extolled his prescient skills. He commented that my father had married twice. When I objected, "No, he only married once," one of the men in the small crowd of onlookers assured me that "it must have been when you were small." As Penangites often call a man's mistress his second wife, I found myself powerless to refute this improbable claim. When the spirit medium began to speak of my elder brother, I realized that it was futile to argue, even though I have no brother. Although the spirit medium's (or the possessing deity's) diagnoses might not always be correct, the god/medium's observations undoubtedly are sufficiently astute that they convince some persons of the god's powers, thereby ensuring continued community support.

I did not witness anyone confront a god whose diagnosis they questioned, but people who were dissatisfied with the outcome of an oracle or a consultation often simply visited another spirit medium to check the validity of the diagnosis. At a regular trance session with the Third Prince, for example, a client approached to ask if advice he had received from another spirit medium was correct:

Client: "Can you gamble in your backyard on the god's birthday if it faces a temple? Another spirit medium told me not to. He said that my luck was dark (*un am, yun an*), and I could meet with problems."
Third Prince: "No, you can gamble there."
Client: "Can I watch a birth?" [Here, he alludes to the fact that things of opposite polarities should not be placed in proximity with one another.]
Third Prince: "Yes, but don't touch water [a *yin* substance]."

Having receiving conflicting advice from different gods-in-their-mediums, the client must then decide which of these authorities is correct in his or her advice, and act accordingly.

Spiritual Collisions

Sometimes people approach spirits to ask for help – with lottery numbers, for example, or for a charm to make a straying lover faithful. But often they come to spirit mediums when they fear that they have inadvertently collided with a spirit.[17] People are not always susceptible to ghosts, but as one temple committee member put it, "When your luck is low, you attract all this." Consequently, when a person's illness does not follow a normal course, many Penang Chinese will often seek spirit mediums while at the same time also seeking medical advice. If the god's diagnosis is that the person has offended (*hoantioh, fande*) or collided (*chhiongtioh, chongde*) with a spiritual being of some sort, then the medium will recommend steps that will persuade the spirit to leave the person alone or, if it is a ghost, that will simply chase it away.

People sometimes use the terms *hoandioh* and *chhiongdioh* as if they were interchangeable, but they have somewhat different meanings. *Hoandioh* means to 'offend' or 'bother.' In a suggestive parallel, the term *hoandioh* also is used to describe getting into trouble, either with the police or with Penang's underworld. Gangsters in particular cultivate their reputations as touchy and violent people whom one should not offend, and in this respect they are like the lower, more passionate beings in the spiritual world. Proper caution often involves avoiding contact with dangerous spiritual beings, including potentially violent deities.

In a ritual context, people use the term *hoantioh* to describe an offense against a particular deity or spirit who could be (but is not always) identified. One research assistant observed that the term was most often used in the offending of Datuk Kong in some way (*hoantioh Natu Kong, Fanzhe Datuk Gong*), with the result that the offender becomes ill and must placate the Datuk spirit with offerings. If ghosts are to blame, then the afflicted person must call on a spirit medium to 'chase' (*koan, gan*) them away. People also sometimes use the more neutral and euphemistic term *tutioh (yude)*, which means 'to encounter.' For example, during a God of Prosperity temple fair, the men who removed the god's statue from its cave temple accidentally bumped it, breaking off the top of the god's head. The participants considered this very bad luck for the Chinese, and also worried that because they had invited me to photograph the statue while they were coaxing it to come with them, I might have an 'encounter' with the deity.

Chinese regard children as particularly vulnerable to committing a spiritual offence. Consequently, adults teach children between the ages of two and four to *pai (bai)* – show respect with a symbolic kotow with their hands – if they urinate outside so that they won't "offend Datuk Kong things." One research assistant explained that Cantonese ranked the Earth God higher than did the Hokkien, because they feared this deity would harm small children who inadvertently disturbed his shrine and didn't know how to apologize (to "ask-no sin" *sia pochue, qing buzui*).[18]

Chhiongtioh, by contrast, means 'to clash or collide.' A Cantonese woman spirit medium whose possessing spirits were the Great Saint and Guanyin, the Goddess of Mercy, explained spiritual collisions to me and my research assistant in Hokkien as follows:

A collision (*chhiongtioh, chongde*) is the same as a ghost entering (*jipkui, jingui*) or getting dirty (*lasam*, a euphemism for ghosts). If this happens, people are mentally confused. You must give them charms to change. If you are really ill, you go to a doctor. If you have cancer, it's very rough. But a spiritual offence can be cured. Dead people collide [with the living].

Although this statement suggests some form of possession by the malevolent spirit, people often regard the trouble as a conflict with a ghost or an animist spirit that triggers retaliation.

People also use the term *chhiongtioh* to describe situations in which the forces of two entities do not agree. For example, if a bride's luck is low (a circumstance that a spirit medium or fortune-teller may diagnose in advance) and she and her wedding party encounter a funeral, she can collide with the *yin* forces of death and perhaps face misfortune. Other events can bring on such an unlucky turn of affairs, including the viewing of a corpse immediately before the coffin lid is put on, or an encounter between persons who are astrologically unsuited (cf. Topley 1974).

Certain arrangements of buildings in space are potentially hazardous: a traditional Chinese would avoid opening a shop opposite a manufacturer of funeral caskets. (Christian friends who believed that their god would protect them took advantage of lower rents for these inauspicious locations when they opened businesses in Penang and Singapore.) A friend noted that a large business, Eastern Smelting, had been built across the street from an Indian temple and that in the evening the building shook by itself. Someone erected on top of Eastern Smelting a statue of a man with an arrow pointing at the temple, which my friend assumed was intended to correct this inauspicious geomantic position face-to-face with the temple.

People regarded women who were impure (*lasam*) because of childbirth or menstruation as being especially susceptible to a spiritual collision. For example, my research assistant noted that when her sister-in-law entered a temple to pray during the hundred-day period of confinement after childbirth it made her very unlucky (*soe, shuai*). As a result she saw a ghost as she was falling asleep, and felt ill and confused afterwards. My landlady claimed that when a menstruating woman attended a Nine Emperor Gods spirit medium ceremony in which the mediums played with red-hot iron balls, the brazier holding the coals used to heat the iron balls tipped over, and she alone was burned. One spirit medium explained that because of the danger of offending the spirits, women did not go into trance very often:

Master Ooi: They don't want to do it. They're not clean during their menses. If a god enters their body then, they will give offense (*hoantioh, fande*). If the woman is not clean, the god will enter and leave. The spirit of the woman might not return. So it's quite dangerous.

Because of this ritual exclusion, most Hokkien spirit mediums are male.

The spirit medium also is potentially vulnerable to spiritual collision. Consider these statements from a research assistant explaining the use of the black flag to cover and protect the spirit medium when he is coming out of trance, but also when processing down streets where the spirit medium is likely to encounter temples or other possessed spirit mediums:

Poh Eng Lip: The black flag is the highest authority when the spirit medium is in trance. It can protect from dirty things and keep the medium from *tiohhoan* when he comes down from trance. . . . The black flag is placed between a medium processing on the road and any other medium temple he passes. It is said to transform into a mountain, and to block the two from any encounter. It has happened that the black flag has been raised, and the two mediums have fought. They avoid (Malay: *pantang*) seeing the idol, or the medium, because they fear *tiohhoan, chhiongtioh*.

Here, the spiritual conflicts that people fear are vividly and dramatically realized as a violent confrontation between two possessed spirit mediums on an urban street.

Mothers and grandmothers commonly consult with spirit mediums when a child cries continuously, leading them to conclude that the child has taken a fright (*tioh chhe^{n}gia^n*, *de qingjing*), a form of soul loss:

Ah Boi had taken a fright. His grandmother went to the Cantonese woman spirit medium, and returned with a treatment: she took gold charm paper of the sort offered to gods, one yellow talisman, and an uneven number of incense sticks, in this case seven. She held them outside the house, facing out, and prayed, then left them burning at the edge of the lawn. Then she brought three yellow talismans inside, and burned them. She placed a minute amount of ash into a pan of water, and washed Ah Boi's face and hands while he continuously protested "Eh, eh! Eh, eh!" [Hokkien baby-talk for "Dirty!"]. While washing the child, his grandmother said "Don't be afraid! Wash your face, wash your hands, don't be afraid!"

Another young mother came to see this spirit medium when she feared that her child had taken a fright. She brought an article of the child's clothing to the god to change the child's luck (*kai-un, gaiyun*), and the spirit medium gave her one charm for the child to eat, and another to paste on his bedroom wall. A friend commented that when children were frightened, it was difficult to bring back their courage (*ta^n, dan*), adding that adults also "prayed to call fear [to go away]" if they fell ill after an argument (*pai kio kia^n, bai jiao jing*).

At quotidian healing sessions, the god discerns whether the person is ill or has offended a spirit, whether his or her luck is dark or low, whether the individual has taken a fear, or if there are other problems. The god may reassure the person that the illness is not due to nonhuman agency, but if the deity diagnoses a spiritual offense or collision, he or she will offer advice for resolution of the conflict. If, for example, the god diagnoses collision with a Malay animist spirit, restitution usually involves placing offerings at the site where the spirit lives, or even placing a small house-like shrine at the tree's base as an altar for regular offerings, and praying to the spirit to relent and allow the individual to recover. (See Chapter Four.)

Saving the World: Two Cases

Let me here discuss two cases of *tiohhoan*. The first gives a sense of how ordinary the diagnosis can be, and how effortless the cure. The second chronicles a far more serious mental breakdown, and is far from typical. In both cases, the symptoms that the spirit medium diagnosed as suggesting spirit retaliation – fear of enemies, inability to sleep, inability to concentrate – would from the perspective of Western psychological models be diagnosed as symptomatic of depression, anxiety, and finally mental breakdown.

In the first case, a young woman consulted the spirit medium, and the Holy Mother (possessing a woman medium) advised her that she had been disturbed by a spirit and described her symptoms without being told them, evidence for believers that the god knew everything even before the young woman had spoken:

> The god offered a diagnosis: "You must wash at night. It's worse at night. Your heart is afraid, you awaken in the middle of the night."
> The young girl objected, "Yes, but not always."
> The god asked her, "Are you married?"
> "No," she replied.
> The god repeated the diagnosis, "You are disturbed (*tiohhoan*) at night. You suppose that there's illness, then it looks like it's gone. You suppose there's no illness, then it looks like it's there."

She concluded the consultation by telling the young woman that the magic had fled, but that she must worship the Bodhisattva of the Southern Seas (*Lamhai Hutcho·, Nanhai Fozu*) – the Goddess of Mercy. She closed the consultation with the definitive statement, "It's nothing."

In a second case, the symbolism of the spiritual offense was worked into a developing mental crisis. Here is an account from my field notes:

One of my friend's mother-in-law's cousins had poured gasoline over herself and set herself on fire on her front lawn that afternoon. She was married and had three children. She and her husband had a food stall in a coffee shop on the mainland and had lived there, but now were waiting to move into a new house near her business. While they waited, they were living with her husband's family in Penang.

She had gone mad after going to her younger brother's wedding in Singapore. On the way back, she started talking about how people wanted to harm her younger brother and her children, and became very despondent. Her relatives recognized her symptoms to be a sign of *tiohhoan* and took her to see spirit mediums. The Inconstant Uncle [a hell official who keeps the books of life and death] in the City God Temple told her to pray to her ancestors. She refused, saying "Look at the gods! Can't you see that they're crying too?"

Her relatives were concerned, and tried to make sure that she always had someone with her so that she wouldn't try to harm herself. But on this afternoon, only one of her sisters-in-law was home, and she stepped out back to hang out the washing. In the few minutes that the cousin was left unattended, she doused herself with gasoline and set herself on fire. She cried out, and people said that she awoke at the last minute.

She was alive in the hospital, but very badly burned, and unable to speak. My friends sat in their living room discussing it, and one young woman challenged me, "Do you dare go and see her?" "I don't dare," I replied, uncertain why they would expect me to do so. Both she and her sister burst out, "You dare to go see spirit mediums, but you won't go see her!"

In the meantime, the woman's family concluded that she had offended the Inconstant Uncle (*hoantioh Po·tiao Peh, fande Wuchang Bo*), probably by refusing his advice that she should pray to the ancestors, and that he had grabbed her soul. Her husband returned to the City God temple to persuade the god to set her soul free. She died soon thereafter, so their efforts were in vain.

Healing with Charms

Ordinarily, a person is cured through ordinary acts of worship. Recovery sometimes involves placating a spirit with food offerings: "After he's eaten he will let you get well!" one spirit medium observed. Some spirit mediums advise people to abstain from bloody foods to purify themselves, or offer their clients prescriptions for herbal remedies. Although the herbs usually appear to be the commonplace tonic ingredients sold at Chinese medicine shops, some spirit mediums claim to have gone to the jungle to gathered rare ingredients for a secret remedy.[19]

Diagnosis involves discerning the causes of the illness, and several spirit mediums mentioned that for many illnesses the client should visit a doctor rather than a medium. Recall Jonas D. Vaughan's 1879 account of the wealthy

Straits Chinese man who lost faith in spirit mediums when he found that a medical remedy was more effective in treating his illness. Spirit mediums are aware that modern scientific medicine poses a competitive threat, but they also know that modern medicine is not always effective in treating spiritual disturbances, which Western scholars tend to regard as psychological in origin and therefore internal to the individual, but which spirit mediums diagnose as having an external source:

> *Master Lim*: When you treat illness, you must diagnose both the physical and the spiritual. The physical can be well and the spiritual sick, or the physical can be sick and the spiritual well. If the spiritual is ill then you need a spiritual cure, if the problem is a spiritual offense (*tiohhoan*). Real illness or *tiohhoan*, you can diagnose [the difference] easily. If the problem is physical, then you give medicine, either Chinese or European.
>
> A lady about 40 came to see me. Her hand was like a claw. Doctors saw her, and the illness was spreading to her arm. It was a real illness. I told her to take Chinese medicine [a boiled tonic], and after three days to come to the temple with an incense urn and worship the immortal ancestors (*siancho·, xianzu*), and to come every week until she got better. She did improve. Everything has its use. . . .

But when a women with a crippled hand, possibly the same person, visited the Third Prince's spirit medium, he calculated on his fingers then advised her to go see a doctor, a response that appeared to discourage her.

This spirit medium later explained ghosts and spiritual healing to me:

> *Spirit medium for the Third Prince*: So he will disturb you. You come and ask, since you will fall ill if he disturbs you. When you are ill you'll come to ask the god. Won't you pray for him to eat now! After he's eaten, he will let you get well. That sort of thing. We don't talk of this but when people worship and celebrate festivals it is worshipping this. Ah. That sort of thing.
>
> Sometimes, it's like you didn't offend a god (*hoantioh, fande*), but the person himself is ill, inside there is illness. Inner illness is different, it's not the same. You need not pray. You see a doctor, and let him give you medicine; you eat it and are cured. . . . Some people don't pray, they just go to a doctor for a visit. After the doctor has seen them, they return, have one dose, two doses, and they still are not cured. Then they come and ask, if they believe in the gods they ask. They've eaten the medicine, taken it, and they know to come. They themselves can know that they've taken the wrong road. Then they find the gods. With many gods, you come and pray for him to eat, he comes, and things are better, your illness is gone. It's like that.

Unlike some charismatic Christian healers who believe that they can cure any illness provided that the person's faith is strong enough – a debilitating assumption that blames the sick person for their inability to recover – spirit mediums discriminate unequivocally between physical and spiritual causes of illness. For example, when I accompanied a friend to a small temple where she prayed for help in finding a job, I asked the two spirit mediums if they could give me a charm for a child I knew who had leukemia. They unequivocally refused, stating with certainty that leukemia was a matter for doctors, and that they could only offer help with spirit collisions and matters of luck.

If the diagnosis is that the trouble is caused by a spiritual collision, however, the spirit medium in trance often dispenses a paper charm together with instructions for its use. The Cantonese woman spirit medium explained her work in this way:

Many races come – Malay, Indian, European. If children are ill, if they take a fright, if someone goes mad, and there is pollution (*lasam*, that is, if ghosts are to blame), if students want success in their studies, then they find me to get charms and 'eat peace' (*ciah pengan, chi pingan*).

Commonly the spirit mediums/gods dispense the oblong slips of transparent yellow tissue paper called *hu* (*fu*), which are stamped in vermilion ink with the temple seal. When the god prepares them for a client, he or she often adds a character in vermilion ink with a writing brush. Occasionally they are even simpler: Master Lim drew a long looping line on plain yellow paper, using no temple seal. The vermilion ink is made with a red powder called cinnabar (*chuse, zhusha*), traditionally a potent ingredient in the Daoist alchemist's quest for an elixir of immortality.[20] According to a Cantonese woman spirit medium, taking the charm prepared with vermilion ink means 'eating' or 'participating' in peace. Although ephemeral, the charms represent an objectification of the god's charisma, which they may take away and apply to their problems (see also Tambiah 1984).

The god dispensing the magical remedy tells the client how to use it, often advising the person to burn one or more charms, then to add some of the ash to a glass of water and drink it. The god may also give the client a charm to paste on the wall or wear for protection. Here, I summarize just a few of the diagnoses and prescriptions that an older spirit medium, possessed by the Imperial Jade Prince, offered clients at two afternoon trance performances:

Before the first client could describe his problems, the Imperial Jade Prince told him that he was suffering from a tired shoulder, a headache, and a dry throat. He told him to wear a rolled-up yellow charm. When the man asked why, the god explained: "In the future there is an obstacle facing you. If you wear this charm, it will open the way for you, and your future will be bright." [The university student who was translating for me found the god's Hokkien very poetic.]

An expectant mother consulted with the god, complaining that her circulation was poor, and that she was having problems sleeping. She feared that she had offended a spirit. The god urged her to be brave, and gave her a yellow charm to burn and take in water.

An older woman consulted on behalf of her daughter-in-law, who was easily fatigued and had no appetite. The god gave her a charm so that "her heart cannot be troubled, her body will have strength" (*sim peiloan, sinkhu u lat, xin buhui luan, shenqu you li*).

Another asked about a child who liked to play, didn't obey, and didn't like to work – a common list of complaints. The god responded, "Give him a charm to eat, so that he know how to listen [in other words, become obedient]" (*ho.i chiah hu, ho.i ehiao tia wa, gei ta chifu, gei ta hui tinghua*).

At temple fairs, the possessed medium sometimes further dots the tissue paper talismans with blood drawn from his tongue by a broken teacup or a ball of nails. Blood represents the life force, and people explain that the blood of the possessed spirit medium is in fact that of the god. For this reason, it has extraordinary demon-expelling, therapeutic power (*lat, li*). Today, fear of AIDS should lead people to avoid contact with blood, but people reason that the god's blood cannot be anything but pure, and at least some continue to ingest blood-impregnated charms.

A person must correctly invoke the appropriate forces before offering the charm or ingesting it. An English-educated temple committee member at a spirit medium temple who was also active in the Heavenly Dao Association (*Tiandao Hui*) compared the ritual associated with use of the charms to use of a computer code or to tuning a radio to the right frequency, suggesting that its effectiveness was rooted in a use of spiritual energy:

Committee member for the Vagabond Buddha: When you pray with the *hu*, you must light three joss sticks and go in front of your house to face heaven. You address the god by name, and tell him your name and your problem. It is like a computer card – you have to punch in the correct code or else it is useless, means nothing. With the *hu*, you need a contact point – it's like tuning in a radio station – and the *hu* provides that point. Even though there are millions of souls, the god will receive the message, and can project a vibration to that person. This is one type of psychic healing, and is very useful.

His explanation underlines the fact that in his view, these phenomena are a part of the unchanging Dao rather than an aspect of human ethics.

Spirit mediums commonly dispensed paper talismans as vehicles of communication with invisible worlds and magical remedies, but some spirit mediums, including the spirit medium of the Nine Emperor Gods festival, also dispensed cloth charms that conferred invulnerability on the possessor and that typically cost $3.60. The use of these body-protection charms is enmeshed in taboos. When I and members of the family I was living with received a yellow cloth body-protection charm (*bo·sin hu, baoshen fu*) from a local spirit medium, for example, the god's followers instructed us to carry it on our bodies or in a bag, not to get it wet, and not to hang it on a wall or let it touch wood. It could be placed on a table but only if placed on paper first.

Spirit mediums and temple committee members promoted body-protection charms with stories of their efficacy. Master Ooi, the Vagabond Buddha's spirit medium, claimed, for example that, "If the person bites this efficacious charm he will be protected against knife stabs in the back. The knife cannot cut." When he feared that one of the young boys at his temple was going to have trouble with the government, he advised the boy to obtain one of these black charms. Master Ooi conferred the protection by hitting the boy's stomach with a sword while he was clenching the black charm in his teeth (see Chapter Seven). A committee member for another spirit medium temple that offered body-protection charms claimed that such a charm had saved the life of a construction worker: a falling object missed him, and when he later looked in his pocket, he discovered that the body-protection charm had torn by itself.[21]

Occult Powers and Spiritual Contests

Although people often suspected their problems to be the result of a spiritual collision, they also visited spirit mediums to undo the workings of black magic (*kongtau*). Often they believed that their enemies had obtained harmful magic from Thai or Malay magicians, but Chinese spirit mediums also were rumored to have the power to harm, sometimes with the assistance of ghosts they commanded.[22]

The discourse of black magic inspires fear. Spirit mediums often described its harmful effects, from the infatuation caused by love magic to physical harm resulting from a magical poison known as *santau*. They noted that sending back the magic involved identifying the source, which is impossible in those cases where the magic went astray from its original target, afflicting the wrong person. In Chapter One I mentioned the story of the woman who picked a flower and was harmed by black magic meant for another. A university student told me a similar story about her former neighbor, who was only a few years older than she but suffered from recurrent headaches. According to this young woman, the neighbor went to many spirit mediums, who invariably told her that she had stepped in the way of magic meant for another person. Because the enemy was not her enemy, she was powerless to find the person who sent it and combat it.

Some Penang Chinese especially feared the black magic of Malay and Thai magicians, whom Chinese may approach for help in harming their enemies or for love magic. Indeed, people attributed especially frightening powers to the magicians of other ethnic groups. Master Ooi, for example, ranked Tibetan,

Indian, Malay, and Thai black magic higher than Chinese, noting that the most dangerous *kongtau* could kill, and that there was no cure. Chinese, by contrast, simply wrote a charm and burned it to make people lose consciousness, a curable affliction.

When Master Ooi rated Chinese magic as the mildest he followed a common pattern in Southeast Asia, whereby people project their fears of those who are not part of their group onto the spirit world, magnifying the occult powers of outgroup practitioners (Golomb 1978: 216). At another meeting, Master Ooi offered a frightening story of a man who had died of Thai *kongtau*: as he described it, the man had a 'knife' in his stomach and could not speak; he had no strength in his legs and he threw up blood. Some people seek protection from black magic by burning the testicles from a dog that is entirely black and wearing the ashes.

There may be some basis for people's intense fear of *kongtau*, because some forms of black magic in Southeast Asia involve the use of actual drugs and poisons. For example, thieves make ritualistic use of a type of narcotic incense called *pukau* in Malay, which they use to put their victims to sleep:

Mr. Lim: Pukau is a type of incense. You chant, and use a white cloth. You chant, and wave the cloth above the incense. The whole household will be asleep. This is a hypnotic drug used by burglars. Whether the effect is due to the smell or spiritual powers we cannot know.

This former spirit medium continued his introduction to black arts:

Mr. Lim: Santau is a poison, an irritant. It is finely ground glass mixed with fine hairs taken from the inside of the bamboo tree, mixed into a paste. You chant an incantation, then flick it into food. You use a tiny bit, but it can make you very ill. This can be combated spiritually.

The Holy Mother's spirit medium also explained that the remedy for black magic was spiritual, observing that: "Sometimes you can be the victim of a charm, you can't see it, but it cuts the stomach. The god can know, can write a charm for the person to eat to cure that person." Although the remedy may be spiritual, a Malay-English dictionary defines *santau* as "a slow and sure poison; not a specific drug, but a compound of several poisons" (Coope 1976: 244).

Although the Hokkien term *kongtau* often describes magic performed in order to inflict physical harm on an enemy, people also suspected the workings of *kongtau* when a Chinese became infatuated with a non-Chinese, in particular a Malay. Here too, the distrust of the ethnic other leads to a suspicion that any attraction must be the consequence of magical forms of entrapment. If they suspect the workings of *kongtau*, the family of the person almost certainly will take the infatuated Chinese to see a Thai monk or a religious practitioner like the Datuk Aunt in order to take action to dispel the infatuation. In defining infatuation with the ethnic other as the result of the workings of black magic, the family has powerful ammunition against a potential match.

At the same time, spirit mediums themselves sometimes tapped into the dark side for occult forms of power, and the yellow talismans that spirit mediums offer as cures for spiritual collisions can also be used in black magic. A former spirit medium who assisted a spirit medium for Taishang Laojun commented:

Mr. Lim: There are many things spiritual which cannot be explained. Take the yellow paper charms. You chant, that is your action. But to them there is a reaction. If you fight you want to know these things. Sometimes people take a yellow charm, they paste it above the door in an obscure place where it is hidden. At night, someone will be knocking at the door. You reach the door and find no one. This you cannot explain, you cannot know the origin. The action leads to a reaction. Whether it is bad or good, it happens.[23]

Whereas curing spiritual offenses or collisions involves mediation with the offended spirit and placation with offerings, dealing with black magic attacks sometimes entails fighting to establish dominance over the spiritual being harming the individual.

I asked Mr. Lim, "What happens when ghosts possess the spirit medium?" and he explained, "The ghosts are more sincere if they come to spirit mediums, since otherwise their deities will retaliate." But when I asked whether this was because the spirit medium's possessing deity was more powerful than the ghosts, he responded:

Mr. Lim: You must define this word power. Good will overcome evil in the end, but at the beginning evil may overcome. So, you may be good at martial arts, and ten persons could not overcome you. Along comes a person with a revolver – you're dead! Evil overcomes good. But if you're warned, you wear a bulletproof vest, and you have protection.

His metaphor points to the fact that the form of protection must be appropriate to the threat, which suggests the appropriateness and importance of spiritual protection against spiritual threats to well-being.

He also explained the spiritual challenge to me:

Someone is sick so you go into trance. The spirit comes, you ask him what is wrong, ask him to help the person. Sometimes he asks for an offering: three types of fruit, red and white candles, three small glasses of water, gold and silver paper.

Generally the person gets cured. But some spirits will not forgive. Depending on the gravity, there will be a spiritual challenge. This is very frightening. If he is compassionate, you will see the deity in a certain form and get a certain force. If he is fierce or evil, you will see a hideous form. Then you must go through the rites and ceremonies and get rid of this spirit.

If there is a black candle it means that a challenge is going on. The flame must not go off, and will not however strong the wind. This is a psychic phenomenon. If the other party is stronger, then the light will go off, and there will be terrible consequences.

A friend, a Malay *bomoh* [magician] was explaining to me his powers. You won't believe. He took a hen's egg and spun. After it spun for some time it stood erect, then he spun a second on top of the first, then a third on top of the second, then a candle on top of that. With a fan on overhead the candle did not flicker. He was challenging someone. He overcame the other party. Usually a truce is called, and there is no outright destruction.

As his highly dramatic stories suggest, Chinese spirit mediums and Malay *bomohs* who, like spirit mediums, are both healers and magicians, perform exorcistic rituals that do battle with invisible spirits or sorcerers to rescue afflicted souls.

One university student offered a lengthy narrative of a spiritual match, describing a contest between Chinese and Thai magic, in which the White-Haired Immortal cured an afflicted individual of a powerful charm. Earlier he had described the White-Haired Immortal to me thus:

The White-haired Immortal (*Pehmo· Sian, Baimao Xian*) is a martial artist. He lives in Ayer Itam, on Jalan Pisang. If you are ill with a charm, he can help you. He is king of the gangsters in Penang. Extortion money comes to him, they pay him homage because of his skill. He can't be killed with a gun, he can walk on water, if you hit him he will fly. He can be three places at once. . . .

One time a man was victim of a charm. A very deep charm. This magic was done by a Thai. Thai magic is very high. So, he went to many black magic immortals. How to take off this magic, so deep. So he went to many places, found no cure.

One day someone said, "If you really have the heart, you want to clear off this magic, you must find the White-Haired Immortal." So he searched and searched and found him. The White-Haired Immortal said, "Okay, la. I know your black magic is very heavy. I want to help you, but it's difficult. But if you really want this, okay la, I'll risk my life for you." So he said, "If you want this, you go and catch 24 frogs, 24 for me, huh? Before six p.m., bring them to me."

The man caught the frogs, and took them to the White-Haired Immortal, and together they stayed in the house. The White-Haired Immortal chanted, and threw the frogs from 6:00 p.m. "He chanted until 6 a.m., threw, threw, threw until 6 a.m." In the morning, all the frogs save one were blind.

The White-Haired Immortal appeared. They asked, "Is he well or not?"
The White-haired Immortal said, "This man is better la."
The man said, "White-Haired Immortal, good dog's life! If those 24 frogs' eyes were all blind, my life would be given to that man to take. That man's magic is much higher than yours!"
Now a few days later, this magician, the Thai magician who made some people mad, he came to find the White-Haired Immortal. The man's eyes were entirely blind.

The White-Haired Immortal said, "Now my magic is higher than yours."

The magician replied, "If your magic is higher, can you kill me or not? Or can I kill you?"

The White-Haired Immortal responded, "If I want to do that, now I can, any time you want to die, I'll do it to you, and you'll have no alternative. You have no magic. But it's a waste to kill a man such as you. Your magic is so high. To kill you is a waste. If you agree to do good, if you agree to not use your magic to kill people, then I'll let you go."

So he said, "Okay," he agreed, and accepted the White-Haired Immortal as his master, and the White-Haired Immortal let him go.

This contest thus resulted not in the destruction of the powerful magician, but rather in his submission to the White-Haired Immortal.[24] Similarly, many of the stories told of Chinese deities imagine them as warriors who fight against evil, transforming demonic enemies into fiercely protective allies. On the journey to India to obtain the Buddhist scriptures, for example, the Great Saint (Monkey), himself a converted enemy, fights and conquers many demons, and with Guanyin's help converts two to become helpers in the quest.

Although magicians usually fight their battles on the transposed territory of the spiritual, sometimes the boundaries between spiritual and human worlds blur. People say, for example, that during the racial riots of 1969, 'bad kids' (*pai gin-a*, *dai haizi*, as gangsters are sometimes known) in Penang and Kuala Lumpur fought with Malays to defend the Chinese community from violent attacks. But according to the student's account, spirits helped them, empowering their knives to fly through the air:

In 1969, the time of the fighting, people were bad. The White-Haired Immortal chanted over the knives. Those knives flew by themselves. They would cut Malay heads. Chinese heads the knife wouldn't cut. When men wanted to kill, the White-Haired Immortal just chanted, chanted, chanted, put the knives down, laid them out one by one. This Kampong Melayu is a Malay place, so when the Malays came to make trouble, the knives hit them.

Here, a magician offered Chinese gangsters magic to animate their weapons so that they could triumph in their battles with the ethnic other, continuing a long history that associates martial and magical arts. The fighters of the Boxer Uprising, for example, used "magic, spells, invulnerability, and spirit possession" in their martial arts (Esherick 1987: 67). Because the knives flew of their own accord, presumably the spirit world took moral responsibility for the consequences of these violent acts.

Despite the insistence that the gods only do good, Penangites accept that some spirit mediums work on the dark side, tapping into demonic powers in order to harm their enemies or to effortlessly obtain money or desired goods. Some described *Mau San* (*Mao Shan*) practitioners, whom they sometimes identified as spirit mediums, sometimes as Daoist masters, as having especially extraordinary powers:

School teacher and amateur numerologist: The black force is called *mo·koai (moguai)*. Mao Shan practitioners are on the dark side. In Balik Pulau there is one. He wears a patched robe and can disappear in front of your eyes. Mount Erskine also has one. . . . Left-handers pray to hell, hell has its own powers.

One Taiwanese-born friend claimed that local Mao Shan practitioners, whose existence at times appeared to be as much urban legend as fact, controlled powerful forms of magic:

Mao Shan Daoists control magic, and they can transform things. They can get money from your purse, for example. There are three rules:

First, they cannot marry.

Second, they cannot keep money. They order ghosts to steal things. If they only use $300 of $500 stolen, they must give it away, they cannot keep it on their body.

Third, they cannot hurt people. The hurt will return to their own body.

She added this story:

At the seaside twenty years ago a Mao Shan spirit medium sat with a few friends. He said to them, "The durian at one stall on Macalister Road is very good. In thirty minutes, they will deliver some to us. Someone has sent them out." Sure enough, the boy came with the durian, and asked for money. The spirit medium said, "We've paid already. Go and ask your boss, these are the serial numbers on the bills."

The boy went back, and sure enough, his boss had bills with those serial numbers in his pocket. But no one had moved. One of the men wondered out loud, "But whom do we thank for this treat?"

The medium said, "You treated! Look in your pocket!"

He looked, and found twenty dollars missing.

Although historically Mao Shan Daoists may have been a powerful and respectable religious lineage (Strickmann 2002), by the nineteenth century the name already was associated with the magic of theft (Dennys 1876: 83).

Although rumors of their powers persist, no Penang spirit medium or religious master has ever identified himself to me as a Mao Shan practitioner. But others once introduced me to a young man with a troubled, violent past that included arson and assault; they claimed he was a Mao Shan spirit medium. In Penang he worked in a nightclub as a bouncer. He also worked at a temple, where he was possessed regularly by a god who 'liked to joke.' When I met the man, I noted that one of his arms was tattooed with an anarchist symbol: two hands and a rose. The wrists had been chained, restraining the hands next to the thorns, but the chains had been broken so that they could reach for the rose.

We have now strayed from the world of spirits into that of society's ghosts – a topic to which I return in Chapter Seven.

Conclusion

In this chapter, I have explored the way Penangites who worship deities communicate with the numinous through divination, dreams, and spirit mediums. I have also looked at the everyday idioms in terms of which Penangites imagine their relationships with the gods and the gods' relationships with one another. I also have discussed the ways in which spirit mediums explain and exercise their powers, both healing and harmful.

A widely shared symbolism of cosmic fundamentals, including *yin, yang,* and the cycle, profoundly shapes Penang Chinese popular religious culture. These cosmic fundamentals organize the habitus of space and time in the periodic practices of popular religious culture, including regular acts of worship at the family altar and the performance of the rituals of the annual festival cycle. People also mobilize these concepts in practice when they interpret everyday events in light of cycles of luck and spiritual collisions, whose negative effects they seek to ameliorate through ritual. When they tell stories, they give aesthetic form to their understandings, which take root in the time and space of their own community, and construct images of the invisible, potent world of spirits.

Let me now examine the trance performance more closely as a chronotope reenacting the habitus of an imagined China that spirit mediums know best from the stories recounted in vernacular literature and traditional theater, stories that contemporary Chinese continue to retell and know through the newer media of film, television, and comic books.

CHAPTER THREE

Possessed by the Past

But let us suppose that the mythical point of view could become subjective; that it could pass over into the active ego and become conscious there, proudly and darkly yet joyously, of its recurrence and its typicality, could celebrate its role and realize its value exclusively in the knowledge that it was a fresh incarnation of the tradition on earth. One might say that such a phenomenon alone could be called the 'lived myth' nor should we think that it is anything novel or unknown.

Mann (1947 [1936]): 423

IN SOUTHEAST ASIA, Hong Kong, and Taiwan, spirit mediums are visible and active religious practitioners.[1] In everyday practice spirit mediums perform a variety of services (which they sometimes describe as 'saving the world' [*kiusay, jiushi*]) that range from the treatment of illness with magical charms or herbs to gambling advice and ambiguously written predictions of lottery numbers.[2] In Penang, some spirit mediums also were teachers who drew on a deep tradition of popular literature and the textual works of the Three Doctrines (*Samkao, Sanjiao*), Daoism, Confucianism, and Buddhism.[3] In the trance performance of Chinese deities, spirit mediums perform the chronotope of invisible spiritual worlds, a chronotope whose imagining is informed by the reading of well-known vernacular literary sources. In this chapter, I explore the use of costume, movement, and language in the performance of military and literary gods. I also review literary sources that inform people's images of the gods and their powers, including the stories of the Great Saint, the Vagabond Buddha, and Nazha.

Some studies of altered states of consciousness have focused on the experience of the trance possession state as an altered state of consciousness and on the therapeutic value of emotional catharsis for the individual.[4] But as Michael Lambek points out, trance as a form of behavior is not extant prior to spirit possession, nor can it be separated from culture (Lambek 1989: 40). Moreover, spirit possession is a performance, and must perforce be considered not only in its psychological dimensions, but also as a patterned (albeit highly variable) form of communication between the possessed spirit medium and his or her audience. As I have demonstrated in Chapter Two, the spirit medium and the patient share a common fund of practices and oral narratives that inform their imagining of invisible worlds – worlds that the spirit medium makes visible when he or she enacts the character of the possessing deity.

Different regions of China have local names for ritual performers, including *wushi, shipo, duangong, shamen, tongzi,* and *shenwu* (Sutton 2000: 2). In Penang, Hokkien speakers call spirit mediums *kitong* (*jitong*), a compound formed from a word meaning 'to divine' (*ki, ji*) and a Min word that linguist Jerry Norman translates as 'shaman' (*tong*).[5] People describe the medium as dancing in trance (*thiautong, tiaotong*), combing a word meaning 'dance' or 'leap' with *tong,* which further suggests the spirit medium's embodied, ecstatic performance.[6] When discussing which god possesses a certain medium, Chinese will say that "he dances the Third Prince," which suggests the way that mediums take on the personality and movements of a particular deity, much as an actor performs a role (see Chan 2006).

People sometimes say that spirit mediums have 'light bones' or a 'light body' (*khin sinku, qing shenqu*), and that they were fated to die young. Some sources explain that this is because spirit mediums have inauspicious horoscopes. Their god saved them and extended their life span for one generation, in return for which the medium undertook to carry out the god's healing work. Most mediums, when asked, say that god chose to come to them. They claim that they resisted at first, because the life of a spirit medium is a difficult one, but the god seized them (*liah, lue)* and forced them to do the work of salvation. For example, a highly respected Master reported that the door god (*muisin, menshen*), the spirit of a Tang dynasty emperor's bodyguard, had seized him: "He stopped me, and I could not move. I called on Heaven and Earth and begged for mercy!"

A Hakka spirit medium observed, "There must be an affinity between the person and the god. Learning to be a spirit medium is not like studying a book. The god must want you to accompany him. The god comes of his own accord." He also commented on the difficulty of my writing about something that I had never experienced, arguing, "To really understand, you must experience this. Unless you taste a glass of water, you don't know if it is sweet or salty. I can tell you that the water is hot. Do you believe me?" I later declined his challenge to go into trance, and therefore cannot speak with firsthand authority,[7] but many spirit mediums were willing to discuss their first experience of trance in response to my curious questions:

Hokkien spirit medium possessed by the Third Prince: Before I became a medium, I was a manual laborer. Then one night I had a terrible headache, and I couldn't sleep. All of a sudden I felt compelled to run, and I ran into a strange house. To this day I don't know whose house it was. The house had an altar to the Third Prince, and before the altar I went into trance and danced. When it was over I went home.

A year later the god appeared to me and told me he wanted to come down to save people and bring good to mankind. I was unwilling, and I tried to run away. Because of this I was crippled by the god, and forced to become a medium. The day when all this is over, when the god has no more use of me, I will be freed and able to walk again.

Hakka spirit medium: I have been going into trance for twenty-eight years, since my eldest son was two years old. At that time, I was working as a vegetable farmer on Penang Hill. Around the time that my mother died, a centipede fell from a tree and stung me. There was no doctor. I was poisoned, but the god came and saved me. In exchange for this, I must do healing work helping mankind. At that time I was thirty-six years old.

Hokkien woman spirit medium, a former beautician possessed by the Holy Mother: When the god came the first time, I was on my knees praying. I found that I couldn't rise. I called mother, called on the Lord of Heaven, and pleaded not to have to do this work. The Holy Mother hit me, she slapped me on both cheeks, and forced me to do this work.

Hokkien spirit medium possessed by the Third Prince: When he approached me, I didn't know what god it was. I'm like this: when I dance, I dance the Third Prince. But you cannot say, man cannot himself decide which god will come. It's like that. He approaches, and you cannot say who comes. It's like that. He wants to save the world.

Chaozhou spirit medium possessed by the Vagabond Buddha: The first time I went into trance, I felt drunk, I had no power to speak myself. But after the god's consciousness entered my body, the god spoke through me.

Spirit medium possessed by the God of War: I met with an accident, and had difficulty walking, then Bodhidharma and Guangong, Guandi [the God of War] came and taught me martial arts.

Mr. Lim, a retired spirit medium who had been possessed by the spirit of a Thai ancestor on his grandfather's side, Nah Phuan, *whom he also called* Nene, *Malay for 'grandmother':* The fifteenth day of the fourth lunar month is my deity's birthday. From 1953 on the events have been within my circle only, there have been no sessions for the public. Before, we worshipped at the incense urn, we had the equipment but no spirit medium. Then an auntie visited a female cousin, and said, "The deity has returned!" I went there and followed closely, and became a spirit medium. I studied Theravada Buddhism in the early stages. Mediumship is actually contrary to Buddhist practice.

Master Lim, describing a mysterious illness episode in 1929 when he was seventeen; he recovered after treatment by a well-known Thai monk: I had never been so sick. For the first time medication had no effect and I was puzzled....Why was it that I could not get well with medical attention, and too, the Chinese physician was not able to do anything for me. There must be things beyond human knowledge. As I was thinking in this strain my room brightened up. It grew brighter and brighter and soon it was brighter than the light of the sun outside. I felt a sense of calm and peace and a brightening inside me that lifted me from the gloom of the previous days. Then when the Light was at its brightest, I heard a voice say to me, "You will not die. Until your work is done you will not die."...The Incident lived in my mind but I did not know what work I had to do (Lim Peng Eok N.d.: 2).

Sometimes at the outset many gods enter, but finally one will 'catch' (*liat, lue*) the medium and regularly possess him or her in order to cure people who are ill because they have offended a spirit:

> *Hakka spirit medium*: My younger brother is twenty. He went into trance for the first time on Tuesday. For him it came on naturally, like my father. I had to try to go into trance, although no one trained me. The first forty-nine days are very difficult. In that period, it is not yet certain which saints (*sin, shen*) will regularly possess the medium, and many deities come. It is like a baby learning to eat.

My research assistant noted that the forty-nine days (or seven weeks) of the spirit medium's apprenticeship is precisely the same as the period of confinement after childbirth. In the four days since the younger brother had first gone into trance, nine deities had possessed him, including seven literary gods and two fierce gods, the Dragon Star Lord and the Wealth Youth. When I returned for a special ceremony several months later, I learned that the younger brother was possessed regularly by the Vagabond Buddha.

Some who take the first steps towards becoming spirit mediums do not progress to being recognized as genuinely chosen by the gods to do their work. For example, one young college student became possessed during a family trance session at which her two brothers were possessed by the Great Saint and Nazha. Rather than incorporate her into their improvised performance, one of her brothers, still possessed, blew water on her face. When I later asked why, he asserted that her trance state had not been genuine. Similarly, Margery Wolf describes a Taiwanese rural woman who began to act as a spirit medium for a *wangye* [divine king] deity. Initially her performances excited great interest, but as events unfolded many came to regard her as crazy, and she did not persist in her shamanic practice (Wolf 1992).

Because the gods themselves are pure, they do not tolerate impurity. Consequently, prior to the trance performance, spirit mediums prepare for the entry of the god into their bodies, sometimes by following a vegetarian diet and abstaining from sexual contact. Some further practice self-cultivation (*siuheng, xiuxing*), including meditation and moral disciplines. The Hokkien term that describes ritual impurity (*lasam*) also names ghosts and female sexual fluids, both of which are regarded as dirty. Because of their alleged impurity, few Hokkien women perform as spirit mediums.

People say that when the god comes, his soul covers (*kham,gai*) the soul of the spirit medium. When I asked spirit mediums about the experience of trance, most replied, "The god comes, then I know nothing":

> *Spirit medium possessed by the Vagabond Buddha*: When the god comes, you can see a very bright light. Being in trance is like sleeping. You must vomit until you're pure, then it becomes very hard to breathe, and everything is confused.

Spirit medium possessed by the Third Prince: If you talk of when the god comes, we only know the suffering (*kankho·, jianku*). When there is suffering, you know that he approaches. You are unconscious. When we do anything, we don't know. We know nothing! Once you have sat in trance, then you can know....It's like we can only experience and talk of the suffering, like that.

Similarly, the Holy Mother's spirit medium explained, "When the god comes, my head hurts. I know nothing, I can heal people."

Some mediums admit that they are conscious of what happens in the trance performance, or will reveal that they remember events and exchanges that occurred while they were in trance. One former spirit medium explained, "There are many types of trance mediums. Some are in a mild stage of trance and are aware of what is going on. A voice will tell them what to prescribe." He added, "The trance state will depend on the temperament of the spirit medium. It depends on his *mind*." The public, however, is firmly convinced that if the trance is real, then the medium will know nothing of what occurred during the trance performance, and that the spirit medium's self is wholly replaced by that of the god.

The Trance Performance

Putting aside spirit mediums' claims for a moment, the trance performance involves the skillful improvisation of one or more characters, and the spirit medium's personal transformation in speech and movement is convincing proof to the audience that a god is truly present. One woman medium was, for example, possessed by each of the Eight Immortals in turn. Even though she had a minimum of props, those present found it easy to identify each of the immortals, and my landlady insisted that the spirit medium's facial expressions changed for each of these deities. Neighbors talked about this impressive performance for days.

Although spirit mediums sometimes fall into trance spontaneously, sometimes those supporting the god invite him by singing or chanting an invocation (*liamchiu, nianzhou*) to the accompaniment of drums and gongs. The invocation (*chiu, zhou*) usually is composed in literary style or deep Hokkien, and although it might be difficult for the listener to comprehend it wholly, its meaning is evident from the context of its performance. A widely available book sold on newsstands that some referred to as the God of Prosperity (Tua Pek Kong) dream book published several invocations. In one 1980 edition, the book's front cover shows an illustration of Tua Pek Kong, and the back describes the book as *The Thousand Character Text and Picture Explanation Book* (*Qianzi Wentu Jieshu*). No author or place of publication is given, but the prominence of the image of Tua Pek Kong, the Sino-Malaysian God of the Earth, on the front cover, the inclusion of Malay, English, and Chinese names of objects, and also the range of objects (which include the pagoda at Penang's Temple of Paradise, Ovaltine, and the ubiquitous small lizard called a *cichak*) strongly suggests that it was locally created and printed.

People referred to this book in order to translate dream images or exceptional events into lottery numbers. But its compilers also included invocations for the Holy King and the Great Saint, and another to 'open the mouth' (*kaikou*), presumably of a new spirit medium in training. The first invocation is designed to invite any saint:

> ### Incantation to Invite the God (*Qingshen Zhou*)
> Three pure joss sticks come to invite the god.
> The youth tending the incense urn stands in front of the altar.
> The first joss stick invites the god to open the bright gates of heaven.
> The second invites the glorious god to consciousness.
> The third invites the bright god to come:
> To ride a jeweled horse and to come out from heaven's terrace,
> To leap on the clouds, and ride the mist of the void.
> One urn of pure incense is in front of the altar.
> Draw a charm in order to save mankind.
> First slay, and then report without tolerance.
> The Jade Emperor grants you this authority.
> Through flying clouds your horse travels to the front of the altar.
> I, your younger brother, sincerely pray three times to invite you.
> [God's name here], descend and approach.
> The god's soldiers are fervent and active, impatient to follow your decree.

The god is imagined as descending from heaven on a horse, and riding the clouds to the front of the altar, where those invoking him describe themselves both as younger brothers to the deity and as soldiers who are awaiting his command.

A second invocation in the Tua Pek Kong Dream Book is an invitation to the Great Saint, or Monkey God. Although the poem invites the god, in it the god apparently speaks, recalling his spiritual journeys to Heaven and India to fetch the Buddhist scriptures, and exhorting his disciples to be wholehearted in their efforts and spiritual:

> ### The Great Saint Equal to Heaven Incantation
> Humbly invite the Great Saint *Sun* [his surname] Equal to Heaven
> Who wears a golden ring on his head and holds the seal
> Tread on the Eastern Sea with your three-inch feet

The Dragon King respected me, and came down to the Elixir [Dan] pool
He bestowed on me a golden dragon golden cudgel
The wild herbs respected me, gathered below,
Everyday I wandered around Taishang Laojun's court
Getting the elixir of life, my Buddha nature rejoiced
Above there is Tripitaka, above Renbai [literally, 'benevolent cypress']
From the east we went to the west for Buddhist scriptures
The golden world has handed down the imperial decree.
The Great Saint Equal to Heaven descended into the human world to save humans from the sea of misery
To remind his disciples to put their hearts into their efforts,
To remind his disciples to be spiritual
The Buddha opens his mouth and does people a favor willingly
Obtaining the elixir of life to rejoice the Buddha nature
His disciples with one heart ask for it three times
Those praying invite the Great Saint to come to the front of the gods
The god's soldiers act urgently as executing an order,
As urgently as executing an order.

The invocation describes the Great Saint as a savior who descends into the world to rescue people from their suffering. His disciples invite him to their altar, praying that he share with them both the elixir of life and his moral teachings.

Once the god has possessed the spirit medium, the person's manner, habit, or style (*khoan, kuan*) changes. If the god is a martial artist, the spirit medium's movements become chaotic and violent, and his assistants restrain him or look after him (*go·, gu*) because, as my research assistant explained, "the person is not aware of his body, so he can become too violent in inflicting harm on himself." Martial artist gods call for their cobra-handled whip (*sinpi^n*, *shenbian* or *sengchoa, shengshe*, literally 'holy snake') and their characteristic weapons – sword, halberd, pole, or spear – and they may ask for rice wine, Guinness Stout, or French brandy.

The spirit medium's movements express the god's identity: the Monkey God announces himself with somersaults and Chinese generals demonstrate their military prowess with spears and halberds. By contrast, a literary god – a teacher, doctor, or magistrate – maintains an aristocratic demeanor and an archaic style of speaking. Like Master Khoo, possessed by Choo Kong in the shrine-grotto, the magistrate walks with stately dignity, and Laozi strokes his long white beard, even though it is only imagined. Spirit mediums who are possessed by local Datuk Kong spirits have Malay tastes; at one festival, a Chinese man possessed by the Malay Red Datuk joined in with the participants to dance in a Malay-style dance to the Dondang Sayang music performed for his pleasure.

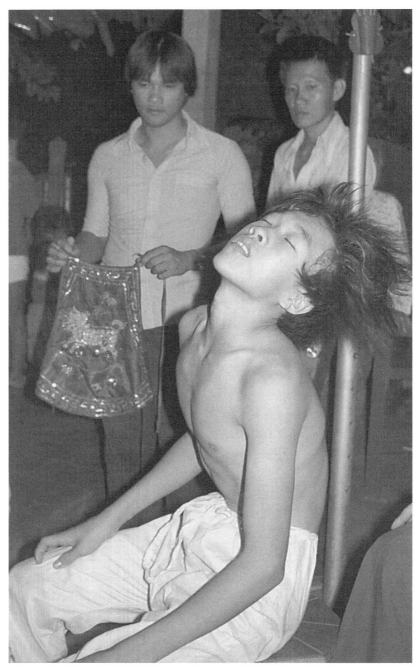

FIG. 22. A young spirit medium falls into a trance, tended by his friend, who will dress him in the god's stomacher and leggings, Penang, 1980. Photo: Jean DeBernardi

F I G . 2 3 . Wearing pure white clothes, a temple committee member ties a headband on the god-in-his medium at the altar of a Nine Emperor Gods temple, George Town, 1980. Photo: Jean DeBernardi

In classifying the gods as either literary or military, Penang Chinese draw on an ancient model of governance through civil and military leaders whose roles complement one another. Although their performances differ, both military and literary gods know what is in the heart of people who come to consult with them, and have knowledge of the past, present, and future and the invisible world of gods and ghosts. Because of this omniscient knowledge, the god can judge whether a client's misfortunes are the result of a spiritual collision with a local animist spirit or a willful ghost and administer the appropriate treatment.

Any spirit might enter a spirit medium, but popular and easily recognized deities are most likely to regularly possess the medium. People are familiar with the personalities of these gods, and can easily identify them by their manner, whether they joke, teach, write poems, or perform martial arts:

Cantonese neighbor: Lala's [Nazha's] habit is that he takes a pacifier. Kuan Kong [the God of War] is very strong. The Monkey God leaps, his habit is to do a somersault. The Inconstant Uncle is a man who ate opium. When he died, white ants covered him over, and people went to worship him. He heals illness. He is an old man, and has no strength. When the medium is in trance, he speaks with a faint voice. People put opium on his face. When the medium is in trance, sharp things – the sword, the nail chair – cannot hurt him, so because of this and the style (*khoan, kuan*), people believe in the medium.

The spirit medium adopts the characteristics of the god, including ways of speaking, special movements, personal taste in food and intoxicants, and insistence on purity or an aversion to baths:

Spirit medium for the Inconstant Uncle: The god is very humble. You must ask him first before giving him gifts. If there are enough people on the first and fifteenth of the lunar month, then he lectures and tells stories.

Even when people invite the gods to do planchette divination, a practice in which two men take the two sides of a triangular-shaped stick and use the tip to write Chinese characters in a three-foot-by-two-foot sandbox placed on the altar, the personalities of the different gods are evident in their manner of writing. Master Lim claimed that they could know which god had descended to write by his or her manner, and that some gods were so fierce that they broke the table. He added that when one participant had expressed doubts at a spirit writing session, the stick had pulled him up off the ground, leaving him speechless and terrified.

Spirit mediums will note and sometimes exaggerate points of contrast between themselves and their possessing deities – preferring tea when possessed by their god when they themselves like coffee, for example. As Raymond Lee points out, these repertoires of behavior are in effect stage props by which spirit mediums distinguish their supernatural self from their ordinary self (Lee 1989: 260).

The transformation of the appearance of the spirit medium is accomplished also through costumes that distinguish the different deities. The Vagabond Buddha wears tattered yellow monk's robes, whereas martial artist gods like Nazha and the Great Saint (Monkey) wear brilliantly colored and embroidered satin stomacher and leggings, which together are called a 'skirt and stomach[er]' (*kundo·, qundu*). The article of clothing that de Groot termed a 'stomacher' is an oval bib of embroidered satin tied at the neck and waist that covers the medium's chest but leaves his back bare, which is sometimes described as an 'embroidered stomach[er]' (*siuto·, xiudu*). The leggings are three long petals of matching embroidered satin tied at the waist, covering plain cotton drawstring pants. Often the costume is yellow (although it may be red, green, black, or white) and typically it is embroidered with dragons and with the name of the god and the temple. Military gods also carry a small satin pennant, also embroidered with the name of the god and the temple, which represents their command (*ling*), the authority that Heaven has granted them to act against demonic spirits.

People regard these costumes as spiritually powerful. For example, one night I walked to a local spirit medium temple that was celebrating a festival only to learn that there would be no trance performance that evening. I attempted to interview the spirit medium but found him to be offhanded and diffident. As a joke, one man who was sitting with the others during this lull in the events put the god's silk stomacher and leggings over his street clothes, sat on the eight-trigrams stool, and demanded, "Photograph me!" I hesitated, disconcerted, then realized that the spirit medium had fallen into trance, saliva running from his mouth. The other men exclaimed, "The god is angry!" as the medium, agitated, fell into a martial arts pose and challenged the joker. The man removed the trance garments and retreated. Meanwhile, the angered god approached the altar and cut his tongue with a spike ball, writing three characters on a large sheet of yellow paper with the blood. The first was *fu* – prosperity – and the other two, less clearly written, seemed to be *lu* and *shou* – status and longevity. When he finished writing, the god's spirit withdrew (*thetang, tuitong*), and he slumped out of trance. The news of these events spread like wildfire in the neighborhood. My landlady described the man who had offended the god as a fool, and reported that he had not dared to leave the temple that night for fear of retaliation from the god he had offended.

FIG. 24. After confronting an impostor, the god-in-his-medium cuts his tongue and writes characters in blood on a large piece of tissue paper, Ayer Itam, 1980. Photo: Jean DeBernardi

Typically, a male spirit medium strips to white or yellow pants, sits on a stool on which the eight-trigrams symbol has been painted (and under which burning paper money is sometimes placed), waiting for the god to approach. His assistants dress him in the god's clothing only after he has gone deeply into trance and the possessing deity has identified himself to those present; the garments are immediately remove when the medium falls out of trance. As this vignette demonstrates, the clothing must be treated with the utmost respect, and indeed, it has powers of its own: when I complained that a Daoist priest was taciturn in response to my questions, my landlady explained that the priest had his powers and knowledge only when he wore his robes, and that otherwise he was just like any ordinary man.

Objects as Power Containers

As Stanley J. Tambiah has noted, charisma is not only a quality of a person or an office; it also is "concretized and sedimented in objects: these objects are repositories of power" (Tambiah 1984: 335). As we have seen, the gods' clothing is powerful. Other crucial power containers in the spirit medium temple are the incense urn, the god images, the gods' weapons and flags (which represent their authority over the demonic), and the temple seal, which is used to stamp charms.

The incense urn symbolizes both the community that forms to worship the deity and the god and his or her powers. The urn collects the ash of burned incense sticks (which symbolize the lives of those who offer incense to the gods) and it is a repository of numinous power. When members carry the urn in procession during temple festivals they often visit the temples of affiliated groups, where they exchange incense as a symbol of their continued bond. When there is no temple, as is the case at the Hungry Ghosts festival in the seventh lunar month, the incense urn representing the association of merchants or neighbors who sponsor the annual event is placed on the altar of the head of the association, who is the 'keeper of the incense urn' (lo·chu, luzhu) for the year in which he is elected. And when a spirit medium temple dissolves, sometimes the only ritual practice that remains is veneration of the deity at the incense urn on a family altar by members of an intimate family circle.

The god images also are containers for numinous power. Daoist priests or spirit mediums infuse them with power in a ceremony to bring consciousness into the images, called 'opening the light' (khui kui, kai guang), or more colloquially 'opening the eyes' (khui bakchiu, kai muzhu). Sometimes the possessed spirit medium dots the eyes of the idol with red ink prepared with powdered cinnabar. Sometimes the god's blood is used:

FIG. 25. A god's dragon throne, draped with the spirit medium's leggings, at Singapore's Wudang Mountain Temple, Woodlands, 2004. Photo: Jean DeBernardi

Two brothers whose family reportedly had founded Penang's original Nine Emperor Gods temple held a private séance for friends and family on the ninth day of the ninth lunar month, which they celebrated as the birthday of Nazha, the Baby God. After offering advice to several people who wanted greater prosperity and lottery numbers, the elder brother, possessed by the Great Saint [Monkey God], cut his tongue and licked a copper plate on which a dragon was engraved. The spirit medium's younger sister explained that the plate represented the god, and the god's essence would reside there once it had been ritually fixed; it would no longer be a mere picture.

After an idol or picture has been ritually infused with the god's consciousness, people may use it to communicate with the deity, making offerings and divining before the image.

Martial artist gods drive out dangerous ghosts with their demon-expelling precious sword (*pokiam, baojian*), engraved with the seven stars of the Big Dipper, the Northern Bushel that controls human fate. They also chase out the ghosts with their snake-handled whip, which Nazha called the 'Holy Snake' (*sengchoa, shengshe*). Other weapons distinguish individual deities: Nazha takes a spear and his circle of Heaven and Earth (*qiankun quan*), a magical bracelet representing the universe; the God of War takes a halberd; Taishang Laojun and the Holy Mother use a blond horse-tail whisk instead of the snake-handled whip. The Holy Mother called this her "holy whip" (*sengsut, shengsuo*). Datuk spirits prefer the Malay-style dagger called the kris.

These weapons have special magical powers. A schoolteacher I interviewed told me this story about a local spirit medium:

Mr. Tan went to Indonesia to do business. His car broke down in the jungle, and he found an old man waiting for him. The old man gave him a sword with special spiritual power, so that he could do good for people. He abused this power and sold lottery numbers, so he lost the power. The sword disappeared, he was paralyzed, and foam comes every night from his mouth.

After telling several such stories, the teacher concluded, "If you abuse spiritual power, your power goes off."

These weapons confer spiritual authority over demons on the possessor, but the gods also turn weapons on the bodies of their spirit mediums. At temple fairs the gods-in-the-mediums beat their backs with the seven-star sword and the prick ball (*chhikiu, ciqiu*), and bathe in burning joss sticks. They sit on a throne-like red chair with a seat of nails (*thihteng i, tieding yi*) or knives (*to-i, dauyi*) and travel in a sedan chair whose seat and arms are constructed of knife blades (*tokio, daojiao*). They sometimes mount a sword ladder or cross a sword bridge or lead their disciples bare-footed across beds of burning charcoal. For the audience, this is one of the most convincing proofs of the reality of the trance performance; they judge that ordinary humans could not endure these punishments without injury.

Flags are another of the charismatic accoutrements of spirit mediums, who often display a long eye-catching row of tall colorful flags to announce their temple festivals to the public. The most important of the gods' flags is the black flag, a large square of black cloth on which has been painted, often in gold, the eight trigrams and the corresponding constellations of the eight directions. The spirit medium's assistants use this flag to protect him or her from demonic influences at points where the medium might be vulnerable to danger: when the medium is cutting his tongue for blood for charms, for example, or when the assistants are inserting or removing a spear from his cheeks. As one research

FIG. 26. Holding his flag, sword, and lit incense, and with the snake-handled whip draped around his neck, a medium possessed by the spirit of a Chinese general pays homage to Nazha, the Baby God, on the occasion of the god's birthday, George Town, 1980. Photo: Jean DeBernardi

assistant explained, "The black flag is the highest authority when the spirit medium is in trance. It can protect from dirty things and keep the medium from *tiohhoan* [*defan*] when he comes down from trance. . . ."

The spirit medium also sometimes takes a much smaller triangular flag on which the character meaning 'command' or 'decree' (*leng, ling*) is embroidered. One spirit medium explained that this flag represents the fact that the Emperor of Heaven has delegated authority to her possessing deity:

The Holy Mother . . . is very high, she is the Lord of Heaven's woman. She is like a general. She fights with a sword, and controls lower gods. He [the Jade Emperor] loves the Holy Mother like a daughter. She has his flag, his command, thus she has the authority to act and then tell him. . . .

Between trance performances, these flags decorate the altar, a mute announcement to anyone who might enter that a spirit medium works at this temple.

Inside a spirit medium's temple typically are placed five flags representing the five spirit armies of the center and the four cardinal points, on which five surnames are written. The yellow flag of the center is placed over the door of the shrine room, above the seat where the possessed spirit medium usually sits. The surname written on the yellow flag is 'Li,' possibly referring to Li Nazha, who is sometime identified as the Central Commander-in-Chief (*Zhongyang Yuanshuai*) or the Commander of the Central Altar (*Zhongtan Yuanshuai*). The remaining four flags – black for North, red for South, white for West, and green for East – are placed in the four corners of the room, each with a surname that identifies the commanders of the four quarters: Lian, Xiao, Liu, and Zhang. Temples also place five flags representing these spirit armies in the red bushel basket, a ritual object representing both the cosmos and human fate that also contains an almanac, a mirror, a set of scales, a lamp, and the seven-star sword. Spirit mediums and Daoist priests sometimes invoke these spirit armies, performing an elaborate ritual to present offerings to the god's soldiers of the four cardinal points and the center (*ko·kun, koujun*).

Chronotopes of Imperial China

In their ritual practice, spirit mediums align themselves with an ancient Asian tradition of leadership through rulers who were imagined to be gods, or at least as channels of spiritual blessings from the invisible spiritual world to the kingdoms that they governed. Consequently, the Chinese trance performance of generals, princes, teachers, and kings of past dynasties resembles the political and ceremonial practices of the Balinese theater state. According to Clifford Geertz, in the Hindu kingdom of Bali the aim of politics was to construct a state by constructing a king who incarnated divinity and embodied the exemplary center. The motor for divine kingship was state ceremony, which celebrated material abundance and imaged the king's centrality and power (Geertz 1980: 128–29; 1983). One of the templates for state ceremony was the mandala, which also provided a "geometrical, topographical, cosmological, and societal blueprint" for the organization of Asian kingdoms (Tambiah 1985: 253). The coordination of the human and the divine was accomplished through systems of classification assumed to order both the cosmos and human hierarchy. As Geertz might put it, the mandala defined a model of the cosmos, and a model for divine and human hierarchies.

The imperial cult itself was a form of theater state. The Emperor sacrificed yearly on the altars to Heaven and Earth – one round, the other square – ritual performances that confirmed his centrality and guaranteed his charisma; his appointed magistrates also performed rituals to ensure cosmic order.[8] The symbolism of the Chinese theater state also deeply permeated the wider society. As many scholars have noted, the Chinese pantheon was imagined as an imperial bureaucracy with an almost Durkheimian precision (Ahern 1981; Feuchtwang 2001; Wolf 1974). Just as the human emperor headed a bureaucracy in which individuals aspired to appointments, so too the celestial emperor appointed meritorious individuals to posts on earth (where they supervised human communities) and to posts in the prisons of earth (where Hell magistrates judged and punished the souls of the dead). The local God of the Earth, for example, was imagined as a Confucian bureaucrat reporting to and following orders from the Lord of Heaven. The divine imperial bureaucracy also had its generals and imperial troops, spirit soldiers whom communities still invoke for divine protection.

The modelling of the divine hierarchy on the human bureaucracy was so thorough that anthropologist Emily Ahern interpreted popular religious culture as a learning game for approaching the bureaucracy (1981). Exploring the relationship further, P. Steven Sangren concludes that, "The reciprocal legitimation of local social structure by official religion and of state authority by local religion depends on the similarities in the hierarchical structures of both systems of thought" (Sangren 1987: 220). In both official religion and local society, power and order are seen to derive from cosmic and natural sources, thereby masking the cultural foundations of social order (Sangren 1987: 216; see also Sangren 1984).

The Chinese imperial state also made use of a form of top-down 'inculturation' to integrate its diverse local populations, one that has had a deep impact on the development of popular religious culture. The state sought to standardize culture and promote unity and integration by supporting the cults of specific deities. In Prasenjit Duara's apt characterization, the Qing imperial state wrote or 'superscribed' meanings over local meanings, claiming, for example, that the God of War was an exemplar of Confucian virtue (Duara 1988: 139–48). Although their efforts to promote shared symbols met with some success, nonetheless the content of belief varied widely, which leads James Watson to conclude that despite the states' efforts to standardize meanings of deities like the Queen of Heaven, people constructed "their own representations of state-approved deities" (Watson 1985: 323). Moreover, many popular deities are not imagined in bureaucratic terms, including Buddhist deities like the Goddess of Mercy (*Guanyin*), Monkey (the 'Great Saint Equal to Heaven,' *Qitian Dasheng*), and the Vagabond Buddha (*Jigong*) (see also Shahar and Weller 1996).

Chinese sectarian movements often claimed a legitimating relationship to the princes, kings, teachers, and generals of the past, whom they worshiped as gods, and who sometimes possessed their spirit mediums. The state perceived such worship as a threat to its imperial prerogatives, and the 1821 law regarding heresies and sects specifically forbade religious leaders to "pretend" to "call down heretical gods, write charms or pronounce them over water, or carry round palanquins (with idols), or invoke saints . . . " (de Groot 1963 [1903–1904]: 137). The state's mistrust was well-founded: spirit mediums who embodied the spirits of the kings and generals of past dynasties sanctified their charisma, but also modeled their flags, seals, and dragon-embroidered costumes on those of the Chinese imperium. For the Hokkien Chinese, the presumption of imperial prerogatives also included their ritual practice of worshipping the Lord of Heaven directly and without imperial mediation. Some scholars view ritual practice as a mystification of power or a mask for domination, but these ritual performances are perhaps better understood as adopting the very face of power. (See DeBernardi 2004: 143–8.)

Contemporary Penang spirit mediums also seek cosmic sources of power, defining the space of their temples in such a way as to confirm their own centrality and authority. As I have discussed, the spirit medium temples of martial deities invariably contain five colored flags of the four directions and the center, placed in the four corners of the room and above the spirit medium's dragon throne. Each of these five flags is associated with camps of spirit soldiers, commonly represented on spirit medium altars by the five generals' heads (*chiongkun thao, jiangjun tou*), a set of five long daggers with five colored heads as handles used as self-mortifying weapons.

Imperial yellow is the color of the flag of the center, and also is the color worn by many spirit mediums in the trance performance, whose satin stomacher and leggings often are gaudily embroidered with another imperial symbol, the dragon. The gods receive their authority from the Lord of Heaven, represented by the god's flag on which the character for 'command' (*ling*) is usually written, and uses the temple seal, modeled on an official seal, to stamp charms to expel demons. Although some of the possessing deities are imagined as the spirits of Chinese generals, other are divine royalty, including princes like Nazha, who is imagined as the commander-in-chief of these spirit soldiers. We also find the spirits of kings and emperors taking center stage in these small back-street temples.

The imperial Chinese state has long since fallen, and the sites and events of popular religious culture now serve not as usurpations of imperial power, but as chronotopes of imperial China. Mikhael Bakhtin defined the term chronotope (which simply means 'time-space') as "the intrinsic connectedness of temporal and spatial relationships that are artistically expressed in literature" (Bakhtin 1981a: 84). In the gothic novel, for example, the castle is the defining space, a place in which we find the traces of the past visible in its architecture, furnishings, and weapons, and its ancestral portrait gallery and archives. He concludes that, "Legends and traditions animate every corner of the castle and its environs through their constant reminder of past events" (Bakhtin 1981a: 246).

Whereas most spirit medium temples are set up in the remodeled front rooms of ordinary houses, nonetheless many are chronotopes that, like Gothic castles, display the past in the present. The temple defines an authoritative space of Chinese-ness, and its sacra include images of the spirit medium's immortal ancestors, the gods' sacred weapons, and the flags and temple seals that mark the delegation of divine authority to the deity. Like the rituals of divine kingship, the rituals of spirit mediumship are designed to ensure harmony, peace, and prosperity. The deity possessing a spirit medium sometimes acts like a king (who himself was imagined as a deity), offering thanksgiving to heaven and expelling demonic forces in order to guard the community and its prosperity.

Embodying the Gods: Physical Discipline

Although the ideology of the trance performance suggests the effacement of the spirit medium's personality, memories, and bodily hexis, nonetheless undeniably the identity, experience, and prior knowledge of the spirit medium significantly informs that performance. The trance performance is highly stereotyped, but it also is a performance art whose effectiveness very much depends on the spirit medium's skills and knowledge, expressed in both physical discipline and verbal virtuosity.

FIG. 27. At a private home, on the ninth day of the ninth lunar month (the climax of the Nine Emperor Gods festival), a teacher who is a trained marital artist but not a practicing spirit medium falls into trance, possessed by the Monkey God, George Town, 1979. Photo: Jean DeBernardi

The traditionalism of the trance performance is expressed in the god's costume but also in his medium's ways of moving. In procession, for example the medium "strides in a rhythmic zigzag," stopping to strike fixed poses and performing the acts of self-mortification when he is close to a temple forecourt (Sutton 1990: 102). There, the spirit medium will beat his naked back with a sword or with the ball of nails, or bathe himself in burning joss sticks. For many, the performance of these self-mortifying acts is the most powerful proof of the spiritual attainments of the spirit medium and the reality of the trance performance. One Hakka spirit medium explained:

In order to become a spirit medium, your heart must be honest and your body clean. The god protects the spirit medium, the medium is the god himself. So the medium can play with the ball of nails, or the fire ball [red-hot iron balls], and not be harmed. It is the same for the Indian god, who enters men who then can walk over coals.

One spirit medium suggested that the martial-arts displays of exorcist trance performers, including his own possessing deity, the God of War, had their origins in the Shaolin martial arts traditions, which several spirit mediums claimed Bodhidharma had brought to China:

Damo Hwatsu [Bodhidharma] is the head of the Eighteen Lohans, who are martial artists. He founded *Siaulim* [*Shaolin*], the science of kung fu [*gongfu*, martial arts....]. Bodhidharma came from India to China and handed over these arts. Before, priests did no work and were clumsy. He reformed them and taught them martial arts in connection with right actions.[9]

According to legendary accounts (which Bernard Faure concludes to be hybrid textual constructions because Bodhidharma has a very shadowy historical existence [Faure 1993: 133]), Bodhidharma came to China from India and taught Chinese Buddhists physical exercises and meditation techniques. Chan Buddhists claim him as their first patriarch, and the tradition spread to Southern China, where an influential Southern Chan school formed in the eighth century.

As Penang martial artist P'ng Chye Khim and his coauthor Donn Draeger describe Shaolin martial arts, they developed into systems that relied on the actions of animals but also on human and supernatural beings, including "Ta-sheng Men, which makes use of the antics of the monkey; the Lohan, or Buddha-like being system; the Er-lang Men, which is based on the actions of a legendary hero; and the Wei-tuo Men, a deity system" (P'ng and Draeger 1979: 20).[10] The replication of the movements of powerful and heroic deities in martial arts performance strongly suggests spirit possession. Indeed, one spirit medium described his own practice of martial arts in Mandarin as "god fighting" (*shenda*): "You invite the god's body to fight, the god enters to let you fight, but when he fights there's no speech."

The Deep Language of the Gods

The enactment of the gods not only involves the performance of standardized physical movements, some derived from Chinese martial arts traditions, but also use of the god's language. As anthropologist and linguist Edward Sapir observed, "Society has its patterns, its set ways of doing things, its distinctive 'theories' of behavior, while the individual has his method of handling those particular patterns of society, giving them just enough of a twist to make them 'his' and no one else's" (Sapir 1949 [1927]: 534). For Sapir, linguistic individuality takes a number of forms, including voice and speech dynamics – intonation, rhythm, relative continuity of speech, and speaking rate – and pronunciation, vocabulary, and style. In the trance performance, all these change, and people often comment on the god's 'deep' (*chhim*, *shen*) language, a depth expressed both in vocabulary and style. Their movements also change, as do their personal tastes and powers.

Master Poh's possessing deity explained to me that this language was 4,000 years old, and contrasted it with Mandarin, which he noted was only 100 years old. The purported antiquity of the god's language is one dimension of the mediumistic recreation of the chronotope of the god's cosmic world, and also is a strategy to distinguish the persona of the spirit medium from that of his possessing deities. By contrast, another spirit medium noted that each of his possessing deities spoke a different language: "The Inconstant Ghost speaks Teochiu [Chaochou]. The Great Saint speaks deep Mandarin, in fact Shanghaiese. Shanghaiese is first-class Mandarin. Cantonese is second-class Mandarin. . . ."

Many scholars who have observed the trance performance in Taiwan and Fujian have described the speech of the possessed spirit medium as incomprehensible. Take, for example, de Groot's account of a trance consultation:

His limbs shake vehemently; his arms knock on the table; his head and shoulders jerk nervously from side to side, and his staring eyes, half closed, seem to gaze straight into a hidden world. This is the proper moment for the consultant or the interpreter to put his questions. Incoherent shrill sounds are the answer; but the interpreter translates this divine language with the greatest fluency in to the intelligible human tongue, while another brother writes these revelations down on paper (de Groot 1964 [1892–1910] Vol. 6: 1274).

Penang spirit mediums also sometimes enact the god's transcendence and the antiquity of their historical age by making their language obscure or opaque; sometimes they speak in a glossolalic register in which no meaning is attached to the sounds produced. Nonetheless, the gods possessing Penang spirit mediums often did communicate with the people who consult with them, usually with the help of an interpreter, in order to offer them advice and ritual remedies.[11]

In Penang, the gods usually spoke – or at least their spirit mediums claimed that they spoke – the 'deep' or literary register of their topolect, a register that with the widespread adoption of Mandarin as China's national language has now all but disappeared from spoken languages like Hokkien (see DeBernardi 1991). Prior to the development of Mandarin, however, the literary register of Southern Min, which Penangites refer to as 'deep Hokkien' (*chhim Hokkien oe, shen Fujian hua*), was the reading pronunciation for Chinese characters in Hokkien-speaking communities. With the development of Mandarin, however, which offers a unified pronunciation for all China, most speakers of Chinese topolects no longer master this literary register. Consequently, China's regional languages have tended to become oral languages of communication, lacking the vocabulary and prestige of the literary tradition.

'Deep' also means 'archaic,' and the enactment of Chinese gods involves their use of rarely used phrases, together with a lack of familiarity with the names and functions of modern objects. Similarly, in Borneo, Iban shamanic healers (*manang*) chant in a 'deep language' (*jako dalam*) rather than the language of everyday life, using "words and phrases of forebears rarely used nowadays and referring to equipment long since outdated, such as rattan door hinges instead of metal hinges" (Barrett 1993: 257). The maintenance of a contrast between everyday modes of communication and the language appropriate for communication with the world of spirits is widespread, and not confined to a contrast between literary and colloquial registers.

Many spirit mediums in Penang use deep Hokkien in the trance performance; some further draw on the moral vocabulary of China's philosophical and moral traditions to teach their followers and clients, offering exegesis on the fundamentals of their syncretic practices. Indeed, the trance performance provides a context in which these teachings are transmitted, and some Penang spirit mediums provide a bridge between the prestigious, literary texts of China's great tradition and the little tradition of popular religious culture, translating China's literary religious traditions into a dramaturgically effective oral performance (a topic that I will investigate in some detail in Part Two of this study). Now that Mandarin has replaced Chinese regional languages as the language in which literacy is acquired, religious performances – including both the trance performance and the chanting of Daoist vernacular scriptures – are among the few cultural sites in which Chinese transmit the prestigious literary tradition of China in Penang's diverse topolects: Hokkien, Teochiu, Cantonese, Shanghai, Hakka, or Hainanese (see also DeBernardi 1991; Lien 1995).

Penang Chinese consider deep Hokkien to be a purer form of speech than they ordinarily use, and indeed the god's language excludes loan words from Malay and English. For example, the word for marriage typically is *kawin*, which Penang Hokkien speakers have borrowed from Malay. A Chinese god might use instead the deep Hokkien expression *kiathun*, which is cognate with the Mandarin word *jiehun* and thus easily comprehended by Chinese-educated participants. Moreover, because I invariably had to ask permission of the god to tape or take photographs, I discovered that the gods were unfamiliar with items of modern technology, which members of the temple committee would helpfully explain to the god-in-his-medium.

The gods possessing their spirit mediums sometimes dictated poems to their assistants, who struggled to write down these compositions. One spirit medium had poems authored by his possessing gods, the Wealth God and the Great Saint, hand-written on large cardboard sheets and posted on the walls of his house-temple. According to the Datuk Aunt, who introduced me to this spirit medium, he was a 'gangster' (*samseng*) whose modern house-temple had been bought for him by a former prostitute. This poem explores the ambiguous relationship between intention and action, appearance and reality, and hints at the interdependence of respectable society with society's dark side, its *yin* and *yang* if you will. This poem, which is composed of seven couplets, each formed of two five-character phrases, he attributed to the Wealth God (*Chaisin, Caishen*), as he called the Inconstant Uncle (*Bo·tia^{n}Peh, Wuchang Bo*). He described the meaning as 'sarcastic':

> There are butterflies in the mountain, but no flowers live there.
> Man speaks eloquently, you hear the words but cannot know the heart.
> You use a brush to write characters; you see the words but cannot see the pen.
> White rice nourishes black men, black water nourishes white fish.
> A new home holds broken furniture; a new cupboard holds old clothes.
> Sugar is sweet but kills ants; the wheat is ripe but kills birds.
> You will study my poem and know what is in my heart.

He also had posted a number of couplets, each formed of two seven-character phrases, also written by the Wealth God:

> The rose has thorns; it is one sort of flower,
> Endure hardships until the time comes when you know my goodness.

And this, authored by the Great Saint:

> Before your eyes you see black gold change into charcoal.
> Whether you do good or do bad, the god sees all.

Although simply written and somewhat clichéd, nonetheless these poems and couplets were written in a parallel poetic form, using metaphorical images to convey this spirit medium's interpretation of the uncertainties and ambiguities of human life. Many promised salvation and justice to those who 'do good,' this despite the fact that the spirit medium himself was allegedly involved in Penang's underworld, stigmatized as someone who 'does bad' (*choephai^n, zuodai*).

Spirit mediums claimed to speak as gods, and some denied that they had studied spiritual matters:

Jean: How do you study these things?
Spirit medium for the Third Prince: Study? No, la! We don't study *angkong* things! This is a god coming! Now, there is chanting sutras (*liamkeng, nianjing*), and this belongs to Buddhism. When Buddha comes, people chant sutras. Now here, it's like the god, like they come to help and people chant incantations (*liamchiu, nianzhou*). They chant the god's incantation for him to hear and he comes. It's like that.

Nonetheless, some spirit mediums did admit that they had studied with masters: Taishang Laojun's spirit medium, for example, said that spirit mediums had both a human and a spiritual master.

The human masters of the spirit mediums I interviewed included Chinese masters but also Theravada Buddhist monks and Hindu gurus. Many appeared to have synthesized teachings drawn from these diverse influences.[12] Mediums may also learn some of their art – including how to write charms and advice on the best times of day to undertake important ventures – from referring to the Chinese almanac, which is an impressive compendium of such information. Even the God of Prosperity dream book (*Qianzi Wentu Jieshu* 1980), which was sold on newsstands for dream divination, included chants for invoking several deities. Because of the lack of any central influence that could shape an orthodox viewpoint, however, each spirit medium who taught me presented a different synthesis of Chinese cosmology. As Donald Sutton observes, this variability has helped spirit mediumship in Taiwan "avoid the ossification and stagnation that Stanley Tambiah (1985: 161–66) among others have noted as a general tendency of ritual" (Sutton 1990:103).

Vernacular Literature and the Trance Performance

Spirit mediumship has no orthodox creed and spirit mediums usually do not practice within institutional hierarchies. Nonetheless the trance performance, which is oral, popular, and performance-oriented, is remarkably consistent. I propose that this consistency is the consequence of spirit mediums' dependence upon China's historical literary traditions, which inform people's images of the gods and their powers. Several spirit mediums explained to me that the stories of the gods were merely parables designed to teach deeper religious truths regarding human morality. At the same time, they taught and healed during the trance state possessed by the very gods who were the main characters in these stories, in a performance designed to inspire deep respect for their authority and for the veracity of their teachings.

Many of the deities who commonly possess spirit mediums are characters drawn from Chinese popular literature; these popular novels were instrumental in spreading gods' cults in China. Indeed, one Chinese historian has claimed that the popularity of the millenarian White Lotus tradition in north China could be attributed to the influence of the *Canonization of Deities* and that the popularity of the Heaven and Earth Society (or Triad) in southern China could be traced to the influence of the *Water Margin* (Shahar 1998: 7). The Boxer uprising in north China, which involved the use of invulnerability magic, was inspired by the influence of these two novels, together with *Journey to the West*

(Esherick 1987: 218). Without a doubt, allegorical fiction has profoundly shaped the Chinese religious and political imagination.

The reading of literature, like the trance performance of Chinese gods, is a strategy for forming a deep connection with the past. Literary critic Stephen Owen has observed that for Chinese, the act of reading is a form of ancestor worship in which the past becomes a presence and through which the past perpetuates itself. Chinese poets used the written word to transmit the content of the self across the gap of time, ensuring their own immortality and the immortality of the historical moments that they experienced and recorded. In turn, Chinese readers were concerned with recovering an intense experience of the past. Poems were one means by which people gained access to historical worlds. Owen uses the trope of synecdoche – the part or image that evokes the whole – to explain the act of reading, comparing the process of recovering meaning to the rite in which an article of clothing is used to recall a soul (Owen 1986: 2). The reader took the text – a mere fragment – and used it to recall the intention of its author and to reconstruct the lost totality of the past.

Like poetry, popular literature transmitted the past in a form that allowed later generations to make contact with the lives of ancient heroes and heroines through the medium of the word. When these ancient heroes and heroines possess spirit mediums, they also meet the present. It is as if Hercules and Socrates, Lancelot and Merlin, Robin Hood and Joan of Arc, could return to earth again to share their extraordinary numinous spiritual energies with the living. I have mixed fictional and historical characters in this hypothetical list, because most Chinese make no distinction between them and regard the stories of the gods as history rather than myth. Whereas Chinese reading a poem felt that they knew the world and mind of the poet through the words of the poem, Chinese reading novels felt that they knew the world and mind not only of the author, but also of the characters the author's stories brought to life.

Take, for example, the Boxer uprising, which is one well-documented case in which the leaders of a sectarian movement drew upon the charisma of the gods of popular literature. In the late nineteenth century there was a resurgence of sectarian activity in northern China. Rather than follow the classic doctrines of the White Lotus society, the groups that emerged turned for inspiration to popular culture and popular novels, including the influential *Canonization of Deities*, which includes the story of Nazha, the so-called Baby God. One sect that formed at the time, known as the Spirit Boxers, drew followers in by offering healing and training in the martial arts of the Eight Trigrams Sect. The most distinctive feature of the Spirit Boxers was spirit possession. In order to go into trance, the group's members kowtowed to the southeast, burned incense, and drank a glass of clear water as a simple ritual of purification. They then sat on a chair on top of a table and called their teacher to come down from the mountain. The gods who possessed them included the Great Saint, his sidekick Pigsy, the God of War, characters from the popular novel *Romance of the Three Kingdoms*, and a number of other martial heroes known to people through theater, novels, and stories (Esherick 1987: 218–19).

In 1898, the group underwent a transformation and began to claim that their rituals conferred invulnerability. At this time, new leadership emerged in an alliance of a martial artist whom the group named Zhu Hongdeng, or Crimson Red Lantern, and a Buddhist monk named Sincere Heart who had studied Shaolin temple boxing. The group's third leader was Yu Chingshui, or At Clear Water, whom a Chinese rhyme described as "a hero, in yellow riding pants and a red plumed hat . . . " (Esherick 1987: 236). The allegorical quality of these names leads me to speculate that their followers may have regarded them as fully incarnated deities, but Chinese officials regarded them as Ming restorationists, accusing Zhu of being a Ming pretender, which the dynastic surname Zhu would suggest. Their militant activities were anti-Christian rather than antidynastic, and at the turn of the century the Spirit Boxers launched a series of brutal attacks on foreigners and Christians, laying siege to the foreign legations in Beijing in the summer of 1900.[13]

The trance performance shapes peoples' concept of the invisible world, but symbolic representations and narratives in turn shape people's images of spirit mediums and their spiritual powers. In the next section, therefore, I will consider the literary and theatrical sources for the pantheon of possessing deities, as well as the cosmological basis of spirit mediums' exorcistic practice. The Hakka spirit medium cited above was undoubtedly correct when he observed that trance is not learned from books. At the same time, the trance performance is significantly informed by the Chinese textual tradition, and many of the basic concepts of these world traditions live in popular discourse.

Popular Literature and Popular Religious Culture

Popular literature has had an enormous impact on the development of Chinese popular religious culture. In a study based on research conducted in Singapore in the 1950's, Alan J. A. Elliott observed that literature and folk tales provide an important and compelling source for belief in the gods and spirit mediumship:

The more sophisticated Chinese regarded these stories as entertaining, light reading; to many illiterate persons, to whom they were transmitted by word of mouth or through theatrical performances, they constituted the essence of historical reality. . . . Furthermore, the heros of these legends often had attributed to them not only historical reality but also the power to bring their miraculous influences to bear on the lives of subsequent generations. (Elliott 1955: 166)

One spirit medium observed that Chinese saints (*shen*) were deified humans who could not perform acts of salvation because they had not escaped the cycle of death and rebirth and achieved immortality. Nonetheless, people commonly regarded these heroic figures as savior gods.[14] Through the performances of popular opera, popular stories of heroes and villains found a wide audience and influence. The character performed on stage undoubtedly provided a model for the savior who possessed a spirit medium at a trance performance, although in the temple the savior god could freely interact with his audience, offering prophesies, teachings, and advice.

Much vernacular literature celebrated martial artists and Chinese knights errant (Liu 1967). Perhaps the most famous example of the transformation of a military hero into the hero of a vernacular novel and a god is the God of War (*Kuan Kong, Guangong*), a historical figure who is one of the heroes of *Romance of the Three Kingdoms*. In China, the imperial state revered him as a military god, rewarding him with titles and declaring him to be "the supporter of heaven and protector of the empire" (Duara 1988: 141). Ironically, he also was, and continues to be, the patron saint of sworn brotherhoods like the historic Heaven and Earth Society and contemporary Triad gangs. Many regard him as a saint who can protect and assist humans, and occasionally he possesses spirit mediums. As a measure of the influence of this novel, Penang Hokkien speakers call professional storytelling "speaking the Three Kingdoms" (*kong samkok, jiang sanguo*).

Although such storytellers are no longer easily found, Chinese opera troupes perform episodes from this and other works of vernacular fiction. Popular novels that employed allegory to teach the basic truths of Chinese syncretic religion also have had enormous influence. As Meir Shahar observes, "The Chinese laity learns about the gods not by reciting canonical scriptures but, in most cases, by reading vernacular fiction, listening to storytellers, and watching plays" (1998: 221). The media of fiction, oral narrative, and drama were vehicles by which the cults of the gods spread widely, and the three worked together to shape people's images of the gods and their powers.

Potential examples abound, but let us take as an example the well-known vernacular novel, the *Water Margin*, which provides a rich fund of episodes for Chinese opera troupes. Like the *Romance of the Three Kingdoms*, the *Water Margin* is a tale of sworn brotherhood and social banditry. In the novel, two brothers encounter one another after a long separation. The homely older brother takes his younger brother, Wu Song, a heroic figure who killed a tiger with his bare hands, home to meet his wife, a former maidservant. When the Emperor calls the younger brother to perform a mission, the wife conspires with a neighbor, an older woman who runs a teahouse, to poison her husband, and she takes up with another man. When the younger brother returns, he learns of his brother's untimely death. He changes into mourning clothes, prepares offerings for the spirit, and addresses him:

"Brother, your soul is near! In life you were weak and timid, and the cause of your death is not clear. If you were abused and murdered, come to me in a dream, and I will avenge you!" He sprinkled wine on the ground, burned the paper money replicas and cried so heart-brokenly that all the neighbors were moved" (Shi and Luo 1981: 413).

He then prepared to sleep on the floor by his brother's memorial tablet. On the third watch, an icy wind swept through the room, and the lamp on the altar went out. Wu Song's hair stood on end as he saw a figure emerge from under the altar table. "Brother," it said, "I died a cruel death!" He said nothing about this eerie experience, but began to investigate his brother's death, finally avenging him and becoming an outlaw as a result (Shi and Luo 1981: 362–427). Although the novel celebrated Wu Song's martial prowess and did not present him as a god, nonetheless (as with Guangong), the novel promoted his later veneration as a god whose cult spread widely throughout China (Shahar 1998: 10).

Although I did not see a Chinese opera troupe perform an episode from the *Water Margin*, in 1980 a Hokkien comedy troupe performed an updated version at a downtown street festival celebrating the Hungry Ghosts Festival, a performance attended by many trishaw riders who normally stationed themselves at a nearby bus station. In the modern Penang satire of this tale, the wife is a barmaid who wears a sleazy kimono, smokes, and drinks beer. She uses her 'English schoolname,' Carol, and is modeled on the high-class bar girls at one Japanese-style Penang bar, who only took successful Chinese businessmen as their clients. She complains that her husband has fallen on hard times: in the past he drove a Fiat, but now he rides a moped and hawks fried banana dumplings. Carol observes to her former madam, Mama Wang, "When he had money, he was handsome. But now?" She falls in love with another man and makes a pass at Wu Song, her husband's younger brother, as well. But Wu Song rejects her, leaving to 'kill a lion' for the King of Africa.

After Wu Song leaves, Carol poisons the homely dumpling salesman and takes up with her boyfriend, Simon. But when the younger brother returns, he encounters his brother's ghost, who demands that he avenge the murder. Wu Song, quaking and terrified, suggests that perhaps the ghost should look after the job himself. Finally, though, he relents and kills Carol, Mama Wang, and Simon, who take a very long time to die. In the process, the actors parody gungfu movies, striking a number of dramatic martial arts poses, naming them as they take each stance. But instead of the 'tiger crouch,' it's the 'shitting crouch,' and instead of a 'fighting cobra,' it's a 'fighting corncob.' The audience responded with hilarity, and was especially lively when the barmaid expressed her materialistic philosophy about men and whenever the madam, Mama Wang, burlesquely played by a cross-dressing actor, took the stage.

Penang's popular religious culture draws many of its deities from classic works of literature, and in the trance performance these characters come alive as individuals with well-defined personalities, just as they do in a staged theatrical performance. Spirit mediums sometimes recommended that I read vernacular novels like the *Canonization of Deities* (*Fengshen Yanyi*), which includes the story of Li Nazha and his father, Li Jing; *The Journey to the West* (*Xiyouji*), in which Monkey plays a major role; the *Romance of the Three Kingdoms* (*Sanguojuan*), a heroic tale in which Guangong (the God of War) is a central character; and *Jigong's Complete Biography* (*Jigong Quanjuan*), which is the story of the Vagabond Buddha. All of these novels were available in Penang's Chinese bookstores; more recently, a number have appeared in abbreviated bilingual comic book form in both Chinese and English. The Chinese opera and puppet troops that perform at temple fairs often draw on this literature, in particular the *Romance of the Three Kingdoms,* for their stories, which often recount tales of imperial oppression and injustice. Many of these stories have now been adapted for the medium of films or animated features, and Chinese also know the stories of gods and heroes through these popular media (see Shahar 1998).

Let me consider the stories of several deities who commonly possess spirit mediums in Penang – Nazha, the Great Saint (Monkey), and the Vagabond Buddha. Each of these stories is an allegory and charter for the exorcizing practices of Daoist priests and spirit mediums, although the stories of the Monkey and Vagabond Buddha claim even higher powers for Buddhism. All express what Bernard Faure has characterized as the tension between the unlocalized conceptions of universal religions like Buddhism and Daoism and the localized ritual practices of popular religion (Faure 1987: 338). As Faure demonstrates, in the Chan Buddhist tradition this tension found expression in a genre of stories that recounted dialogs or confrontations between Buddhist monks and local deities, often imagined as snakes, dragons, or tigers. Daoists tended to absorb these local deities into the inferior levels of the Daoist hierarchy, whereas Buddhists converted or subdued the local deities, often thereby acquiring spiritual power (Faure 1987: 341).

Li Nazha

The story of Li Nazha, whom English-educated Penangites often call the Third Prince or the Baby God, is found in the *Canonization of Deities* (*Fengshen Yenyi* n.d), a compendium of stories that contains many heroic myth-histories. Xu Zhong Lin compiled *The Canonization of Deities* after the mid-Ming dynasty, basing it on an actual historical event, the attack by King Wu on King Zhou during the Shang Dynasty. He developed it, however, into an allegorical story of good and evil, in which Daoist deities defeated monsters. One of the main supernatural characters in the novel is Li Nazha, a clever, youthful rebel who is six feet tall by the age of seven, and already a skillful martial artist. He even fights his father, and if the Chinese have an Oedipus myth, Nazha is its hero.[15]

Nazha is one of several child martial artist deities imagined as princes that possess Penang spirit mediums, and Penangites tend to call all these child deities 'baby gods.' Nazha is realized in the trance performance as one of three brothers. The eldest is Jinzha, the second Muzha (or Moksha), and the youngest Nazha. Other baby gods include the Jade Emperor Prince and the Crown Prince of the House of Feng. These child martial artists embody the exorcizing power of *yang*, and we find a similar identification of *yang* with the child among the Daoist Eight Immortals, who are eight deities correlated with the eight trigrams that form the basis of the *Yijing*. By contrast with the *Yijing*, the inventor of the Eight Immortals associated the trigram representing *yang* strength and creative power not with the fully realized masculine power of the patriarchal father, but rather with the chaotic, exuberant energy and potentiality of the child.

Nazha's story also is a mythic charter for the practice of spirit mediumship.[16] According to the tale, Nazha's father, Li Jing, was a general whose wife became pregnant but did not give birth for three and a half years – an omen that this child would be no ordinary human. Finally, Nazha was born in a ball of flesh. When his father cut open the ball a baby boy emerged, his right wrist wrapped in a gold bracelet and a piece of red silk fabric covering his chest. He was, in fact, the avatar of a deity. Immediately after his birth, a Daoist priest visited the family and identified the bracelet and silk as magical treasures from the Calm Cave on Mount Heavenly Primordial: the gold bracelet was the Circle of Heaven and Earth , the red silk damask was Chaotic Heaven silk. Here, it seems no coincidence that the word for silk damask puns on the word for spiritual efficacy (*ling*). The Daoist priest gave the child a secret name and became the child's master.

When Nazha was seven (and already six feet tall!), he was restless and left the fort with a servant to find a cool place to relax. They found a river and the young

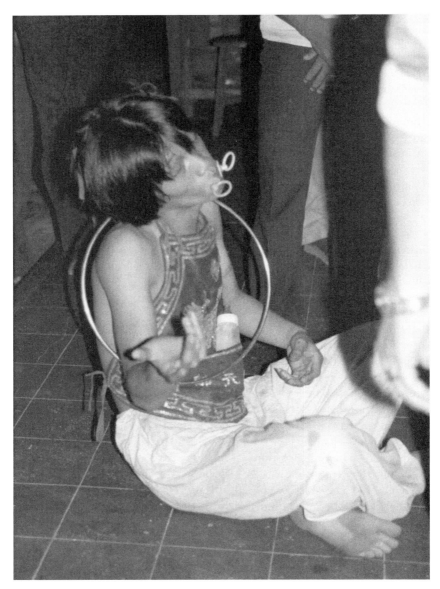

FIG. 28. The Baby God Nazha, possessing his spirit medium, takes pacifiers, a bottle of milk, and his weapon, the Heaven and Earth circle that represents the universe, George Town, 1981. Photo: Jean DeBernardi

Prince bathed. He dipped his seven-foot Chaotic Heaven silk damask into the water. The red silk agitated the water, disturbing the temple of the Sea Dragon King at the bottom of the ocean. One of the Sea Dragon King's officers tried to seize him, but Nazha killed him with his magical ring. Next, the Sea Dragon King's third son challenged Nazha, and Nazha killed him by flinging balls of fire from his Chaotic Heaven silk. The Sea Dragon King left his river to visit Heaven to lodge a complaint, but Nazha ambushed him and ripped his scales off before he arrived at Heaven's gate, sparing him only on the condition that he not lodge a complaint with the Jade Emperor.

The Dragon Kings did complain to the Jade Emperor, however, and also to Nazha's father, who was very angry with his son. When in retaliation the four dragon kings went to arrest Nazha's parents, Nazha asked if they would leave his parents alone if he killed himself. They agreed, and he killed himself with a sword. His spirit went to the Daoist priest, who advised him to beg his mother to build him a temple, which, surreptitiously, she did. While he was waiting to be reborn, Nazha's spirit visited this temple, speaking as an oracle through a statue. Traveling with his troops, his father saw the road crowded with pilgrims and learned of the temple. His father regarded Nazha as a false god, and destroyed his temple.

The Daoist Master then produced a new body made from lotus stalks for Nazha, and he was reborn, more powerful than before. The Daoist also gave Nazha two weapons, a spear and fire wheels, and he met his father in battle. Unfilial behavior indeed! Unhappy with this turn of events, the Daoist armed Li Jing with a magical weapon, the nine-story, eight-sided pagoda with which he could control Nazha. The pagoda has the same number of levels as heaven and the same shape as the eight trigrams that are basic to the model of order represented in the *Yijing*. Undoubtedly Heaven and the Dao finally control the Baby God, and order is reestablished (*Fengshen Yanyi* N.d.: 96–121). The Jade Emperor appointed Li Jing the Generalissimo of the Twenty-Six Celestial Officers, Grand Marshal of the Skies, and Guardian of the Gate of Heaven (Werner 1986 [1922]: 319), and together he and Nazha fought against an opposing dynasty (*Fengshen Yanyi* N.d.; Poh 1973: 23–25; Werner 1986 [1922]: 305–19).

The tale is a transparent allegory for the Daoist magician's power over chaotic and potentially destructive forces. Nazha is an avatar of a deity, born with two magical weapons, the gold bracelet that is the Heaven and Earth (Universe) Circle and a red silk garment that gives off brilliant golden light and causes the ocean to boil, a transparent symbolic representation for the demon-exorcizing power of *yang* energy. As a child, he represents the *yang* vitality of youth, for as the *Daodejing* teaches, "One who possesses virtue in abundance is comparable to a newborn babe. . . . It does not know the union of male and female yet its male member will stir; this is because its virility is at its height" (Lau 1963: 116). After he triumphs in this conflict, Nazha assures his parents that his Daoist master can protect them. But the Daoist priest also constrains Nazha (who misuses his magical power in fighting his own father) by giving his father even greater magical power. Only then does Nazha submit to his father and to Heaven.

Thus far, I have discussed the story as a Daoist allegory of demonic control, but the story also suggests that spirit mediums are agents in this control. The link with spirit possession is strongly suggested when Nazha commits suicide (giving up his human body) and returns to inhabit a speaking image in his temple. There, his disembodied spirit speaks as an oracle, drawing worshippers from far and wide. The story also suggests spirit mediumship in its details: artists depict Nazha wearing a child's undergarment that covers his chest and holding his magical Chaotic Heaven red silk, which together may provide the model for the silk embroidered stomacher and three-paneled pants worn by spirit mediums in trance when they are possessed by martial artist deities like Nazha, the Emperor of the Dark Heavens, and Monkey.

In the contemporary trance performance, Nazha is a martial artist who calls for his magical weapons but also for a pacifier or a baby bottle filled with milk. He offers magical cures, but also displays his skills as a martial artist. Indeed, Master Ooi described him as the "small one who rules the whole world."

The Great Saint

The syncretic Buddhist allegory that Arthur Waley translated in abridged form as *Monkey* (Waley 1980 [1943]) – which Anthony Yu translated in its complete form as *The Journey to the West* (Yu 1977–1983) – suggests a similar interpretation. Although episodes in the story have antecedents in other texts, in its literary form *The Journey to the West* was published in 1592 in the late Ming dynasty. The story recounts a Buddhist monk's pilgrimage to India to obtain Buddhist scriptures, which he accomplishes with the assistance of Monkey, Sandy and Pigsy. Although the novel is an allegory for Buddhist teachings, the story is deeply infused with Daoist themes, including *yin-yang* five phase cosmology (Yu 1977–1983: 45–53).[17]

The imperial state often attempted to superscribe meanings on deities in order to integrate its diverse population.[18] Many popular deities were not elite Confucian literati, but rather rebels and eccentrics who playfully inverted Confucian values and sometimes offered alternative value systems (DeBernardi 1987; Shahar and Weller 1996). Monkey, for example, cared so little for Confucian notions of propriety and social order that he revolted against the heavenly hierarchy. Meir Shahar concludes that characters like Monkey might simply offer the reader (or worshipper) an opportunity for emotional catharsis; nonetheless the Chinese pantheon also offered "symbolic resources for revolt" (Shahar 1996: 205).

Like Nazha, the Great Saint (*Thai Seng Ia, Taisheng Ya*) – whom many English-speaking Penangites affectionately call the Monkey God – is simultaneously a chaotic and childlike figure and a powerful martial artist. He achieves immortality through study with a Master and acquires a powerful magical weapon from the Dragon King of the Eastern Sea: an iron pillar that expands or contracts on command and with which the Milky Way was pounded into existence. Like Nazha, he offended the Sea Dragon King, who reported him to the Jade Emperor. Soon thereafter, while he slept, his soul was arrested and taken to hell. Indignant (because he was, after all, immortal), he erased his name from hell's registration books, together with the names of all the other monkeys in his kingdom.[19]

Concerned about the mounting complaints against Monkey, the Jade Emperor invited him to heaven, hoping to subdue him by giving him a post in the imperial stables. When Monkey discovered how lowly a position this was, however, he was indignant. He returned to earth and awarded himself a lofty title, "The Great Saint Equal with Heaven," agreeing to return to Heaven only if the Emperor accepted this title. On his return, Monkey behaved even more badly, however, stealing peaches from Heaven's peach garden and stealing the elixir of immortality from Laozi's laboratory.

Finally, Buddha imprisoned him in a rock for 500 years, and he remained there until Guanyin, the Buddhist Goddess of Mercy, released him. She placed a metal band around Monkey's head, which tightened when a special prayer was said. Thus controlled, he used his magical arts to help a Chinese monk who makes a pilgrimage to India to obtain the Buddhist scriptures. Along the way they have many adventures, and Monkey's courage and sense of adventure ensure the safety of the timid monk.

Unlike Nazha, the Great Saint is not a heavenly avatar, but rather a stone monkey born of a rock – a force of nature. He also is a shamanic rebel who assaults the rulers of the three realms of the cosmos: the watery underworld, Heaven, and Hell. Because he is armed with Daoist immortality and a formidable magical weapon, even Heaven finds it difficult to control him. By contrast with Nazha, it is not a Daoist priest but rather Buddha and Guanyin who finally succeed in taming him by use of a magical device. This is an allegorical assertion of Buddhism's superiority to Daoism and its power to tame autochthonous spirits. With the Great Saint, as with the story of Nazha, we see a parallel message, which is that spiritual means – in this case, Buddha's magic – may be used to control powerful but chaotic beings like the Monkey. At the same time, the allegory suggests that once people have used religion to harness and control the demons, they will serve and protect humans.

The Vagabond Buddha

Finally, I consider the story of Jigong, the 'Mad Monk' who is the main character in *Jigong's Complete Biography* (*Jigong Quanzhuan* N.d.) Although earlier versions of his story exist, the version available for sale in Penang was a reprint of a popular novel first published in 1898 whose author probably was Guo Guangrui (Shahar 1998: 233). His story is an allegory of superior spiritual power vanquishing powerful and dangerous demons. Like the story of Monkey, and by contrast with Nazha, here it is a Buddhist saint rather than a Daoist master who overpowers autochthonous spirits – a snake spirit and a fox spirit. Jigong dispenses moral justice: he rewards good people by helping them but punishes the bad, including corrupt, venal Daoist priests and Buddhist monks. In many episodes, he also demonstrates that his spiritual power is superior to that of the Daoist priest.

As Meir Shahar observes, "eccentric, rebellious, and clownish, [Jigong] in-habits a world in which defiance and deviance are the norms" (Shahar 1998: 16). Because he turns the world upside down, he is an appropriate patron saint for society's rebels but persons who live their lives within society's conventions also worship him. Shahar concludes that, "Jigong has been worshiped simultane-ously by rebels, bandits, and members of the elite" (1998: 17).[20] In Malaysia, Jigong is the patron saint of a network of Malaysian moral uplifting associations (*dejiao hui*), including one whose members came to one spirit medium temple wearing gray robes to offer formal worship on Jigong's birthday. His worship also is associated with the ritual practice of the Unity Sect (*Yi Guan Dao*), a sectarian group whose leader declared himself to be an incarnation of Jigong in the early twentieth century (Shahar 1998: 198; Jordan and Overmyer 1986: 236). As I discuss in Chapter Seven, one spirit medium in Penang who worked on the dark side also was possessed by Jigong, and in trance he emphasized the trickster aspects of his personality rather than his Buddhist moral teachings (see DeBernardi 1987).

Jigong, like Nazha, was not an ordinary human.[21] Jigong's father was a mil-itary governor who retired to his home community. Lacking a son, he and his wife prayed at the Yongning Temple. When they offered incense at the hall of Arhats, or Buddhist saints, the fourth statue fell to the ground and the Abbot predicted that they would have a son. A few months later the child was born but cried until the Abbot visited the family. The Abbot accepted the baby as a disci-ple, and named him Xiuyuan. This episode is parallel to the episode in Nazha's story in which the Daoist who has given him his magical weapons names the child.

His parents died, and Xiuyuan did not have the means to sit for the imperial examinations to obtain a post in the official bureaucracy. He decided instead to become a monk and entered a monastery, whose chief abbot greeted him as the incarnation of an Arhat from the Western Heaven, renaming him Daoji ('the Dao heals'). Despite this lofty beginning, Daoji was a scruffy trickster who ate dog meat and drank rather than fasting and abstaining, and others regarded him as mad.

Let me just give one episode from *Jigong's Complete Biography* to illustrate his style. In this episode, Jigong maneuvred himself inside the house of a Magistrate in order to rescue a young girl whose father had indentured her there. The father had worked to earn the money to redeem his daughter but then he lost the money and with it all hope. To gain entry, the Vagabond Buddha offered his services to cure the Magistrate's ailing mother. A servant haughtily dismissed him, saying that the family had already arranged for the services of a famous doctor and the Vagabond Buddha was not needed:

The Vagabond Buddha met the Doctor, and in order to prove that his own skills were superior to the Doctor's, he set him a challenge, asking him, "For what problem is 'Freshly Baked Bread Right From the Oven' the cure?" The Doctor mulled this over, and finally responded: "I don't know. It's not in my medical books." The Buddha retorted: "Why, even the most basic things you don't know. And you call yourself a doctor! 'Freshly Baked Bread Right from the Oven' cures hunger!"

The Vagabond Buddha was allowed to see the Magistrate's mother. His prescription was dirt from the road rubbed from his body, and *yin-yang* water, which was cold water mixed with hot water.

In the novel as well as in some spirit medium temples, the Healing Buddha allies himself with a martial artist god. In the novel this is Wei Tuo, whom several spirit mediums described to me as a Protector of Buddhism (see also Stein 1991 [1981]). In the novel, however, Wei Tuo is a hungry young man who agreed to 'do' Wei Tuo for a price. For him, taking the part of Wei Tuo involved stealing back a magical charm that had been stolen from the Vagabond Buddha. I perceive a parallel between the alliance of the Vagabond Buddha and Wei Tuo in the novel and the alliance of the Vagabond Buddha and Nazha, who also is a martial artist, in a spirit medium temple that I will discuss in Chapter Seven.

In Singapore and Malaysia, Jigong's story is available in a comic book edition that is a collaboration between a Beijing Professor of English and a Malaysian illustrator (Goh 1996). The episodes selected for this brief volume epitomize well the themes we are discussing here. In one episode, for example, a wicked Buddhist monk murdered a virtuous abbot so that he could take over his temple. A snake spirit in the guise of a Daoist priest approached the wicked monk, who requested financial assistance from the boa spirit. In response, the snake spirit offered to use his black magic to poison the river and make villagers in the region ill. He advised the abbot to make money by announcing that an Iron Buddha would descend to earth to heal the sick. The abbott made the announcement and people thronged the temple, seeking cures for the illness that the alleged healer had in fact caused.

Meanwhile, Jigong heard of the epidemic and of the cure offered at the temple and decided to go see what was going on. As he walked he sang this song: "I roam the world by land and by water, I mix with the common people, do good and punish the evil. Ghosts and monsters have no place to hide." As he approached the temple, Jigong encountered a young woman whom the Iron Buddha – like Nazha, a speaking statue – had coldly turned away (because she had no money to donate in exchange for the cure) with the words: "We don't operate on credit here. No money, no drug." Jigong entered the temple and stole a peach from the altar. When the wicked abbot challenged him, he responded, "You use Buddha to get food and clothing, so why can't I even eat a peach?" Jigong then chanted in front of the image of the Iron Buddha, who revealed his true identity as an evil snake spirit.

Jigong fought first the huge snake and then the wicked monk. Before the match with the monk, Jigong accused him of harming the villagers, thereby violating Buddhist dharma, and asserted that, "Evil is repaid with evil." They fought, and the monk transformed himself into a fierce tiger. Jigong transformed the tiger into a cat. The monk flung fire at Jigong, who deflected it back to the monk, destroying him – an allegorical statement of the karmic principle that evil turns back upon its perpetrator. Jigong then provided the villagers with ten vats of magic water to cure their epidemic (Goh 1996: 68–88).

Jigong is an extraordinary being, a Buddhist saint. Like Nazha and Monkey, he is chaotic and earthy rather than smooth and refined: when high-ranking officials visit his monastery, for example, he turns cartwheels, revealing his naked buttocks. As his song suggests, he identifies with the common man. And although he is a Buddhist monk, he drinks too much, eats dog meat, and jokes. He is, however, the wise fool who sees through pretense and chicanery: again, as his song reveals, his goal is to 'do good and punish the evil.' The moral of the story is transparent: Jigong cures those who are virtuous and fights with those who harm and cheat others until their own evil destroys them. He is the Buddhist principle of karma made incarnate.

Performing the Vagabond Buddha

In the trance performance, the deities whose stories people know through novels, television series, movies, or comic books come alive as individuals. People say that the gods must have an affinity (*yuan*) for the mediums they possess; elsewhere I have argued that for some socially marginal individuals, antinomian or rebellious gods like the Vagabond Buddha and Nazha symbolize their values (DeBernardi 1987). At the temple that I discuss in Chapter Seven, for example, the spirit medium emphasized the Vagabond Buddha's trickster qualities. No necessary relationship exists, however, between the worship of deities like the Vagabond Buddha and social marginality, which suggests a great degree of freedom in the way that spirit mediums interpret the personalities of the gods in performance.

Let me compare two temples, one that elaborated the Vagabond Buddha's trickster image, the other his healing powers and moral teachings. At the first temple, a spirit medium from another temple performed after-hours as a guest, and a large crowd gathered for the event. The regular participants introduced me to a large man with tattooed arms who had a rather pleasant and expansive demeanor, almost to the point of looking simple, but with an alert edge that made him seem anything but simple. The medium sat on the chair facing the altar, donned his greasy brown cap, and blew his nose three times very loudly, into his fingers, then wiped his hands on the boy (himself a spirit medium regularly possessed by Nazha) who was tending him. Ah Tat tried to dance away but got caught, and complained, "You're so *dirty!*"

The Buddha then took burning joss sticks and held the lit ends to his back so that his body was bathed in smoke, making contented sighs and grunts. Ah Tat helped the Vagabond Buddha into his yellow robe, and the Buddha called for his Dragon Throne. As he aided the Buddha in putting on his robe, Ah Tat asked in a stage whisper, "Are you wearing pants?" alluding perhaps to a scene in the novel where the Vagabond Buddha does cartwheels at his Buddhist monastery, revealing his naked behind to a wealthy patron. Ah Tat lifted the robe to help the Buddha onto the throne, announcing in a loud, official-sounding voice: "Cannot look at the Healing Buddha's ass!"

The Buddha settled into the throne of nails, bouncing up and down a few times, and with an "Ahh!" of satisfaction, took his glass of Guinness Stout, and chanted "Amitofo!" Then, more seriously: "The Healing Buddha is here to settle matters." Ah Tat yelled: "The dirty man has arrived! Come, come, come!" Amitofo is the Hokkien name of Amitabha Buddha, and Pure Land Buddhists believe that by chanting his name they will enter his Western Paradise of endless

FIG. 29. Wearing dirty robes and a hat on which the character for Buddha (*Fo*) is written, the Vagabond Buddha drinks a glass of Guinness Stout, George Town, 1981. Photo: Jean DeBernardi

light on their death. In chanting the name, the spirit medium both identified himself as a Buddhist and parodied this act of simple devotion.

The first client, a young boy, took his place by the altar table. He complained that a woman had stolen money from him. The Healing Buddha spoke Chaozhou to the boy. As Ah Tat struggled to translate, the Vagabond contradicted him and hit him with his fan. "Brr, Brr, Brr," the Buddha rumbled, and he asked the boy if he owed money to anyone. When the session was over the Vagabond Buddha dictated a poem to his interpreter, who painstakingly wrote down the composition.

His performance was parodic: when the Buddha arrived, instead of demonstrating his Buddhist identity by chanting a sutra and holding his hands in a mudra, he blew his nose in a mocking exaggeration of a lower-class habit that middle-class and wealthy Chinese view with distaste, wiping the snot on the young spirit medium tending him. In the meantime, the younger man consistently referred to him disrespectfully and familiarly as "the dirty man." In parody of the self-important actions of temple committee members who surround ritual events with taboos and exclusions, he declared a taboo on viewing the Buddha's naked posterior. It was a coarse, male, lower-class present that was evoked here, rather than a sacred and literary past.

By contrast, at another temple the Vagabond Buddha's spirit medium cooperated with members of the True Heavenly Dao (*Zhen Tiandao*) association to emphasize moral teachings and spiritual healing. The temple distributed free morality books (*shanshu*), including several written through planchette divination. One of these was the *Journey to Purgatory* (*Diyu Youji* 1978), a widely known morality book published in Taiwan whose authorship people attributed to the Vagabond Buddha.[22] One committee member explained that people should read this book to their children so that "when they grow up, they won't be bad-hearted" (*phai^n sim, dai xin*). On the god's birthday they distributed another morality book that included essays attributed to God (*Shangdi*), the Vagabond Buddha, and a variety of lesser-known deities (*Shiquan Jiuku Pian* 1980).[23]

The True Heavenly Dao (*Zhen Tiandao*) traces its origins to the World Red Swastika Society, a moral uplifting association (*dejiao hui*) officially established in China in 1922. According to a 1949 pamphlet that one of the group's members gave me, the Red Swastika Society is a charitable body that teaches that the five principle religions (Christianity, Islam, Confucianism, Buddhism, and Daoism) all have the "same origin in God," and seeks to "foster universal brotherhood and world peace" (Wang 1949: 5–16).[24] One member drew a tree to explain this to me, labeling the tree's roots as the Heavenly Dao and its branches as the five religions. He concluded by writing, "Falling leaves return to the root" (*loye guigen*). Although the group venerates a unitary god, they also venerate the founders of these five religions and a variety of saints, including General

Montgomery, who went to Japan during World War II and there achieved heroic status.[25] This group met weekly on Sunday morning for thirty minutes of chanting and forty-five minutes of meditation, which they performed wearing what a member described as "old Chinese dress." The group also gathered to celebrate the birthdays of Mohammed, Buddha, and the Vagabond Buddha.

Like members of many moral uplifting societies, the members of the True Heavenly Dao offered special veneration to the Vagabond Buddha, whom they call the "Living Buddha" (*Chekong Hoahut, Jigong Huofo*), but they emphasized his work in relieving human suffering rather than his antinomian antics. One of the members whom I interviewed knew the god's story well and retold it for me in some detail:

> The Vagabond Buddha was born 800 years ago, in the Song Dynasty in China, to the Li family. This family was very rich. They were a leading family in their district. But they had no son, so they went to a temple to pray. There were eighteen statues of Buddhas [Lohans] in this temple, and as they prayed one statue fell down. The wife then conceived, and her son was this Buddha made incarnate.
>
> The child was very intelligent, and he conformed to the wishes of his parents while they were alive. Once his parents died, though, he gave away his property and went traveling. He had many adventures, and is a sort of trickster. He might use funny methods for cures to frighten you – give you dirt rubbed from off his skin to eat for instance – but if you believe, he will cure you. People come to this god to be cured. If danger is coming, the god warns them. He can also help with family troubles. Even if you come to tell him about the illness of others, he will know about your own illness.

He further claimed that the Vagabond Buddha had authored through planchette divination a long moral poem written in four-line verses with four-character lines. This poem is reprinted in the *World Red Swastika Society Prospectus* (Wang 1949: 4–11). Allow me to cite three verses as translated in the pamphlet:

> To preach the gospel through different apostles,
> At different times in different localities,
> They were born to be Archangels of God,
> Together with many good qualities....
>
> The five religions are Christianity, Mohammedanism,
> Confucianism, Buddhism, and Taoism.
> With no difference from the outset,
> They are the same under God's Kingdom.
>
> To develop them into many branches,
> There were countless thinkers of the past.
> They followed strictly the human nature
> To prove all things good and hold them fast.

The spirit medium at this temple went into trance regularly to perform healing rituals, including healing with charms, but he refused requests for numbers for gambling in the lottery and, at least while I was at his temple, scolded anyone who asked for them. Although he did distribute body-protection charms for a modest fee, the medium did not fall into trance during the temple festival celebrating the Vagabond Buddha's birthday on the fifth day of the fifth lunar month.

Instead, members of the True Heavenly Dao, wearing gray robes, gathered to formally offer the gods incense and a table laden with offerings including fruit, flowers, and a stack of their newly published morality book, which they later distributed to participants. In this text, this Song dynasty Buddhist saint transcended space and time to reinterpret his moral teachings for modern Chinese seeking regulation, order, and a better world in the spiritual disciplines of charity, prayer, and meditation. They performed a Hokkien liturgy that encapsulates some of their cosmology and ideology in song.

Their liturgy opened with a Greeting Incense song (*Zhu Xiang Ci*), which the group sang three times as they burned incense to establish a connection with the gods:

> Every sort of pure incense revolves in the sacred emptiness,
> Incense revolves in the sacred emptiness,
> Gods and people are connected,
> Gods and people are connected just through their heart's feelings, the heart's feelings believe,
> Incense transforms into the azure sky.
> At the Nanwu Heaven's cloud-sea you can meet every immortal and perfected one.

They next chanted a song entitled "Start Praising" (*Qizan*), a verse that offers an account of the cosmic origins of their religious ideology at the very moment of creation:

Yin and *yang* divided, and our elders the sun and moon dawned in the sky. From chaos came the five phases, and Heaven and Earth [the universe, *qian* and *kun*]. Royal virtue, mysterious yellow, joined the transforming nurture, establishing wisdom and reason, cultivating the true root.

Next, they invited all the gods of their 'Virtuous Association' (*Dede She*), including the Star Lords of the four quarters and the center:

> We make offering to and invite the Eastern Quarter Wood-virtue Star Lord.
> We make offerings to and invite the Southern Quarter Fire-virtue Star Lord.
> We make offerings and invite the Central Earth-virtue Star Lord.

FIG. 30. Members of a moral uplifting society offer morality books to the gods. Later they will offer them for free distribution at a spirit medium temple whose main deity is the Vagabond Buddha, Ayer Itam, 1980. Photo: Jean DeBernardi

We make offerings to and invite the Western Quarter Gold-virtue Star Lord.
We make offerings to and invite the Northern Quarter Water-virtue Star Lord.
We make offerings to and invite the Virtuous Association's every Buddha, Immortal, and Elder.

They chanted their scripture, which venerates their highest deity but also promotes morality as a means to return to the true (*zhen*), the perfected state of being that Daoist adepts seek through meditation and purity. The result, the scripture promises, is a utopian world in which there are no troubles, disasters, or worries:

Mysterious Heaven High God, Jade Emperor the Great Heavenly Elder, mercifully consider the final calamity in the dust [the human world], recommend infinite compassion and mercy, promote transformation through the great religion, save us from every bitterness and distress, save all the common people, all the benevolent ones, religion cannot be separated from morality, morality cannot be separated from the body, heaven's command decides nature, human nature returns to the perfected state [*zhen*], . . . amass essence into spirit, you will not see flood, fire, or war disasters, you will not meet with epidemic diseases, you will find peace and comfort and be fulfilled, the will of wisdom is clean and pure, always rely on the Holy Canon, correct awareness, ask for wisdom, be free from worldly cares and transform to a perfected state [*zhen*], you will have no worries or anxieties and will gain weight, the family will be peaceful, . . . the way transforms into principles, pious feelings reach the numinous.
Nanwu Great Compassion Great Mercy Devil-subduing Great Emperor Every Virtue Society Highest Old Buddha Jade Emperor Great Heavenly Elder (three times).

The members of the Heavenly Dao concluded their liturgy with the "Keep the Scripture Poem":

Jade Emperor Great Heavenly Elder, your righteous energy fills Heaven and Earth [Qian and Kun], you loyal heart is as red as the sun, your purple [royal] virtue is the pinnacle, the high way, if you wish to use this doctrinal canon, spread salvation all over the world, together climb to the Pure Land, together ascend to enjoy happiness in Heaven (three times).
Nanwu All Virtue Society Every Buddha, Immortal, and Elder (three times).

Although the event celebrated the Vagabond Buddha, this simple poetic composition repeatedly venerated the group's highest deity, the "Old Buddha Jade Emperor," imagined as an exemplary ruler and savior, but also extolled the virtues of loyalty, benevolence, and honesty as a means to ascend to Heaven.

Conclusion

In this chapter, I have investigated the trance performance as a habitus that is significantly informed by visual, oral, and literary representations. These representations provide those who visit the gods with images of the magical power of the gods to reverse negative influences in an individual's life, ranging from bad fate to a spiritual collision with an unseen spirit or ghost.

The divine heroes of stories like *The Journey to the West* and the *Canonization of Deities* are characters whose allegorical adventures vividly realize the unending struggle of the spiritual to overcome the material. These stories dramatize the cosmological struggle between good and evil, health and illness, luck and misfortune, expressing people's powerful desire to attract blessings and drive away misfortune.

Sinologist Benjamin Schwartz points out that although Chinese religion was never rationalized and disenchanted, the gods' roles were fixed by their functions in the larger cosmic order, and they were never entirely liberated from their roles to take on the rich mythic existence of Greek or Roman gods (Schwartz 1998 [1975]: 190). Whereas many of the deities who possess spirit mediums are very much alive as personalities for Chinese who know their stories, still Schwartz is correct that many others represent metaphysical realities. Often the gods are transparently archetypal figures and Chinese recognize this when they classify them according to their distinctive attributes as military or literary gods, child warriors, virgin goddesses, earth gods, or wealth gods. A Hokkien proverb has it that, "The same rice nourishes one hundred types of person."[26] The trance performance takes inventory of human diversity in a *commedia dell'arte* of humanity's stock characters: male and female, child and adult, warrior and scholar, trickster and bureaucrat, Chinese and Malay.

In the trance performance, however, we find that for a time this allegorical, fictional world becomes people's primary experience. Thomas Mann described this process eloquently as a "lived myth," produced when the mythical point of view became subjective, passed "into the active ego," and became "conscious there, proudly and darkly yet joyously, of its recurrence and its typicality" as a "fresh incarnation of the tradition on earth, and as a 'lived myth'" (Mann 1947 [1936]: 423).

This is precisely what happens in the Chinese trance performance, since the myth becomes conscious in the self, as a "fresh reincarnation of tradition on earth." Allegory becomes primary reality as gods come to earth to offer recovery, escape, and consolation to those who invite them. At the same time, people form an intimate connection with their tradition as they encounter the spirits of Chinese magistrates, generals, and teachers embodied in their mediums.

PART II

Spirit Mediums

I N P A R T T w o I present case studies of four spirit mediums and their teachings. Many authors have described Chinese popular religious culture as pragmatic, piecemeal, and unsystematic; some scholars regard spirit mediums as religious specialists whose level of knowledge is low in comparison with the textual and performance skills of Daoist priests. Kristofer Schipper concludes, for example, that from the ritual master's perspective, the spirit medium is his puppet, "merely a disciple, an interpreter of the art, an instrument of his power, filling the place that a doll might occupy in other circumstances" (Schipper 1993 [1982]: 47–48).[1]

Stephen Owen has observed that China's historical civilization is above all "the structure of its own perpetuation" (Owen 1986: 19). If so, then the trance performance is implicated in this process, because it provides a structure through which the past can speak and act again. The spirit medium is a puppet to the extent that he or she learns the stereotyped ways of moving and speaking that I described in Chapter Three in discussing the performance of military and literary gods. But this account does not consider the considerable creative energy that some spirit mediums pour into their practice, which is in a state of constant transformation as they engage with their clients and disciples in the time and space of a trance performance event.

One foundation that ensures the conventionality of spirit mediumship is its transmission within small family groups. Spirit mediums often claim that the spirits chose them, but the practice of spirit mediumship often is passed on within intimate circles. Several spirit mediums I interviewed had followed their fathers in the practice, and occasionally two brothers fell into trance together at a temple or family séance. But I also encountered a husband whom people reverentially addressed as "Master" who apparently had trained his much younger wife to perform as a warrior woman saint, and I twice learned of an aunt mentoring a nephew. And sometimes a family member – often an older woman whose own father or husband has been a spirit medium – encourages a boy with aptitude to go into trance as a means of continuing a family or small temple tradition. Without these family pressures, some young people probably would not submit to the disciplines required of them in their practice as spirit mediums.

At the same time, family pressure may prevent a person from becoming a spirit medium. As I briefly mentioned in Chapter Three, two brothers (one a teacher and trained martial artist) in a family that once had managed Penang's first Nine Emperor Gods temple fell into trance at a private home, possessed by the spirits of the Great Saint and Nazha. Their younger sister, a university student who had invited me to the event, unexpectedly fell into trance, and led an excited small crowd from the interior of the house to the roadside. On her return, one brother, still in trance, sprayed water on her face to take her out of trance, and later declared the trance to have been false.

Although some spirit mediums learn their craft within intimate circles, spirit mediums also form networks with other spirit mediums, and some claim to have entered into master-disciple relationships with famous religious masters. People address these spirit mediums as Master (*Sinse^n, Xiansheng*), and the title commands considerable respect and deference, at least among Chinese traditionalists. Most of the individuals whom Penang Chinese regard as masters performed as spirit mediums, possessed by a range of deities, sometimes falling into trance simultaneously with their disciples. By contrast with younger spirit mediums, these 'masters of mediums' (*kitang e suhu, jitong de shifu*) train disciples; some also teach religious doctrine to their followers, including individuals who are not preparing to become spirit mediums.

Spirit mediums also sometimes identified the founders of sectarian religions as their spiritual masters. Master Lim called these founders Ancestor Patriarchs (*cho·su, zushi*) or immortal ancestors (*siancho·, xianzu*) and looked to them for inspiration and teachings. He further claimed that the *real* Chinese religion involved the worship of these ancestral patriarchs, and that only these deities could save humans. Spirit mediums in Penang identified as Ancestor Patriarchs Bodhidharma, the Pure Water Patriarch (*Qingshui Zushi Gong*), also known as the Snake God (whose worship I discuss in Endnote 6 of the Introduction to Part One), the Emperor of the Dark Heavens (*Xuantian Dadi*), and one of the Daoist Eight Immortals, Lü Dongbin.

The worship of ancestral patriarchs hints strongly at a connection between spirit mediumship and sectarian groups like the Great Way of Former Heaven (*Xiantian Dadao*), whose practitioners claim a connection through a chain of masters to the sixth Chan patriarch, Hui Neng, and indirectly to the so-called White Lotus tradition of sectarian Buddhism. As anthropologist Marjorie Topley described it, the group organized itself by rotating leadership among Five Lords, high-ranking members who became transformed into deities, including the group's highest deity, the Mother Goddess (Topley 1963: 378). Members of the Great Way of Former Heaven performed the group's salvation work by pursuing a pure lifestyle, abstaining from sexual relations, and following a vegetarian diet, a list of abstentions that contemporary Penang spirit mediums call on all members of the community to adhere to during the annual Nine Emperor Gods festival.

The last Chinese dynasty suppressed sectarian organizations, which have remained unpopular with subsequent Chinese governments. Qing dynasty law regarding heresies and sects, in the 1821 revision, specifically forbade religious leaders to call down "heretical gods." The law described a set of practices that resemble those of contemporary spirit mediumship:

> Religious leaders or instructors, and priests, who pretending thereby to call down heretical gods, write charms or pronounce them over water, or carry round palanquins (with idols), or invoke saints, calling themselves orthodox leaders, chief patrons, or female leaders, further, all societies calling themselves at random White Lotus communities of the Buddha Maitreya, or the Ming-tsun religion, or the school of the White Cloud, etc., together all that answers to practices of tso tao [the tao of the left] or i tuan [heterodoxy]; finally, they who in secret places have prints and images, and offer incense to them, or hold meetings which take place at night and break up by day, whereby the people are stirred up and misled under the pretext of cultivating virtue,– shall be sentenced, the principal perpetrators to strangulation, and their accomplices each to a hundred blows with the long stick, followed by a lifelong banishment to the distance of three thousand miles (de Groot 1963 [1903–1904]: 137).

In both the nineteenth and twentieth centuries, some religious practitioners threatened by Chinese government policies fled to Southeast Asia. In Malaysia and Singapore, British colonial rule promoted religious tolerance in the multireligious communities created by labor migration and the modern Malaysian and Singaporean governments have taken great care to protect religious harmony and tolerance. Consequently, practices that the Chinese government still criticizes as superstitious and antimodern flourished with fewer controls in Chinese communities outside its political borders.

Remaking Religious Practice

Although Penang Chinese often insisted on their conservatism and respect for tradition, nonetheless a close study of their religious culture reveals the degree to which they have remade those traditions in the contexts of modernity. Even traditionalists who devoutly worship ancestral patriarchs seek novel sources of religious inspiration. Vehicles for religious transformation are many, from the simple expansion of the popular religious pantheon to incorporate new deities to the promotion of new syntheses through the written word and teachings. Recent innovations include the use of modern media to promote popular religious culture: temples now use glossy color posters to advertise their events and they commonly produce video CDs of major festival processions.

Ongoing renovation of religious practices is an inevitable consequence of change through time. Charismatic religious practitioners retire and must be replaced, old buildings decay and must be renovated. At the same time, the expectations of audiences and clients change. Medical advances ensure that Penang no longer suffers the periodic devastation of epidemics of smallpox, cholera, and diphtheria; exorcist and *chingay* processions that Chinese once organized on an ad hoc basis to avert epidemics and devastating crises are now routinely performed as periodic events of the lunar calendar. Nonetheless, when Penang suffered a downturn in 2002, devotees of the healing Life-Protecting God (*Baosheng Dadi*) mobilized temples to perform a special *chingay* procession of brilliantly illuminated floats through the streets of urban George Town as a collective prayer for economic recovery.

Penang is a Chinese-dominated city within a nation-state whose identity is largely defined by Malay language and culture, including the practice of Islam. I have argued in *Rites of Belonging: Memory, Modernity, and Identity in a Malaysian Chinese Community* (2004) that an important religious revival that occurred in the 1970s and 1980s was a form of reactive nationalism, and that traditional Chinese turned to their popular religious organizations to fortify their community. Spirit mediums also responded to the dominance of Islam and the increasing popularity of modernist forms of Buddhism by seeking to strengthen and remake their religious practices.

As I discuss in the Introduction, Daoist priests, Buddhist monks, and the leaders of moral uplifting societies and sectarian groups now commonly present their lay followers with catechism-like formulations of religious precepts and moral guidelines. Religious leaders also recognize that a new, literate generation wishes direct access to sacred texts rather than mediated access through religious teachers and ritual practitioners, and some sects make strategic use of mass media to reach a wider audience. Southeast Asian Buddhists have successfully borrowed evangelical Christian organizational strategies, forming youth groups, offering social services, and scheduling regular classes to teach lay practitioners.

Most spirit mediums are independent entrepreneurs, offering their clients diagnoses of unseen sources of personal misfortune and luck-altering rituals and charms. Robert Weller proposes that the individualism of self-interested worship may be explained in light of the impact of capitalism, arguing that contemporary Taiwanese worship at ghost shrines, for example, expresses a "world of individualistic, utilitarian and amoral competition" (1994b). Although Malaysia's Chinese capitalists also seek the assistance of their gods, I conclude that their individualism is rather a consequence of the widespread practice of ascribing personal hardships to the unique action of fate and luck. Individuals seek to mitigate a stark determinism by using divination to discern luck's ebb and flow and performing rituals to change or mend luck.

Although I prefer not to see the individualism of their practice solely as the product of the influence of modern capitalist structures, I do regard Penang's spirit mediums as interpreters of the postmodern condition. They practice in Penang, an urbanized, multiethnic, religiously diverse setting, and they express respect for differences of race and religion. They analyze the differences, but also claim that all gods are true, all religions are the same, and all peoples share a single humanity. Indeed, they draw the same conclusion as scholar Max Müller did when he argued that the comparative study of historical religions would lead us to see that the gods of different religions were "nothing but names for what [is] beyond all names" (Martin 2000: 52).

Scholars may proclaim the "death of Christian Britain" in the postmodern era (Brown 2001), but in postmodern Malaysia, many people assert that in order to be moral everyone must have a religion. Islam enjoys unique prestige as Malaysia's national religion, and Malaysia's *Rukunegera*, or national principles, takes as one of its five foundations a belief in God. Three scriptural religions – Islam, Christianity, and Buddhism – link Malaysian adherents into national, regional, and global networks through print and mass media, traveling speakers and evangelists, and pilgrimage to sacred centers like Mecca, the Holy Land, and Buddhist sacred sites.

Unlike Islam, Christianity, and Buddhism, spirit mediumship has no formal theology, no religious schools, no centralized administrative hierarchy, and no method of credentialing its practitioners. Although scholars may have difficulty in defining religion as a comparative category, many nonscholars decisively reject the idea that spirit mediumship is a form of religious practice, regarding it instead as mere folk superstition. The connection of some spirit mediums with black magic and the underground economy of Penang's black societies further promotes their stigmatization.

Spirit mediums may not have created formal institutional structures, but they do participate in informal networks with other spirit mediums. And although they have no central administration, they recognize sacred centers and many now lead their disciples on pilgrimages to sacred sites in China, venerating the Goddess of the Sea (*Mazu*) at Meizhou Island in Fujian, Guanyin at

Putuoshan in Zhejiang, or the Emperor of the Dark Heavens at Wudang Mountain's Golden Peak in Hubei Province. They study no formal theology, but spirit mediums recognize a corpus of sacred books, including popular novels like *The Journey to the West*, the *Canonization of Deities*, and *Romance of the Three Kingdoms* along with moral tracts like the well-known *Taishang's Treatise on Action and Retribution*. Master Lim further emphasized the antiquity and wisdom of Chinese sacred texts like the *Daodejing* and the *Yijing*. They seek to instill in their disciples a sense of Chinese identity and pride, but also sometimes downplay stigmatized aspects of Chinese popular religious culture, including its so-called superstitious and folk dimensions.

In seeking greater social honor in a modern, urban, multireligious setting, some spirit mediums now emphasize teaching and exegesis as a complement to ritual performance. Master Lim claimed that he was the only person in Penang to really teach Chinese religion, and he identified a modernist Sri Lankan monk as a key influence. We may easily trace the source of that influence back to the late nineteenth-century reform of Theravada Buddhism, a reform movement that was deeply interwoven with modernity as a response to colonialism, to proselytizing missionaries, to new rhythms of work and leisure, and to a higher standard of education and literacy. But we also find striking continuities with the past. Like the post-war builders of new Taiwanese temples, Penang Chinese spirit mediums seek "to conserve ideas and practices that have been regarded as ageless, and to make them, with minimum formal alteration, personally and collectively useful for today" (Sutton 2003: 44).

Overview

Each of the four chapters in Part Two presents the teachings and ritual practice of an individual spirit medium occupying a different position in Penang's complex social and linguistic landscape: Nonya Chinese; Hokkien Chinese immigrant; anglicized Straits Chinese; Mandarin-educated Chaozhou. These compound identities point to complexities within the Chinese community produced by migration from linguistically diverse areas within China, intermarriage and hybridity, and education in modern schools that teach national languages (Mandarin, English, and Malay) as languages of literacy, marginalizing but never quite replacing Chinese regional languages like the three Southern Min topolects (Hokkien, Hainanese, and Teojiu), Cantonese, and Hakka (see also Carstens 1983).

Chapter Four explores the syncretic, mediumistic practice of a woman spirit medium possessed by Malay animist spirits. As a woman and a spirit medium whose possessing spirits are Southeast Asian, not Chinese, she is not typical of Hokkien Chinese spirit mediums, who are overwhelmingly male and whose possessing spirits usually are drawn from a standard Chinese pantheon of martial and literary deities. Instead, the Datuk Aunt has based her practice on a syncretic fusion of Southeast Asian and Chinese animisms based in a mutual recognition of deeply shared cultural roots.

Etymologically, the term syncretism refers to the alliance of warring groups against a third party, and supposedly derives from a Greek term describing an alliance formed by previously antagonistic Cretans against their enemies. The term suggests, then, the strategic overcoming of differences. For many centuries, however, the term syncretism has referred more narrowly to the blending of elements from separate religious traditions. In many religions we find traces of syncretic fusions, but Chinese religious practitioners are often self-consciously syncretic, combining elements that practitioners identify as Daoist, Buddhist, Confucian, and even sometimes Christian. Indeed, practitioners regard syncretism as evidence of their tolerance and universality.

Like language, spirit mediumship is layered, stratum upon stratum, and a Chinese spirit medium may combine elements of widely shared ancient practices of communicating with spirits with moral teachings or forms of spirit writing rooted in the historical experiences of a bounded social group. The Datuk Aunt established her practice on one of spirit mediumship's most universal strata – that of providing remedies for spiritual collisions with ghosts. In a multicultural setting the spirits of the dead also are multicultural; the Datuk Aunt reported encounters with and ritual strategies for placating Indian, Malay, and Chinese ghosts.

Chapters Five and Six explore the sectarian teachings of two religious masters. Both of these spirit mediums applied a religious ideology based on the Three Religions – Daoism, Buddhism, and Confucianism – to the circumstances and dilemmas of life in Penang. Like the Datuk Aunt, both offered their clients magical remedies for spiritual collisions, but they also taught moral doctrines and the disciplines of self-cultivation and meditation as means to human moral perfection. Consequently, these two moral mediums (to borrow Philip Clart's apt term) form a bridge between China's written traditions and contemporary audiences and settings, using oral performance as a vehicle for the transmission of authoritative teachings.[2]

Master Poh had immigrated to Penang from China, and recalled that after the revolution in China, people wanted to split open and 'wash' old-fashioned minds. He defended tradition against these attacks and taught a syncretic doctrine of self-cultivation. In his lectures, he presented a detailed exegesis of classificatory and ethical terms deriving from Daoism, Buddhism, and Confucianism. He further taught how to escape from the cycle of death and rebirth through moral cultivation, including meditation and moral action.

By contrast, Master Lim was an English-educated, Straits-born Chinese who followed his father in becoming a spirit medium but also worked as a teacher in a prestigious British school. He called Daoist immortal Lü Dongbin his ancestral patriarch, and claimed a modernist Theravada Buddhist monk as a major influence. In his classes, he taught texts like the *Daodejing* and the theosophist poem *Light of Asia* (Arnold 1995 [1879]) to a small class of elite disciples; he was widely famous and respected in Penang.

Chapter Seven explores the reality-reversing, looking-glass world of the antinomian Vagabond Buddha. Although most spirit mediums use their charismatic presence to influence people to follow a moral path, some use the power of performance to sanctify socially marginal activities. This spirit medium developed a religious antilanguage to valorize a perspective on moral values that existed in tension with that of the larger society. In the Conclusion, I reflect on the way that the quotidian trance performance of the spirits of magistrates, kings, and princes, coupled with liberal expenditure on exuberant festival events, stages the spirit medium's charisma and magnifies the god-in-the-medium's reputation for spiritual efficacy. But I also consider contemporary challenges to the mystification of the gift and of the spirit medium's charismatic power.

CHAPTER FOUR

Domesticating the Dead

THE PLACATION OF GHOSTS and local spirits is a practice of great antiquity. In the volume of *The Religious System of China* devoted to "Demonology," Jan Jakob Maria de Groot concluded that the belief that ghosts and animistic spirits caused illness and mysterious death were folk conceptions that probably were much older than Confucianism (de Groot 1964 [1892–1910] Vol. 5: 495). Shamanism and animistic practices provide a substrate for a variety of religions in Southeast Asia; local folk religions often combine participation in world religions like Islam and Buddhism with the magical and healing practices of spirit possession (see, for example, Geertz 1976 [1960]; Spiro 1970; Tambiah 1970).

The Penang Chinese offer special worship to local animistic spirits known as Datuk Kong (*Datuk Gong*).[1] The term 'natu' or 'latu' is the Hokkien pronunciation for *datuk*, a Malay word meaning elder or tutelary spirit, and *kong* is an honorific Hokkien term meaning 'duke' that is commonly used in gods' names. The placation of these local spirits derives from Malay practices associated with worship at *keramat*, which are places, objects, or persons invested with sacred power that commonly include sites like a striking outcrop of rock, an enormous tree, a hilltop, a whirlpool, and the graves of saints (Winstedt 1977 [1924]: 54–59).

Throughout the Malayan Peninsula and Indonesia, local peoples venerate *keramat* that include the tombs of community founders, kings and sultans and the spirits of the warriors and learned men (*ulamas*) who contributed to the Islamicization of the region. The cult of Muslim saints probably was introduced to Southeast Asia together with Islam, but many *keramat* shrines are pre-Islamic sacred spaces, some of which have been Islamicized (Chambert-Loir 2002: 138–39). This syncretic fusion bridged Islam and a variety of autochthonous substrata whose practices included ancestor worship and the veneration of local

FIG. 31. Datuk Keramat shrine in Singapore dedicated to Keramat Datuk Loyang. The *keramat* shrine is located between a popular temple whose chief deity is Tua Pek Kong, the Chinese God of Prosperity, and a small Hindu temple, Loyang, 2004. Photo: Jean DeBernardi

spirits (Chambert-Loir and Reid 2002).[2] Many contemporary Muslims condemn these practices as superstitious, antimodern, and polytheistic. Nonetheless, the practice of venerating *keramat* with prayers and offerings persists among Islamic peoples in Southeast Asia.

Chinese also venerate *keramat* shrines throughout Southeast Asia, where the practice apparently arose in the creolized Chinese communities formed through intermarriage between Chinese male settlers and indigenous women, including the *peranakan* Chinese of Java (Salmon 1991) and the creolized Baba Chinese of Penang, Malacca, and Singapore. The creolized Chinese retained many of the identity-maintaining practices of Chinese ancestor worship and popular religious practice, worshipping in temples that were chronotopes of the Chinese cultural world (Skinner 1996; Vaughan 1854; 1971 [1879]). But the Nonya/Baba Chinese also adopted the worship of local spirits, retold Malay ghost stories, and gave credence to the spiritual claims of Southeast Asian magicians and trance performers, seeking them out for magical cures.

Chinese who came to the region recognized in Malay *keramat* shrines an analogue to Chinese veneration of their own protective deities, and reworked their image of the Earth God (*Tho·te Kong, Tudi Gong*) to incorporate indigenous elements. Throughout Southeast Asia, Chinese call him the God of Prosperity (*Tua Pek Kong, Dabo Gong*) and his veneration typically incorporates elements of, or is juxtaposed to, the veneration of *keramat* spirits. In Java, for example, Tua Pek Kong's oldest temple dates to the mid-seventeenth century, and is associated with a Moslem tomb regarded as a *keramat* where both Chinese and local people worship (Salmon and Lombard 1980: xviii, xlviii). Penang's oldest Tua Pek Kong Temple is the Sea Pearl Temple in Tanjung Tokong, which was established in this fishing village no later than 1792.

Penangites describe the Tua Pek Kong at the Sea Pearl Temple as the spirit of a community founder who died beside a boulder and is buried there. These details parallel the Malay veneration of *keramat* sites associated with community founders who often are said to have died beside a sacred stone, or to have been transformed into stone on death. In another suggestive parallel, Chinese say that the tiger is the God of Prosperity's seat or, alternatively, his bodyguard or that he can transform himself into a tiger to protect his territory. Malays also report that tigers and crocodiles, and sometimes snakes and scorpions, protect *keramat* sites and the communities that worship there (Winstedt 1977 [1924]: 52; see also DeBernardi 2004: 149–54).

One of the first places I visited as a novice researcher was a cluster of small shrines, each just large enough to protect a spirit medium in trance, backed onto a mountain cliff behind the modern housing estate where I rented a room. According to the caretaker, the spirits at this popular shrine include Datuk Aceh, the senior spirit, whose actual tomb was deep in the mountains and difficult to reach but for whom a simulacra of a tomb had been constructed; the Black Knight (Malay, *Panglima Hitam*), who is the spirit of a Bugis warrior; and the Red Datuk, whose shrine had been relocated to this site when his original shrine was claimed for redevelopment (but only after obtaining Datuk Aceh's permission). Other spirits included Datuk Nana, who was mute but who gave lottery numbers; Datuk Rimau (Malay, *Harimau*), the Tiger spirit; and Tua Pek Kong, the Chinese God of Prosperity.

The caretaker and the main spirit medium at this shrine center were Chinese, but an Indian spirit medium also worked there. The Chinese spirit medium went into trance every afternoon between three and seven; when I visited, more than twenty Chinese clients – five men, the rest women or schoolgirls – waited to consult with him. When the medium fell into trance he sat Malay-style, cross-legged on the floor beside the saint's tomb, inhaling the fragrant incense that his assistant fanned into his face from a modest clay incense burner. The datuk-in-his-medium spoke *kampong* (village) Malay, which his interpreter translated into Hokkien or Cantonese. My first landlady praised this spirit medium as 'very good,' saying that when she went to ask the spirit about her father's illness, he told her that because her father was very old nothing could be done, and he correctly predicted that her father would die in the fifth month.

In this chapter, I explore the stories and practices associated with Penang Chinese placation of local spirits. In particular, I explore the teachings of a woman spirit medium known as the Datuk Aunt (*Natu I, Datuk Yi*). The Datuk Aunt specialized in providing magical remedies for persons troubled by local spirits at a house temple that combined on a single altar the images of popular Chinese deities and the ritual arcana associated with Datuk Kong spirits. My research assistant and I interviewed her twice, and I attended the festival celebrating her possessing deity's birthday. At her invitation, I also drove her to meet with a spirit medium possessed by the spirit of the Inconstant Uncle, an official in hell regarded locally as a Wealth God (*Caishen*). (See DeBernardi 1994b.)

China's literary tradition, including the textual works of the three doctrines (Daoism, Buddhism, and Confucianism), deeply informed the teachings of the two male spirit mediums I discuss in the next two chapters. Some of the Datuk Aunt's teachings on morality and immortality echoed theirs, and she gave me a popular Daoist morality book, a small pamphlet edition of *Taishang's Treatise on Action and Retribution* (*Taishang Ganying Pian* N.d.), that she herself had obtained at another temple. Although she focused on the placation of local spirits and ghosts, in her conversations with us she described widely shared habits of interpretation and practice that inform Chinese reliance on their spirit mediums for magical assistance.[3]

Colliding with Datuk Kong

The placation of Datuk Kong spirits is a cultural practice common among Penang Chinese. Although Malays sometimes consult with these spirits, the caretaker of the cluster of shrines that I mention above noted that they usually brought a Chinese friend with them to ask on their behalf since Muslims, like Christians, are prohibited from engaging in this form of animistic worship. To some extent, Datuk Kong spirits have been assimilated to the Chinese concept of ghost, and Chinese treat them much as they treat ghosts. They respect (Malay: *hormat*) them by giving them an honorific title (*Natu Kong, Datuk Gong*) and by offering them flowers, camphor incense, and food, including many Malay dishes (but never pork, since most of these spirits are considered to be Muslim).[4] The objects used for worship and the language describing acts of worship define two parallel but distinct unseen worlds.

As my landlady described it, there were many Datuk spirits and you could learn their names through a spirit medium. Just as they do with Chinese saints, they invited these spirits to enter the body of the spirit medium in order to diagnose spiritual conflicts and to help humans. Chinese judge some spirits to be more useful than others: one of Penang's Datuk Kong is Japanese, no doubt the spirit of a Japanese soldier who died in Penang during World War II. But when he possesses the spirit medium no one understands him, so they ask him to return. Many Penang Chinese spirit mediums do speak some Malay or Thai or Indonesian, so they can communicate with Datuk Kong spirits. The names of the spirits are many: Datuk Haji, Datuk Ali, Datuk Aceh, Datuk Koya, Datuk Hang Jebat, the Red, White, Black, Blue, and Green Datuk spirits, and the spirits of the crocodile, snake, and tiger.

Chinese go to Datuk spirits for help, but as my landlady warned me, "Datuks can be bad. You don't want to play with them!" She added that a relative of hers had gone into the mountains to ask a Datuk spirit for lottery numbers, and two days later his wife died. My landlady's teenaged son also had a story about a visit to the popular Datuk shrine that I describe above. As he stood before the spirit medium, he claimed, he actually saw the Tiger Datuk; this visual hallucination convinced him of the reality and seriousness of Datuk spirits.

Another friend reported that one of Penang's graveyards had a Datuk spirit whom Europeans had disturbed when they developed the land. Local people advised them to offer the spirit a feast (Malay: *kenduri*) before developing the site, but the Europeans refused. Finally, the developers agreed to hold a *kenduri* but the ritual placation came too late – the spirit already was provoked. Several individuals committed suicide on the site and rumor spread that the spirit would take twenty lives.

Because they can be dangerous, many parents teach children as young as two years old to show respect to Datuk spirits when they urinate outside. They instruct the children to place both hands together, lowering and raising them several times in a symbolic bow (*pai, bai*), just as they do to show respect for the gods when they enter a temple. Otherwise, the parents fear, the children might inadvertently offend "Datuk Kong things" (*hoantioh Natu Konge migia, fanzhe Datuk Gongde dongxi*).

Often the only trace of Datuk worship is a small clay incense burner filled with ashes or the charred ends of a bunch of joss sticks at the base of a tree or boulder, but sometimes people construct for the Datuk spirit a small open-fronted shrine in the form of a miniature house no more than two or three feet tall. People place offerings of flowers and fruit on plates on the floor of the shrine, and burn camphor incense (*phangchha, fangchai*) in a small terra-cotta incense burner. Shrines are sometimes placed by the roadside, or other times in a yard, next to a large tree or boulder.

FIG. 32. A roadside Datuk Keramat shrine – a miniature house that stands beside a tree and a large rock, with a small stone altar for offerings that displays an Islamic-style star and crescent moon, Ayer Itam, 1997. Photo: Jean DeBernardi

To give but one example of a consultation with a Datuk Kong spirit: when an air force pilot and his wife bought and remodelled a house on a back street to use as a residence and sewing factory, they also decided to replace a dilapidated Datuk Kong shrine that stood at the base of a tree in the compound. The pilot explained to me that they prayed to the spirit "for safety to do business." He and his wife prepared the appropriate offerings, and late in the evening a Chinese medium whom the Monkey God regularly possessed went into trance. Although my grasp of Malay is elementary, the possessed medium spoke slowly and I could easily follow his words:

At 11:00 p.m. the medium sat cross-legged in front of the shrine and the man assisting him threw incense onto the burner and fanned it so that he was enveloped in camphor smoke. Meanwhile, inside the Buddhist center across the road an odd rattling started. The neighbors, Buddhists themselves, came to watch from the other side of the fence, but they seemed uneasy with the proceedings.

After five minutes or so the medium began beating the ground with his hands. The medium's breath became rasping as he went into trance, and he began to speak, a jumble of syllables *dut dut dut pu deh dat din*... until the name *Datuk Puteh* – the White Datuk Kong – emerged from the jumble. The Datuk spirit had arrived.

The pilot asked him, "Will my business be successful here?" Datuk Puteh responded that yes, he would succeed. The spirit also specified his needs, advising him that his new house should be higher than the old one, and asked for prayer and other offerings (Malay: *sembahyang*). He requested that a caretaker (Malay: *jaga*) tend his shrine, because Indian kids had been stealing the fruits left for him. The pilot promised to lock the newly installed gate. Although Datuk Puteh-in-his-medium spoke a very simple form of Malay, he was concerned that his clients would not understand him, and asked them several times, "Do you children understand Datuk Puteh?" (Malay: *Chuchu paham Datuk Puteh?*).

After the important business had been transacted, those present implored Datuk Puteh for lottery numbers, and gave him a pen and two sheets of paper. One number was not clearly written, so the pilot asked him to write it again. The crowd became intensely involved at this point, but I could not photograph the intimate gathering since I had not yet asked permission of the spirit. Finally, the pilot introduced me, and asking very politely, "Can the American woman (Malay: *perumpuan de Amerika*) who is studying in Penang take a photograph?" I had tried to ask permission of the spirit medium before the trance session, but he had told me that I had to ask the spirit, who now responded, "Okay (Malay: *boleh*), but she cannot pray to the photograph."

When the consultation was over, one man crouched behind the spirit medium, catching him as he slumped out of trance. After a minute, he nudged the un-conscious medium, and offered him a glass of water. The medium recovered consciousness. Soon thereafter, the pilot and his wife installed the new shrine at the base of the tree, and the sewing factory opened its doors.

Chinese say that you can collide with Datuk Kong, just as you can with all manner of invisible spirits, sometimes comparing such a collision to a human interaction in which there is a social error that gives offence. As one research assistant explained, when a person's luck is low, all manner of spiritual collisions may occur:

You may become ill by encountering Datuk Kong; *chhiongtioh Natu Kong. Chhiongtioh* means 'to rush or charge, to encounter in battle.' If you are not fortunate, if your luck is not high, then you must avoid the spirit medium in trance, or else you might get ill. . . . If your luck is low, then you will see a ghost, if your luck is high, then you see nothing.

At a shop close to the factory where she worked, for example, the owner illegally filled gas tanks as a commercial sideline. When one exploded, killing the owner, she reported that a fortune-teller had advised him that this year would be a very bad year for him unless he gave money to charity to save himself. There were other ominous omens: when he came back to the shop at night, he heard footsteps on the stairs and the light switch turned on and off of its own accord. He went to a spirit medium who told him that the trouble was caused by a Datuk Kong, and that he and his family should pray. She concluded, "You have to believe in Datuk Kong – they are everywhere," adding a story about her sister-in-law's uncle's nine-year-old son, who snatched kites that had become lodged in trees, disturbing Datuk Kong. After three days he was dead, the victim of a spiritual collision. Penangites told many such stories to warn of the dangers of offending Datuk Kong spirits.[5]

People sometimes go to spirit mediums to learn whether or not they have collided with a Datuk spirit. If the diagnosis is positive, the Chinese god possessing the spirit medium may refer the troubled person to a spirit medium like the Datuk Aunt who is possessed by Datuk spirits and who can communicate with them in Malay. Through the medium, the spirit communicates the person's wishes, and the afflicted individual can then make restitution by making offerings at the site where the Datuk spirit resides or even by establishing a new shrine there so that the spirit will relent. But Chinese also visit spirit mediums possessed by Datuk spirits to ask for lottery numbers, for the curing of intractable illness, and to get dreams – which is another way of securing winning lottery numbers.

Penangites offer Datuk spirits the foods and incense appropriate to entertaining a Muslim Malay, together with all the accoutrements needed to enjoy betel nut, a mild intoxicant.[6] People concurred that the proper food offering for a Datuk spirit is a Malay dish called 'yellow rice' (*nasi kunyit*), which is rice cooked with turmeric and curried chicken prepared and cooked by a Malay. This ensures that the meat was slaughtered following correct ritual prescriptions and is therefore *halal*, or permissible for a Muslim to eat. Pork cannot be offered, and a person cannot approach a Datuk Kong if she or he has eaten pork that

F I G . 3 3 . Devotees burn camphor incense and sing a Malay invocation to invite the Red Datuk to enter his spirit medium. Here the Datuk-in-his-medium prays at the Lord of Heaven altar, Ayer Itam, 1981. Photo: Jean DeBernardi

day, as pork is *haram*, or forbidden, by Islamic law. People also offer camphor incense in a pottery incense burner; sometimes they offer the betel nuts, cire leaves, and lime combined in betel-nut chewing.

In the habitus of ritual practice, Chinese set out the Datuk spirits' Malay ethnicity in a form of worship that neatly parallels Chinese practices. We see this, for example, in the offerings of food, incense, and refreshments appropriate to Malay taste and Muslim proscriptions. Moreover, Chinese say that ghosts fear the emperor's sword, but that Datuk Kong will submit to the authority of the Malay sultans:

In cutting down trees, people are frightened that there is a Datuk inside. But the Datuk has to obey higher authority and move if requested to do so. So, when they take down lots of trees to put in a highway, for instance, they first post an announcement from the Sultan that they plan to do so, then there's no problem.

The basis of the Sultan's power is magical:

Ham [*xian*] is power, strength, a type of force, awe. The king has *ham*, so for instance if a forest has to be taken down to make way for development, and it is thought that Datuk Kongs reside in the trees, then the only way to proceed with the work without fearing retaliation from the angered Datuks is to have the king order them to leave, to move out. Kings have this special power.

The word she uses to describe this power (*ham*, *xian*) literally means 'a horse's bit,' but it also means 'control' or 'official title.' The king's power extends to a charismatic and magical form of authority over potentially dangerous spirits.

The Datuk Aunt

A series of coincidences let me to the Datuk Aunt. During the Hungry Ghosts Festival, my research assistant and I set out to find a spirit medium who specialized in calling ghosts up from the grave (*khanbong, qianmu*), a practice common during the seventh lunar month. The first spirit medium we visited did not object to our presence, but she had no customers, so we went in search of another medium whom we had heard worked in a house at the base of Penang Hill. Lost, we stopped at a bus stop to ask directions of an elderly woman wearing the Malay-style costume of the Straits Chinese. This woman, who lived in a women's vegetarian society that tended a small temple (the *Shanding Dimu Miao*), decided to postpone her planned errand and guide us to the spirit medium's house. We found it easily, but the spirit medium refused to allow us to observe a trance session. Our guide offered to take us to find another spirit medium she was certain would be willing to be interviewed, and she introduced us to the Datuk Aunt.

The Datuk Aunt lived in a small house in a modern housing estate. She was a woman in her sixties, perhaps, younger than the woman who brought us to meet her but by no means young. She too had her long hair knotted on the back of her head in the Malay-style coiled bun called a 'snail' (Malay: *siput*). She wore the *sarong kebaya*, a long-sleeved, embroidered, and often diaphanous blouse coupled with a Javanese-style finely flowered sarong. She spoke a creolized Penang Hokkien filled with Malay words. At first she directed her comments to me in Malay.

The front room of the Datuk Aunt's house was both sitting room and temple. In the central part of the altar she had placed statues of the Goddess of Mercy, Nazha, the God of Prosperity, the Great Saint or "Monkey God," and Buddha. To the right was a stand with seven small triangular silk flags in seven colours: pink, white, blue, green, yellow, black, and red. Beneath these flags were seven krises, each with a coloured ribbon attached to the handle. These flags and daggers are the banners and weapons of seven datuk spirits, each identified by color, like the White Datuk whose trance performance I describe above. These flags and weapons parallel the flags and weapons used in the trance performance of Chinese martial artist deities who call for their flag, which is the god's mandate, and a weapon. When Chinese martial gods possess the spirit medium, they call for the double-bladed sword, or a halberd or spear. Datuk spirits instead call for the Malay dagger with its sinuous blade.

In front of the section of the altar that held flags and krises was a lower table on which the Datuk Aunt had laid out offerings. This table held both a Chinese brass incense burner for joss sticks and a pottery incense burner for the camphor incense burned for Datuk spirits. Other offerings for worship of these Malay spirits included a tray with flowers of many colors and varieties and a brass bowl that held all the accoutrements of betel-nut chewing: betel nuts, cire leaves, and powdered lime.

Although I visited with her several times, I only saw the Datuk Aunt in trance during her temple festival. The Datuk Aunt's main possessing spirit was Datuk Lai Huat, a spirit whose name appears to combine the Malay term Datuk with the Hokkien expression meaning 'Come Prosperity.' She described Datuk Lai Huat as a male 'baby god' who cured sickness, and she and her friends celebrated his birthday on the eleventh and twelfth days of the twelfth lunar month. Ordinarily she wore a very feminine sarong and kebaya blouse, but to prepare for trance she donned a pure white suit – pants and a tunic – and used flowers to purify herself. When she fell into trance, she knotted a white scarf spangled with gold around her forehead. Barefoot, she danced in the courtyard to the music of a Malay-style Dondang Sayang ensemble. Later she exchanged her white headband for a yellow scarf, and performed ritual healing at the altar table.[7]

When her small temple celebrated the Datuk's birthday, the offering table overflowed with many-colored flowers heaped on a round brass tray, and large bowls of food, including yellow rice (*nasi kunyit*), chicken curry, rose water ice, a variety of sweet cakes associated with Straits Chinese cuisine that are made with sticky rice, coconut, and palm sugar, and also a Western-style birthday cake. Other offerings included incense, cire, and betel nuts, stacked up sacks of sugar and rice, fruits heaped on trays, rice powder for a woman's face, the round, bright-pink breads called 'tortoises' (*miku, miangui*), red paper charms, candy, and red candles. One of the participants explained that the offerings were all made "to bring luck and blessings [*ong*], and to take away bad luck." Another explained that they made food offerings to 'eat peace' (*chiah pengan, chi pingan*), which she explained as good luck and health. Although the festival fêted Malay spirits, nonetheless the Datuk Aunt and her followers placed a tall red altar in the temple courtyard for the Lord of Heaven, a practice followed at all Hokkien temple festivals (see DeBernardi 2004:143–48).

The celebrants had placed tall banners at the perimeter of the yard, one of them a black flag bearing the name of a Malay martial artist spirit, *Panglima Hitam*, the Black Knight. Panglima Hitam was a Bugis man who migrated from Indonesia to an area near the Thai border in 1813, where he married a local

FIG. 34. On the occasion of his birthday and possessed by the datuk's spirit, the Datuk Aunt blesses the birthday offerings of food and flowers, Ayer Itam, 1981. Photo: Jean DeBernardi

princess. Malays recall him as the grandfather of the man who founded S*ilat Gayong*, a Malay form of martial arts practiced in Malaysia, Indonesia, and Singapore, and Penang Chinese venerate him at a small temple in Kimberly Street in the center of George Town's original commercial district.

To the hypnotic musical accompaniment of violin, drums, and gongs, two Malay women took turns singing improvised verses in the small courtyard in front of this house temple. Finally, they sang an invocation, repeatedly inviting a guest to come: "Come, Red Datuk!" As they sang, the male medium – the Datuk Aunt's nephew – sat inside the small temple facing the altar. He already wore his trance costume, a tunic and pants made of a brilliant red fabric shot through with gold threads, and he waited for the spirit to enter his body. When the Red Datuk arrived, the spirit medium put on his red hat and took his kris, leaving the altar room for the front courtyard. He first danced a *ronggeng* with the Malay singers, later dancing with the Datuk Aunt, also in trance, and finally with the anthropologist. He reentered the temple to fetch a tray heaped with fruit. Seated in front of the temple, he distributed slices of orange and apple, representing blessings, to a crowd of children, including his own two young daughters.

The Datuk Aunt's Stories

When we three arrived at the Datuk Aunt's house-shrine, the spirit medium, anticipating that we were there to consult with her possessing deity, placed camphor into a pottery incense burner on the altar. But when the older woman explained our reasons for visiting her, the Datuk Aunt sat down with us instead. She was puzzled at my interest in studying her religious practice, but she overflowed with fascinating stories about black magic, Datuk spirits, ghost, exorcisms, and battles with malicious spirits. Prompted by our questions, she also shared stories about the Goddess of Mercy, Buddha, the Wealth God, and the origin of the ancestral tablet. In retrospect, my interest in knowing the stories of the gods probably distracted her from a narrative in which she was laying out the premises of her own practice. Nonetheless, she seemed willing to answer our questions.

She immediately introduced us to her skills, claiming that she and her possessing spirit could cure people of black magic (*kongtau*):

> To make a charm, you must chant. Malays like to do this. The Datuk Aunt can give a paper charm to combat this. You can tell that someone has cast a spell over you, or your friends can tell, if you are giving many things to a person, always go to find them, think about them often, then they've put a spell on you....

FIG. 35. Possessing his spirit medium, the Red Datuk dances to Malay-style music in the temple courtyard at a festival, Ayer Itam, 1981. Photo: Jean DeBernardi

The first time I was possessed, my Thai ancestor entered my body. My elder brother's son is also a medium, possessed by Datuk spirits. He has the same seed. Datuks easily approach him. The Datuk healed a person who had a hole in his heart. He healed a child who was in the hospital with terrible stomach pains, also a person with a cataract. Another person had a broken leg, the Datuk joined the break. The Datuk is very efficacious (*xia, ling*). The Datuk comes to save the world (*giusay, jiushi*). Malays believe that Datuks are ghosts. Chinese believe. Malays use charms to hurt people; they give things to people to eat. My Datuk saved me, I didn't die.

For most Chinese, these miracle tales are a sort of curriculum vitae for the god and the god's medium, an account of their special powers and actual achievements. Although temple committee members who attend trance performances usually provide this kind of personal attestation, the Datuk Aunt here provided her own, offering us immediate evidence of her practical competence and the miraculous powers of her possessing deities. She also claimed that both she and her nephew had a special seed that allowed these spirits to approach them.

At the point when I met the Datuk Aunt, I had many questions about the Chinese pantheon that remained unanswered. Many male spirit mediums had referred me to popular books like the *Canonization of Deities* or the *Jigong's Complete Biography* to learn the stories of the gods. Like them, she first referred me to books as authoritative sources for the information that I sought. But she knew stories and was willing to perform them for us. We asked her about the deities on her altar, including Nazha, whom Penangites regard as three brothers, and the Goddess of Mercy, Guanyin:

The three-year-old doesn't know how to speak, he doesn't listen, and he runs around chaotically. If he is bad, you must call the name of Mother Pusat (*Pho·sat Ma*), Mother Guanyin, then they will be obedient, they follow her. . . .

Guanyin is three sisters. Two sisters were married, but the third was not yet married. The father tried to force her to marry, and kept trying to 'do' her [harm her], to trick her. He tried to make her eat meat, and dipped a needle in meat then poked the needle into the bean sprouts she was to eat. When she ate it, she threw up. In any case, so little would make no difference, particularly if she washed it clean.

When the father was sick, Heaven sent Li Tok Gwai (*Li Tieguai*), a god-doctor to talk to him – he is connected to heaven. Guanyin suffered hardships. The doctor said that the illness was serious, but that a daughter would heal him. She had left home, and was living in the mountains. Someone found her, and took her hand for the father to eat, but he took the wrong hand, he chopped off her right. The next time her father was ill she gave him her eyes, and he got well. He rode his horse to find her and ask her to return, but she was not there. She had become a Bodhisattva, Guanyin. Her married sisters followed her and became her hands in the southern sea.

Here in Penang they are going to make a statue of Guanyin. When the world is troubled Guanyin will cry. When the world had an epidemic, the Guanyin in Pitt Street cried real tears.

She asked me what religion I practiced. I explained that I did not practice any particular religion, but that I prayed to Guanyin, an answer that seemed to satisfy her.

She continued with her own story:

> At 49, I had more than I have now. But in the old days, life was bad. I lived in a garage, beside the toilet, a widow with children to raise. I have the house that I am in now because someone who struck the lottery bought it and rents it to me cheaply, for 150 dollars a month. My life hasn't reached the stage of buying a house. My Datuk doesn't make me rich, I only get enough to eat. I have two unmarried daughters. One is old-fashioned, the other is very sporting. They both work. If you don't sweat, it's no good, you must work.

She asked how we had met up with the woman who had brought us to her. We explained that she had taken us to find the medium that calls back souls from the dead, and the Datuk Aunt remarked that it was better not to call back souls because "the dead person is sure to want money, or to want you to do things that will cost money."

She described her temple's annual festival, then explained Datuk Kong spirits to me:

> At the festival, we serve *nyonya* cakes and *nasi kunyit* (yellow rice with curry). The cost is 2,000 dollars. People who strike the lottery generally sponsor the event. My own expenses are 70 dollars a month for telephone and water plus rent.
>
> Malays think that Datuks are ghosts. There are good and bad Datuks. The good ones are good people who die. The bad ones are trishaw pullers, cart pullers, people who haven't studied, who can't read. They live by the roadside, the ones who live in trees are also like this. They swear at you and scold you. The Datuks who have houses are good. The ones by the roadside might let you strike the lottery, but if you don't repay them as much as they want they might want your life back in exchange. You won't know yourself, you will be in a trance. If you offend (*hoantioh, fande*) Datuk Kong, come to find the Datuk Aunt.

Oon Hooi asked her which Datuk spirits were good, and she gave us a rapid inventory:

> The green-faced one – he's the worst, there's no hope of saving you. The most forgiving ones are Yellow, White, and Haji. Datuk Haji has been to Mecca, he's religious. The Blue Datuk is no good. Good Datuk Kongs can ascend to heaven. The Black Datuk looks after the sea, fishermen pray to him, he is a wind god. The Tiger God, *Harimau*, tends the mountains. You should worship him before going to the mountains. The Crocodile Datuk has entered my body. When this happened, I slithered like a crocodile, and plunged into the well. This Datuk also is bad.

She then described a Malay spirit that possessed her nephew, Hang Jebat, the brother of a famous Malay hero, Hang Tuah.

In the standard version of this story, the two men were warriors. Enemies slandered Hang Tuah and the Sultan ordered him killed. Hang Tuah went into hiding and the Sultan bestowed a high rank upon Hang Jebat. He also gave him Hang Tuah's magical kris, named Taming Sari, which could leap out of its sheath and fly through the air whenever Hang Tuah was threatened by his enemies. But Hang Jebat was enraged at the injustice done to Hang Tuah and went on a rampage at the palace. Because he had Taming Sari he was invincible. The Sultan saw no alternative but to pardon Hang Tuah, who was the only one who could defeat the traitorous Hang Jebat. Hang Tuah put loyalty to his Sultan above loyalty to his friend and killed Hang Jebat. Later he threw Taming Sari into a river and disappeared.

But rather than being a tale of court intrigue, the Datuk Aunt's version of this story was a gruesome family drama. By her account, Hang Tuah and Hang Jebat were like brothers and Hang Jebat's parents had been murdered. Hang Jebat was naughty: he played in a stream and the water washed him away. By a strange twist of fate, the person who had killed his parents picked him up and raised him. He fell in love with the daughter of his adopted parents and wanted to marry her. Hang Tuah's spirit was living in the river, but it emerged when his magical kris fell into the water. He killed Hang Jebat in order to prevent him from unknowingly marrying the daughter of his parents' murderer, then returned to the river.

Although she may have known an idiosyncratic version of his history, she was very familiar with Hang Jebat as the spirit medium performed him. As she described it, when he possessed her nephew, Hang Jebat wore yellow clothes and liked apples: "He skewers them on his kris," she noted. "It's very pretty!" Her nephew also was possessed by the Red Datuk who, she claimed, had fixed a broken leg. She described her nephew's practice:

My nephew in Kuala Lumpur calls Cantonese opera, he is more Chinese, but Datuk spirits enter his body. With Datuk spirits, you must practice certain taboos (Malay: *pantang*; 'abstain, practice avoidances'). There is dirt (Hokkien: *lasam,* also means ghosts) and pregnant women can hurt themselves. Three actresses and an actor support my nephew's temple, they take care of the money. It's enough! They spend 10,000 dollars a year.

Oon Hooi urged her to tell us more stories, and the Datuk Aunt described other Datuk spirits for us:

The one with a walking stick is Datuk Koyah. His tomb is very old. He became a Datuk because he stole from the rich to help the poor. He is like Robin Hood. Datuk Koyah. My friend, a woman medium, was possessed by him. She was snatched, she took a fear, she had diarrhoea and died.

You pray to Datuk Musa if you are studying for English exams. He speaks English. Taite-ia [*Dadiye*, more formally known as *Baosheng Dadi*] is a doctor, in Jelutong there is one temple. People do sorcery, they chant prayers to make something happen over there. Datuk Sakai [a name referring to an aboriginal people] eats raw things, when he comes, he paints his face like a cat. When we have a festival, it's very lively. My nephew comes. Bad Datuks can enter my two nephews.... Datuks won't help Malays since they don't believe. They don't help (Malay: *tolong*) the Datuks.

Oon Hooi asked where the Datuk spirits lived:

White ants' nests – that shape. Datuk spirits like to live in tamarind trees. Siloban, Langsiah, these are ghosts. The silk cotton tree ghost, the ghost of this type of tree, looks like an unmarried pretty woman. She hypnotizes young men, who want to follow her into the forest. If your friends don't call you, then you die of fright. She sucks blood.

At our second interview with the Datuk Aunt, she added:

Flowers also have flower spirits. At night they sleep, you must not pick them. But if there is a fragrance by the roadside at night, that is dirt (*lasam*, ghosts). Langsiatlai has a high-pitched laugh. The Gami mountain in Glugor has this type. It comes as a pretty woman to entice skirt-chasers (literally, 'five-haired chins,' men who chase women). Malays know that going into the hills is no good. If they see someone wandering off, they will call out, "Who are you looking for?" (*Chari siapa?*), and they call them to return. The silk cotton (*Kapuk*) tree ghost is very pretty. It looks like a woman. The ghost lives in this kind of tree....

She added that people could also control the spirit world to do dark things:

The Siloban child. Sometimes babies die at birth, and people bury them at night, not in the morning, because they don't want people to see. People can do black magic, raise a spirit, take his spirit, raise it, and order it around. People in Malacca are like this, they like to play with these things. At night, when people are asleep, the head of the person who raises the Siloban flies, it goes. [The other woman added, "It sucks blood."] We still have this....

With that she concluded this horrific account of black magic.

But dangerous ghosts also include the spirits of those who die tragic, premature deaths, who are imagined to be especially vengeful unless they are worshipped, or find another soul to replace them and release them. At our second interview, she explained this:

A girl hanged herself in a tree behind a house, and the servant could hear her cry. The gods called them to worship her. If you die like this, you must stay on the site until your proper age of death arrives. They are like a person in jail, they cannot be reborn. But they are released if they find a person who replaces them.

Penangites not uncommonly explained suicides in these terms. For example, when we transcribed the tape of our interview together, my research assistant recalled more than twenty people had jumped to their deaths at the Rifle Range flats. Someone asked a Datuk spirit through a spirit medium why there had been so many suicides. The spirit responded that in a mass grave on the site, the Japanese had buried Chinese they had executed, and the dead needed to take back sixteen lives. My sceptical Christian research assistant added, however, that she thought they had taken their lives because they had no money or work, or else were sick, and also remarked that the number of suicides had grown to twenty.

The Datuk Aunt worked as an exorcist, and recounted her experiences with a mischievous child spirit:

When children are ghosts, they are very clever and powerful. There was a family with a husband, wife, and child, Monijia. The father died, and the mother remarried. Then the child died at eight years of age of strep throat. She was buried next to the father. The father called the daughter to come out to tease the second father. She did things like move his typewriter and she disturbed things. I called my Datuk spirit to talk to the girl. The girl said that her father put her up to all this. They asked her not to disturb them, and built a house for her inside her parents' house, and every week offered her cakes, cake from the Tip Top Restaurant, and large prawns. But she said she didn't want this house. She agreed to move to the Temple of the Reclining Buddha [the Thai temple, Wat Chaya Mangkalaram], to the columbarium there, but then she refused. Finally when her own mother died she stopped disturbing people. It was very difficult to catch her to talk to her. She ran about randomly, sometimes entering people, then immediately leaving again, impossible to catch. The stepfather remarried, but he had no more troubles.

In this instance, the Datuk Aunt's spirit failed because the child ghost was impossible to catch and would not accept the offerings made to her. Her story demonstrates, however, that the dead may be jealous of the living and interfere in their lives unless their spirits can be enticed to move out of their homes.

Indeed, the Datuk Aunt dramatically described her own frightening experience when the ghost of her deceased husband sought to take her life:

When my husband died, my younger sister's daughter came to live with me. She struck the lottery, and had a party. My dead husband was jealous, and wanted me to die. He made me breathless and ill. The Datuk scolded my husband. I burned a replacement body [*thoesin, tishen*, a small paper bundle representing the person]. He wanted to take me to die. The god said [to the husband], "She must look after her children!" The god and the ghost quarrelled until the incense burner fell over. I burned the image during Qing Ming.

Here ritual action deflected the jealous ghost: she used a paper replacement body of the sort used in ceremonies to change or mend luck in order to placate her husband, who accepted the substitute, sparing her life.

Knowing my interests, my research assistant next asked the Datuk Aunt about the Nine Emperor Gods, demon-expelling gods who rid a community of plague and calamity, who also are known in Penang as the Nine Divine Kings (*Ong Ia, Wangye*). People consider the Divine Kings to be dangerous and easily offended, and they were especially reluctant to discuss these spirits during the nine-day period of their festival when they were said to be on earth.

The Datuk Aunt prefaced her comments on the Nine Divine Kings with a story explaining the origin of the worship of divine kings (*ongia, wangye*). One of the actors in this story is a Daoist priest named Immortal Master Zhang (*Tiao^n Sensu, Zhang Xianshi*), who, she noted, could be found in a temple in Malacca:[8]

A rich man called a Daoist priest (*Sai Kong, Shigong*) and wanted to test the Daoist's magical potency (*hoat, fa*). Ghosts were disturbing him. The Daoist chanted, and the ghosts were stilled. Then some people disturbed the rich man, and he asked the Daoist to kill them. The Daoist asked, "Are you willing to bear the weight of the sin?" The rich man said, "Yes." So the Daoist priest did away with all of them.

The eighteen dead persons continued to disturb the rich man, asking him for things, and he called the Daoist priest back again. Immortal Master Diao^n [*Zhang*] suggested that they be awarded with a title (*hong, feng*). The rich man appointed them to be divine kings. Wherever they go, they eat well, and they live in a minister's house! They help people.

She added that the Nine Divine Kings were similarly awarded with their rank by the emperor and that consequently they became savior gods:

The Nine Emperor Gods were nine beggars. They lived in a broken down, dirty house, but they did good deeds. The Nine Divine Kings ate vegetarian food and they had good hearts and saved people, so the emperor invested them with their rank. Now they help people.

During their festival, people eat vegetarian food. These gods are very efficacious. If you are sick, you go to hospital. But if you don't get better, then you go to see the gods (*angkong*). The nurses also know this.

She added the stories of the God of the Earth and the Kitchen God, all of whom suffered misfortunes before being elevated to their lofty positions in the celestial bureaucracy:

The God of the Earth is five brothers. Their mother died, and their stepmother mistreated them. Heaven invested them with their position.

The Kitchen God (*Chau Kun Kong*) is the last son of the Lord of Heaven. He was very ugly, deaf and mute, but very playful. He likes to see women. He is served by people in the kitchen. Whenever you move your mouth he thinks you are scolding him! If you criticize him three times, then he will go to Heaven and sue you. Some don't want to serve him because they think that he always goes to complain. He likes to be in the back of the house where he can watch women. He is also called *Chau Kun* [*Chu Shen*].

After this brief excursion into discussing Chinese deities, she returned to her explication of Datuk spirits:

> There are good and bad Datuks. In Medan there is *Gunung Api* (Malay: 'fire mountain,' a volcano). It puts out smoke and fire, it is a volcano (Hokkien: *hesua*^{n}, *huoshan*). With some Datuks, if you offend them, you'll die within three days. If they trouble you, going to see a doctor will do no good, you must find a spirit medium. Your eyes close, you can't eat, you are tired and out of breath. A Christian came and asked me to pray to the Datuk. He followed some friends who went to ask a Datuk, and they didn't pray for him, so he fell ill. He came to me and got better.

After a few moments of silence, she volunteered the story of another Chinese deity.

During the Hungry Ghosts Festival, the image of the Inconstant Uncle was everywhere in Penang. The Datuk Aunt knew his story, and retold it with apparent relish:

> The Inconstant Uncle was a gentleman, but unfilial. He was working in the fields one day, and his mother brought him food. He hit her, and she grew frightened of him. Then one day he saw young goats sucking milk from their mother, and he sang: "The mother goat knows how to love her kids, and lets them suck milk. Now I am so unfilial to my mother, and this is not a good thing." This god is a God of Wealth.[9] As soon as you see him, great wealth.
>
> He holds a fan. He was very unfilial. He was in China.
>
> His mother was frightened until she trembled. She brought rice for him to eat, and still was frightened until she trembled. Even beasts know how to love their mothers. His mother cooked rice for him very early. He was remorseful and ran, ran, ran to kneel before his mother. She was scared that he would hit her again, and jumped into the well and died. When his mother died, an ancestral tablet floated to the surface of the water.

Thus according to the Datuk Aunt, this story explains the origin of Chinese use of the ancestral tablet. The ancestral tablet is placed on family altars to represent the deceased, and remorseful descendants have the opportunity to make amends for filial lapses through posthumous acts of respect and merit-making.

She also knew the god personally. She had gone to see him, and she attested to his good character:

> The Inconstant Uncle is a very good man. I have talked with him. The medium can call him up. I joked with him at the temple. I asked him, "Is my time up?" He said, "No, your name isn't written." He gives numbers too! Some are scared to ask this god questions, but there is no need to be frightened. He called me his advisor. I joked with him and asked him to write me a check. He said, "My check would surely bounce!"[10]

The Datuk Aunt again asked somewhat doubtfully who I was, and why I was interested in these stories, then volunteered the story of the Prince who was unfilial to his father, a story that I recount in Chapter One. She used this tale as a vehicle through which to convey the message that some years in the human life cycle were perilous for men, others for women. She then asked where we lived, and after a few minutes of gossip about neighbors she commented on shrines and spirit mediums near our street:

There is a Snake Datuk in that area, Datuk Sari (Salleh?). There was a Vagabond Buddha in a roadside temple, but he is dead now, there is a new spirit medium. I won't go, I'm afraid of Chinese male mediums. They can fool you, they are more daring than women, and sometimes they are not truthful. My place it's all women, they come to find me.

With that, our conversation ended.

A Second Conversation

Four months after this initial interview, we returned for a second visit with the Datuk Aunt. I asked a few questions to follow up on points that I had not clearly understood in the first conversation, but again she led the discussion into areas that I could not have anticipated. I was curious to know more about the apparent resemblances between the God of Prosperity (*Tua Pek Kong*) and the Datuk Kong spirits. In answer to my question she observed, "If your heart is good, you can turn into a god after death. It is easy to confuse the God of Prosperity and Datuk Kong, since both were men turned into gods."

She offered us a story about a trishaw rider who became a Datuk spirit and visited a spirit medium at a well-known temple in Ayer Itam. The story explores the paradoxes of his situation in a story that we may read as an allegory for the position of the Chinese minority in Malaysia:

A long time ago, in the period of the Japanese occupation, there was a man named Ah Chheng, a trishaw peddlar. He used to ride his trishaw to Tanjung Bungah to eat pork dumplings, and there he was killed by a Japanese bomb and became a Datuk Kong. He then resided in Tanjung Bungah, in a tree behind the house of a rich Chinese man, So Chu Teng. He's there because he died there, and now his spirit resides together with the Red Datuk.

He visited a spirit medium at the Thai Siong Lo Kun [Taishang Laojun] temple, a medium who normally was possessed by the Snake Datuk [Natu Sari]. But this time Ah Chheng entered his body.

Ah Chheng said to the medium: "Don't you remember me? We used to eat pork dumplings together at the same coffee shop! We used to eat together, in a thatch-roofed coffee shop in Tanjung Bungah. I know that things are hard for you now, so I've come."

The medium asked, "Can you help me? Can you give me something?"

And Ah Chheng, who was China-born, said, "Sure (*way*), I'll write a number for you," and he gave him lottery numbers to sell.

Then the medium asked him, "What do you want in exchange?"

"I want to eat pork dumplings," he replied. So they gave him pork dumplings to eat. But after he had eaten them, he had to rinse his mouth. "Otherwise," he said, "the Red Datuk will scold me and press me into the mud."

The story is a neat parable for Malay-Chinese relations. Ah Chheng died tragically in Penang, the victim of a Japanese bomb. Because he died a violent, premature death, his spirit could not leave the site of his death. Thus he stayed in a tree in a rich man's garden compound together with a local Malay spirit, the Red Datuk, waiting until his appointed time of death arrived so that his spirit could finally leave earth. Chinese offer the Red Datuk fruits, flowers, and yellow rice, but never pork. But Ah Chheng still craved pork dumplings. In exchange for a taste of his favourite food, he was willing to help the spirit medium (see DeBernardi 1994a).[11]

The Datuk Aunt reiterated her earlier point:

Humans become gods (*sin, shen*) as the result of their efforts (*tekto, dedau*). Malays call them ghosts, so they help Chinese not Malays. The Datuks are awarded with their titles on earth [literally, below heaven]. These matters are not controlled by Heaven. If you don't respect (Malay: *hormat*) the Datuks, they can make you ill.

She next told us the story of Buddha's renunciation of the world, and the tests he endured while meditating:

Buddha was an Indian King's son. His coachman and he rode horses to go out. He saw how people suffered, wearing tattered clothing, with no money. "Why is his leg like that, so ugly? It's no use being human."

He waited until his wife was asleep, then he ran away. He didn't want to be human (*choelang, zuoren*). Illness, all these illnesses. He was humble. He chanted, worshipped, meditated, did yoga. When he was tested, he could sit. Pretty women were sent, and he took no notice of them. Fairies came to shave his head for him. . . . He wasn't afraid, but his wife and son would not stay. Many things came, snakes and ladies. His wife and child were sad since he left his home.

She continued, contrasting Maitreya Buddha, the Buddha of the Future, with Shakyamuni Buddha, the Buddha who controls the present age, whom she claimed won his powers through trickery:

The fat Buddha, Maitreya, is the elder brother. He's good. The younger brother, Shakyamuni, has a bad heart. Heaven wanted to decide who would control the land, and he gave each of the brothers a lotus flower to care for. Whoever's lotus bloomed first would control the world. The elder brother slept, and didn't tend to his flower, and his opened while he was asleep. The younger brother saw this and exchanged the flowers. This is why the world is the way it is. If the elder brother ruled, men would never get old or die. The younger brother rules, so it's not so good. . . .

Consequently, the world is ruled by the small, and people must contend with the suffering of old age and death.

Dreams and Divination

The Datuk Aunt also described for us spirits in objects that humans could control. Although these spirits did not speak through spirit mediums (because they are, after all, inanimate objects), they did give dreams whose images gave clues to winning lottery numbers:

> The Basket Aunt, if you chant her chant she will come. You can get numbers, and ask questions. But the spirit cannot speak. You dream. The Basket Aunt was bullied by her elder brother's wife and she died. She died in a basket in China, and became the Basket Spirit. She will run away if you call 'sister-in-law' since her sister-in-law killed her.
>
> I borrowed a basket to control (*koan, guan*)[12] the Basket Aunt. You must dress the basket in a pink dress, put in one flower, and put in a soup ladle. You chant, and the basket moves. The basket is a Teo Chiu [Chaozhou] type, and you chant in Teo Chiu. It turns, and your arms get tired. You chant: "*Na lu-e sing, chhing ling ling, pua sua gue nia, din jiu chhin.*" You must put in face powder and flowers.[13]

People also used other household objects to divine lottery numbers:

> People used to steal a mortar and pestle, and use it to call the spirit. Someone would go to find their mortar and pestle, and would curse! Then the person who borrowed it would return it with money [after they had struck the lottery]. You call the mortar 'ma,' you call the pestle 'child.' If you call it, it will give you dreams. The Kinta Lane one was good. You must give it a human form, [dress it in] real clothes, draw a face. You can hear it thump along the floor at night "dum, dum, dum, down it comes!"
>
> You can also use brooms. You steal an old broom. Brooms are in the house washing the floor all day, they are slaves. So you take them for a ride in a trishaw.

Whereas ghosts are won over by offerings of food and simulacra of human life, people court the help of their household slaves by giving them clothes, a face, a name, and time out of the house and away from their labors.

But the Datuk Aunt explained that bookies also had spiritual allies:

> Bookies worship the God of the Earth. Bookies also worship the rice sieve spirit (*bithai sin, mishai shen*). If you chant the spirit's rhyme, you can call it. For the sieve the chant is: "If you worship the rice sieve, you can dream, but you cannot guess."

The bookie prays that their clients will not interpret their dreams correctly, and the aid of the rice sieve spirit helps them thwart their clients' success at discerning winning lottery numbers.

The interview continued at some length. She discussed death and mourning rituals, ways of communicating with the dead, and even ways to snatch the dead back from hell. She complained that old taboos were no longer observed either in the rituals of burial or marriage, and finally she told another story of trance possession:

> A friend went into trance, a man, behind an Indian temple in Ayer Itam. He sat at this man's place, and a girl ghost entered. Then she [the spirit-in-the-medium] came to my place. The girl wanted a brush and a broom, she wanted to wash the bathroom. After she washed it, she wanted to eat coffee and bread, but she would only eat the heels of the bread.
>
> "What?" I asked her, "Why do you want to eat that? Who are you?" We pitied her, she wanted to eat like that.
>
> [The girl's spirit in the male medium replied]: "I liked, I got close to this man. . . . and my boss's wife killed me. She put lye into the bread."
>
> She [the murdered girl's spirit] used to live in the European area. They offered her good foods, but she wouldn't take them.

The Datuk Aunt added that people were wicked in the olden days, and that people sometimes killed the women they bought as slaves when the women grew old, secretly burying them. Those houses, she warned, would be troubled by ghosts, and she guessed that the wicked mistress would be reborn as a pig or a dog.

Conclusion

In my interviews with the Datuk Aunt, we often were following separate paths. I found her stories about Guanyin, Buddha, and the Inconstant Uncle entertaining and memorable, and sought more stories of the gods. But she invariably resumed telling eerie stories about spirits and ghosts, laying out the basis for her own exorcistic practice. Indeed, such ghost stories enhance the credibility of spirit mediums, and stoke people's need for their exorcizing powers. I found especially puzzling her reminiscences about her use of ordinary household objects to obtain lottery numbers in dreams. For the Datuk Aunt, even household tools – the stone mortar and pestle, the basket, sieve, and broom – had spirits with their own powers, histories, and grievances, and when shown proper respect they could act as channels of communication with spirits.

The Datuk Aunt's teachings draw from a rich fund of ghost stories and an oral literature of significant proportions in Penang. Today, rows upon rows of popular books of ghost tales are available for sale in bookstores in Singapore and Malaysia, books with titles like *True Singapore Ghost Stories* (Lee 1995 [1989]). Written down, these tales seem one-dimensional and formulaic, but spoken as occult gossip they kindle curiosity and fear. "Is it true or not?!" the audience usually exclaims, finally concluding, "You have to believe it."

The ancestral cult presents images of an ordered relationship between the living and the dead that is maintained through regular ritual offerings during the Chinese lunar calendar. These include generous food offerings at Chinese New Year and at the midpoint of the seventh lunar month during the Hungry Ghosts Festival, and at visits to gravesites during the spring Qing Ming festival. The dead may be vindictive, jealous, and mischievous, and the spirits resident in rocks, trees, and volcanoes, together with their animal protectors – tigers, crocodiles, and snakes – also have powers to harm or help humans. But just as Chinese use ritual to maintain ordered relationships with their potentially disruptive ancestors, so too they domesticate Datuk Kong spirits with miniature homes, placating them with food offerings, intoxicants, and ritualized expressions of respect, transforming potential adversaries into spiritual allies.

CHAPTER FIVE

Self-Cultivation and the Dao

M R. L E E, a civil servant who was a committee member for a Nine Emperor Gods temple in a densely populated, poor part of George Town,
introduced me to Master Poh. At the opening procession for the nine-day festival, a prominent politician had greeted me, shaking my hand. "You're very
lucky!" Mr. Lee exclaimed, and he introduced himself. He offered to bring me
to meet a spirit medium who could help me in my work, and he did so on the
following day.

We met at the Nine Emperor Gods Temple, and Mr. Lee drove to a rundown
urban hotel to pick up a man who wanted to consult with the medium. Leaving
town, we drove toward the center of the island into a squatter area not far from
my own neighborhood. On the way, Mr. Lee described Mr. Poh's deity to me:

If you are falsely accused by the police, this god can help keep you out of jail. He makes
it so that when you speak, the police will be sure to believe you. Or he'll say if you are
going to jail. Either way it sets your mind at rest. This god is very powerful. We have a
thousand-over members.

He warned me that there were many dishonest people in Penang who would
try to take advantage of me, then reflected that I didn't seem to be the sort of
person who was easily fooled. Mr. Lee also observed that the medium's Hokkien
was very deep.

We drove down a long dirt road to a simple wooden house that faced onto a
large open clearing fringed with trees and a few houses. In the main altar room
I found an altar that was uniquely arranged. On the wall behind it was painted a
Chinese unicorn, the *qilin*, whose mouth emitted a cloud with a book. In place
of the more typical arrangement of deities to the left and right of the main god,
here the spirit medium had placed his god images in a three-level arrangement.

On the middle and lower steps stood images of two other gods, both red-faced; I was told these were the eldest and youngest of the 'Baby Gods,' Jinzha and Nazha.

On the top level was the black-faced Pure Water Patriarch (*Chheng Chui Cho·su Kong, Qingshui Zushi Gong*), who also is known in Penang as the Founder God (*Cho·su Kong, Zushi Gong*) or Snake God. The Snake God is a healing deity whose worship is attested in Penang as early as the 1830s. His most well known temple is the so-called Snake Temple in Sungai Kluang, more formally known as the Prosperity Palace (*Hok Heng Keong, Fuxing Gong*), which was built there in 1850.

To the left of the Snake God stood Iu^n Chen (*Yang Jian*), who also is known as Erlang.[1] The spirit medium noted that he was the son of a general and had three eyes (the Daoist sage Laozi gave him the third); the medium also called him the Eastern Quarter Second Leader (*Dongfang Er Yuanshi*). According to Master Lim, Erlang was the Jade Emperor's nephew. One of his teachers taught him seventy-two arts – the same number that the Great Saint mastered. But then Erlang captured a magical dog using a mirror given to him by a barefoot immortal, thereby adding a seventy-third. Master Lim added that Erlang was the spirit of the constellation Orion, and that his dog was Canis Major. In one episode in *Journey to the West*, after other members of the Jade Emperor's army had failed to subdue the rebellious Monkey, Erlang defeated him with the aid of Vaisravana, Nazha's father.

When we arrived the medium already was in trance, possessed by the god. An older man with close-shaven hair, the medium wore white pants but no costume; Mr. Lee explained that he was in mourning. The medium spoke in a deep Hokkien that I found difficult to follow, but I photographed and observed from the side of the altar. After Mr. Lee's friend had finished his business, Mr. Lee urged me to go and ask the god a question. I took my place by the side of the altar table and asked, "I'm writing a book about Chinese religion. Will the project be successful?" The god-in-his-medium not only predicted success, but he also began to lecture me on the Great Ultimate and the Dao. Out of trance, he agreed that he would teach me more if I returned to his temple.

Previously, I had watched a trance performance and interviewed a spirit medium only after he or she fell out of trance. Most spirit mediums enhance the contrast between the personas of their divine visitors and their ordinary selves by stressing how ordinary they themselves are, and that they know little, while the god is all-knowing. When a god (rather than a mere mortal) conveys his moral teachings, this significantly enhances the weightiness of his message. After this encounter, I was bolder in approaching the altar to ask the gods questions about religious matters. I found myself entering into the performance myself, enacting the role not only of anthropologist but also disciple.

FIG. 36. Master Poh calculates the future on his hand. Because he was in mourning, he did not wear the spirit medium's stomacher and leggings in trance, Penang. 1980. Photo: Jean DeBernardi

Master Poh was born in mainland China, and in retrospect I wish I had asked him questions about his life before he came to Penang. China's communist leaders denounced spirit mediums as witches in antisuperstition campaigns, tormenting them and forcing them to undergo 'reeducation,' especially during the Great Leap Forward in the late 1950s and in the Cultural Revolution (1966–1976). It seems very likely that he experienced persecution after 1951. Master Poh mentioned that after the revolution, people no longer kept the Dao, and in his didactic lecture to us he debated an imaginary other who wanted to split open and wash old-fashioned minds. He responded to this other by comparing tradition to a shade tree whose broad, sheltering crown grew from deep roots, concluding, "It's praise to call you old-fashioned!"[2]

Perhaps because Master Poh was in mourning, trance sessions at his temple seemed infrequent and irregular compared with those at other temples. Nonetheless, during the festival celebrating Iu^n Jen's birthday on the fourth, fifth, and sixth of the tenth lunar month, the temple committee hired a costly Teo Chiu (*Chaozhou*) opera troupe from Thailand at MR1,000 per night. They performed on a temporary stage erected in this clearing, and despite heavy rains that swamped the field, a large crowd of neighbors and devotees gathered to watch the opera performances. In the course of the three-day festival, Daoist priests performed rituals to honor the god, and the spirit medium gave talismans anointed with his blood to the group's inner members, whom Mr. Lee called his disciples. The members also selected a new temple management committee, placing the names of aspirants before the god and using the divining crescents to discern the god's preferences. Generous food offerings had been prepared for the event, including a whole roast pig. The food was divided among the new temple management committee, and the pig's head reserved for Mr. Lee's wife, who had been chosen as the new keeper of the incense urn.

On the final day of the event, almost 200 people attended a lavish ten-course banquet in the paved courtyard in front of the temple. At the table where I sat, all the guests came from the George Town street where I had first met Mr. Lee during the Nine Emperor Gods festival. Other members came from every part of Penang, although most appeared to be part of a network of kin and friends from urban George Town and Jelutong. Mr. Lee complained that many members had not returned for the yearly reunion, and perhaps this was because Master Poh's reputation had waned.[3] At the conclusion of the banquet, the new management committee carried on a discussion of whether they should consider a less costly form of entertainment in the following year, talking on until the caterers insisted they surrendering the rented table.

I interviewed Master Poh twice with the help of a research assistant, a young university student who had grown up in George Town. Although he was a committed Christian, Eng Hok was knowledgeable about popular religion, largely due to the influence of an uncle who had insisted that he disciple himself to a spirit medium. Master Poh appeared to like Eng Hok, and lectured us at length. To my surprise, however, at the temple festival Mr. Lee discouraged me from coming with the student again, adding that the spirit medium was afraid that Eng Hok, who wore a gold cross on a chain, might influence me against his teachings.

Master Poh had worked as a spirit medium for the previous decade at this small house temple, which a group of people from Jelutong had established around 1970. Nonetheless, he insisted several times in the course of our two extended interviews that he had not taught the Dao or exhorted people to do good (*khoansian*, *quanshan*) since 1965. He did not tell us where he had taught about morality and the Dao in the earlier period of his career, but many of his teachings evoke the moral doctrines of syncretic moral uplifting (*dejiao*) associations, which have enjoyed great popularity in Malaysia since World War II. These groups are universalistic and egalitarian in their doctrine, proposing that all religions should work together to "eradicate religious, class and racial conflicts for the attainment of world peace and brotherhood" (Tan 1985: 64).

Master Poh argued for a similar universalistic outlook, exhorting us to see that all religions are the same; that people should not look at appearances but should treat all people equally; that all races are fundamentally the same, although they speak different languages. Typically, however, spirit mediums were not involved in the moral uplifting associations, which instead employed planchette mediums who used a y-shaped divination stick to write divinely authored texts in fine sand. Master Poh did tell us a little about his earlier career, emphasizing his exceptional ability to meditate on the sun, which he called the golden flower, and tracing the roots of his meditation practice back to the teachings of Bodhidharma, the Indian Buddhist monk whom Chan Buddhists claim as their founding patriarch.[4]

Master Poh's discourse was filled with exegesis of classificatory and ethical terms deriving from Daoism, Buddhism, and Confucianism. Daoism provided him with the classificatory framework of the five elements or phases, and he further classified the world's creatures in light of a Daoist tripartite division of the cosmos into the realms of Heaven, Earth, and Water. His lectures emphasized keeping the Dao, which included both the spiritual practice of meditating on the sun, or 'entering the golden flower' (*jip kimhoa, ru jinhua*), and the moral practice of 'doing good' (*choeho, zuohao*).

I did not receive any religious tracts from Master Poh's temple, but he lent me his tattered copy of *The Canonization of Deities* (*Fengshen Yanyi* N.d.) and referred me to the *Journey to Purgatory* (*Diyu Youji* 1978), a book published in Taiwan and widely distributed for free in Penang's spirit medium temples. He also recommended another book that he called the *Ultimate of Non-Being Heavenly Book* (*Bochi-e Thiansu, Wuji Tianshu*), which I was not able to locate in Penang.

In his teachings he stressed the notions of karma and rebirth, a doctrine that historically is Buddhist but that deeply permeates Daoist moral teachings. In Penang, more than a few spirit medium temples distributed Daoist morality books, including *Taishang's Treatise on Action and Retribution* (*Taishang Ganying Pian* N.d.), which unequivocally teaches that "good and evil will always be rewarded just as shadow follows form." The longer version of this text teaches this lesson through didactic poems and moral tales, all of which say that the gods reward good deeds with longevity and success and punish bad deeds with poverty, failure, and a poor rebirth (see Bell 1996a; 1996b; DeBernardi N.d.a). In his teachings, Master Poh similarly described the rewards for moral behavior and punishments for evil in light of a system of divine retribution.

Master Poh suggested that the desire to be reborn is strong, but that on being reborn, or 'crossing the sea of blood,' people experienced the sorrows of life. Although he described a religious path that allowed people to achieve immortality, to take their bodies and ascend heaven, he repeatedly insisted that these days, everyone went to hell. Even so, he presented arguments for moral behavior, explaining that one's rebirth is determined by one's deeds: "You must have good deeds and good morals, then you will have good rewards." Bad deeds, by contrast, would lead one to be reborn with "the animals of Heaven, Earth, and Water" rather than as a human being.

At times he directed his exhortations at us as if we were the unreformed sinners he deplored. Indeed, my research assistant believed that at the second interview, Master Poh took advantage of a request to clarify the meaning of a phrase to scold us for not showing him greater gratitude, and the assistant felt slightly affronted:

> Eng Hok asked, "What does 'disloyality and injustice' (*buttiong, butgi; wuzhong, wuyi*) mean?"
>
> Master Poh replied, "Disloyality and injustice is immorality (*loanlai, luanlai*)! I don't know if you are good, or if you are bad. But now I help you people in a special way. I help you, you have difficulties and I save you. But you are ungrateful and unrighteous (*pong-un pueki, wangen beiyi*)! You get rich and don't mix with me even though I took care of you. This is called 'disloyalty' (*puttiong, wuzhong*). I saved you, but you don't think of it, you are unfaithful (*bochintiong, bujinzhong*). You hurt me even though I took care of you. . . . I helped you to progress, you don't understand that you should come and repay (*tap, da*) me. [Eng Hok felt that Master Poh directed this remark at us.] This is called 'disloyal, unjust, unfilial.'
>
> "This is called 'benefactors' (*kuijin, guiren*). Benefactors help people, they save people. They save people from dying, and people must repay them, it's correct. But people will say 'you go away.'" He added a proverb, "'A boat crosses the water and leaves no mark' (*chun koechui bohun liao, chuan guoshui wuhen le*). I saved you, and now I am a mess. You go into the world, and you see that I have not got enough to eat. This is what is called 'ungrateful and unjust.'"

Perhaps Master Poh did criticize us for ingratitude, but this mode of exposition also was a rhetorical strategy that pitted his own moral views against the reprehensible behavior of an imagined other.

Master Poh debated this imaginary 'you' when he explicated moral terms for us, as he did here, representing opposing viewpoints in the dialogic style that Russian literary critic Mikhail Bakhtin termed double-voiced discourse (1981b: 324). Bakhtin used the term to describe texts that, though seemingly uttered from the point of view of a single speaker, will in fact convey two voices or two points of view. Parody is an obvious example: in a parody, the words of another are cited, but also mockingly distorted. The person who parodies represents both his own sceptical attitude as well as the words of another speaker. Other verbal forms may be double-voiced with varying degrees of obviousness, and to some extent there is always a tension between the individual's use of a term and the uses that precede it. Master Poh frequently debated with an imaginary interlocutor who defended his or her immoral actions. He countered the other's argument that rewards in this life are superior to deferred rewards with the threat that immoral deeds would compromise one's future rebirth and the welfare of as yet unborn future generations.

He also exhorted us to be filial, explaining the basis of obligation to us:

This filiality (*hau, xiao*) is very deep. You cannot repay your parents. If people follow them and please them, then that is good. You must do this and that to please them. Follow father, follow mother. You must not oppose father, oppose mother, you must not oppose Heaven and Earth. To follow (*sun, shun*) you must recognize that he is big, you are small. He is the elder, and in a certain instance he is wrong. He is the one who taught you and raised you, and now clearly he is wrong. But he's still right. You must not correct him to his face. When he has passed by, then you can speak. This is called 'to follow.' People must not oppose their elders. We are small, and he is big, and she is the mother who gave us life.

In the section that follows, I present a translation of Master Poh's teachings as they unfolded in the first interview, adding some details from the second interview, which in many respects duplicated the first.[5] He claimed not to have taught the Dao in many years, but nonetheless lectured us fluently.

Although the student helping me asked Master Poh a few questions, on the whole we were a passive audience in the face of this moral exhortation. By contrast, my interviews with other possessed spirit mediums were far more interactive and sometimes even playful. Master Poh's discussion had greater depth and internal consistency, however, and he provided a more integrated exposition of the basic principles of the Three Religions than any other spirit medium was able to provide me.

We started by asking Master Poh about his possessing deity, Erlang. At first he was reluctant to answer, saying that he didn't know the stories of the gods: "To tell the stories of the gods, you must talk about 5,000 and more years of history, 5,000 years of ascending to Heaven. You couldn't tell it all." Eng Hok asked him about another deity, *Sam Po* (*Sanbao*), the deified spirit of the Ming dynasty admiral Zheng He, and this time the medium responded more expansively, explaining that the history of the gods could be divided into three periods.

The three periods included a cosmologically creative Upper Period during which the Ultimate of Non-Being produced the Great Ultimate, and Heaven and Earth were opened; a historical Middle Period during which the heroes of the *Canonization of Deities* and of the *Journey to the West* – Monkey, Pigsy, and the Monk – were made saints, and the Spring and Autumn Period, the setting for the famous *Romance of the Three Kingdoms*. At our second interview he further clarified that gods, immortals, and Buddhas all were "transformed human beings"– living people who had followed the Dao and ascended to Heaven, thereby achieving their immortality. Indeed, his teaching on this point is identical to that of *Old Ancestor Taishang's Daoist Scripture*, which proposes that "Saints, immortals, Buddhas, and humans all practice the Dao, their reward is that they ascend to Heaven and stand on a cloud. . . . " (Chun 1914: 1).

After a halting beginning, he continued more fluently: "The Ultimate of Non-Being produced the Great Ultimate. The Great Ultimate opened Heaven and Earth. Heaven and Earth produced creatures, then humans. First there were animals, then there were humans. People began to worship the gods in the Middle Period; people from the Upper Period passed this on to them."

He broke from his narrative to express his uncertainty as to our motives in wanting him to teach us: "I must influence you, and help you. I don't know your hearts in doing this. Good, bad, I don't know. I can tell you how to behave, how to worship, things like that, and then I can influence you. You must cultivate yourselves (*siu, xiu*). Do it like that, do it like that.

"Humans definitely come, but they don't definitely return. Return, they can return."

Eng Hok responded, "It's difficult!"

"They can return. How do you interpret this? But for people today, they can't, this is no more."

Eng Hok proposed, "You can meditate a lot, and eat a vegetarian diet."

Master Poh continued, "One way is to pray, to follow a vegetarian diet, to meditate. Do you understand? . . . You must know this. I will discuss Daoli for you"

What followed was an extended lecture on morality, which I present here in its entirety.

Master Poh's Lecture on Self-Cultivation and the Dao

> The Ultimate of Non-Being produced the Great Ultimate.
> The Great Ultimate opened Heaven and Earth.
> Heaven and Earth produced creatures, then humans.

Animals – chicken, duck, pig, cow, goat, dog – these have two souls. Humans have three souls. Trees, grass, have one soul. Humans are divided into five types. Red race – *Kolo*; yellow race – Chinese; black race – Indian; white race – European, beige race. . . . Red hair, white hair, black hair, blonde hair.

The five elements of the body are also the same. Inside there are five persons – gold, wood, water, fire, and earth. Inside of this is the Three Religions, Daoism [he touches his forehead], Buddhism [he touches his left shoulder], Confucianism [he touches his right shoulder].[6] The three religions divide nine streams (*kiuliu, jiuliu*). We ourselves are the nine streams. We must do this, we must carry the Dao.

You must keep the Dao. Humans can come, and they must return. But now there is no one who wants to return. No one meditates and goes to Heaven. Why not? This is because today men are greedy for office, greedy for women, greedy for money, greedy for power. Once you come to the revolution (*kekbeng*, *geming*), those keeping the *Dao* were no more. Men cannot return; they all go to hell. When you are born, you will come. When you die, it's not definite that you will return. Now, everyone goes to hell. What is it to return? You meditate. Soul and matter, you take these and return. If you go to the prisons of earth, your flesh and bones all go. It's not that you can't return, but you must know how to go back.

We humans all have sin. I have sinned, you have sinned. Humans have sinned, but they still have desire. What is desire? You see the world is so nice, there is much of this in Heaven. The people above want to come down, to accompany each other down. They are asked, "Do you want or not?" "Yes, we want it." This desire is very deep.

People have desire, but they do not know the sorrow. If you know sorrow, you know how to keep the Dao, how to be human. If you want to take the sins, to suffer them, how can you take them? After fifty years, humans can return to Heaven.

This is called 'Following Heaven, following Earth.' Heaven is man's grandfather, father, mother. Earth is our elder brother, elder sister, younger brother, younger sister. This is what you call discussing daoli (*kong toli, jiang daoli*). Now people call this the Dao of association (*poe, pei*). Man's association with woman's Dao is called *ngo bio*; woman's association with man's Dao is called *bok gong*.[7] This human is an example. You must keep the Dao, then after fifty years you can go to Heaven. But you must not be greedy for money, material things, and fame.

You must go to a deep forest, to a clear mountain, and practice the Dao. You practice, and go to Heaven. You must not hear or see men's shadows. You don't want to hear sounds, even the echo of human voices. What do you hear? You hear the sounds of Heaven. Heaven's sounds, Heaven's voice, Heaven's shadow. You hear the sounds of Earth, see the shadows of Earth. Then only can you study the Dao. You don't want to see people. You live in the deep forest, and call the creatures of Heaven and Earth.

What are the creatures of Heaven, what are the creatures of Earth? Creatures that are born of bird's eggs are creatures of Heaven. What are the creatures of Earth? Animals, animals and beasts. Snakes also belong to the Earth. What are the creatures of Water? Tortoise, fish, snake, turtle. Above, bird's eggs, below, pig, dog, beast. These are part of the class of Earth creatures. They have two souls. The Heaven class also has two souls. The Water class also has two souls. If you kill them and compare them, they are the same as humans. The five elements [organs] and the body are the same. He also has a liver, he also has lungs, he also has a heart, he also has a bile, he also has a stomach. They have two souls. If they want to keep the Dao, it takes them 500 years. If humans want to keep the Dao, fifty years. The tree has one soul. If the tree wants to keep the Dao, 10,000 years. He can then rise to become human. This is daoli. In the three religions and the nine streams, no one teaches daoli. No matter what religion it is, it doesn't teach daoli. Daoli is very deep. It is difficult to discuss.

I kept the Dao, and took things lightly in 1945 and 1946. I then began to teach. This thing, the atom bomb, had not yet come. Radiofusion had not yet come. The whole world suffered an epidemic, and I put out a circular, and called men to pray, to do good, to call on Heaven and Earth. I also helped people get food. . . .

If you want to keep the Dao, you must go to the seaside. All five senses are aware, and I am looking. It is like a clock ticking. Monks also sit, but they cannot compete with me. Monks practice empty head meditation. The monk is afraid to get wet in the rain. Monks are like that. If you meditate with closed eyes, this is called practicing Empty Head. Our eyes are open, and all five senses are aware. From this, sun comes out. It's like that. Daoli is very deep.

Humans today, humans from 1951 onwards, changed. How did they change? They changed, then said, "You're old-fashioned," they took the 'old-fashioned' [people] and wanted to split their minds open and wash them.

I said, "Not yet, hold on. To call us old-fashioned is to praise us, it is good. Where do you come from? Let me compare it with this tree. After walking in the heat of the day, people are hot. They stay at the foot of the tree where it is so cool, and they praise the tree. But where does the crown of the tree come from? From whence? The tree's leaves, its beauty comes from where? Below is the shadow of the tree, its broad span, this tree which is so beautiful above us is from where?"

Eng Hok responded, "From the seed?"

Master Poh rejoined, "No! From the 'head' [roots]. If there are no roots, then there will be no crown. [Literally, "If there is no head, there will be no tail."] It's praise to call you old-fashioned! Now they want to eliminate old-fashioned heads. What I say is true." [Having emphatically established his point, he resumed lecturing us.]

I say, you don't know how to return father, return mother, how to return father, return mother with gratitude. You must repay them. You mother bears you for ten months in the womb, bears your burden for ten months. Not a full ten months, but exactly 295 days. You are born then.

When you are born, this is called 'crossing the sea of blood' (*ke huih-hai, guo xuehai*). Below you, all is blood. Your mother is swooning, as if dead. Below is blood. You must cross the sea of blood. When you come, your eyes are open, and your hands are also open. You see the sea of blood and are frightened: your eyes close, and your fist clenches. Your mouth is plugged by blood, dirt (*lasam*) blocks the mouth and your fist clenches. When your eyes meet the blood, they close, the eyelids close, and the hands make a fist. The blood must be removed from your mouth, then you let out three cries: "Wah, wah, wah!" After crossing the sea of blood, you must cross the sea of suffering. The three cries are the sea of suffering.

Now you reject your father and mother. You are unfilial to your parents, to your father, to your mother, to your elders. This is wrong. When you are born, your parents must bear you, they bear eight parts of your sin. Children have what sins? Parents take eight parts, you bear two parts. When you eat, when your parents serve you food, if they don't know how to control you, "This is rice, this is excrement," you don't know anything, everything is just paste. You don't know that this is sin. If your mother doesn't look after you, she will bear eight parts of the sin, you two parts, until you are sixteen, and go out of your mother's home. You arrive at your real self, you worship Heaven and Earth, worship the gods. The mother who gave birth to you gives you life. After you are sixteen, it is your business to repay your sins. She bore you for ten months, and you repay your parents with gratitude.

A bird understands filiality. How is a bird born? From an egg, hatched from a layer of shell. We men are born from the womb. You speak of birds, a bird can repay his parent's love. You are human, but you don't understand how to repay the kindness of your parents. The eggshell hatches what bird? A crow, and in three years the crow must moult. He has no feathers and cannot fly, and will starve. When his stomach is empty, he can cry "Wah, wah, wah," and his grandson will know to feed him worms until his feathers have grown back again. This is called 'repaying kindness.'

You speak of humans, they don't understand how to repay their parents' kindness. You ask, "Is this true or not?" The bird has only two souls, we humans don't understand how to repay our parents' favors. Birds know how. Humans are ungrateful, they don't remember. We humans are born of wombs, we are mammals. Those animals that are hatched from one membrane, from a shell, know how to repay their parents. Humans don't, they don't know how to be a filial son.

Speaking of animals of the earth, which is the most filial? Take the goat. He is born from the womb, like humans. The goat's mother also has tears, like us. When the kid is born, he faces Heaven and kowtows – one, two, three – then he gets to his feet. When he stands up, he is hungry. He kneels on his front legs, and suckles his mother's milk. The goat also is born like humans, and he understands filiality. He eats, and then a bit later, his mother bleats 'Meh' to ask if the kid has eaten his fill yet. This animal cannot speak, and to answer he must nod his head three times, and run against her udders three times. This kid knows how to find his mother when he is hungry, and he knows how to be a filial son. If you are human, you must know how to be a filial son.

Speaking of being bad, the tiger will attack men, tigers can eat people, but you can teach tigers to be obedient. Now tigers are so bad and eat people, but you can tame them. You are a human being, but no one can teach you to be good.

This is born-of-the-womb. Pig, cow, horse, tiger, goat, dog – all are born of the womb. What is it to be righteous (*gi, yi*) or upright (*cheng, zheng*)? Men forget gratitude, and are not righteous. They fail us in loyalty, in righteousness, in filiality (*butdiong, butgi, buthau; wuzhong, wuyi, wuxiao*). If you raise a dog, he cannot speak, but he is the most grateful and the most faithful creature. Now, today, if he does something wrong, he knows that the master will hit him. But he won't keep resentment in his heart. He doesn't criticize or blame the master. Now you go away and return, he sees you and wags his tail. This is called 'having righteousness and loyalty.' A dog understands righteousness and loyalty. You must not be unrighteous and disloyal.

Humans won't listen. Those who are born from eggs, who are wrapped in a single membrane, can obey. You don't know how to obey. A chicken, a duck. This house has chickens, that one has ducks. If you let them out to play, then you call for your chickens, if the master calls for his ducks 'gu gu gu,' they'll understand and return home to eat. Other people's chickens or ducks don't come near. A chicken or a duck can obey. You are human, and you don't obey. This is true, no more, no less! You just let them go, call, they'll return. What use are people? They're no use.

These things, daoli, are very deep, very long. If you want to study the Dao, it is very deep, very long. If you want to study the Dao, you must not covet money, or power, status, or women. You must take the world lightly, and refuse money. You must seek perfection (*choe totek, zuo daode*). You must go to the deep forest to study. After fifty years, you can become an immortal.

These days, people are greedy for women, for power, for money. They hurt people, kill people, set fires – they dare to do this sort of thing. We have this sort of thing. After the Spring Period, no one ascended to Heaven. Gods, immortals, Buddhas – all are humans – but they don't die, and then they do this. Their flesh and bones all return. This is really ascending to Heaven.

You must know, all go to hell. I also will go to hell. You say there is no Heaven, you can see none? Now, people don't know anything. This is called 'escaping' (*thoat, to*).

What soul doesn't die? The heart soul doesn't die. The material soul (*imhun, yinhun*), the intelligence soul (*lenghun, linghun*), the heart soul (*simhun, xinhun*). One doesn't die, two die. The heart soul flies. I don't know what it wants to join up with. This soul must go and combine. How to combine? You must have good deeds, good morals (*totek, daode*). A good rebirth is a reward for your good deeds. Then only can you combine with a human womb and be reborn.

If you're not good, you will go and join with animals of the Heavens, Earth, Water. These animals, worms, grass. Grass also has one soul. If there is no soul, there is no life. You must not misunderstand. Trees also have one soul. If you are a tree and want to migrate (*chian, qian*), you cannot go so fast, you need 10,000 years. You want to know these things. These matters are very deep.

If you want to talk, I haven't talked of this for many years. If I'm to speak, I must speak the whole thing. Twenty or more years I haven't lectured people to do good (*khoansian, quanshan*). In Singapore they called me to write a book, they called me to exhort people to do good. I said, "I don't want to do it, I take the world lightly. If you have money, the money is yours. But when you're born, you don't bring it, and when you die, you don't take it." Life is like that, good or bad, you don't know.

Every child must pass four months. Four months, 120 days, then only the hand can open. If not, it doesn't open. One day less than this, the hand will not open. If you study this just right, before four months the hand will not open. Close, open, close, open . . . not so readily.

After that, the hand is open. Good, bad, you still don't know. When the person leaves, only then can you see. You go to Hell empty. You don't go to Heaven. If you go to Heaven, flesh and bones go, you leave no bit behind. If you don't go to Hell, then you don't even leave a hair behind on earth. You want to know heavenly things. When all is taken back, only then is this called Heaven. No matter how you worship, everyone goes to Hell.

You go to Hell, the prisons of earth. You cannot go to Heaven. In the prisons of earth, you have one name. Monks are also the same. Do you go to the West? No. To the Western Paradise? No, you go to hell. You call the monk and ask him. He says *A-mi-to-hut* (*Amitofo*), but he also goes to hell. What is *to*? What is *hut*? *Hut-to*, where is it? *La-mo-o-fi-to, la-mo-o-fi-to* — what is that? What explanation is there? This is very deep.

This question of how the gods came, this matter we cannot discuss very clearly for you. History, if you want to hear this you must find someone 200 years old, then you can know. If you want to know about going to Heaven, there is a living prophet. He will know. China has these people.

This prophet is living. When he dies, he also goes to hell. Every generation has living prophets. These people can clarify this matter of going to Heaven. Others won't know. Others must do good deeds, be moral, save the world, then they can know a little bit, but they cannot know these things to the bottom. These things are done like this: when you believe, they appear, a shadow that men can see, they can move and walk, already this is good. If you hurt men, then no more.

This tree must cultivate morality (*siuheng, xiuxing*) for 10,000 years. Humans must cultivate morality for fifty years, then they can become reborn at a higher level. Sky animals, Earth animals, Water animals, after 500 years they can be reborn on a higher level. These things are very deep.

Now, I don't have the heart. Twenty years ago I let go. Now I don't meditate. If you want to meditate, you must go at dawn, at 4:00 a.m., go to the seaside and sit in a lotus position and watch the sun rise. You must open your eyes, you cannot close them. The body is aware. Your eyes are facing toward the sun, looking. At night, there's the moon. It's called 'entering the pure flower.' You also can do this with the setting sun. When it is dark, and there is moonlight, you cannot meditate. This is called 'entering the pure flower.' You cannot do any good things, any bad things.

In the early days, when you are inexperienced, you will know things that you did when you meditate. You will be afraid, you won't want to do these things again. Things that have passed, you will see, and they will frighten you.

In the world today, people do as they like. There is no distinction between men and women, and people are immoral. No one knows how to divide Heaven and Earth, no one understands principles. They lack reason. Officials, those in the government, are the same. They also don't 'follow the road.' Do you know what this is called? This is a 'gold-money world.' If you murder someone, you can fix it so that there's no trial. The money is given to you [by your fate], and in a 'gold-money world,' money buys a life. It's true. If you have money you can murder men. It's a gold-money world.

If you have money, you can talk. If you have no money, no matter what you say, it's not the truth. I call this a 'glass' but you say 'cup.' I say that 'glass' is more correct, but I don't have money. You have money, and you say that 'cup' is more correct, so it's 'glass' that's wrong. If you have money, everyone speaks your language. He says 'glass' is right and I say 'cup.' I have no money, so even if I'm right, he will say I'm wrong. It's like that. Most people call this a 'biscuit' but he calls it 'cake,' even though most people say 'biscuit.' If you have money, people will speak your language.

People see what is good. Everyone says that they want to be filial, and that people ought to be honest. No one intends to do people in recklessly, or to injure them by talking behind their backs.

Do you want to obey me or not? If not, I can repeat myself a hundred times, you know. If you don't want to obey, then think it over slowly. If you understand how to think about people, then you will hear me and know that I'm right. You must study this yourselves. Good.

Now, I tell you not to hurt people, but you defy me. You say, "No," you don't want to hear this. I say, "Don't go and steal." You say, "If I don't steal, I don't eat." But 'Heaven will not starve people to death.' You want to have your needs satisfied, you want your children to eat. 'For every blade of grass a drop of dew.' The grass is dry, but if a drop of dew touches it, it will grow so green and beautiful. It will be so dry and withered, but will bloom with a drop of rainwater. 'One blade of grass, one drop of dew.'

But you want to do things like that. You tell him not to, but he wants it like that. He definitely wants to be a success. These days people are like this: "Do it now, get it now, it's okay now." They say that if you 'do good' then your descendants get nothing. If you 'do bad,' then at least they'll get something: 'Be fierce, be poisonous, ride a horse, ki-kok. Good heart, good manner, no food to eat, no clothes to wear.' That sentence you will understand – it belongs to the old language. He says, "If I do good, I don't get anything: Good heart, good manner, no food to eat, no clothes to wear." Bad-hearted people say, "Be fierce, be poisonous, do bad, set fires, ride a horse." He rides a horse [enjoys high status], but there will be a day. The next generation will suffer. No one takes notice of people who are good. But the future generations will be better off. These days you cannot find three consecutive generations rich. After two generations, the wealth is gone. If you are impatient to get, you are not thinking of the next generation. Have you no concern for your children and grandchildren? If you want to understand, it's like that.

Now I don't need to do it. People are proud, they won't take notice of you or mix, you're hurt. These things are like that. I don't look at you and ask what religion you practice. Daoism is fine, Buddhism is fine, it doesn't bother me. I want to call you to do good. The real religion is the Three Doctrines (*Samkau, Sanjiao*).

This divides into five types. Red, yellow, white, black, coffee. Also four types of hair. Red hair, yellow hair, black hair, brown hair. The same, all together the same. The organs are the same, the body structure is the same. But when men speak, their speech is not the same. He speaks English, he speaks Hindi, he speaks Bengali, he speaks Malay, he speaks German, they all are different. Within the Chinese race, the yellow race, there are also differences. Within the Chinese race there are Hok Chiu, Teo Chiu also belongs to the yellow race, Hong Kong also belongs to the yellow race, he is Hainanese, he also belongs to the yellow race, Shanghai, Keng Hua, all are part of the yellow race. The languages they speak are not the same. Inside the five races, these divide into red, yellow, white, black, and brown. There are also four types of hair: red, yellow, black, brown. The elements and the body are the same. We are all part of the Nine Streams.

In our bodies are eight 'people.' Three: Daoism [he touches his forehead], Buddhism [he touches his left shoulder], and Confucianism [he touches his right shoulder]. Inside, there are five elements. Gold is the heart, wood is the liver, water is the stomach, fire is the lungs, earth is the kidneys. There are five 'people' inside. Dogs are the same, birds are the same, pigs are the same. If you kill them, their organs are the same. But they only have two souls, and their eyes are on the side. Their eyes are not centred, are not parallel with the ground. If their vision is carried straight, and their eyes are parallel to the ground, then they can see ghosts. Ah – you can understand.

Birds have vision on the side. There are four types. The four types of birds are called: night birds, they are also called 'ghost birds.' Their eyes are straight like humans, owls are like this. These are birds [he only tells about one type of bird]. These are birds. Birds have one membrane. Man, pig, horse, dog, goat, tiger, these are born of the womb. Taishang Laojun (*Laozi*) says that if it has ears on the side, then it is a mammal. Birds have one membrane, they are born from the shell. They are also animals. Chickens and ducks are the same. Fish are also from eggs. They are born of a membrane. After the bird's egg comes out, it has a hard shell. When it is just born it is soft, but when exposed to air it becomes hard. . . .

When they are born, people encounter air. They blow out air. Ah – you want to understand. It's not that this is a big breath, when you are born you are small. But when you encounter the air, you take a large breath. To understand, you must know the reasons. These things are very deep. I must prove these matters fact by fact. For over twenty years, I haven't talked about this. If you want to talk, it's very easy – we must find a quiet and serene time.

If you want to meditate, I also can challenge you to sit. I can do all of these things. If you want to challenge me to see how long I can bear to sit in meditation, you can. I can meditate for three days and three nights.

In Tanjung Bungah, someone claimed he could meditate for forty-nine days in a glass cabinet with no gaps or crevices. I asked him, "Are there air holes or not?" He said, "No." I gave him seven days, challenged him to sit for three days, even. He managed one day and one night. He could not do it. He could do it in the open air, he could meditate for a month. If he had had fresh air he could have done it. But in that cabinet even ants would have died. If you haven't kept the way enough, you must not try this sort of thing.

Indians, in India, have this magic power. If you dig a hole and bury someone for forty-nine days, when you dig them up, they'll still be fine. They have the skills to do this. If you haven't studied enough, no one will acknowledge you, you speak of immortals – "Not true"; you speak of Buddha – "Not true"; you speak of the gods – "Not true." No one will acknowledge you. If you meet the standard, people will acknowledge you, no matter what you say, they will have faith in you. If you say, "Immortal" – "Immortal." If you say "Dao" – "Dao." You can talk about anything – you have met the standard. You can say anything, name anything.

Our Bodhidharma lived on the wall, for three years he didn't touch the ground. Bodhidharma became a god, became a saint, by hanging on the wall.[8] This is 'going to Heaven,' 'performing miracles.' Bodhidharma was from India, but India doesn't have this sort of person. They themselves influenced China. Did you know? They spread these arts, and gave them to us Chinese. China now has this sort of man. They came across, bringing books, and showed people how to do things. Bodhidharma came and opened up the road. They taught exercises, how to walk, how to let the blood circulate. This is Bodhidharma's art.

If you want to 'climb,' to practice, you can. But you can also do this in your home. Before these books were produced, before they came to China, people could do these things. If they meditated they could, when they slept they also could. I can make sounds without any movement, I can still do this even after I've done it a hundred times. I can release my veins like that.

This is the power of Immortals, of Buddha, of the Dao. The Dao, Buddha, the Immortals. This method is very deep. You cannot say all. If you do not control your breathing, you cannot perform.

In a life, you are given just so much money. You speak of money as yours, and if you have lots it's better. These things are borrowed to use, lent to you to use, if you have money you can eat. We come to earth for a few decades, only a few decades. It's not to say that you have eternal life.

In the old days, people lived for several centuries. Ancestor Pi (Pi Cho) lived for 803 years, have you heard of her? Ancestor Pi lived until 803 years old. In the end, what happened? Small ghosts discovered her age, which had been kept a secret. They took her and sent her to hell.

Every generation asked why this person was still here, 803 years old! Hell sent these small ghosts to take her, to see. They went to a river (here we call it *kang*, in China they call it *kuei*), and they set to washing charcoal. She asked "What are you doing?" and they said, "We're washing charcoal until it's white." She said, "I've eaten for 803 years, and I've never seen charcoal that could be washed white!" So, they took her.

China still has people who live until 140. They're still strong, they can ride a bike, they can travel around, can walk. China also has people who are 160 – you can go and see. Before, people had long lives. Now, they only live a few years. See the story, "The Princess causes the Downfall of the King." These old men don't even shiver in cold weather, whereas men in their thirties or forties shiver (he imitates their teeth chattering).

You must look in *The Canonization of Deities* and the hell book for stories about hell, the fairy fox. *The Canonization of Deities* has all the stories of the Middle Period. Immortals, Buddha, the Dao, Hell, everything is there. These things are very old, several thousand years old. They go back, they begin when Heaven and Earth were opened and go on until the present. These things are very deep. They date back to the beginning of the Middle Period."

He gestured to the altar, to a candelabrum with seven small oil lamps. "That was given by a Christian, a Catholic. He lit it for a month." (In retrospect, perhaps he hoped that I would make a similar offering as evidence of my respect for him and his teachings.)

He continued:

If you don't keep correctness (*siucheng*, *xiuzheng*), then even if I teach you, it's no use. You must have patience, and have a sincere heart. Men don't interfere with these things. It's like, with these things, it's like the clock will go, the clock's gears. If you meditate, you cannot practice, then stop, practice, then stop, study, then stop. You must keep to it and practice. If you want to get things, to do things, you cannot. You must have time, and you must control your heart. You must have time to do this, time to go. You eat, but when the time comes, you must practice and study. It's like that. You must have the time. Some will gossip, will say that this is not the path, people are like that.

If ordinary people eat one bowl of rice, the person following a religious path won't even get this, he will eat half a bowl of rice. But this man really practices to the right degree. Saints come to test you. These saints you cannot see. He comes, and you don't know what to say. He is wealthy, but you won't know what kind of man he is. These people will test you. They wear dirty clothes. But the man is a saint. He tests your heart to see if there are good deeds, if you have a good heart or not. But you chase him away, like you would chase an animal, "Ke! ke! ke! ke!" You look – "Ke! ke! ke! ke!" You must not look high, you must not look low. You say, he has money, so I come, he hasn't got any, so I'll cut him. You cannot. He still is the same man. He comes to save men. You must know these things.

Good children, how old are you? A few years ago, did you see the paper? There was a man who carried a broken vegetable basket, he carried a broken basket, wore filthy clothes, and carried a broken umbrella. He wore his clothes until they were filthy. The government caught him, and in his basket, his broken basket, was $6,000 and checkbooks for three banks. He was a beggar. If you gave to him, okay, he didn't bother you. He walked along the road, and whether or not you gave to him, he would just walk on. The government caught him.

. . . What sort of man is this? He is a boss. In Butterworth there was a man who carried a broken umbrella, he owned half of Butterworth but he walked on the road. People would look at him and tell him to go away, "Ki! ki! ki!" People like this are different. But people cannot see it. This is called 'to rise above' (*tengseng, shangsheng*).

When you're born, you bring nothing, when you leave, you take nothing. You have enough to make life enjoyable. I lack, and life is not enjoyable. You have plenty, I do not. . . . You're more comfortable, I don't have any, if I want to use it, I don't have it. Your life is better, mine is worse. It's like that. These things are very deep.

There are many deep doctrines. The Three Religions is not divisive. All the same, it does not call people to be divided. This is done by people. They don't follow the law. "Now I want to do it." Ah! "This is more true, that's not true." Inside all [religions are] the same, but this is done by people. The god doesn't ask you to be like this, the religion doesn't ask you to do this. Buddhism, Daoism, Confucianism, all call you to follow the law. Men call you to do this, do that, they belong in order to find excitement. It's like that. It's done by people. Gods, no. "You want to believe, come." You want to believe, call a god to descend. You want to believe in Buddha, Buddha descends. You want to believe in Jesus, Jesus comes down. He doesn't call you, no. You don't want to believe, he also doesn't call you, no. Does he come down to save you? No! People save you. We people save ourselves. Heh – you say that your god is more efficacious. "No! Mine is more efficacious! Yours is not true." These things are done by people. Like this, we are forever splintered. The gods of Chinese religion do not call people to be like this. These are the faults of people. Our minds are too cunning, our hearts don't obey.

Your mouth says this, but it's not in your heart. The black race understands, but we don't understand. You ask the Malays [he speaks Malay], "If you want to be a Haji, what do you need? If you want to be a Haji, what must you take?" "Your heart. You must wear your heart. If your heart walks on the right path, then you can pray and become a Haji. Otherwise you will not meet Allah." These things cannot be seen.

Conclusion

Master Poh's teachings describe a moral stance rooted in Confucianism, Buddhism, and Daoism. His discourse emphasized an order that distinguished Heaven and Earth, above and below, elder and junior. His discussion of moral virtue based that virtue on a logic of obligation: for example, people owed filial gratitude to their parents because they had taken on the burden of their children's sins and the responsibility for their moral education. He also stressed the naturalness of these virtues, suggesting for example that goats knew how to feel gratitude toward their parents, dogs were loyal and forgiving to their owners, and birds took care of their elders when they moulted and were helpless. Indeed, he concluded that by contrast with animals, people were 'no use.'

Master Poh's teachings also contextualized human life in the larger framework that stressed again and again that all humans are fundamentally the same despite their different colors and languages. As he noted, we share a common biology: our internal organs are the same and we are all born in exactly the same way. He contextualized humans in the natural world, identifying them as mammals, by contrast with animals that laid eggs. He classified the natural world (including humans) into Heaven, Earth, and Water classes, a fundamental cosmological triad that I suggest elsewhere also underlies Penang's three major festivals to the Lord of Heaven, the Hungry Ghosts, and the Nine Emperor Gods (DeBernardi 2004; see also 1992). In turn, he ranked the natural world in terms of the number of souls (trees have one, humans have three), and the length of time that it would take for various living beings to achieve transcendence of the cycle of death and rebirth.

Let me close with Master Poh's recollections on his mediation practice. In our second interview with him, he vividly described his extraordinary ability to meditate as a foundation for his religious authority, but also as a source for visions, prophecies, and teachings that spirits gave him to pass on to others. As he explained it, when he meditated by the seaside, he absorbed "a ray of the golden flower." He could see his past deeds, but he also received messages from the spirits calling him to "explain these things to people, print books for men, and call people to do good." As the result of his meditation practice, he even was able to know the future.

He noted that while he meditated, poisonous things tested him, but his own soul protected him from harm:

Gods, Immortals, Buddhas, they come to test you. We call this *lengtong*. This *ling* soul, this intelligence, itself appears. This magical appearance is *lengtong*. Do you know, this heavenly spirit nourishes you, he comes to save you. Dirty things, powerful things, poisonous things try to approach you. How is it when these things approach you? You must be firm. These things, your own *lengtong*, these pure things come to protect you. He protects you, but you don't see it. You can't see it.

Thus the heavenly spirit is both within and without.

Although he had been famous in Penang for his meditation practice and spiritual powers, Master Poh had ceased to meditate and to teach others, disillusioned with the 'gold-money' world in which he lived. He explained:

I studied the Dao and saw through life's vanities (*khoaphoa; kanpo*), and in 1948 I exhorted people to do good. This was before the time of the atom bomb, before electric lights, television, or Radiofusion. One year, the world suffered from an epidemic. I called on people to worship Heaven and Earth. I put out a circular calling them to pray with fruits and flowers, to do good, to call on Heaven and Earth, and I helped people get food. But some fooled people, and cheated the gods. They took wax fruit and called it 'fruit,' they took fake flowers and invoked Heaven and Earth. How could they fool people with wax fruits? The cheaters said: "People make money." I saw that it was like that, and I didn't want to bother any more.

The substitution of fake fruit for real fruit in worship is an image for a materialism and greed that leads men to esteem profit over value. Chinese offer the 'essence' to the gods before enjoying food offerings themselves: wax fruit has no essence for either gods or humans.

CHAPTER SIX

The Teachings of a Modern Master

B Y THE LATE NINETEENTH CENTURY, anglicized Straits Chinese in the Straits Settlements (Penang, Singapore, and Malacca) had embraced Enlightenment ideals of scientific progress and representative government and they contributed to the reform of China. Although the anglicized Straits Chinese were progressive and modern in their outlook, that did not mean they abandoned Chinese culture. Indeed, some self-consciously fashioned themselves as culturally dualistic mediators at the crossroads of civilizations, cosmopolitans who innovated and reformed and revitalized traditional cultural forms in light of their experiences and knowledge.[1]

As I discuss in Chapter Five, in the mid-1960s Master Poh retired from proselytizing his sectarian worldview. The spiritual master whose teaching I discuss in this chapter, by contrast, developed healing and teaching practices that addressed the desire of modern, literate, urban Chinese to know their own traditions. English-educated, in his youth Lim Peng Eok had aspired to further education in England and studied for the Cambridge Exams, with the Bible as his special subject. He failed those exams, which he attributed to his 'never agreeing' with his teachers, but he had a successful career teaching art in one of Penang's most elite English-language secondary schools, the Penang Free School.

Master Lim's approach to instruction differed in two important ways from that of other spirit mediums. First, many of the other mediums recommended that I read popular narratives like *The Canonization of Deities*, but few directed me to read classics like the *Daodejing* or the *Yijing*. Master Lim himself had translated the *Journey to the North* into an English version for his followers, providing important names and terms in both Hokkien and Chinese characters, and several of his disciples mentioned that he was a well-versed storyteller. But he pointed out to me that the worship of deities and the histories of the gods were less important than an understanding of the Dao, and in his classes he taught the *Daodejing* and the *Yijing* as the foundation for that understanding.

Second, spirit mediums sometimes offered their teachings during the staged, formal context of the trance performance while they were possessed by the gods. By contrast, in Master Lim's class, we read the texts together and he offered authoritative commentary on chapters of the *Daodejing* in a side room of the temple, wearing ordinary street clothes. Although his style was unconventional, nonetheless Master Lim's devotees regarded him as an incarnate deity and a spiritually powerful ally.

Like other spirit mediums, Master Lim had disciples, but these were not youthful students of martial arts; rather, they were English-educated, middle-class Chinese, including a medical doctor, a professor, and a stock analyst. During the period in which I joined their class, they met with Master Lim every Saturday to read and discuss the *Daodejing*. Usually the discussion lasted an hour, followed by a fifteen-minute period of meditation in the main hall of the temple. After this, the temple caretakers served a light vegetarian meal to the class, and informal discussion continued for another hour or so.

In these Saturday classes, Master Lim alternated between reading the English translation and reading the original Chinese text in 'deep' or 'literary' Hokkien, and his commentary and the discussion also moved back and forth between English and Hokkien. He commented on the *Daodejing* by recounting his life experiences, and also told stories that transformed Penang's social and physical landscape, its ethnic groups, families, streets, and trees into images of the Dao. In adopting this method of instruction, Master Lim bridged the gap between cultural and linguistic traditions for his students.

As an integrative cosmopolitan, he often juxtaposed lines from the *Daodejing* with lines from the Bible or from English poems, and found congruent or parallel messages in the two traditions. He did not confine himself to the teachings of a single tradition, and although he focused his teachings on the Dao, he cited a Sinhalese Theravada Buddhist monk as one of his important influences, and also recommended to me books by two Western authors who had gone to the East to study Hinduism and Buddhism.[2] He claimed to have been Penang's only religious teacher for over thirty years. He said that he had done this on his own, adding that if the immortals did not save humans, then human life would be hopeless.

Many aspects of his teaching practice, however, do suggest a universalist background similar to that of Master Poh. Both insisted that *real* religion should be distinguished from dogmatic sectarianism, and that there were many paths to salvation. Both also emphasized that the individual should follow a path of ascetic self-cultivation in the form of physical and moral self-control. Physical self-control focused on meditation and breathing exercises, whereas moral self-control included obeying elders, following a simple life, and knowing how to be human.

Like Master Poh, Master Lim promised that humans could escape from the unending cycle of death and rebirth if they achieved the Dao through self-cultivation. He, too, distinguished between saints and immortals:[3]

> Confucius is a saint (*sin, shen*), not an immortal (*sian, xian*). He is not so deep. Saints and immortals are not the same. 'Immortal' means enlightened, and immortals are worshipped. Saints are not worshipped. Immortals have power, they can help people, they can save people. Saints cannot, immortals can. Men who achieved the Dao can change into immortals. If you pass over the ninth plane of existence, or life, then you can become an immortal.

At another meeting with him he explained that immortal ancestors (*siancho·, xianzu*) were saviors born of the light of god. "No one teaches about this," he added. "The Daoist priest won't know. He is afraid to tend immortal ancestors. To teach this is Chinese, to really worship deities." We may also translate *Cho· (Zu)* as 'patriarch' or 'founder,' as this kind of ancestor is usually the founder of a religious sect. Among the deities worshipped at this temple as immortal ancestors were Shakyamuni Buddha, Amitabha Buddha, the Goddess of Mercy, the Emperor of the Dark Heavens, the hero of *Journey to the North*, and Lü Dongbin, who is one of the Eight Immortals.

He explained the salvation work of immortal ancestors as being a form of spiritual healing, and attributed some illnesses to collisions with unseen forces:

> When you treat illness, you must diagnose both the physical and the spiritual. The physical can be well and the spiritual sick, or the physical can be sick and the spiritual well. If the spiritual is ill, then you need a spiritual cure, if the problem is a spiritual collision (*tioh hoan, de fan*). Real illness, or a spiritual collision, you can diagnose the difference easily. If the problem is physical, then you give medicine, either Chinese or European.

After describing a few miraculous cures, he concluded, "Everyone is the same. To be human is this heart."

Master Lim's work as a teacher who wholly embodied an ancestor-teacher (*cho·su, zushi*) may be rooted in a Chinese sectarian tradition of leadership through founding patriarchs (*zu*) who are believed to have exceptional supernatural powers, including the power to become reincarnate Buddhas or deities (Topley 1963: 376). We must consider whether the textual construction that is the patriarch's life does not include a very real form of immortality, as he lives generation after generation, incarnated again and again in the bodies of his disciples.

Although he may have been influenced by one or more sectarian movements, either through participation or the study of written works, he undoubtedly also innovated in developing new ways to practice and teach Chinese religious culture. Master Lim's father also had been a spirit medium, but he nonetheless claimed that no one, including his father, had taught him the inner meaning of Chinese religious practices. Indeed, he concluded that because Chinese popular religious culture remained unsystematic, its meanings unexplained to its practitioners, Chinese had no choice but to go to Theravada Buddhist temples to study religion.

In his autobiography, Master Lim also mentions in passing the intriguing detail that he had attended meetings of the Penang Theosophical Society. As I discuss in the Introduction, Theosophy was a Western universalistic movement based on a syncretic amalgamation of Hinduism, Buddhism, and Western esoteric philosophy that introduced and popularized Asian religious and philosophical ideas in the West but also among English-educated Asian elites. Master Lim taught his students Buddhism using *The Light of Asia*, an epic poem written by theosophist Edwin Arnold and published in 1879 (Arnold 1995 [1879]), together with the Heart Sutra, a short sutra embraced by Chan Buddhists that teaches the ultimate insight that all form and consciousness are identical with the void and nothingness.

Master Lim also was deeply influenced by the modernist form of Theravada Buddhism that Sri Lankan missionary monks introduced to Malaysia. He identified as Malaysia's chief priest the head monk at a well-known Sinhalese Buddhist Temple in Kuala Lumpur, and praised him for teachings. Although he did not name the monk, he undoubtedly referred to Ven. K. Sri Dhammananda.

In 1895, Sinhalese Buddhists formed the Sasana Abhiwurdhi Wardhana Society in Malaya, which established Kuala Lumpur's Maha Vihara on Brickfields Road. Although initially built to serve the needs of the immigrant Sinhalese community, this center became especially renowned after Ven. K. Sri Dhammananda joined it in 1951. In post-war Malaya, Christian evangelists, blocked from entry into China, were actively seeking converts among Chinese and Indians. Ven. Dhammananda decided to embark on Buddhist missionary outreach, initiating a lively program of itinerant evangelism, regular lectures, and publication in order to reach Malaysians of all ethnic backgrounds.[4] He had the benefit of an extensive course of Buddhist training, including training in Sanskrit, Pali scriptures, and Buddhist philosophy at Vidyalankara Pirivena Buddhist College in Sri Lanka and a Masters degree in Indian Philosophy from Benares Hindu University (Sasana Abhiwurdhi Wardhana Society 2002).

When I first was in Penang, still undecided as to the final focus of my research, two university students who were keen Buddhists visited several times to discuss

Buddhism with me, and made gifts of a number of pamphlets written by Ven. Dhammananda. In 1962, he established the Buddhist Missionary Society. By 1980 the society had published twenty books, a magazine (*Voice of Buddhism*), numerous cassette tapes of Pali chanting and Buddhist talks, and nineteen pamphlets for free distribution (Buddhist Missionary Society N.d.). The outreach effort has continued, and many of these publications are now available for purchase or download on a website created in 2002 to celebrate Ven. Dhammananda's fiftieth anniversary in Malaysia (Sasana Abhiwurdhi Wardhana Society 2002).

Many of Ven. Dhammananda's essays argue for the compatibility of Buddhism with modern values. He openly debates Christian missionaries and modern materialists, noting that in the course of 450 years of foreign rule, colonial rulers and missionaries often suppressed and denigrated Buddhism. To give but one of many examples, he cites a poem that a Bishop Herber wrote in which he describes the Sinhalese people as blind heathens:

> In vain with lavish kindness
> The gifts of God are strewn
> The heathen in his blindness
> Bow down to wood and stone.

Ven. Dhammananda concludes that this poem demonstrates that the missionaries had an evil motive when they tried to introduce their religion "in the name of social advancement and foreign education," and praises the brave Sinhalese who protected their religion against this foreign incursion (Dhammananda N.d.a: 4).

In his pamphlets, Ven. Dhammananda argues that far from being superstitious, Buddhism is a rational, pragmatic religion that is fully compatible with the findings of modern science. He compares Buddhist teachings to those of Western philosophers, psychologists, and scientists, noting, for example, that Buddhist teachings are not incompatible with Darwin's ideas:

This is a religion which always encourages man to face facts of life without acting as a hypocrite and to accept the truth what or whenever it may be. Therefore, Buddhists do not reject the facts pertaining to worldly matters discovered by great thinkers and scientists (Dhammananda 1977: 9).

He also describes Buddhism as "scientific, modern, and essentially progressive" (Dhammananda N.d.b: 41). Buddhism, he notes, is a practical religion that teaches people how to behave in relation to those around them, promoting responsibility, humility, gratitude, tolerance, patience, understanding, forgiveness, and moral action (Dhammananda N.d.c).

When he sets out the Buddhist moral and ethical code, Ven. Dhammananda stresses that Buddhism is not a religion of faith, but rather "a religion based on morality, concentration and wisdom." He argues that the religion is necessary for all humans: "By practicing a rational religion he can train himself to live as a cultured man and finally to be able to achieve eternal peace and happiness. His wealth, academical knowledge, name, power and other embellishments cannot give him his peace of mind and happiness" (Dhammananda N.d.b: 37).

In his pamphlets, Ven. Dhammananda provides extensive advice for the lay Buddhist, describing correct conduct in moral obligations but also promoting moderate reforms in the way that Malaysian Chinese practice religion, replacing costly Daoist funeral services, for example, with religious or charitable donations (Dhammananda 1976: 14–16). He also promotes a doctrine of self-reliance. In the pamphlet entitled *You Are Responsible*, for example, he argues for human agency, asserting that a person's sorrows and miseries are not caused by a family curse, or the original sin of some ancestor, nor by the God or the Devil or Mara, but rather by the person's own self. "Your sorrow is your own making. You are your own jailor; you are your own liberator" (Dhammananda N.d.c: 1).

Finally, although many have noted the contribution that Buddhism made to the development of Sri Lankan nationalism, Ven. Dhammananda emphasizes its universalism:

The kinship of blood and race and the welding power of nationality, these are nothing compared with the kinship of ideas, for instance, like those of universal compassion and harmlessness put into action and spreading wide the spirit of a true culture. . . . The power of the kinship of pure consciousness is better and firmer than that of family or nation. Great and pure ideas can unite peoples living far apart who have not seen each other or who have not directly contacted one another. That is the real power of truth. . . . (Dhammananda N.d.b: 44).

Because his approach is inclusive, he can claim that Buddhists comprise a quarter of the world's population (Dhammananda 1977: 4).[5]

Many of these teachings find an echo in Master Lim's, including the emphasis on the importance of morality, spirituality, and self-reliance. But Master Lim critically noted that no teaching – apart, of course, from his own classes – was being done in Chinese temples:

Chinese religion explains all. But people who came here did not know, no explanation was available to them. It is very intricate. My father didn't teach me these things. I went to worship, and the gods scolded me!

He recalled that he had begun praying at the time he left Penang to take up a teaching post in Singapore in 1932.

Master Lim's life story, as recalled in his autobiography, suggests that although his stature as a spiritual leader was high, his spiritual training in Chinese religion was improvised and eclectic. Whereas Ven. Dhammananda pursued higher degrees in Buddhism and Hinduism in Ceylon and India, no such options were available to a Chinese in colonial Malaya who was keenly interested in China's Three Religions. Nonetheless, in his practice of spirit mediumship, Master Lim sought to create a form of Daoist religious practice that would appeal to modern, educated Malaysians, without over-rationalizing its mysterious foundation. Although he may have admired Ven. Dhammananda, he did not engage in an ambitious program of missionary outreach and publication like that of the Sinhalese Theravada Buddhists.

Becoming a Master

In his autobiography, Master Lim explains in some detail how he developed his spiritual gifts in his teens and twenties. As I mention in Chapter Two, when he was seventeen Master Lim became ill and recovered only after a Thai monk tended him. At that time, he heard a mysterious voice tell him, "You will not die. Until your work is done you will not die," but he did not know what that work would be. But when he went to Singapore he began to develop his healing powers, and the mysterious voice advised him that if he were to touch someone with his hand, that person would recover. He did not entirely believe this, and did not practice healing by touch until his return to Penang just before the end of World War II.

Before he went to Singapore, he trained in Penang to qualify as a teacher. He offered a story describing difficulties he encountered under the colonial system, hinting that his turn to Chinese religion was a form of resistance against racial and cultural arrogance that he encountered there:

At that time, I was doing my training to be a teacher. A Miss Lukas was then head of the program, and she came and sat in on my class to evaluate my teaching. I was teaching English, and I taught the word 'municipal.'

She interrupted and said: "Excuse me, but you're teaching that incorrectly. It should be 'muni-_ci_-pal.' "

"No," I said. "Mu-_ni_-cipal" is correct."

"No," she said, "Muni-_ci_-pal."

So I went after class and found the largest dictionary that I could find, and I went to her office. I said, "Look. It's 'mu-_ni_-cipal.' "

She looked and said, "Yes. But anyway, you shouldn't disagree with me."

This was 1932. The British were like that. They were the 'first eldest' (_toe it tua, diyida_).

Master Lim added that when he got his results, he learned that he had a distinction on the written part of the examination, but had failed the practical. On learning what had happened, the Inspector of Schools, T. A. O. Sullivan, arranged for him to retake the practical, which he passed. At that time, however, no jobs were available in Penang. He accepted a job in Singapore, and remained there from 1932 until 1944.

In Singapore, he lived with an aunt whom he described in his autobiography as a "rather pious woman," and he accompanied her to the Goddess of Mercy (*Guanyin*) temple on the first and fifteenth of every lunar month. At that time, he began to have vivid dreams of Gautama Buddha and Guanyin, from which he usually woke up at 3:00 a.m. In one of these dreams, Guanyin appeared in the sky above him as he stood on a high cliff that overlooked the sea. Frightened, he ran home. The goddess pursued him, and an excited crowd gathered. People tried to touch the hem of her robe for luck, but the goddess evaded them, stopping at the door of his aunt's house. She called his name, and when he did not respond, she waved her whisk and the front door flew open. She entered and came directly to Lim. He knelt down, and she asked why he had not come when she called him. He replied, "All the others could not get near you. How could I?" She responded, "Oh, no, you must not speak like that. Next time I call you, you must come." He assented, and she took a scroll from her robes and gave it to him. He took the scroll and woke up.

Master Lim's dream narratives all point to the conclusion that he had special spiritual powers. Like the narratives explaining how spirit mediums came to be possessed by their gods, his stories suggest that he was chosen by the gods to do spiritual healing, and that his powers were innate. For example, he recounts that while he was in Singapore, a friend invited him to celebrate Buddha's birthday at his uncle's house. Although he did not know how to chant sutras, he listened to the chanting, and had an uncanny experience:

I felt the whole scene vanish in front of me. Everything grew dark and I felt drawn back into the past. It was as if I was taken back a few thousand years. There was a bright light on the top of my head and I heard the sutra being chanted softly but distinctly. I remained in that state for as long as the chanting of the sutra lasted. Then I felt myself being transported back to the place where I was sitting" (Lim 1969: 5).

Later he asked his friend to read to him the sutras that they had chanted that night, and discovered that it was the *Prajna Paramita Hridaya*, that had put him into this extraordinary state. This work, popularly known as the Heart Sutra, is attributed to the salvific bodhisattva Avalokitesvara, whom Penangites venerate as the Goddess of Mercy (*Kuan Yin, Guanyin*). He discovered that he could recite the text without looking at the book.

His friend's uncle gave him a book of sutras, and a month or two later Lim put out three small cups of tea, some flowers, and three lighted joss sticks as offerings, and prayed. Although the extraordinary experience did not repeat itself, he did feel "a quietness of spirit in me." He prayed again the next night, and again on the third night. This time he had another powerful experience:

That night after reading a few pages of the book I happened to glance up into the dark sky. As I looked I saw a white speck of light. The white speck became a vertical line and soon became the three sides of a door. The door opened and light shone out of it. The light was very bright and at the bottom of the door, steps appeared leading from the door to my window sill. As I looked, many Buddhas in yellow robes came out from the door. They descended the steps one by one. All of them were shining with light, each had his own individual light and they seem to light up the sky. As each one reached the window he stepped into the room and took his place alongside the wall, until the room was filled up. All the while I was awe-struck by what I saw, and instead of reading the prayers, I watched silently at the proceedings before me. In my heart I was afraid that I had done something wrong, so I knelt there in silence. But as the last Buddha came in and took his place with the others he looked at me and told me to go on reading. I went on as instructed. When I had finished all of them turned towards me and bowed, I bowed too and one by one they ascended the steps. When the last one had entered, the door closed and all was as it were before. I got up and went to bed (Lim 1969: 6).

Shaken by this vision, Lim stopped praying for a time until his friend's uncle convinced him that was had happened was good.

During the war, he wrote a number of poems in a Western poetic style that he gathered into a small anthology and published (Lim N.d.). Christian archetypes, including God, the Law of Love, and Mammon, permeated many, but others suggest Eastern religious imagery. For example, the following poem (which he dedicated to his father) hints that his father, who also was a spirit medium, had escaped the cycle of death and rebirth to "the home of peace and bliss," thereby achieving immortality:

> Freed from the bonds of being,
> Purified by its tears,
> Through death the end of life
> He lives eternal years.
> Into his own he comes,
> Triumphant and secure,
> Past human joys and woes,
> Radiant, Enlightened, Pure (2.9.42 [Lim N.d.]).

Master Lim further suggests that his father was an avatar of deity. He recalled visiting a small temple in Bata Pahat where he met a Daoist priest who had seen a vision of an old man standing on a cloud dressed in white, carrying a long stick in his hand. This "very old saint" told the Daoist priest that Master Lim was his son and predicted that Lim would stop by his temple on his way to Malacca. Master Lim further recalled that some years earlier his father had revealed to him that "he was very old and that he had a white beard and his home was very far away" (Lim 1969: 4-5).[6]

In his twenties, Lim learned to meditate, and was never tired or worried. On his return to Penang in 1944, he continued to meditate, and discovered that he had developed special powers:

Then too I found that I could see many strange things. For example, I could see the pain that hurts, I could see the troubled mind, and too the restless spirit of a person. Thus I tried to diagnose diseases and find the right cure for them. I found that certain diseases could be better treated with Western medicine and in certain cases Chinese medicine was efficacious. There too when spiritual disturbances caused trouble medicine was of no avail. (Lim 1969: 12)

In this period, he also had a dream in which he saw five figures descend from the sky, then stand on clouds in a row above the table. The figure in the center was dressed in the robes of an official, and the remaining four wore the costumes of a soldier, a worker, a teacher, and a philosopher:

The worker looked hard at me and smiled and I saw that he looked exactly like me. As I looked at him, he said, "Don't you know me? I am You." All at once he leapt on to my back and entered into my body. With a shiver I woke up. It was nearly 3:00 a.m. (Lim 1969: 16).

The story reveals his modesty in imagining his spirit self, which although divine still is not the grand official or the philosopher, but rather the humble worker.

As Lim described it, when he returned to Penang in 1944 food was scarce, and people were dying in the streets or in the five-foot walkways of houses in George Town. He found many of his old friends were ill, and he began to do spiritual healing in a house on Stewart Lane. Soon 200 people a day would wait to see him. He also resumed teaching, and eventually taught art at one of Penang's most prestigious British schools. In his autobiography, he recalled that after World War II he meditated every evening, and on Sundays he went to a temple in Glugor to meditate. Although he did not name it, this temple is likely to have been the Jewel Moon Palace where he practiced as a spirit medium.

He described his meditation practice in precise detail, ascribing his growing spiritual powers to his developing ability. He claimed:

I had been able to shut out all hearing, seeing, smelling, touching, and taste. I had been able to gather myself at the centre i.e. the solar plexus. I had fixed my mind at the house of the heavenly heart and I had sunk into the place of power. There I had experienced the warm glow of the mixing in the centre. I had experienced the separation of the spiritual from the physical body. (Lim 1969: 18)

In a section of his autobiography entitled, "The Experience," Lim noted that, "The mixing of spirit and power gives birth to a spirit body in the place of power and before this can come about, one must sink deep into the quiet atmosphere of the self." The spirit body then ascends to the head, "the spiritual home of the true self," and strives to free itself of the body. Finally, the person meditating is able to "break through the mind barrier": the essence "comes out" and spreads over the head like a halo, where it remains until the mind breaks off (Lim 1969: 19).

His powers included not only spiritual healing, but also giving advice to Penang's entrepreneurs, who commonly consult spirit mediums to check their luck and to get advice before embarking on risky ventures. In one of his classes he recalled that in the 1950s, speculators invited him to Perak so that he could advise them whether or not they could safely blast a large boulder. He counseled them to wait for two years, but they were impatient and blew up the rock. Afterwards they found a huge white snake on the site, and because they had disturbed it, they were forced to shut down the mine. He claimed that people had offered him money and shares to help them, and that one entrepreneur had even offered him a full-time job, but his response had been, "Then I would be in your employ rather than divine employ."

Teaching and Healing

Master Lim engaged in healing and teaching in a well-appointed temple, but there was no special drama to his trance performances, and he wore no costume. A teacher who was an amateur numerologist told me that Master Lim was a reincarnated deity, adding that monks went to him for help after exorcisms. He noted that Master Lim did not go into trance, and that he had five disciples. The numerologist also interpreted a red birthmark on his face as evidence that Master Lim's powers were inborn. Master Lim himself made no such claims directly, though he did mention that a friend, seeing the red birthmark, read it as a sign that Master Lim could meditate. Many Penangites, including several spirit mediums, mentioned to me that Master Lim had powerful and successful connections, some of whom were his former students at the elite secondary school where he had taught art. Some knew of his friendship with Penang's former Chief Minister, and also had heard that he gave his intimate associates good advice on the stock market.

FIG. 37. Baoyue Gong, the Jewel Moon Palace, Glugor, 1999. Photo: Jean DeBernardi

By contrast with most spirit medium temples, which were often converted front rooms in small bungalows, the Jewel Moon Palace (*Pogeh Kiong, Baoyue Gong*) was a spacious and well-built temple with walled-in grounds. The interior had three altars. On the central altar, the North Pole Immortal Ancestor (*Bakkak Siancho·, Beiji Xianzu*) stood to Shakyamuni Buddha's right at the back of the altar, and Amitabha Buddha, the Buddha of Boundless Light and ruler of the Western Paradise, was placed at the altar's center. In front of Amitabha stood four deities, the Jade Girl and the Golden Boy to the left and right, with an image of Immortal Ancestor Lü (*Lü Dongbin*) and Bodhisattva Wei Tuo between them, and another image of Immortal Lü in front.[7] On the Buddha's left-hand side, the side of greater honor (which is on the worshipper's right), Guanyin was enshrined on a separate altar. On the altar on Buddha's right-hand side (to the worshipper's left) was the altar for the Ancestor Gods. The North Pole Immortal Ancestor and the God of War stood at the back, and in front of them stood the Goddess of Birth and her two attendants. At the very front of this altar stood the Queen of Heaven (*Ma Cho· Po, Mazu*) and her four attendants, the "Four Great Diamonds," who are the four Diamond Kings of Heaven, or Four Heavenly Kings, Buddhist *devas* who protect the four cardinal points as defined by the world's center, Mount Meru (Werner 1986 [1922]: 120–22).

Immortal Lü is Lü Dongbin, who probably is best known as one of the Eight Immortals. Artists often depict him carrying a child, which symbolizes a promise of gifted, intelligent children. He also is the patron of those concerned with the teaching of Daoism (Poh 1978: 55).[8] According to a popular text called *An Illustrated Account of the Eight Immortals' Mission to the East*, Lü was born in Shanxi in 798 AD. On a journey he met a Fire-Dragon who gave him a magic sword that enabled him to hide himself in the heavens. He also met the Immortal Quan Zhongli, who instructed him in the arts of alchemy. He decided that he wanted to assist in converting mankind to the true doctrine, but he first had to overcome ten temptations. Once he had overcome these, he gained extraordinary supernatural powers, and spent the next 400 years using his supernatural powers to rid the earth of evils (Koh 1996; Werner 1986 [1922]: 297–99).

For many years I believed Master Lim's temple to have been demolished when the city widened the road that ran before it and replaced a roundabout with a major intersection. In 1999, however, I searched for it with a friend's help, and we discovered that it still existed, now hidden from view by the new roadway. I learned from the lay vegetarian nun who tended the temple that Master Lim had died, but that his disciples had commissioned an artist to make a 'golden image' of him. The gilded statue – an excellent likeness of Master Lim – now sits on the temple altar on Guanyin's right hand.

Healing and Teaching

Master Lim held healing consultations in the main shrine room of the temple several mornings a week, but his Saturday morning class met in a side room furnished with round tables and chairs. In both his healing and teaching practice, Master Lim did not follow the conventions for the spirit medium performance. He wore street clothes for his consultations and teaching sessions, and simply walked into the temple and sat down at a small desk at the side of the temple's main shrine room when he was ready to see clients. When people came to consult, he gave them advice, using no interpreter, although often one of his disciples was present to assist him.

Some regarded Master Lim as a reincarnated deity; others thought that although his practice was unique, nonetheless he was a spirit medium. The vegetarian nuns (*chhaiko·, caigu*) who tended the temple and prepared simple vegetarian meals for the class, for example, commented that when he fell into trance there were no visible signs. Mediums depend on the contrast between their ordinary selves and the manner of the god who possesses them to convince the public of the genuineness of the trance state. With Master Lim, the lack of

FIG. 38. Master Lim's golden image on the altar at the Jewel Moon Palace, next to Guanyin's image, Glugor, 1999. Photo: Jean DeBernardi

contrast between his ordinary self and the self who was teacher, healer, and mediator simply elevated his status into that of a total avatar of the god.

When I asked him what happens when the god enters the medium, he responded:

> The god covers him, covers his soul. The spirit medium (*kitang, jitong*) doesn't know. If you examine his heart it is beating very fast. The god can enter through the nape of the neck. If it is something *lasam* [Hokkien, impure, a ghost], then any part of the body can be entered, he can harm you. Keep pure. This is protection against *lasam*. Once he enters, you will start dancing. A real god [Hokkien, *angkong*] wants to enter through the neck, the medium must first purify himself.
>
> If it is a real god, then the medium can't speak at first, you must open the mouth, give him a charm so that he can talk. If it is *lasam*, then he can talk right away. When the god returns, the medium slumps and the people are called to look after him. If it is truly a big god, then there is no slump, and the medium simply returns to himself. The simpler it is, the greater the spiritual power. Power is high if it's like this. The lower gods are more violent. If it is real, then you believe.

Thus the simplicity of his practice confirmed his transcendent powers, distinguishing him from spirit mediums possessed by lower, more violent gods.

An English-educated temple committee member at the Taishang Laojun temple had advised me at a temple fair to seek Master Lim at this temple, and to ask him for a book that he had translated and published in English, the *Journey to the North*. When I first went to the temple, the caretakers told me to return for his Saturday class. When I arrived, he invited me to join the class and I sat at the round table with a dozen or so men and women. Some read Chinese, but most were English-educated Hokkien speakers.

They were already well-advanced in their study, and were discussing verse twenty-five of the *Daodejing*:

Chapter 25
There is a thing confusedly formed,
Born before heaven and earth,
Silent and void
It stands alone and does not change,
Goes round and does not weary.
It is capable of being the mother of the world.
I know not its name
So I style it 'the way.'
I give it the makeshift name of 'the great.'
Being great, it is further described as receding,
Receding, it is described as far away,
Being far away, it is described as turning back.

Hence the way is great; heaven is great; earth is great; and the king is also great.
Within the realm there are four things that are great, and the king counts as one.

Man models himself on earth,
Earth on heaven,
Heaven on the way,
And the way on that which is naturally so (Lao Tzu 1963: 82).[9]

Master Lim commented on the verse in a mixture of Hokkien and English, explicating how humans follow the Dao:

To be empty means to give. To cultivate Daoist conduct (*siuheng, xiuxing*). If you follow the Dao, you will have followers with you, virtue will be with you. You give things. It is natural to give speech, gossip is not natural. If you lead a simple life you can avoid trouble. But you must not eat recklessly, you must not speak recklessly. You must have control of yourself. You must not eat to excess. You must control your tongue. You must not talk too much. Men who achieve the Dao are followers of the law of the Dao. The Dao is the great law.

According to the *Yijing*, Earth follows Heaven. The principle (*li, li*) of Heaven, the principle of Earth, the principle of Humans. You must be in line with Heaven. Alone, it's no use. Heaven, Earth, Man are the basis of the *Yijing*. The three lines are doubled, giving six lines. The wind and rain of heaven fall on the earth, and this leads to fruition, and the 10,000 things depend on this.

When the calendar began to be invented, man followed heaven, he watched the cycle to time the harvest, this is the principle of heaven. The Dao is law, *li*, heaven and earth, *yin* and *yang*. Nature is deeper than the Dao.

He continued, alternately reading verses and offering commentary and interpretation.

The class took a break to meditate, and I took the opportunity to ask him for the book that I had heard about, a privately published and divinely endorsed English translation of the *Journey to the North*. He gave it to me, explaining that there was a story for each cardinal point:

The North is the story of the gods. The East is the story of Immortals, The *Journey to the East*. The South, the fire god, born of light: The *Journey to the South*. The West, Monkey, The *Journey to the West*.

I had known of the *Journey to the West*, which Arthur Waley translated as the highly entertaining novel *Monkey*, but I was unaware of these other journey stories, which were written in the late sixteenth or early seventeenth centuries and compiled together as a quartet no later than 1811 (Cedzich 1995: 138).

The *Journey to the South* tells the story of the God of Fire (*Hoa Kng, Hua Guang*, 'Magnificent Radiance'), whereas the *Journey to the East*, also known as *The Eight Immortals Cross the Sea*, tells of the Eight Immortals' adventures (see also Chan 1996). The object of my quest that day, The *Journey to the North*, is an allegorical tale that tells of the rebirths of the Emperor of the Dark Heavens, who is also widely known as the Perfected Warrior (*Zhenwu*). A divine being, the god came to earth because of his desire for a jeweled tree, then sought to return to heaven by following a path of self-cultivation. After many tests and some failures, he finally achieved enlightenment, but then returned to earth to save humans from all manner of disasters (*Park Yew Kee* 1974; see also DeBernardi 2004: 208-14; Seaman 1987).

Master Lim immediately turned to discussion of the Dao with me, however, and was unwilling to say more about these stories:

> The *Daodejing* is a book of great wisdom. I have tried to discover who is it who wrote this, and found that it was not written by any mortal. It provides guidance to an understanding of man's spiritual self.[10] I have been healing for thirty years. This temple was build by Khor Pen Cheng's great grandmother, she handed it down.
>
> People don't learn to think for themselves. The Dao is a way to find one's spiritual self. Names are man made. All ways are wrong except for the way that lives in your heart. The name god is given by humans, he himself has no name. When we are born, we have no name. A name is only a label to differentiate you from others.
>
> The *Daodejing* dates to 60 BC, the *Yijing* is 2000 plus years old, the Chou Dynasty.[11]

As the students drifted back from meditation, Master Lim defined two terms for me:

> *Chesian* (*zuochan;* to 'sit Chan') is not meditation. Meditation is deep thought only. In *chesian* we find our spiritual selves, enlightenment. Self-cultivation (*siuheng, xiuxing*) is self-discipline, self-control, ridding oneself of bad habits. Bad habits are not good, you can hurt people. This is the essence of the path to self-realization. You must do good, help others. The highest sutra is the Heart Sutra."

His students had reassembled after their meditation, and with that comment he returned to teaching them the *Daodejing*.

I also had two visits with him on days when he was available for consultation in the temple, which I present here as teachings conveyed in dialog. In the section that follows these accounts, I present his teachings to his class, following a more thematic approach to illustrate his strategy of teaching through illustrative anecdote and allegory.

A Visit with the Master

After attending several classes, I visited the temple on an afternoon when he was consulting. Four clients were already waiting when I arrived, so I burned incense to the deities and waited my turn. The first couple asked about illness, and he gave them a strip of yellow tissue on which he drew with red ink a long looping line. He advised them to burn the tissue paper charm to ash, then drink it in water in the conventional fashion. The second couple asked about starting a business, and after some discussion he advised them to throw divining crescents to consult with the gods. When my turn came, I impulsively asked if he could introduce me to the gods. He laughed abruptly and motioned toward the altar, saying, "You ask them yourself!" He invited me into the side room to talk, and only responded to my request some months later.

When we had sat down, he began to lecture me: "What is important is not the story of the gods, but what I've been teaching them [the class]. The *Daodejing* concerns all men, what is inside. What is inside is what is important, what is outside, rituals, are all show, they mean nothing."

"But surely these things also have meaning," I objected.

He explained, "In real faith healing, there is no intermediary between the client and the healer. Faith is direct from above. I experienced this when I was young. My eyes were concerned. I had a white spot on my eye after an operation. I prayed with joss sticks for three days, and a miraculous flame shot up from the incense burner when I prayed. I returned to the doctor, who wanted to know what medicine I had taken."

He again stressed the importance of study: "A person studying the *Daodejing* must go on to the *Yijing*, he must read and reflect. People want religion according to man, men quarrel over religion. Christians quarrel among themselves, Buddhists and Muslims are the same."

I observed, "People use religion as a means to power."

"Real power never hurt. What men have is only pseudo-power. Men are acknowledged as this, as that, they think they have power. Real religion lives in the heart. It is the sorriest thing to see people quarreling about religion. They have vanity, pride, they claim that this knowledge is better than what others have. What is knowledge? To pass an exam you needn't be brilliant, no, you need a good memory, with a good tape recorder you pass. . . . If you really know life, it is not like that. Everyone is the same, everyone is human. No one wants to be born a beggar, yet there are beggars. No one wants to be born a tiger, yet there are tigers. You must accept the world as it is. A power has made the world the way it is."

He continued his argument with a story, "A fellow came to see me, and tried to convince me of the correctness of Christianity, to preach to me. I said to him, 'You are trying to cut down all the trees in Penang, and to only plant coconut trees. Then once there are only coconut trees in Penang, you'll go to Province Wellesley and do the same. Can you do that? It's very silly to plant just one sort of tree. What of rambutan trees, and bananas, and durian?' . . . The people in charge of religion, the priests, teach the wrong thing. People are too much attracted by what is outside, the attraction of the outside is too strong."

He then returned to discussion of the *Yijing*. "The eight trigrams are about the workings of nature. The creative is opposite to the receptive, heaven is opposed to earth, fire to water, stillness to joy, thunder to wind, force to gentleness. Thunder is a hidden force that comes from above as well as below, as a force from earth, like earthquakes, or volcanos. It is the life force, a spiritual force that gives life. If you plant a seed in the earth it comes up. *Khi* (*qi*) is the breath of wind, this is hard to say. Fire and water complement each other more than destroy each other. Thunder is spread with the aid of the wind. These four things have been going on since time immemorial. It comes from the law of heaven (*thi^n-e li, tianli*). It is the working of the *li*. The second trigram shows the working of the *li*."

He opened the book to a diagram and explained it:

East is Spring, thunder, the spiritual force in nature. Southeast is wind, which disperses everything. South is fire. Southwest is earth. All things come out from here. West is joyous, happiness. Autumn fruits come out from the earth. Northwest is creative, spiritual force. North is the abysmal, water. Standing still. There you have gone one full cycle, to the point of death and rebirth. It seems like standing still, but the seed contains everything that there is, the seed condenses a tree. From there again you break forth into spring again, so the cycle goes on. You can count it also as a day, from morning to night. The cycle goes on for lord knows how long, the cycle of change that returns to the original. The tree is contained in the seed. Plant the seed and it becomes a tree again. In human affairs it is the same. But this book is very difficult. It also discusses the eight directions and yin and yang.

If the immortal ancestors don't save us, then it's the end of the road. The sacred ancestors are born of the light of god. Guanyin, Buddha, Jesus, are not earthly beings, they are from above, they come down to help and then return. The Buddhas are all immortal ancestors.

The human race is all one, we are separated by this, by that, by conditions of weather and all that. What is the greatest wonder of the world? It is in your self. We all have the same set of teeth, the same tongue, and yet when you twist the tongue, one set of sounds, one language comes out. Take the dialects of Penang: Hokkien, Teochiu, Cantonese, Hainanese. This is one of the wonders of the world. If you think of the human race as one, then you can reach god, then you are humble, you are not a peacock. Money divides. The poor are together, the rich lead separate lives.

I can talk a lot, [I am] in contact with the top level, I also can go to basics. The chief priest for Malaysia is at the Buddhist Center [the Sinhalese Maha Vihara] at Brickfields Road [in Kuala Lumpur]. He is a Theravada Buddhist. His message was that prayers are not enough. You need to discipline yourself, to control yourself. [Here, Master Lim referred to Ven. Dhammananda, who as I discuss above developed a highly regarded modernist program of Buddhist missionary outreach in Malaysia.]

Master Lim continued:

Monks who memorize the thinking of one school of thought cannot answer questions. They narrow themselves down to that one way of thinking. But life is not like that, it is all-embracing. Many crimes are committed in the name of god. In the end we try to find peace, but instead we seem to find the pieces of a jigsaw puzzle! Man makes religion good, religion cannot make man good. A book is a guide to thinking. If you take it as limiting, then you are fanatical. If man is good he makes religion good.

Chief Minister Lim Cheong Eu sent the former Prime Minister Tunku Abdul Rahman to see me. The Tunku suggested that I do a degree in comparative religion, since my learning was so broad. I replied, "You are born with heart and head. Look into your heart and find god. Look outside your heart and find trouble." The Tunku went back to Datuk Lim and said, "Your friend's thinking is very deep – it's hard to talk to him!"

With that story, our interview ended.

An Encounter with the Holy Mother

After my fourth visit to his class, I again consulted with Master Lim in his temple, this time to ask for his interpretation of a vivid, dream-like image I visualized while meditating in his temple during the break. I had quickly written down a description, which I gave him to read. My description, which I later published as a poem, was this:

> A woman with a crown stands before an
> altar she holds my soul my heart
> has been torn out and eaten I
> have been humbled,
> slain, low, eaten by eagles
> who she controls with her two hands.
> And spiraling up, quickly, shooting,
> dispersing, my body lost,
> abandoned
> to a cave under the sea.
> "You've met us before," the
> sea lions say. "You ignored us,
> rejected us, you gave us away.
> But you've returned to ask again,
> and if you ask, there will be a reply.
> Do not complain at the heat,
> At the pain.
> You asked, you asked
> We reply.
> You cannot return.
> You are ours." (DeBernardi 1985).

This waking dream image is a composite of phrases and images from Master Lim's teachings and Penang Chinese popular religious culture: I encounter the goddess known as the Holy Mother (*Seng Ma, Sheng Bou*) – although I cannot see her face – and from the Tsimshian myth of Asdiwal (which I had reanalyzed as a shamanic journey in a paper for a seminar on structuralism taught by Michelle Rosaldo). These images gave vivid form to my own fears about events unfolding in several spirit medium temples whose members had hinted at the darker side of their practice (see Chapter Seven). Although I was fascinated, I also feared being drawn too far inside that world.

But Master Lim saw a different meaning in my vision. Initially skeptical, he took the divining crescents, knelt in front of the gods, and threw them. He returned to the table and commented, "Yes, they showed this to you. You must have been religious when you were young." He was mysterious about the meaning, but implied that I had a religious calling, observing that I could not yet know what form that would take. He then told me a story about an encounter he once had with Mary, the Lady of Fatima:[12]

Many years ago, a statue of Mary was brought to Penang and placed in Saint Xavier's Church by the Old Esplanade. Many people crowded in to see it. I myself waited outside and saw a woman in white and another woman, Mary Magdelene, approach me. The woman in white asked me, "Why aren't you going in?" I replied, "I'm not a Christian. If people see me they will ask what right I have to go in." She said, "Oh, you too! I'll come and talk to you in three days." Before she entered, there was a bright light on the porch where she had stood, and glorious music played. Then, as she entered, a column of light appeared over the statue on the altar, which calmed to a glow. Three days later I was in my schoolmaster's flat, and she came. And she said: "Remember? I said I'd come." I asked, "Can you help me?" and she replied, "Close your eyes, then look." I did so, and when I opened my eyes, I saw my hands, and knew that I would have all that I needed to help myself.

Whereas the assumed-to-be-Christian anthropologist encountered a Chinese goddess in a popular religious temple, the Chinese spirit medium encountered a Christian goddess in Saint Xavier's Church. She identified herself as a non-Christian, and like a Chinese deity, came to inhabit her image on the day of the festivity when throngs of people crowd into the church, not alone but accompanied by Mary Magdalene. When the event ended, she visited Master Lim, who asked for help – a very characteristic Chinese way of interacting with divinity. Instead she gave him a hint that he interpreted to mean he must not expect her to save him, because people must save themselves.

He followed this story with another about people's motives for seeking a spiritual master. Here, he distinguished between his own spiritual practice and the claims that guru Sai Baba (whose followers believed him to be an Indian avatar of Shiva) had been making for his powers, including that he could magically produce wristwatches and gems for his followers:

> One day, I went to see a friend who owns a dispensary on Pitt Street. He told me that Sai Baba could produce a gem by turning an orange pit in the flame. I said to him, "That is not religion. That is not religion. If I took this teacup, and made it lift from the saucer and move around the room, would you follow me? Every man I speak to would have a different answer to that question. I'll show you – we'll ask whoever comes in."
>
> The first man came into the shop, and I asked him: "If I took this teacup and made it lift from the saucer and move around the room, would you follow me?" The man answered, "Yes! I think I could make something of it!" [in other words, a profit]. The second man came into the shop, and I asked him, "If I took this teacup, and made it lift from the saucer and move around the room, would you follow me?" He replied, "Yes! If you can do that to a teacup, what could you do to me?" The third came in, and I asked him, "If I took this teacup and made it move around the room, would you follow me?" He said, "Yes, I'd follow you. I'd like to know how to do that."

Master Lim suggested that disciples who follow religious leaders do so because they desire profit, or fear the spiritually powerful, or wish to apprentice themselves to a master. He also observed, however, that the real religion was in the heart, and that faith healing was between the heart and the divine, and required no medium.

Although he responded to the question of the genuineness of my vision as a divine revelation, he did not comment on the edge of fear revealed in it. Turning the conversation toward an occult world, associated with some spirit mediums, that I had only glimpsed, I asked Master Lim if he remembered a particular spirit medium who claimed Master Lim as his master. This medium had said of Master Lim, "Master Peng Eok's Lü Dongbin is a gentleman, and very good-looking. He will come down and fall in love. Gangsters worship him because he is skillful in martial arts." Master Lim had hinted that he was a master of spiritual martial arts, mentioning that a friend had urged him to go to the United Kingdom during the war to make money, because he could kill using his hands and mudras. But he no longer appeared to practice or teach martial arts, and he responded, "At one time, many mediums came to me for help. Some of them would listen, but their eyes would look at the floor. They dared not look at me."

I probed, "Why was that?"

"These mediums were on the dark side of things. There is a difference between heavenly spirits, above, and that below. These mediums control the dark side."

I recalled a class in which he commented in response to a question that 'bad people,' *samseng* (Penang slang for 'gangsters'), could quietly come and help, acting as a person's *kuijin*, or benefactor, and asked him, "Can the dark side help?"

He responded, "That side can help, but only in the short term. These mediums want money. If an ordinary man goes to them, he can fall in their clutches." Perhaps my line of questioning suggested to him that I doubted his own motives, for his next comment was, "I do not do this work for financial gain. People have offered me money, shares, one offered me a full-time position as his counselor, but I said, 'Then I would be in your employ rather than in divine employ.'"

Let me now turn to a discussion of his exegetical teachings.

The Real Religion

For Master Lim, the real Chinese religion was a path to self-realization and to the achievement of internal wisdom. He stressed simplicity and that which is internal to a person, by contrast with what he regarded as meaningless ritual expressions. For him, understanding itself was internal and inexpressible, a point of view that resembles the Chan Buddhist school. For example, he wrote to me that:

If you get the right way of looking at it, everything in life opens up for you and realizations will dawn and you will be at a loss for words. For there are things that live in the heart that are too deep for words to express. Few people realize this and that is why human beings depend on books and the result is confusion. The only way to reach the Ultimate is to use correctly the heart and head but this way will not get you a PhD!

Compare this with an often-quoted excerpt from Chapter 56 of the *Daodejing*, "He who knows does not speak, he who speaks does not know." It is this knowledge that lives in the heart, which, he said time and again, was the way to know god.

For Master Lim, self-control was an essential part of the practice of religion. He taught that spiritual development involved self-discipline and self-purification as means to spiritual enlightenment. In his moral teachings, he also taught that a life of self-cultivation involved both positive action in helping others and restraint in not harming them through malice or the pursuit of egoistic satisfactions. Like Ven. Dhammananda, Master Lim promoted an ethic of personal responsibility, observing that, "Whether or not something is your fate is the result of your own action." He added, "As to gambling luck, I hope that the first time he plays, the gambler loses!"

According to Master Lim, self-cultivation was a path to spiritual transformation, and meditation was one means to achieve it:

Chanting is like meditation. You must not allow yourself to be distracted. You must learn how to 'fix.' The spiritual fire, when it comes, moves from the head to the heart. When it comes, you cannot bear it. When you worship the gods, you must follow a correct path. You must cultivate yourself (*siuheng, xiuxing*), and slowly, gradually, you will transform until your mind changes. The person is no longer the same. Jesus in the wilderness went to transform, as did Buddha in the forest. The body transforms, and it is no longer the same.

At the end of the journey, you will eat vegetarian foods, pure foods. This is the last step. . . . Once you have reached this stage, you have new feelings inside. You have no worries. What used to be a worry is now nothing to feel confused about. If a man is changed, you can be scared. When you change, you feel ill. But this is not fever. It is spiritual fire. It is more painful than a high fever. When you meditate, your heart stops. There is no pulse. You cannot hear, and your breathing is slow. This is only the beginning. If you really meditate, it is really severe.

Indeed, for Master Lim, meditation and self-cultivation were at the heart of Chinese religion.

Master Lim also proposed that the sage should keep his life simple:

The sage follows the *li* of humans. Life is simple. To the world this is confusing. When he could drink wine he has water. You give him so much wine, he will not drink it. When he could eat Kentucky Fried Chicken, he follows a vegetarian diet. When he could wear silk, he wears plain clothes. He leads a simple, natural life.

A simple life involves the ascetic renunciation of desire and the distractions offered by man-made things, symbolized here by the luxury of silk garments and wine, but also by faddish Western food sold in a local restaurant incongruously housed in an ornate colonial mansion.

As a teacher, Master Lim regarded himself as a guide who led people to the experience of self-realization. He related Chapter 68 of the *Daodejing* to the art of leading without dominating:

> One who excels as a warrior does not appear formidable;
> One who excels in fighting is never aroused in anger;
> One who excels in defeating his enemy does not join issue.
> One who excels in employing others humbles himself before them.
> This is known as the virtue of non-contention.
> This is known as making use of the efforts of others;
> This is known as matching the sublimity of heaven (Lao Tzu 1963: 130).

"You use the Dao with people, to deal with people," Master Lim commented. "This means unity with heaven. The fighter is not angry, the winner is not vengeful. Ali still wants to be champion. If you are humble, does it mean not aggressive?"

A student offered: "The man of the Dao does not say 'I am the boss' to bend people to his will. He thinks of the staff also. He is not proud. He does not think highly of himself."

Master Lim responded, "The employer does not assert himself. He speaks to them as he speaks to anyone. He is humble in that way. He is not oppressive or tyrannical. Humble ... there are many types."

Student: "Does it mean to be simple?"

"Yes. 'If you can walk with kings and not lose the common touch. . . .' There is a physical side, but also a materialistic side. You want a bigger house, and yet again a bigger house. . . . You must know how to lead a simple life or you will never know the meaning of humility. You need a correct mental approach. People who are easygoing (Hokkien, *chhinchhai*) are humble. If they are *chhinchhai*, then they are humble. But be careful. You may just see his manner. Humility is inside. How does it gain expression outside? In simplicity. But sometimes people don't have it inside. Is it manners? No. The good winner is not vengeful. When your mind is at a stage where there are no strong likes and dislikes then you can achieve this. You are not petty about a friend's job when you don't like how someone else has done things."

Master Lim followed this reflection with a story to illustrate the usefulness of noncontention or inaction in teaching:

Being a teacher is the worst job on earth. If you really want to teach, if you are sincere in your teaching, then your head must be terrible. Most of us do not teach. The uncle instructs the child in the correct way to put a toy together. Then he finally does it for him. The child is quiet, he is scared. He has been told that this is wrong, that is wrong. But you must let them find out for themselves. Otherwise they won't learn. If you dominate them you will hurt them. You must not interfere.

I remember my little fellow. When my son was a small kid he liked to play with matches. Then the mother used to chase him and scold him: "You mustn't play with this! It will burn you!" No good. Didn't do him any good. One day I saw him playing with the matches when the mother was in the back. . . . The mother came in and yelled at him like the blazes, scolded him. I told her "Keep quiet. Let me do it my way." [Then to his son,] "So, you want to play with these matches. Don't worry about the mother. You like to play, is it." So, in front of me he played. He played with it, and said, "Very nice!"

"Burn your hand, you know."

"Ouch!"

After that no more matches. He learns. Realization comes from that. Everything is self-taught. No one can teach you if you don't want to learn. If you stay quiet, people will rectify their own mistakes. This is the virtue of not striving (*wuwei*), of not taking part. If people are clever at doing this or that, then let them do that. You must leave it to them. Heaven keeps still and everything is done.

When I was teaching at the School, a supervisor came into my art class and complained, "The students are undisciplined!" I replied, "These are the sounds of learning going on."

Thus, Master Lim interpreted his approach to teaching in light of the Daoist virtue of nonstriving (*wuwei*) and the importance of experience and self-realization.

In an interpretation that reflects his education and teaching career in British schools, Master Lim also contrasted an education that emphasized character development to one that merely taught a trade. He translated part of Chapter 64, "A journey of a thousand miles starts under one's feet. The sage learns not to hold onto ideas. . . . And because he does not lay hold of anything, loses nothing."

He commented:

This Number 64 talks of men with no stamina [he spoke Hokkien, but used the English word]. The British educational system taught Latin in order to lead out. Now no schools do this. Literacy is not the same as education. Schools now prepare students for a career. Memorization is not realization. Training alone does not make a doctor.

Knowledge makes a man proud. Wisdom makes a man humble. I know a Queen's scholar. He went to the racetrack and said, "The horse weighs nine stone six." He could not read the betting sheet. What was that? The jockey's weight, of course! Education brings out a man's character. Socrates taught this way. Does anyone know how Socrates died?

A student replied, "Poisoned."

Can you change a coward into a hero by teaching? Cannot. Cannot. In wisdom there is much grief. And he who increases knowledge increases grief. You look at the atom bomb and know this.

In an earlier class, he had shared a story about an experience that he had after World War II:

After the Japanese occupation, I was living on Perak Road. I was thinking about the atom bomb, worrying about it as I was falling asleep. I heard a voice say, "Ecclesiastes." The next day, I went to the God of Prosperity temple at Datuk Keramat Padang, and again I heard a voice saying, "Ecclesiastes." I looked, but I saw no one, then the voice instructed me to go to a Chinese school. I went, thinking "Well, why not." Then I felt embarrassed and turned back. As I turned back, I encountered a friend on a bicycle. I asked him if he had ever heard of the Ecclesiastes. He said, "Yes, it's part of the Old Testament," and he lent me a copy. I looked at it, and there I found: "The more man increases his knowledge, the more he increases his sorrow." This was the answer to my thoughts on the atom bomb.

Here, as elsewhere, Master Lim concluded that knowledge did not guarantee people happiness, stressing the difference between knowledge and wisdom.

The Dao and the Cycle

The idea of the Dao, a word that literally means 'path' or 'way,' is a foundational concept in the Chinese religious tradition. According to the *Daodejing*, the Dao is unnamable: "The way that can be spoken of is not the constant way." The Dao is empty, deep, and dark, but still is endlessly creative, giving birth to the 10,000 creatures: "It is capable of being the mother of the world, I know not its name, So I style it 'the way.'" (Lao Tzu 1963: 82). The *Daodejing* describes the Dao as a 'mysterious female,' also comparing it to a low-lying *yin* valley, the marshy land to which all the world's life-giving waters flowed. The marshy land is imagined as being like a woman who passively takes the lower position and attracts her lover to her, and the sage advises his ruler also to take the lower position, like the woman, and to attract followers to him by his charismatic virtue.

The Dao also is a model of process, change, and transformation, and this aspect of the Dao finds its fullest expression in the *Book of Changes* (*Yijing*). The *Book of Changes* combines straight (*yang*) and broken (*yin*) lines into trigrams, which generates eight possible combinations. The trigram formed of three unbroken lines represents the strength of *yang*, the trigram formed of three broken lines represents the yielding passivity of *yin*. The remaining six trigrams commonly are arranged to form a circle that represents the transition from *yang* to *yin*, then from *yin* back to *yang*. Both *yang* and *yin* contain the seed of their opposite, and in the course of cyclical change, change into their opposite. The eight trigrams model the cycle of seasons, the human cycle of birth, maturity, decline, death, and rebirth.

The *Daodejing* and the *Yijing* were designed to provide models and guidance for human behavior, and their original audience was China's ancient rulers. But Master Lim localized the metaphor of the path (*dao*) to the streets of Penang and the problems of contemporary life when he commented on Chapter 53: "Were I possessed of the least knowledge, I would, when walking on the great way, fear only paths that lead astray. The great way is easy, yet people prefer by-paths" (Lao Tzu 1963: 114):

> The main road is the way of the Dao. One day, I was sitting at home. I was told that a girl had come to find me. She was the wife of one of the teachers, a Roman Catholic. She asked, "Do you recognize me?" and she asked for help for her child. I asked what the matter was, and she said, "I feel so sad. I feel so sorry for him. He is studying medicine, and he has gotten entangled with a girl. He returned home, and now he can't study, can't eat, can't sleep. Master – do something! Make him forget!"
>
> I said, "What! Do you think I'm a magician!" I talked with him. Later, she complained, "He's still the same."
>
> I told her, "You don't realize that boy is a man now. Let's say you go to the Clock Tower [in downtown George Town] and you want to go to the Ayer Itam Market [in the

center of the island]. You start off, walking. Walk, walk, walk ... you come to Penang Road and you see that it's very nice! There are so many beautiful things, so many shops. Then you pass Campbell Street, and it's even more beautiful and full of lights. So you say, 'Wait la, I'll take a detour.' So you walk down Campbell Street, then you see Cintra Street. Wa, more beautiful lights! You forget Ayer Itam. But then you tell me that you still want to go, and you return to Penang Road."

You cannot reach Ayer Itam by wandering along Campbell Road and Cintra Street. You cannot. Even if you grow a beard too you cannot reach Ayer Itam by that route. If you keep in your mind that you want to go to Ayer Itam, you just close your eyes and go. Problems come up by themselves. Keeping to the main road is not easy. People love to stray away. Even if you get to Ayer Itam, you've seen how pretty Campbell Street is, so you might just go back.

This story is an extended parable on the idea of the path, using the relation between Penang's main roads and its business side streets as a model for the relation between the Dao – a life of simplicity and self-cultivation – and life's distractions. Master Lim's use of place names provided vivid analogies through which his listeners could localize this abstract concept in the time and space of their lives.

Another basic image in the Chinese religious tradition is that of the cycle, which is represented by the alternation of *yin* and *yang*, that most fundamental of complementary dualisms:

Chapter 52
[It began with a matrix,
The world had a mother.]
When you know the mother
Go on to know the child.
After you have known the child
Go back to holding fast to the mother,
And to the end of your days you will not meet with danger ...
(Lao Tzu 1963: 113; the first two lines are Master Lim's own translation).

Master Lim taught, "At the beginning of the universe, the Lord of Heaven came. Then comes the mother. You know the mother, then know the sons. Knowing the sons, do not forget the mother, the natural law of heaven. The mother of all things is the heaven's law (thi^n-e $hoat$, $tianfa$). The sons are heavenly principles ($thi^n e$ li, $tianli$). The mother is law, the son is order...."

He then turned to discussing the *Yijing*, emphasizing that although many had used it as an oracle, its predictions were the predictions of a science that looked at the patterned cycles of nature in order to anticipate the future:

What are the 10,000 things? They are from nature, they are not man made. They are rivers, animals, grass. If you return to the simple and natural, you can then understand the depth of nature. This has much to do with the *Yijing*.

The opinion in the West of the *Yijing* is that it is an oracle, you ask questions and throw shillings. This is a misuse of the *Yijing*. You must know what it is. Look at the rambutan tree. You take the seed and throw it away as useless. Is it useless? No! That whole tree is condensed and put into that little seed by nature. Take the seed and plant it – a rambutan tree. It reveals itself again. It's not useless. But you don't think that far down the road.

Some use the book as an oracle. They want to know the future. The gist of the *Yijing* is that if you can know the past, so you can know the future. If an egg is hatched, another chicken. You know the past, so you know the future. And knowledge of the future depends of your knowledge of the past.

That is nature. You needn't be a mind reader or look at crystal balls. You must return to nature in its simplicity. People don't want to look. It's like the tree. The tree grows, produces fruit, the fruit dries and the seed grows. It's also the same. The tree changes into its original form again. That is a cycle. All things are the same – they change. The 10,000 things go and come – they are the same. It says this in the Bible, in Ecclesiastes. "There is no new thing under the sun." Solomon himself said this.

But Master Lim also contrasted human differences that arose out of the natural order with those that were the product of human culture, suggesting that humans were both part of and outside of nature. As he explained it, "Man made and natural are two things." He followed this statement with a chiasmic play on words – "*Lang choe- e si choe lang*," which translates less euphonically as, "Things that are man made do men in." He explained, "Things that are for sale are mostly man-made things – a house, a car. Necessities are simple, not expensive. Your heart can open, your senses can respond to man-made things. These waste much money. Things made by people cheat them every one (*lang choe- e lang pien-e galiao*). Heaven doesn't kill men. There is plenty: shortages and rising prices are man made. Human beings are outside of nature because people think, and they destroy. The cycles of nature are predictable by comparison with the future of human beings: the son does not necessarily follow his father in the same way of life." Thus by his interpretation the laws that govern the cycles of nature do not determine human history.

At another teaching session, he discussed Chapter 28 of the *Daodejing*, which calls on people to be virtuous and to "return to being the uncarved block" (Lao Tzu 1963: 85). Master Lim interpreted this verse to mean that people should seek to return to the simplicity of nature, observing that, "Money removes us from understanding what is necessary and what is unnecessary. It is very hard to return to the state of the uncarved block. Is there any place where people live naturally? Cannot. Utopia, Shangrila, are ideas, concepts, they are not truth. This is not practicable." Nonetheless, he exhorted his students to simplify their lives. "We are all perfect. We over-fashion ourselves, and make our complications."

Being Human

Master Lim used the *Daodejing* as the foundation for his observations on how to be human (*choelang, zuoren*). He discussed virtuous conduct (*tekheng, dexing*) and the real religion that lives in the heart, contrasting the principal (*li*) of heaven with the *li* of being human. Heaven's law is inexorable, and makes no distinctions among people. Human law is by contrast relative to context and circumstance, and not everyone is created equal.

He commented that one must *ehiao jou lang* (*dong zuoren*), which he literally glossed in English as "understand to be a man," adding that there was no way to translate this expression. He stressed that being human meant knowing how to live a life in harmony with others: "He doesn't fear evil men, he does not get angry, he is not clever at fighting. This doesn't mean that he is deathless. But there are no quarrels because he knows how to be human. He does not go astray; he follows a peaceful road." By contrast, passion and anger lead to quarrels and an immoral life.

He took certain principles as fundamental to human life, which by extension determined human moral rules. Take, for example, his discussion of Chapter 47:

> The world may be known without leaving the house.
> The way may be seen apart from the windows
> The further you go the less you will know.
> Accordingly, the wise man knows without going
> Sees without seeing, does without doing [Master Lim's translation].

He glossed the general meaning of this verse, "You stay in the room to know your spiritual self. Knowledge is outside, wisdom is in your own self."

But Master Lim also illustrated the verse's meaning with a story demonstrating the importance of *li* or principle in human affairs:

> The principle (*li*) of heaven is that one generation follows the next. The *li* of being human is that it is not for one generation to quarrel with another. One day, a young man and his sister came to find me. The man had borrowed money from his mother to do business, and had failed at the undertaking and could not repay her. She decided to sue him. I talked to her, and told her that this was against human principles (*lange li, renli*). She would not listen. I told her, "The world is in disorder if you do not follow reason (*li*). You are not distinguishing large from small. If you go against reason you will suffer."
>
> The mother lost her case. She appealed, and she lost the appeal. If you know the principles of heaven, you will know what is right and what is wrong. You do not need to know all the facts. When I called up the mother, I didn't need to hear her side of things. I told her, "What you are doing is wrong."

In an orderly world, elders are "big" and juniors are "small" and elders protect and nurture their juniors. The mother's punitive actions violated these norms, nor would she accept Master Lim's role as mediator, preferring to settle the affair in a court of law.

He continued with another story, this time suggesting that acting against nature would lead to karmic retribution: "I have a friend who loves shooting. He wants to kill all the bats in my *chikus* tree. Can he kill them all? The bats eat only half of the fruit, the rest is mine. The plant is not mine, it belongs to the earth. The fruits belong to mother earth, and are there to feed living beings. Rice feeds men, fruit feeds the bats. One can kill when one needs food. If you destroy for fun it is very bad. This man's wife's father is the same. His wife has no children. If you go against *li*, you will suffer."

Master Lim added another example to illustrate that human morality is relative to one's social identity: "If a doctor's wife goes to pray to the Goddess of Mercy for her husband's business to improve, this is not appropriate. This is the *li* of men. If the wife of a shopkeeper on Carnarvon Lane prays, then it is okay. The *li* of heaven is different. It makes no distinctions among men (*bohun lang, wufen ren*). All are the same." For the doctor's wife, of course, business is good when people are ill; to pray for good business is to wish the suffering of others. Thus the relativity of human life contrasts with the inexorable operation of natural law. This is not an ethical relativity, however, but rather a relativity that asserts that one's actions are judged by one's position in society. The elder generation has one set of responsibilities toward the younger, the younger has another toward its elders. Profit for the shopkeeper and profit for the doctor are two different things.

Master Lim also emphasized that knowing how to be human meant that people should know how to negotiate their way in the world without conflict, showing respect for the cycles of nature and tolerance of the diversity of mankind. Like Master Poh, Master Lim observed that humanity was one, but the existence of different languages separates humans. He wrote to me that the "true insight" into life was contained in a four-character phrase that was engraved on a board in the Temple of Heaven where Penangites offer worship on the ninth day of the first lunar month: "One heaven, ten thousand humans."

On Benefactors

The author of the *Daodejing* applied the Dao as a model for governance and the social order. One pervasive argument made through the poetry of the text is that it is better to rule through passivity and virtue than through force. Master Lim elaborates on this aspect of the text in his comments on a passage from Chapter 50 from the *Daodejing*:

Three in five follow a death road, these are immoral. If you follow the life road, you live life to the fullest. And for one who knows how to live, there is no place the tiger's claw can grip, or the buffalo's horn can jab, or where the soldier's sword can pierce him.

Why so? In him there is no place of death. [Master Lim's translation]

He commented, "He does not fear evil men. He is not angry. He is not clever at fighting. This does not mean that he is deathless. But there are no quarrels, because he knows how to 'be human.' He does not go astray. He follows a peaceful road."

"What are *kuijin* (benefactors, *guiren*)?" he asked his students.

"Good people," one replied.

"Can bad people be *kuijin*? What are *kuijin*?" he asked again.

"One who helps you."

"One who helps you find a solution to a situation when you're in a difficult position."

Master Lim added: "They are people. He who helps you is a *kuijin*."

A student gave an example, which was designed as a compliment to Master Lim and a testimonial to his powers:

"My child had a fever. The doctor did a spinal check and found nothing. He was discharged at our risk from the hospital, and we took him to see the Master, who helped, who took us to the Guanyin temple to pray to *Hutcho·* (*Fozu*). The Master was our *kuijin*, my son recovered."

The stockbroker added, "My adopted father helps me do business. When I get tips just when shares go up, it's because I'm helped by *kuijin*."

Master Lim: "*Jinkui* or *kuijin*?" he joked, reversing the Hokkien term for 'benefactor' (*kuijin*), and asking if these tips were not in fact 'very expensive' (*jinkui*). He continued to tease, "If they help you, they're *kuijin*, but if the shares drop, they're 'small people' [*siaujin*, enemies or detractors]!"

Another of his students spoke, "People who want to help you are *kuijin*."

Master Lim returned to the stockbroker's comment:

"Why are the people who give you tips not *kuijin*? You have no difficulty. When people face hardships, then *kuijin* come. When it's so hard that there's no way out, then *kuijin* come to help you. He doesn't talk of taking credit. The *Daodejing* says, 'Retire when your work is done.'

"He helps you, looks out for you, when there are problems he comes to help you. When men are not in trouble, he doesn't come. In your suffering, you will meet someone who will help you. He does it, then forgets it. If you are ill … there are many instances of this.

"Bad people can be *kuijin*. He can be a bad person, a *samseng* [gangster], but quietly he will come and help you. It was like this in May '69. I will give you an example of *kuijin* who were very bad. Bad people did good. May 13th in Kuala Lumpur, they all were gangsters. Some did not go out, but many died, and they saved many people. You cannot know where they will come from, but if you encounter problems, then you can find *kuijin*. . . . "

He proposed a moral relativism here, arguing that although those who saved others during the violent racial riots of 1969 were "bad," nonetheless they risked their lives for the good of their community and should therefore be praised.

Conclusion

Master Lim taught Chinese religion to an elite group of disciples who eagerly listened to his didactic exposition of the *Daodejing* and the *Yijing*. English-educated himself, the texts that he selected for exposition were ones that had been translated into English and became best-sellers in the West. In his teachings he appropriated them for his Penang Chinese audience, translating key terms into Hokkien and claiming the authority of divine insight into their deeper meanings. Indeed, he transmitted messages to us from Laozi himself to encourage us in our studies. Other spirit mediums knew of him and respected him, and even those on Penang's dark side sought his help. His practice was uniquely prestigious. At present, there is no teacher or spirit medium working in the temple in Glugor, but traces of his influence persist in Penang in books that his students have written promoting modernized forms of Daoism; his disciples now venerate his golden image on the altar of the temple in Glugor.[13]

In the next chapter, I turn to a temple whose spirit medium played with symbolic inversion as a way of reworking moral values. Although some of his teachings echo those offered by Master Lim, nonetheless his performance emphasized his martial prowess and wit rather than the morality of being human. Let me now turn to my final case study.

CHAPTER SEVEN

Drawing on the Dark Side

T HE MOUNTAIN SPIRIT PALACE stood on an unpaved lane in a
remote area of the island, facing onto a large open clearing. 'Palace' is
perhaps too grand a term: this spirit medium practiced in a house whose front
room had been transformed into a shrine. The house was in an established community, and the large clearing it faced had ample space for a temple festival. The
main spirit medium, Master Ooi, held healing consultations three times a week;
in 1979 he was just beginning his second year of practice at this location. The
temple was geographically marginal but symbolically complete as a microcosm
of the universe, with altars to the Lord of Heaven, the gods, the immortals, the
Buddhas, and the Gods of Earth.

The temple committee here was tightly knit, and committee members who
attended the healing sessions to help out frequently stayed at the temple for
hours after the last client had left. Sometimes the spirit medium entertained the
committee with further trance performances; other times they all sat around and
visited, often with guests from other parts of Malaysia. In ritual performance
the spirit medium used symbolic landmarks that hinted at a connection with
Penang's tradition of sworn brotherhoods, as did his use of a distinctive slang
register.

Historically, Chinese have formed sworn brotherhoods and sisterhoods for
many purposes, ranging from mutual assistance and protection to economic
predation. The leaders of sworn brotherhoods and sisterhoods used the ritual
process to ensure their members' loyalty and commitment to the group, seeking
to sanctify the bond of belonging. Their rituals of belonging could be as simple
as the swearing of an oath before the gods, or as elaborate as the nineteenth
century Heaven and Earth Society's highly scripted, historically resonant rituals
of initiation. In nineteenth century Penang, the sworn brotherhoods further

maintained temples where they celebrated an annual round of festival events, gathering to offer prayers of thanksgiving during Chinese New Year, and for an annual feast during the Hungry Ghosts festival. Here, as in Taiwan, "An incense burner, or later, a festival and a temple, represented a form of self-organization and defense," and the performance of communication with the gods was itself "the organisation of an association" (Feuchtwang 2001: 84).

Penang's contemporary sworn brotherhoods may be socially marginal, but their members sometimes glance backwards to a period in which their community associations were powerful and their leaders influential. Before the British suppressed them in 1890, five sworn brotherhoods existed in Penang, the most important of which were the Ghee Hin and Kian Tek Societies. The Ghee Hin (*Gi Hin, Yixing*, 'Justice and Happiness') Society was a branch of the well-known Heaven and Earth Society (*Tiandi Hui*), also known as the *Hongmen* or 'The Vast Gate.' Chinese who came to Penang from Burma or Thailand probably established Penang's first Ghee Hin group in 1801; Straits-born Chinese who were disaffected with the Ghee Hin broke away to form the Kian Tek Society (*Jiande Tang*), which the British called the Tua Pek Kong Society, in Jelutong in 1844.

Initially, the British adopted a policy of indirect rule in the Straits Settlements that empowered the leaders of the sworn brotherhoods and of Penang's major community temple, the Kong Hok Palace. Indeed, the strength of the Heaven and Earth Society in the Straits Settlements and Malaya was undoubtedly a product of the British policy of indirect rule, since the British held Chinese community leaders responsible for governing their followers, and those leaders included the headmen of the sworn brotherhoods. The colonial practice of farming (or contracting) the sale of opium also empowered the sworn brotherhoods, since opium farmers often enlisted the brotherhoods' help to protect their economic interests.

The British feared that the Chinese had formed an 'empire within the empire,' and a crisis erupted when leaders of the sworn brotherhoods would not uphold the British prohibition on gambling. The colonial government suppressed the groups in 1890, and at the same time promoted a new form of secular leadership with the creation of Chinese Advisory Boards. Although the British rulers of the Straits Settlements continued to suppress both the sworn brotherhoods and their rituals of initiation – even possession of ritual arcana could lead to a person's arrest – their own policies of religious tolerance did not allow them to suppress other ritual expressions. Consequently, some of the sworn brotherhoods were able to maintain temples at which they venerated their ancestral deities and performed festivals of the annual lunar cycle. (See DeBernardi 2004: 68–78.)

The traditional sworn brotherhoods may have been stigmatized and suppressed under colonial rule, but the contemporary media now reports the role that diverse modern sworn brotherhoods (often referred to as the Triad, a term misleadingly suggesting that they are a single entity) play in global crime. The 'black societies' (*o· siahui, hei shehui*), as they are commonly known in Penang, retain a cachet of danger and excitement, and many stories circulate about Penang's gangsters. The Hong Kong film industry and martial arts novels further romanticize those involved in underground economics as chivalrous swordmen (*xia*) and social bandits. But unlike the nineteenth-century sworn brotherhoods, modern gangs no longer work in concert with community leaders, and many people deplore their violence and lack of order. Their activities are risky and dangerous, and society's "ghosts" sometimes turn to their most powerful gods for protection and assistance.

The Temple

I found the main spirit medium at the Mountain Spirit Palace, Master Ooi, to be touchy and mercurial, and as the Vagabond Buddha, his possessing deity, later pointed out to me, he had a bad temper. When he overheard one of his assistants tell me that a certain religious practice was the 'superstition of the Chinese,' for example, he exploded: "It's very simple! I dress up in a costume, and act the fool, and the people who come here are all crazy." As he stalked away, the assistant addressed his retreating back with a sarcastic, "Master!" Mr. Ooi demanded face. At one point, in explaining his occasional unwillingness to give exegesis, he commented to the person acting as interpreter that, "I'm not immoral. But sometimes I don't want to talk. She must understand that I'm larger [than she]." He assumed the role of elder in his temple community, but he was not always accorded the respect and loyalty that he expected from his temple committee.

In the first year of my research, I went to a fair at his temple, which celebrated Nazha's birthday on the fifteenth day of the ninth lunar month. My Hokkien tutor prompted me as I attempted my first interview in Hokkien. In response to my awkwardly phrased questions, Master Ooi described his healing practice and the experience of trance:

> I am the master of the mediums (*kitang e suhu, jitong de shifu*). I am in residence to cure and help people. Money left over from the donations is given to charity. I teach meditation and martial arts (*gongfu*) and I have five disciples. I can swallow a two-inch nail. Once I was interviewed, and I did this. The next day I was x-rayed in the hospital, and no trace could be found of the nail.
>
> The god is true. You cannot know if the god really enters the medium. But if the medium's heart is true, he can walk through fire, or dip his hands in boiling oil. If a person is ill, the medium will know what illness he has from touching the pulse of the

sick person. But if the sick person is a woman, then he doesn't touch her. He uses the wooden end of a joss stick to touch her pulse instead. If you go into trance, you must be clean. You cannot mix with women for three days before, or during the period of the festival.

Throughout the interview, Master Ooi also insisted on the importance of purity, exemplified here by sexual abstinence and propriety in his relationships with women clients, and described himself as moral, strict, humanitarian, and ascetic. By contrast with Master Poh and Master Lim, both of whom emphasized self-cultivation and the philosophical aspects of the Chinese religious tradition, Master Ooi stressed his ability to perform self-mortifying acts that demonstrated his invulnerability to pain while possessed. This was a means of establishing his credentials, and as Mr. Poh observed, once this is accomplished, the medium's words are accepted as true by his followers.

I next asked, "What is it like when the god comes?"

He responded, "When the god comes, you can see a very bright light. Being in trance is like sleeping. You must vomit until you are clean, then it's hard to breathe and everything is confused. This god is always on earth, unlike the Nine Emperor Gods. He goes back one week only at the end of the year. We send the god back on paper horses, and offer vegetarian dishes."

"How did you become a spirit medium?"

"I have been a medium for twenty-one years. Before I went into trance, I didn't pray. Then one day I was walking down the road, and the god entered. I went to find the Holy Mother (*Seng Ma, Sheng Bou*). She is like Mary. I cannot say that there is no god Jesus. I have seen him. All gods are true, only people are divided into camps. I saw Mary carrying a baby all dressed in white. Then Jesus in a robe with the sleeves folded up. I could see his chest, he wore no shoes. The robe was brown. This was seven years ago at the Saint Anne's Pilgrimage [a Catholic pilgrimage that takes place on the mainland near Penang]."

Here, Master Ooi, assuming that I was Christian, politely acknowledged Jesus and Mary. Indeed, like Master Lim, he claimed to have seen Christian deities, and to believe in them. At the same time, he pointed out that worship of these deities often segments people into groups, just as worship of different deities in the Chinese pantheon provides different focal points for group formation and self-identification.

He continued, "Once the god has entered, he will tell you what to do. You must wait for instructions from the god. I have gone into trance in Pangkor, Taiping, Kerow, Kuala Lumpur, Penang, and Singapore." Master Ooi's mention of places that he has performed in trance is another legitimating act. It is an honor for spirit mediums to be invited to perform at other temples during their fairs, and a medium who has fame within the larger network of medium temples has won the respect and recognition of others.

He instructed us on proper behavior in the temple, and told us something of the temple's three festivals: "You cannot smoke inside the temple, you must listen. If an ill person is consulting, you cannot write down their name. The god has healed thousands, the blind, the lame. There are two types of blindness. One can be healed. But if a vein is broken, then it is impossible.

"The images in the temple are presents from persons who have been healed by the god. The band for the festival was paid for by a person who won $10,000-over in the four-digits lottery: he was told to bet on his car number. The person is from another place.... This is the second festival this year. The temple has been here for two years. This year is the first year with so much activity. There are also festivals on the fifth day of the fifth month (that one lasts for five days), and on the twenty-fifth day of the tenth month, for six days. That one has walking on coals and burning oil."

I asked one final question, "Why don't women go into trance very often?"

He responded, "They don't want to do it. They're not clean during their menses. If a god enters their body then, they will be ill (*hoantioh, fande*). If the woman is not clean, the god will enter and leave. The spirit of the woman might not return. So it's quite dangerous."

Mr. Ooi identified women as potentially polluting to spirit mediums both as sexual partners and during menstruation. During menstruation or after child-birth, they 'have impurities' (*lasam*) and their presence at a temple is considered dangerous to themselves as well as to the medium. In a later discussion, Mr. Ooi criticized Penang's monks for marrying when they should have been celibate. Ironically, one of his possessing deities, the Vagabond Buddha, commented that his medium was a lady's man, and suggested that it was improper for him to have two wives.

A number of deities possessed Mr. Ooi, including the Vagabond Buddha, the Crippled Immortal, the spirit of a Chinese king, and the Holy Mother. In trance he usually spoke 'deep Hokkien,' but he sometimes slipped into Teochiu (*Chaozhou*), a closely related Southern Min topolect, and occasionally switched into Mandarin and even English when speaking with me. Although I observed him go into trance possessed by the Crippled Immortal and the Holy King, my interactions were exclusively with the Vagabond Buddha, a trickster who is the hero of the popular novel *Jigong's Complete Biography*. As I have discussed earlier, this comic novel is a memorable satire of Buddhist and Daoist religious orthodoxies. By contrast with the heroes of morally correct works, the Vagabond Buddha is not especially virtuous or courageous, but rather outwits his opponents with cunning and showy magical tricks (Ruhlman 1960: 153).

Mr. Ooi performed the Vagabond Buddha wearing a tattered yellow robe and a greasy brown hat, which epitomizes one of his nicknames, the 'dirty Buddha' (*lasam Hut*, lasam *Fo*). As he enacted the role, the Vagabond Buddha was an avid gambler who liked to joke and drink Guinness Stout. He confounds opposites, because he is simultaneously pure and impure. Often playful in his speech, the Vagabond Buddha was a poet and teacher as well as a trickster, and his teachings were less memorable for their content than for their highly charged style of presentation.

The Buddha's fondness for Guinness Stout is based on a complicated play of meanings in Hokkien. According to his story, the Vagabond Buddha eats black dog meat, which is an especially impure food but also a powerful prophylactic against black magic. Penang Hokkien-speakers found the name Guinness difficult to pronounce; because the label was illustrated with a bulldog they called it instead 'black dog' (*o·kau, heigou*). Because Hokkien-speakers use the same word for 'eat' and 'drink' (*chiah, chi*), drinking Guinness Stout is 'eating black dog.'

Master Ooi also went into trance possessed by Li Tok Kuai (*Li Tieguai*), called by some the Crippled Immortal but referred to by the Vagabond Buddha in trance performance as the Lame Ghost (*Paikha Kui, Bojiao Gui*). Li Tok Kuai is one of the Eight Immortals, and his story is told in the popular novel, *Eight Immortals Cross the Sea* (*Baxian Guohai*; see Chan 1996). Perhaps because he retained control of every interaction, I never asked Master Ooi for the stories of his possessing deities. During my second interview with Master Poh, however, he spontaneously told me the Crippled Immortal's story:

Li Tok Kuai was very handsome. This affair came to pass before his time had arrived. He was in the mountain, mastering the Dao (*hakto, xuedao*). He said to them that he would go for forty-nine days, and then this happened. He was in the mountain meditating, and they pulled him, he was meditating and they came. The time had not yet arrived, it was short one day, and they came and burned his body. He came back and couldn't find it. A beggar slept by the side of the road. Before, Li Tok Kuai was a gentleman-scholar (*suseng, shisheng*), he was very lovely, very handsome, did you know this? Li Dok Kuai was very handsome, he wasn't a beggar. His body is that of a beggar who slept by the road, his soul took that body.... Nowadays nobody becomes immortal. ...

Master Poh's story suggests that appearances can deceive: the deformed immortal with a beggar's body is in fact a handsome gentleman who achieved a remarkable level of moral cultivation.

Master Ooi's other main possessing deities were the Holy King (as the Vast Favor Venerable King [*Kongtek Chunong, Guangze Zunwang*] is commonly known), and his wife, the Holy Mother. In Fujian Province, the Holy King is a widely popular savior god, equal perhaps to the Goddess of Mercy (Dean

1993: 131). When possessed by the Holy King, the spirit medium distorted his speech by alternating nonsense syllables with meaningful ones.

My quest for the Holy King's history met with failure, but Tua Pek Kong's *Dreambook* included an incantation that tells something of his history and moral virtues:

The Holy King Incantation

We humbly invite the Fengshan Holy King Guo
Who because of his loyalty and filial piety was conferred by the emperor
and became a god
The Jade Emperor bestowed him to establish a Buddhist country
Emperors of each generation conferred titles upon him as the honorable king
Living in Liangshan he achieved the right way.
He guarded the state and pacified the people by displaying his magic power.
After eighteen years, his body was transformed.
Brilliantly radiant, he rendered outstanding service
He [transformed] his presence and saved the emperor and the country
He was entitled Guangze, the Great Honorable King
He protected people from dangers and helped people in a state of emergency
He had great magic power (*shentong*) and displayed his prowess
He was a filial son whose home place was at the An River for generations.
His incarnation at Nan An extended his magic power
He made his home at the Fengshan temple
His powerful spirit was eminent and spread everywhere
He was loyal and filial, and moved Heaven and Earth
He was respected as the Great Honorable King everywhere
Buddha's power transforms without any limitation
Three pure incense sticks invite the Holy King
Your younger brothers sincerely and humbly pray to invite you three times,
Pray to invite Guangze the Great Honorable King
Mount the clouds and ride the mist and come down
Come to the front of the altar and display your magical power
Help the needy and relieve the distressed with your merciful will
Use this way to save the world and display your magical power
The spirit medium comes to give [convey your] instructions
Open his mouth so that he can convey your instructions and perform
outstanding service
The god's soldiers act urgently as executing an order,
As urgently as executing an order.

As Master Ooi performed him, the Holy King was a martial deity who wore yellow embroidered stomacher and leggings. When possessed by this god, he performed self-mortifying acts, hitting his back with the seven-star sword or the prick ball, or strafing his body with burning joss sticks. I never saw him possessed by the Holy King's wife, the Holy Mother, but Master Ooi reported that when he went into trance possessed by her spirit, he preened and asked for makeup.

Several other spirit mediums also went into trance at this temple. Two who attended regularly were possessed by the martial artist deities, Nazha (whom the spirit medium called the Central Commander-in-Chief [*Zhongyang Yuanshuai*] and whose story I summarize in Chapter Three), and the Five Thunder God (*Wulei Gong*). These two spirit mediums often performed in the courtyard out-side the temple, and according to Master Ooi they protected the temple so that bad things (for example, ghosts) could not enter. They sometimes performed next to an enormous tree outside the house compound's gates, where resided, according to Master Ooi, the spirits of seven Datuk Kong who were brothers.[1]

The trance events at this temple were marked by both humor and intimida-tion, and the mood of the crowd would often shift from awe and fear to laughter. At one temple fair, for example, the Great Saint-in-his-medium performed an impressive acrobatic display, then took the snake-handled whip and began to whip invisible ghosts in the temple courtyard. The frightened crowd fell back. But when the god began to aim his whip at muddy puddles, splashing the temple committee member tending him, the audience laughed.

At Nazha's birthday in 1980, four spirit mediums fell into trance. Two were possessed by Nazha and the Great Saint; people induced a third to enter a trance state for the first time, which he tentatively did. Master Ooi fell into trance possessed first by the Crippled Immortal and then by the Holy King. Once all the spirit mediums were in trance and a large crowd of worshippers and curious neighbors had assembled, the gods led a procession through the neighborhood, stopping at every crossroads to burn paper money and three joss sticks. The four spirit mediums first entered the God of Prosperity Temple near the marketplace to offer their respects, then they led the procession down the same narrow lane to another Daoist temple. But as they approached a small modernist Buddhist temple, one of its members opened the gates and decisively turned on the lights.

The Holy King, possessing Master Ooi, appeared to hesitate, but finally he entered the hall alone while the temple committee held the crowd back. He beat his back vigorously with the prick ball, and blood flowed. I wondered what Buddha would think of that violent, bloody display, which seemed entirely out of place in this tranquil setting, but one of the temple's members seemed enthralled as he took photographs. The gods continued their passage, next entering an old Daoist temple, where they beat the temple's resonant, deep-voiced drum and bells. The newly initiated spirit medium tripped over a tennis shoe, but managed to stay in trance. They returned to the Mountain Spirit Palace, where Nazha led the worshippers, some holding small paper replacement bodies, through two gates constructed of bamboo and paper. These represented the Northern and Southern Bushel stars, the stars controlling death and life, and passage through them enacted a ritualized prayer for longevity and peace. At this temple festival, the spirit mediums also performed the more violent displays of mediumistic machismo: the gods here led their followers across red-hot coals; they beat their backs with swords; and they played a cosmic game with red-hot iron balls.

The next year I returned to attend a temple fair celebrating the Vagabond Buddha's birthday on the fifth day of the fifth lunar month. The god was doing a brisk business, dotting god images with red ink to infuse them with spirit, and he clowned for the audience, drinking glass after glass of Guinness Stout. I observed the trance performance, and chatted with devotees and temple committee members. Let me turn to my field notes to describe what happened next:

> Suddenly, outside the temple there was a great rush, and I thought it had begun to rain. After a minute someone came to speak to the Vagabond Buddha. He made a mudra, then his forehead hit the table. He stripped off his robe, and raced out of the temple. I followed, and saw him lead a young boy whose shirt was soaked in blood to a stool. He took off the boy's shirt, and massaged his back. I raised my camera, but then lowered it, realizing that this was not an event that I should document. Feeling nauseous, I left and went to a friend's house. They were unsurprised by my news, and explained the gangs to me. They knew quite a bit because a restaurant owner who is their friend knows gangsters and detectives, and 'mixes around' a lot. Apparently gang fights sometimes break out at temple festivals, since the gangs gather at these events and take advantage of them to locate their enemies.

Later I learned that the boy almost died because no one was willing to report the fight. People were reluctant to drive him to the hospital for fear he would die in their car and his ghost would remain there, a vengeful spirit. Someone finally took the risk, and he survived. Still, I wished that I had stayed and helped him, since I did not share their fears. I thought less of the spirit medium for refusing to drive the boy to the hospital in his new white car.

After this event, I avoided Master Ooi's temple for many months, and became a more frequent visitor to the entirely respectable Vagabond Buddha temple that I describe in Chapter Three. But I did finally decide to continue my research at this temple, and stopped in to see the trance performance a few more times. Although he cancelled trance sessions several times (apparently because he had been called upon to perform exorcisms in other cities), when he did meet with clients, many attended. Before the trance sessions he gave therapeutic massages to some men, and during the performances dispensed magical healing. Possessed by the Vagabond Buddha, he often joked with his clients. Allow me to give two examples.

In the first case, two women (probably a mother and daughter) came to consult with the Vagabond Buddha. The Buddha described the older woman's symptoms to her, and she agreed that he was correct in his diagnosis. He suggested that she pray to the gods every day on rising, and every evening at 9:00 p.m. He also recommended that she abstain from eating 'bloody things,' in other words, meat, at least one day a week. After he finished, the younger woman said, somewhat telegraphically, "Went to the doctor. Still not well." The Buddha looked surprised, and asked, "Is the doctor sick?!" Both women laughed, and the younger one said apologetically, "I don't know how to talk!"

In the second case, a young couple brought an infant to see the Vagabond Buddha. The Buddha had the mother turn the child over so that he could examine her back, and he felt the bumps on the infant's back and head. The baby's older brother ran to the altar table and hoisted himself up so that he could see what was happening. "Mom! He can't see! His hat covers his eyes!" The Buddha regarded him for a moment, clearly amused. He took a sheet of paper money, dabbed red ink on it, and rubbed the inked paper over the child's head. He joked, "She's not growing snakes [bumps that wrap around your body like a snake], she has dog fleas!" The afflicted child's elder sibling laughed with delight.

As my fieldwork drew to a close, I decided that I wanted to document all phases of the trance performance on slide film. I returned to the Mountain Spirit Palace since I knew that even at ordinary trance performances, several spirit mediums would fall into trance and they did not object to my taking photographs. I initially believed that the temple had merely been the site of the gang fight, but later I learned that members of this society were on the dark side as defined against ordinary popular religious groups. This was not safe or comfortable knowledge to possess. I will say little more in this chapter about the form that their marginal activities took: in any case I learned very little, because this was not, after all, the focus of my research. I will, however, discuss the group's reworking of language to create a new moral foundation for their activities.

For reasons that are still unclear to me – the desire for vindication or admiration, perhaps? – Master Ooi opened up the group's occult world for me to a surprising degree. Like the other Masters I have discussed, he also taught me about their values, although often in a language of symbolic inversion that valorized the group's unique social perspective. He also sometimes contradicted himself, however, which suggests that at least some of these teachings may have been performances improvised for the occasion, or that they were designed to mislead rather than guide me. I present his teachings as four vignettes. The first

I call "The Black Charm"; the second is "Teaching the Ethnographer"; the third is "The Gods Gamble"; and the final is "The Ghost Dare."

The Black Charm

On this Monday evening, I was present to observe the regularly scheduled healing practices of the god, with permission to photograph the trance performance. After the clients who came for healing charms, advice, and lottery numbers had left, the Vagabond Buddha called everyone into the temple, then called to his side an ordinary-looking young man wearing a bright orange shirt and shorts.

"How old are you?" the god asked.

"English or Chinese years?"

The interpreter, exasperated, interrupted: "Chinese years! He's Chinese, isn't he?!"

"Twenty-three."

The Buddha calculated on his fingers, then advised the young man: "In the coming year, you will encounter trouble. Have a small heart, be careful. Otherwise you will give offense (*hoan tioh, fan de*). But you won't offend ghosts, you'll offend officials."

"He means the government," the interpreter noted.

The Buddha continued: "Some people's hearts are no good, some are not straight, but here, we are all friends. Your heart is confused, isn't it?" he asked, in a deliberate, insinuating tone.

"Yes," the young man agreed.

"Do you want the Buddha to help you?"

The young man, clearly intimidated, again replied, "Yes."

"Then I will give you a black charm at the next trance session. You must avoid eating bloody things."

The interpreter explained, "You cannot eat beef or congealed blood [an ingredient in a popular noodle dish]."

The Buddha continued, "If you eat pure things, peace will come" (*chiah chhengchheng, lai pengpeng, chi qingqing, lai pingping*)."

Another boy, nicknamed Fatso, took out his black charm and began to unfold it to show the young man, but the Vagabond Buddha sharply said, "Cannot!" The Buddha then advised the first young man, "If you want to receive the charm, your stomach must be cut with a sword. You must learn to endure pain in silence (*lun, ren*)."[2] The god-in-his-medium instructed the others to get down a sword. They tested it for sharpness, and again advised the young man that the black charm would be conferred on Wednesday night. The Buddha called for a handsome young medium and instructed him that the Third Prince [Nazha], wanted to possess him. (As we know, Nazha is a child martial artist, an anarchist who in his myth-history overcomes the son of the Dragon-King of the sea, then fights with his father.) The senior medium then went out of trance under the protection of the demon-repelling black flag.

In observing this encounter, my attention was drawn by the Buddha's surprising use of language. The Buddha opened the scene by predicting that the young man would give offense. In the context of a spirit medium temple, normally this prediction would mean that the person would offend a ghost, who would then retaliate by causing illness or emotional distress. It is, after all, spiritual collisions such as these that bring most people to spirit mediums for magical cures. The ghosts that cause such misfortunes are sometimes said to be touchy criminal elements in the prisons of earth (as hell is known) who may be brought under control through an appeal to the divine bureaucracy. But in suggesting that the young man will encounter a human opponent rather than a ghost, the Vagabond Buddha relocates the opponent *inside* the bureaucracy rather than outside of it in an act of symbolic inversion.

On Wednesday I went to the temple early and observed a variety of clients consulting with the Buddha. I stood to the side and was joined by a man who had failed a degree in engineering in London and now owned a small business on the mainland at some distance from Penang. He was there with his mother, waiting while she consulted with the Buddha about exorcizing a ghost from her home.

The woman complained to the Vagabond Buddha: "There is a spirit in our house that comes to bother us (*chhaloan, chaoluan*). It walks in the rafters every night at 2:00 or 3:00 a.m., *pimpo, pimpo*." The god-in-the-medium diagnosed the problem swiftly: "There is a piece of wood from which someone hanged themselves before the wood was part of the house." He prepared a yellow charm for her, and advised her to add it to water, together with rice and salt, and to sprinkle it in the house. He concluded by noting, "Eviction takes time. You must send a notice and invite the spirit to leave."

Then something curious happened. On that Monday, after regular clients had left, one of the men who frequently was at the temple sat in the client's seat and jokingly asked the Buddha, "When will the woman I am fated to marry enter my life? What astrological sign will she be?" The Buddha, impatient, replied, "Horse, Goat, Duck, how do I know?" There was general mirth, since duck is not one of the animal years in the Chinese astrological system. The scene was repeated again late on Wednesday night, but this time when the Vagabond Buddha said, "Horse, Goat, Duck," the man standing next to me said suddenly, "Duck," and the Buddha fixed his attention on him.

The Buddha then prepared to give the black charm to the young man from Monday night, marking the black cloth with red ink. When this was done, the spirit medium's assistants took the young man into the open courtyard in front of the temple. The Buddha began to follow him, then turned back into the temple and his interpreters said to me, "He wants you to speak to him in English." Although it was already quite late, I went over to him and said brightly, "Good morning!" The interpreters turned to him and translated this into Mandarin, "*Dzauan!*" then, confused, changed it to "*Wanan,*" "Good evening."

The Buddha gave me an intense look from under his hat, and said that we couldn't converse in English, "Becoz I dok sai veddy veddy *chhim*!" ["Because my English is too deep!"].

"I speak Chinese!" I responded.

He exclaimed, "Why didn't you tell me before?"

Outside in the courtyard, the assistants aided the young man in stripping off his shirt and removing his gold chain. "It'll be nothing!" they said. "Don't worry, it won't hurt."

The assistants instructed the young man to hold the folded black cloth charm in his teeth, and to raise his arms over his head, palms together. The Vagabond Buddha took the double-bladed sword, wiped it on the soles of his bare feet, made a few practice swings, then swung in earnest and hit the youth in the stomach with a resounding thud. The young man's relief was palpable when he realized that it really didn't hurt as badly as he had feared. My own response was to feel tense with concentration as I photographed the scene, but then to laugh with relief. The younger spirit medium again fell into trance, possessed by the Baby God, and playfully grabbed the Vagabond Buddha's hat, then remorsefully offered him his pacifier. The Buddha called for the divining crescents and entered the temple with his entourage.

This series of events demonstrates the enormous interactional power that the spirit medium has when possessed by the god. The possessing deity is socially superior to his or her followers, and this superiority is expressed through the medium's ability to command cooperation and obedience. The contrast between the authority and omniscience of the deity and that of the spirit medium is striking. Spirit mediums are not wealthy or highly successful by the standards of the larger society, and do not command the same respect as their possessing deities.

Often the god behaves in a parental fashion, scolding people or praising them or, as in this case, testing their loyalty to the group. Both threat and moral persuasion are employed verbally, although this pressure is exerted through innuendo: here, a vague prediction of trouble leads to a public test by the sword. This hazing, designed to develop the young man's ability to 'bear up,' at the same time conferred a black charm, a form of invulnerability magic.[3]

Teaching the Ethnographer

After conferring the black charm, the Vagabond Buddha remained outside and consulted privately in an area past the fence with the man he had nicknamed 'Little Duck.' On his return, the Buddha called for his Dragon Throne and sat outside facing the altar to the Lord of Heaven. To my surprise, Little Duck called me over. He said that the Buddha wanted to talk with me, and that I should ask him things. Before I had a chance to speak, however, the Vagabond Buddha began. His words were translated into Mandarin and English by the men present, so the teaching unfolded fairly slowly:

"Heaven and Earth's clouds have seven layers. Some people say that man went to the moon, but it's not true. Man only went to the outer surface. All gods are true. At some temples that you've been to, people don't want to talk to you because they are afraid that you are Christian. You've been to many temples now. Is that true?" I agreed, though in fact I had learned far more at other temples than I had learned at this temple. "Humans can break the law of earth. The British were good at this, and they sought to destroy the geomantic balance of the Chinese. The stone lions at the Guanyin [Goddess of Mercy] temple used to dance."

"This is true!" added the bystanders.

The Vagabond Buddha continued, "Under British rule, the Chinese were very prosperous and controlled trade. The geomancy of the Goddess of Mercy temple of Pitt Street helped the Chinese, and people like Yeap Chor Ee [a Chinese millionaire] would go to the Goddess of Mercy and pray to her before speculating on sugar, and he would always profit. The British were very jealous, and tried many ways to combat the Chinese. So the British consulted their own spirit medium."

One of the men asked me to identify the British spirit medium: "Who would that be?"

"Maybe they asked the Archbishop of Canterbury," I speculated.

The Buddha resumed telling the story: "They tried to find a way to destroy the prosperity of the Chinese, to make it so that when the Goddess of Mercy spoke, she wouldn't speak the truth, she would give false answers when the businessmen went to ask. So the British dug a well in the temple and installed a clock to block the view of the Goddess of Mercy so that she could not see clearly. But instead of blocking the Goddess of Mercy they killed the two lions. In the old days, the lions would dance at night, they would run down to the seaside and drink water. But now they are dead, they can no longer dance. The Goddess of Mercy took care of the clock. It has four sides, and the angle facing the Goddess of Mercy always breaks down. It has been repaired numerous times, but it never strikes correctly at twelve. It always strikes before or after."

Note that the British attack on Chinese geomancy was an attack on both Earth and Heaven: the well penetrated Earth, and the clock's elevation was designed to block Guanyin's view of the sea. Although the attack on Earth was successful – the stone lions no longer dance – the attack on Guanyin's oracular vision failed.

The Vagabond Buddha then ranked five martial artist gods, all of whom possess spirit mediums. He named them with their formal titles, and the men interpreting gave them their colloquial names:

"The gate of heaven has nine steps. I will tell you of five. Not all can be told, some things must remain secret. Heavenly things must not be written.

"On the lowest step is the Great Saint Equal to Heaven (*Qitian Dasheng*)."

The interpreter added, "The Monkey God, like Hanuman."

"Then, *Sam Lang*,"[4] whom the interpreter explained was Erlang Shen, Master Poh's possessing deity, who more commonly is called *Yang Jian*.

"Then, the Central Great One (*Tiong Toa, Zhong Da*), the Commander-in-Chief (*Oansoe, Yuanshuai*)." Again, the god paused, and the interpreter explained: "The Baby God, Nazha." The Vagabond Buddha noted, "There are three ages of Nazha: the eldest is 11; the next is 7, and the youngest is 3. The three-year-old is very willful: he has no Heaven, no Earth.

"Then, the Pagoda Heavenly King (*Thah Thian-ong, Ta Tianwang*)." The interpreter translated this formal name into the god's better-known one, *Li Jing*. Again the Buddha explained for me, "He is Nazha's father. He controls the eight-angled pagoda, which Nazha fears. Nazha always wins; he loses only to the eight-sided pagoda, which his father controls.

"Last, the God of War (*Kuan Kung, Guangong*). Every dragon year there is a revolution, and the new head is elected. The former head will live in seclusion, and won't take care of heavenly matters any more. The next head will be Li Jing."

The god then advised me, "You should consult *The Canonization of Deities*, and ask questions of the medium. He has studied for twenty-two years." Referring back to the ritual that had just been performed, he added, "The sword is real – it can cut – and the stomach is the weakest part of the body." Next, the god demonstrated his omniscient knowledge, observing: "When you come here, you needn't spend your own money. When you mix with people, you must be alert. If you believe people too easily you will come to trouble. Say what is necessary and no more." One of his young followers snorted, and the Buddha silenced him with a stern, "What?"

The Buddha continued: "If you want clear explanations, come here. Other places condemn Christians, here there is respect. Here there is respect for all religions. Christ came to teach men to be good, to scold people to be good. You use candles to worship Jesus, joss sticks to worship the Vagabond Buddha. The gods are all sacred. All spirits teach man good, people teach them to be evil. The most wicked is the monk. The teaching of the sutras is true, but here priests make money and marry. Priests and nuns ought not to marry. Gods teach men to do good, they don't teach men to do bad. . . ."

He next explained the reversed-swastika symbol used by moral uplifting associations like the Red Swastika Society to represent the unity of the world's religions. He noted that the moral uplifting picture (*tekkau-ui, dejiao hua*) depicted founders of the five major religions at the center and on the four arms of the Buddhist reversed-swastika (*wanzi*): Christ (Christianity); Mohammed (Islam); the Rulai Buddha (Buddhism); and the Eight Immortals (Daoism); the god-in-his-medium neglected to mention the fifth founder, who I assume to be Confucius.

The Vagabond Buddha then listed Buddhas in ranked order. Although my notes are unclear, he seemed to list only three: Rulai Fo, who his helpers explained was the 'large-stomach Buddha' – Maitreya, the Buddha of the Future; Guanyin, the Goddess of Mercy; and Shakyamuni Buddha. Like the Datuk Aunt, he ranked Maitreya higher than Shakyamuni.

One of the men suggested that the Vagabond Buddha liked to joke, and the Buddha then introduced himself:

I am called the 'dirty Buddha' (*lasam Hut*). I don't fast. I eat dog meat. I bathe once every three years. I am the only savior among the Buddhas. I am the chief of the 108 Lohans. My real name is Li Siuhong (*shoufeng*, keep the wind; slang for a bookie?). My fiancée is named Suh Kek Niao. She is the daughter of the Empress Goddess. I am born a Buddha, and cannot marry. I am a Lohan come to earth.

Note that he also identified himself as the chief of the 108 Lohans, alluding to the Buddhist saints who protect Buddhist law at all points of space (Levi and Chavannes 1916: 189). According to some Mahayana Buddhist texts, the Lohans are ascetics who already have achieved nirvana, but they hold back from entering into that state until the Law has penetrated time and space, and Maitreya Buddha arrives in the world (Levi and Chavannes 1916: 202).[5] In claiming that there are 108(12 × 9), rather than the more common 18(2 × 9) Lohans, he uses a symbolic number that refers to the governed universe as the sum of two other significant numbers, thirty-six (3 + 6 = 9) and seventy-two (7 + 2 = 9).[6]

The Vagabond Buddha next detailed the kinship of the gods related to the Jade Emperor:

The Jade Emperor. His brother, the kitchen god, Tiau Kek Lim. His third son, Tiau Kek Su; his second son, Tiau Kek Chun, he doesn't care for anything. His father, Tiau Thian Su, he also is called the Old Jade Emperor. His mother, Wangbu Niuniu (*Wangmu Niangniang*, the Empress of Heaven). She is also the mother of Sok Gek Neo [the Vagabond Buddha's fiancée]. The Vagabond Buddha can return to heaven after he is transformed.

The god-in-the-medium added, "The medium here has a bad temper, but he knows everything, you must ask him," then went to fetch the Third Prince for a photograph. But he came back alone and crossly said, "He won't come," before slumping out of trance.

There is poetry and imagination in the story of the Stone Lions, a story of warring spiritual forces designed to express and sustain community resentment against the British. In this war, the temple protectors are killed but the Goddess of Mercy, who is a key symbol of community for the Penang Chinese, thwarts her opponents. The story has added meaning in its performance context: the Vagabond Buddha offers it to me as an explanation for the suspicion that I have encountered in other temples. At the same time, I am reminded of the boundaries that exist between this group and me: I am not Chinese, and they guess that I am Christian (see also DeBernardi 2004; Wang [Ong] 1999).

In a curious coincidence, one of my research assistants arranged for me to interview a numerologist soon after my encounter with the Vagabond Buddha. I asked him for the story of Koantek Chunong, the Holy King who possessed Master Ooi and was also the main deity in a temple in which this numerologist was actively involved. He began to recount the history but stopped, saying elliptically, "The Stone Lions at the Goddess of Mercy Temple used to dance." He then changed the subject. Whereas the Vagabond Buddha possessing Master Ooi had told me this story to explain why people at some temples refused to talk with me, this man seemingly recalled it to remind himself not to reveal sacred knowledge to me. We may compare this interaction with Keith Basso's analysis of Apache place-names, in which mention of places recalls the didactic stories associated with those sites (1984; see also 1990). Even without the retelling of the tale, mere mention of the place or, in the Chinese case, the story's name, will accomplish the interactional work of veiled criticism.

The spirit medium, possessed by the Vagabond Buddha, also ranked Buddhas, and revealed more of his identity. It may be significant that Maitreya, the Buddha of the Future, is ranked above Shakyamuni Buddha in this scheme. Occasionally people hinted that the Vagabond Buddha was none other than Maitreya, and this may be implied here, because the Buddha follows mention of Maitreya with a description of his own impure habits, hinting at the great importance of this deity who is the "only savior" among the Buddhas.[7] By the norms of orthodox Buddhism, the Vagabond Buddha is deviant: Buddhism is associated with ideals of purity and the control of desire; by contrast, this Buddha never bathes, doesn't fast, and eats black dog (or its symbolic equivalent, Guinness Stout), which is the most ritually impure food. This is a curious Buddha who defies all the laws of Buddhism, then declares that monks are wicked.

The Medium Predicts My Future

Duckie helped me review my notes, then Mr. Ooi joined us and retold the story of the Stone Lions. As he talked, the ten or so men present gathered, and we sat in a circle until well past midnight. Mr. Ooi began the discussion by bragging about his spiritual abilities: "I am a geomantic expert. I can look and know the contents of a house. I can predict when someone will die. I can swallow hot coals, a three-inch nail, acid I can drink. I have studied these things for twenty-two years – I'm not pretending!"

Answering a question that I had asked him unsuccessfully many months earlier, Mr. Ooi explained the symbolism of two bamboo posts that represented the armies of the gods, emphasizing that the Third Prince controlled them:

"The two posts are controlled by Nazha, and they represent North-South-East-West. These are the camps of the god's soldiers. I can tell you how many are in each camp: the Eastern Camp, 9,982; the Southern Camp, 8,888; the Center Camp, 7,360."

Duckie interpolated, "That is the center, the headquarters."

The god continued, "The Western Camp, 3,760; the Northern Camp, 300 generals. Nazha's real name is Li **** ****. This must not be repeated. . . . He controls the center, he is the boss [Hokkien slang, *antua*]. He can control the whole world, he is the small one who controls the whole world. He is the only god who can control them all, including the gods of the Northern Camp."

"Like a Tiger General," added Duckie.[8]

"The Northern Camp has 300 generals, they are the fiercest and bravest. They are also the most difficult to invite. Only the Third Prince can control them." He continued: "You cannot hypnotize me! If you can, I'll eat paper. I can hypnotize people, eat paper and ask them to eat it."

"This," said Duckie, "is a challenge to you."

I wondered if some of his followers had accused me of attempting to hypnotize him in order to elicit the information that I sought. At the same time, I found it remarkable that he bragged that he could hypnotize people to eat paper, because almost certainly he referred to his healing practice with yellow tissue charms.

Mr. Ooi continued very politely, "If you know anyone with ghosts in their house, please introduce me." Then a bit fiercely, "I like ghosts, I don't like men." Here again there is ambiguity: does he really speak of ghosts, or is it society's "ghosts," the hedonist, the Gambling Ghost, and the Opium Immortal, whose company he prefers?[9]

The discussion continued with the medium's assertion of his respect for Christianity: "I wouldn't dare offend Jesus or Saint Anne. They are real. Jesus never married. He was reborn on the third day. His death was an apparition,

FIG. 39. A bamboo post represents the world axis connecting Heaven and Earth. Nazha's weapons, the spear and the circle, have been placed by the shrine to show the relationship of vertical and horizontal axes, representing the union of Heaven and Earth, Penang, 1981. Photo: Jean DeBernardi

FIG. 40. A second bamboo post uses four cups to represent the spirit armies of the four directions, Penang, 1981. Photo: Jean DeBernardi

his soul left and returned. I have seen Saint Anne. She wore a coiled hat, a white dress, no shoes. She was not carrying a child, her hand was open, and the palm had a torch. In the other hand she carried a candle."

"No, that's Saint Mary," objected one of the men.

The spirit medium ignored him. "When I was small, I didn't believe. Now I believe in the Dao, in saints, in Buddha." Here, like Master Lim, he identified points of congruence between Christianity and Chinese popular religious culture. He assimilated Jesus, Mary, and Saint Anne to Chinese saints, and expressed his fear of offending them, just as Chinese fear offending spirits. Jesus' spirituality is confirmed by his purity in not marrying, and Mr. Ooi interpreted his death and resurrection in terms that evoke the detachable souls of Chinese saints.

Duckie then prompted Mr. Ooi to tell my fortune, and Master Ooi turned to the task: "You don't know how to suspect people. Wherever you go, people disturb you, and they try to be intimate with you. You have no ulterior motives; you speak only of your research. People look at you and see you are a woman, your body holds you back. Here you have a good life, when you return it will not be so good. In America someone jilted you, you lost hope and came to Malaysia in order to recover face by doing this research. Your father married twice."

Here I objected, "No, he only married once."

One of the men assured me, "It must have been when you were small." I recalled that people sometimes used the term 'wife' to refer to a man's 'second wife,' or mistress, and concluded that this was what they implied.

Master Ooi insisted, "I will crawl to Gurney Drive and crawl into the water if it's not true. Go back and ask him. Your elder brother is somebody [I must have looked doubtful, as I have no brothers], but still lacks the opportunities he deserves. He's smart, like you. [By this point, I knew better than to object.] When you want to do a thing, you go after it. Once you find the road, you are running. I'm not immoral. But sometimes I don't want to talk." He then addressed Duckie: "She must understand that I'm 'bigger' than she is. I'm not after her red packets (gifts of money, *angbao*, *hongbao*)."

He addressed me again directly, this time with predictions: "In April, you should drive carefully. It's nothing serious, but you might have to spend money. From your eyebrows I know this. You have three moles: one top right, two on your spinal cord. Don't remove them – they help you. You have had small accidents, but have never gotten hurt, these moles have helped you a lot. I'm not a simple man. I eat only one meal a day before 12. I don't drink tea. Neither am I a 'five-hair chin' [a lady's man]." Finally I left, well past 1:00 a.m., and his parting words were, "Good morning."

I took with me two small gifts – a stamp of the temple's seal on a sheet of pink tissue paper and a handwritten copy of a poem that the god-in-his-medium had dictated to his assistant, which prophesied the fulfillment of people's desires at the approaching New Year:

> The year is changing, the year is ending.
> In the spring, human affairs and wishes are fulfilled in the springtime.
> The Wealth God comes, and the five blessings approach the door.
> People have their wishes fulfilled.
> All success hinges on human effort, and Heaven is satisfied.
> People travel in four directions, their luck is perfect and complete.
> Everyone comes to celebrate, and they received prosperity and luck.

The poem is not elegantly written, but its message is auspicious and inspiriting.[10]

The Gods Go to Heaven

The next night, I went to the temple for the ceremony to send the gods back to Heaven for Chinese New Year. When I arrived, a member explained: "They leave tonight and return to earth on the ninth day of the first lunar month, which is also the day that people worship Heaven and the Jade Emperor." The men had set up five paper horses to send the gods back to heaven, and the Third Prince was dotting the horses with red ink to bring them to life. When this was done, the Master of the Incense Urn knelt before one of the two posts and invited the Holy King (*Seng-ong, Shengwang*) to come. As the Master of the Incense Urn threw the divining crescents, the Third Prince called in a plaintive voice, "Dad, I'm calling you!" Finally, Master Ooi fell into trance, and those tending him dressed him in the yellow costume of a martial artist god, this time a king. In trance, he spoke rhythmically, introducing nonsense syllables into his speech.

The Holy King cut his tongue with the ball of nails, then with broken glass, and dabbed the blood on four yellow paper charms. One was burned and put in a bowl of water. He called for a bowl of Guinness Stout, drank it down, then went outside to the offering table and dotted a set of smaller paper horses and large folded bales of gold god money. The men covered him with black flags to protect him from a spiritual collision as he wrote lottery numbers on gold paper and folded them. They placed these papers in the mouths of the large paper horses, which had been surrounded by bales of paper money, grass, oats, and a tea cup. Finally, he wrote, "Sending the gods is lucky business" and the time for the ceremony, 11:30, on the table in red ink.

Mr. Ooi then went out of trance as the Holy King, and was possessed by the Vagabond Buddha. His first words were, "I hear that man is sending off the gods. I hear that they won't send me. Buddha doesn't get to ride a horse!" He leaned close to the horses to inspect them in a nearsighted way, his hat covering his eyes, then tapped his fan over each of the wine cups on the altar to the Lord of Heaven. The Third Prince's medium, now out of trance, teased him, and the Vagabond Buddha, apparently affronted, responded with an aggressive challenge, "Do you want a fight?" The boy retorted irreverently, "You scolded me first, you unwashed monk!" Soon the boy went into trance again, possessed by the Third Prince, and the gods gambled to pass the time before the ceremony.

The Gods Gamble

The Third Prince and the Vagabond Buddha sat on the ground in front of the bamboo post to the north of the Lord of Heaven shrine, and they played a hand of 'Twenty Points.' The Third Prince contributed a bag of peanuts to the party, and the Vagabond Buddha offered to share his glass of Guinness Stout. The Third Prince (who is, after all, a child) tasted it, made a face, and called for a sweet drink. In the meantime, the temple committee members gathered around the two gods, and the mood was light-hearted, almost euphoric, as they watched the Third Prince and the Vagabond Buddha gamble.

The Third Prince, exasperated with the Vagabond Buddha's clumsiness in shuffling the cards, commented, "*You* don't know how to do it. *You're* big, and *I'm* small, but you don't know how to do it." Finally, the Third Prince hit on a plan. He distracted the Buddha by pointing at something behind him, then grabbed the cards to shuffle and deal. The crowd giggled, and someone said, "The child fools the adult!" recognizing that a common strategy for distracting a child in order to wrest something away from him had been used here. "*My* friends do it like *this*," said the Baby God, shuffling expertly and dealing.

The Buddha took his cards, but before looking at them he held the cards in one hand, with his other hand held in a mudra, and recited a Buddhist sutra. Then he hit the cards with his fan, and turned them over. A terrible hand, to general hilarity. The Third Prince had a perfect score of twenty. The Third Prince now dealt four cards to the committee, and they placed the cards by the yellow paper horse representing the center. The Vagabond Buddha took the cards back in order to deal. He did an immensely tricky shuffle-cut-shuffle-cut-deal in which he moved quickly and cards seemed to be flying in all directions. He dealt the cards, but just at the crucial moment when the audience was to see the result of these seemingly brilliant maneuvers, the Third Prince said, "No more!" in a childish tone, and the dealt cards vanished back into the deck. There was laughter all around. It was then 11:30 and time for the ceremony to send the gods back to heaven, so the card game broke up.

In this parody of a card game, the child outdoes the adult, and the magician bungles his act. There is an inversion of the roles of 'large' and 'small,' the Vagabond Buddha's general ineptness contrasting with the professional manner of the Third Prince. There is but one serious moment in this comedy, in which the gods deal four cards to the committee members, a prediction of a lottery number.

Master Ooi slumped out of trance, retched, then went into trance again, this time possessed by the Crippled Immortal, Li Tok Kuai (*Li Tieguai*), wearing gray robes and a silver crown and hobbling with a crutch. He scolded the Third Prince, then sat in the dragon seat, facing out, while the Third Prince took water prepared with the bloody, burned charm to which flowers had been added. The inside members carried joss sticks and the first few knelt before the Third Prince, but he said, "No need," and the rest stood. The Third Prince took a leaf and used it to draw water from the basin, which he tossed on their bodies: their eyes, mouth, two hands, genital area, and feet.

The small group of men then heaped the five paper horses that the gods would ride on their return to Heaven together with a huge mound of paper money outside the gate and lit it. They walked around the blazing fire in a circle, led by the Third Prince. The Crippled Immortal went out to join them, first bowing politely to the anthropologist, and the Third Prince returned to the temple, followed by the Crippled Immortal and the members. At this point I left, impressed by the intimacy of that circle of men moving around the fire, and feeling myself an outsider.

The ritual to send the gods back to Heaven invoked the spirit armies of the center and the four quarters, whom the Vagabond Buddha had explained to me were invited by the Third Prince, the 'small one who controlled the whole world.' The Third Prince also blessed the members, using water, flowers, and a burned charm prepared with blood that the older medium provided as he was possessed by the Holy King. The men renewed the bonds of belonging through the blessings bestowed by the god's blood, and the powerful act of walking together in silence, circling the fire at midnight.

The Ghost Dare

When I returned with copies of the photographs from the evening's events, I discovered to my disappointment that the communitas of the previous event's intimate ritual performance had given way to suspicion. I had another conversation with the Buddha, this time in the shrine room. The Vagabond Buddha, after drinking a large swig of French brandy, opened by saying, "You are smart to know Chinese. You know how to take care of yourself. Some people say that you're bad." One of the men added in a disapproving tone, "Chinese are like that."

The Vagabond Buddha then turned to teaching, but this time the hierarchy of deities that he offered made little sense to me, and I guess that he might have deliberately jumbled it:

In front is the Western Heaven. Behind are the Eight Jewels, the 10,000 blessings eight precious gems. On the left are the Buddhas, on the right the Lohans, in the center is Amitofo. On the seats of the seven heavens, in the seven palaces: the first is large Gods and Buddhas; the second, Shakyamuni; the Third, the Emperor of the Dark Heavens; the fourth, Maitreya Buddha; the fifth, Immeasurable Blessings; the sixth, the 18 Lohans; the seventh, Hindu lamas; the eighth, the 10,000 blessings precious people.

Although this cosmology resembles that of Pure Land Buddhism, with its emphasis on the Western Heaven and the centrality of Amitabha Buddha, in other respects it rings false. When he offered to teach me about the seats in the seven heavens, for example, the Vagabond Buddha listed eight rather than seven seats. What followed was a standard invocation to do good not bad, but he also probed to find out if religious teachings are truly all that interest me.

"From this it follows that you really investigate god's lives. I can know. You will return after two years, the Saving Buddha can know. But when you return, you are born into a poor family. You are lucky to come here."

I agree, "Yes, being a researcher is like that."

He then dictated a long moral poem in what seemed a parody of an overly serious Chinese teacher. "Do you understand?" he asked, I thought a bit facetiously.

"Could you please explain it more simply?" I replied.

He swiftly summed up a predictable moral message: "So, gods all command men to do good deeds. You must be in accord with heaven and control your actions, because to do things well is to be a proper human being. . . . Religions tell people not to be immoral. . . . Why isn't she writing this down?"

"She has a tape recorder," the men explained, struggling to describe this piece of modern technology to him.

I had asked to tape that evening's trance performance, and received permission from the temple committee members but not from the god himself. Here, the possessed spirit medium draws people's attention to the fact that he is an individual from a different historical epoch by professing unfamiliarity with this item of modern technology, which of course would be unfamiliar to a Song dynasty Buddha, thereby reinforcing the chronotope of pure Chinese-ness and the past that he seeks to create.

Satisfied with their explanation, he continued. "Her nature and mind are troubled. Do you know? On the outside she seems happy, but inside she is troubled, no one knows. Ask her if it's so or not." He then added, "You receive instruction from someone."

The men struggled to interpret this: "Like, you receive instruction from someone, there's an order or something, to interview la, to do your work a certain way, someone tells you like this, so you do it like this."

The Buddha continued, "I want you, if things are not clear, to come and ask me. I can settle matters having to do with worship." He then introduced a five-fold classification of people that echoed a classification that another spirit medium, Master Poh, had offered me earlier. Like his invented hierarchy of the gods, however, this classification seemed hollow in comparison with Master Poh's, which was integrated into a far more complex discussion of humanity and universality:

"Black people, yellow people, white people, blue people."

"Blue people?" I asked.

The interpreter explained, "'Blue people' are aboriginals, Malays, *Sakai*."

"There still remains *youren*. What are *youren*? *Youren* are Indians. South Asians are *you*. They were awarded by Heaven." [*youren* = 'original people'?]

One of the men offered an explanation: "They also are Buddhists."

To my surprise, the Vagabond Buddha then issued a challenge, daring me to confront a ghost during the second or seventh lunar month:

"I tell you, in this foreign country, what is this place with a Queen?"

"England," one of the men volunteered.

"Oh. In England, isn't there a place with a ghost? Ask the foreign lady if she is brave. In the second month, or the seventh month, you yourself can come with me and see."

The men interpreted: "Do you dare to go?" "If you want to see it. . . . "

Still not comprehending, I asked "England?"

They responded, "To see ghosts!"

The Vagabond Buddha said, "I myself will let you see!"

One of the men translated, "If you want to see, if you're daring, in the second month or the seventh month the Vagabond Buddha will take you to see. Do you dare?"

I said, "Sure I dare!" – not feeling at all sure.

"Ghosts la!" The Vagabond Buddha added, "But when you see the ghost, I won't be there. I won't be there. Although I want to protect her. . . . "

"No one will accompany you, just you alone. Seeing ghosts. Do you dare?"

I stalled for time, "I don't know. Where?"

"One lonely house," responded the Buddha dramatically.

"A house no one lives in," said one of the men, more prosaically.

The Buddha added, "You will be inside. I will be outside. It is in Penang."

"In Sungei Ara," added one man.

The Buddha continued, "Men call her the Black Water Aunt. There is a house." The crowd named the house, and the Buddha confirmed the location. "A young female ghost. She changed to steal men's lives. Are you brave enough? You're very famous in Penang."

Again, one of the men asked me, "Do you want to try?"

This time I equivocated: "I'll tell you next time."

"Tell her, she will be inside, I will be outside."

"You will go inside alone! One house."

The Buddha said, "I myself am afraid, afraid to go there and fight with her. Moreover, the territory is hers. Fighting skill is not enough. She is seventeen."

An older man summarized the dare in broken English: "One girl. Seventeen years old. She die already. The house inside. Want to go to see her? One person go inside!"

The Buddha repeated in English, "One person inside!" then reverted to Chinese. "You are inside, I myself will stay outside, watching you. You're a researcher."

Finally I made light of the dare, proposing, "Why don't *you* go inside, and I'll wait outside."

The Buddha responded swiftly, "No! *You* will be inside. I'll be outside. Watching you. You're the researcher."

Then to the men: "She says no, never mind, gods and spirits pass along that road, but there are no humans, you need not control that."

The interpreter said, "This god says okay. That ghost is very fierce!" Another man added, "What can you do, fierce is fierce. Whoever sees it will know."

The Buddha added, "That kind of ghost has no children. The tree has no branches. One hundred lives must be given to her. She has no children, so no one to do a *gongtek* (merit-making) ceremony to rescue her."

One of the men exclaimed, "I don't want to be her adopted kin!"

The god explained, "She is asleep now, but when she awakes she is very fierce. . . when she awakes she is very fierce!" He rapped on the table as he spoke. "But we Chinese are very ungrateful. She helps men, but man doesn't help her. Until today no one has done the ceremony for her." The Buddha laughed maniacally as the committee interpreted his words. "Do you believe or not? If not, then go and see."

The Buddha then changed the subject, and offered a dare of a different sort: "Is your house poor?"

"Not really," I replied.

He came back quickly, "Is it wealthy? If you're not poor, then why come to Malaysia?"

"Research is like that," I weakly explained.

"Is acid strong or not?"

"Yes, it's very strong."

"The Vagabond Buddha's medium can put acid on his arm, and only a little skin will peel off. So, if this is true, you can donate a temple, if it's not true, I will give you $10,000."

Somewhat puzzled, I responded, "There's no need to do this."

When I refused both his dares, he turned to advising me, and approached the question that was truly on his mind:

"Tell her, she now is working fast, her head and heart will be tired."

The older man translated this as, "You're working too hard."

The Buddha then warned me:

"Tell her, on earth there are bees, on earth your bees' 'red packet.'"

This was mangled in the translation, "On earth, la, when you give red packets. . . ."

The Vagabond Buddha interrupted, speaking more bluntly: "You are a single flower. I hear that people have intentions."

This the men finally translated as: "Be careful – you're a single woman. There are many bees – bees like flowers, right?"

He repeated, "Ask her, do bees like to eat flowers or not? Do you understand? People will do you in, be careful."

The main interpreter translated the warning in general terms: "Going out alone is dangerous for you. Be careful."

"Have you studied *gongfu*?" one of the younger men asked, laughing.

The Vagabond Buddha then took a new direction in the conversation, and said:

"I tell her, there are five precepts that I keep in mind in my life: First, dog meat is very tasty. Second, there must be good wine in the mouth. Third, drifting and tattered is the Dao (way) of humans. Fourth, following the road is the Dao of humans. Fifth, in the bright heaven is the Dao of the Daoists and Buddhists."

In this much-appreciated performance, the Vagabond Buddha offered his Five Precepts. For comparison, the five precepts of Mahayana Buddhism are as follows: 1. To abstain from taking life; 2. To abstain from taking what is not given; 3. To abstain from illegal sexual pleasure; 4. To abstain from lying; 5. To abstain from drinking. On all these counts, members of this temple's inner circle probably would not want to be judged.

After quizzing me again about my family, the Vagabond Buddha returned to advising me:

"After three years, things will be very good for you. Tell her, after being here, she will go to Hong Kong."

"Yes, I would like to go there."

"I know your heart, what you think in your heart I don't know?"

He patted my head with his fan, and the translator chimed in, "If you think something in your heart, he knows."

"I'm also thinking of going to Beijing," I added.

"No," the Buddha responded. "Hong Kong."

He added further advice. "Tell her, do you understand or not, if she goes to a foreign land, it is very important you understand, if you go around, you must be suspicious. Be good, men are suspicious of women alone, there are unsuspected dangers, people will gossip, they will not know if you are good or bad. When you go out, some people recognize you. Some people watch your movements, like coming here, coming to this country, fierce people take notice of you."

The translator explains, "Probably the government takes notice of you."

"Probably," I agree.

"You come here secretly, I want to say. Tell her! Tell her!"

He beat the table with his fan. The men resisted, "This isn't easy to tell her, this."

"She understands, but only a little," another added. Finally the older man who spoke a little English bluntly translated. "He says you come here, the police will mark you, you know." The translator added a comment in Hokkien: "Government people are not good, they bully people."

"Have a small heart – be careful. Don't get caught."

Although I had cultivated the art of responding to everything surprising, from tongue cutting to ghost dares, with equanimity, registering no reaction to anything I thought I should not admit to seeing or understanding, I finally said, "Yes, I understand."

The Buddha took his warnings a step further:

"The Vagabond Buddha's good must not be told on the outside. When you go out there is a man who follows you. Be careful . . . a thief child follows you. Tonight, I want to teach you clearly."

The men are confused, and one vaguely warns me of 'difficulties.'

The Vagabond Buddha repeated his warning in Chaozhou. "Now someone follows you. Careful! You've come tonight, and I want to teach you clearly. You've come to Malaysia for two years. Tell her, a thief-child follows you." One of the men translated, "Someone from the government will bother you." I wondered if he referred to the university student who sometimes assisted me, whom Master Poh also had distrusted (I thought because he was Christian), and whom they appeared to suspect of being a detective.

Then, to everyone's surprise, he seemed to seek to draw me further inside the group by hinting that he could offer me benefits that I will not describe here in exchange for my photographs. But, he warned, there would be risks.

After this warning there was laughter: "You terrible person!" And to me, "You mustn't study this!"

The Buddha exclaimed, "I'm only teaching her the Dao!"

"The Buddha doesn't understand," said the tall, well-to-do man. "*You* had better study the Dao yourself," he scolded the Buddha.

"I just want to tell her to be careful!" protested the god. "I'm blocking with a black flag." Then to me, "You must be careful. If you're not careful you won't be able to stay here long. But if you come here to study, 'wind' [*hong, feng*, Hokkien slang for police] matters need not trouble your heart. You're invited alone. But someone follows."

He was incoherent for a few moments, "You come-a-la...."

The translator guesses, "You come to Malaysia...."

"No! Cam-a-la...."

"Your camera!"

"You photographed me, your photographs are very outstanding. I am veddy thank you! I am, do you understand, hep you. No veddy popolam." He reverted to Chinese: "You come to Malaysia, do you understand, siding with the Vagabond Buddha is siding with good.... Happy to be able to teach. I will help you, no problem."

"You will get your PhD," added the translator, and the Buddha seemed surprised. "Good," he said, "Then find a gentleman-husband. Don't go out again once you're married. But now you pretend to have one, I know."

"The Vagabond Buddha knows everything."

"Your work is not yet done. You're writing sutras like the Buddhas. You're clever at raising the cups of ghosts. I want you to put out."

The tall man explains, "If you come here again, you must buy this wine [the Guinness Stout] and bring it. You must buy this wine to show respect to him."

The conversation closed with a discussion of the temple, and the men reminded me that the Buddha had taught me a great deal.

Then the Buddha said, "You've been to many temples, and studied a lot of gods. But other places don't teach you as much."

A committee member added, "We help you progress."

The Buddha advised me, "You have this responsibility. In your writing, you must say that we settle things for people, give medicine to ill people. The news seldom reports these things. Here there's a lot, other places there is less of this." The Vagabond Buddha offered to burn himself with charcoal, and again I resist the suggestion that he provide me with proof of his spiritual powers.

The Buddha then asked me, "You've been many places. Are they stronger at other places, or are we stronger? Ask her, is this house more strict, or are other houses more strict? You have written a lot, this I can know. . . . Is this place more honest, or are other places more honest? If you ask, there will be a response. Do we take red packets here?"

A tall man who drove an expensive imported car added, "Other places want lots of money. They look at how much people give, but here, two dollars is okay, twenty cents is okay, we don't have this sort of thing. . . ." Another person noted, "If you put a red packet here, the Vagabond Buddha will scold you and send you away without fulfilling your hopes. Here we don't want people's money. This god settles matters for people. He doesn't want money."

The Vagabond Buddha interrupted, "I, the Healing Lord, am getting ready to go. . . . You haven't thanked me yet. Tell her! Bring the ball of nails, and I'll hit my back."

The translator noted, "Ordinary men can't do this. There is a God there, so the medium can do it."

"Go and get the spike ball, I'm not pretending."

Again I protested, "There's no need, I don't need that kind of proof, I've already seen it."

Then, to my surprise, the Vagabond Buddha advised me, "The spirit medium is a playboy. Tell her. Tell her, his children are all grown up."

A translator explained, "He asks you, now the Vagabond Buddha himself doesn't like this, he is so old that spirit medium, but still he takes a young wife. Now he has two wives."

"Little brother, tell her, because I the Healing Buddha am good, when I come to stay, if there are any problems tell me. If the medium misbehaves, I will investigate." He switched to Mandarin, "If the medium misbehaves, I will punish him. Please excuse me. . . ."

He called over the tall man, and went out of trance, looking ill and disoriented.

In this final performance, the Vagabond Buddha has taken hold of me in much the same way that he confronted the young man who was offered the black charm. He began by daring me to fight a ghost. I am praised for my courage, told that I am famous, but I am also dared to put my courage to the test. I am also reminded that I am, after all, a researcher and it is implied that if I want to understand Chinese religion, I must experience it. I am not offered the protection of invulnerability magic, however, and indeed the god suggests that while he would like to protect me, he cannot. When I ultimately decline the dare, I sense that they are relieved.

The tone of veiled warning continued, however. The god advised me that I was 'working too hard.' He used a clichéd poetic metaphor comparing a woman to a flower, and man to a bee, to advise me of my vulnerability as a woman researcher. Finally, he warned me that the government took note of me, and the men are more frank about expressing their real concern, which is that I might be followed to their temple by a detective.

In these interactions, the spirit medium replaced symbolic disguise with a frank warning that in participating in their activities, I am risking trouble with the authorities. Unvoiced but also heard is their fear that I might betray their secrets to the authorities, and they remind me of my responsibility to them, and of all that they have done for me. I hear in their warnings a threat, and return for only one last visit to give the spirit medium photographs, and for one final interview with the spirit medium. But I sense that I have exhausted my luck, and leave the Mountain Spirit Palace for the last time.

Religious Antilanguage

Although most spirit mediums use their charismatic presence to attempt to help people follow a moral path, some use it to sanctify socially marginal activities. In this respect they are very much like nineteenth-century Chinese sworn brotherhoods whose doctrines enunciated and taught a moral code, at the same time that the group's leaders and members engaged in illegal activities deplored by the governments of every territory in which these groups existed.[11]

Spirit mediums claim to speak in the voice of their possessing deities, and to be divinely inspired in their interpretation of the sacred texts. But a few spirit mediums use the authority of the gods to radically reinterpret received wisdom regarding the meaning of those traditions, and to redefine as moral and good behavior that others regard as amoral. In order to defend themselves against the negative judgments of the orthodox, they rework meanings, stigmatizing those who seek to stigmatize them. They borrowed the sanctity and authority of religious framework of meanings, including the forms of religiosity – ritual, or the authority of the sacred printed word – to validate alternative moral codes. In particular, socially marginal spirit mediums used religious forms and ideas to sanctify behavior that others regarded as sinful, amoral, and bad. They represented their values in an idiom of inversion, for example through worship of a dirty Buddha who violates all norms of purity.

Recall Master Ooi's subtle identification with ghosts: "If you know any-one with ghosts in their house, please introduce me. I like ghosts, I don't like men. . . ." We must also consider Master Ooi's description of his possessing deity, the Vagabond Buddha, who he introduced to me as a "dirty Buddha" who doesn't fast, eats dog meat, and bathes only once every three years, but also the "only savior among the Buddhas." In a later teaching session, he further listed the Vagabond Buddha's precepts, which emphasize his impurity, his peripatetic, drifting life, and his respect for Daoism and Buddhism. Allow me to repeat them here:

I tell her, there are five precepts that I keep in mind in my life: First, dog meat is very tasty. Second, there must be good wine in the mouth. Third, drifting and tattered is the Dao (way) of man. Fourth, following the road is the Dao of man. Fifth, in the bright (*ming*) heaven is the Dao of the Daoists and Buddhists.

Although the Vagabond Buddha's five precepts are not a symmetrical inversion of the five precepts of Mahayana Buddhism, which forbid murder, theft, illicit sexual pleasure, lying, and drinking – activities that are not unknown to members of the black societies – nonetheless they do neatly capture the god's antinomian ethic.

Master Ooi appropriated and transformed the language of popular religious morality as the basis of an antilanguage that redefined moral values. This language of inversion is not a totally new innovation. Rather, it represents continuation of a tradition in which Chinese sworn brotherhoods executed a social contract that created solidarity. At the same time, they also legislated a strict morality among insiders but did not regulate moral behavior toward outsiders. Indeed, Heaven and Earth Society jargon long has included many slang terms for illegal acts of violence, and this master's teaching continues that tradition.

The richness of this slang might of course be the result of the need for secrecy or the search for fresh modes of expression (Jesperson 1946: 135; see also Maurer 1964 [1955]). Linguist Michael A. K. Halliday went further, however, and suggested that the slangs developed by socially marginal, secretive groups served their need to construct an alternative social reality. This form of linguistic elaboration, which he termed 'antilanguage,' exists in tension with ordinary reality. He observed:

An antilanguage is the means of realization of a subjective reality: not merely expressing it, but actively creating it and maintaining it. In this respect, it is just another language. But the reality is a counter-reality, and this has certain special implications. . . . It implies that social meanings will be seen as oppositions: values will be defined by what they are *not*, like time and space in the Looking-Glass world (where one lives backwards, and things get further away the more one walks toward them (Halliday 1978: 172).

For the individual, this reverse world is a means to rescue the self from the negative judgments of conventional society. But the alternative social reality of this

Looking-Glass world is under constant pressure from society, and participants struggle to defend its counterreality.

Religious discourse is profoundly concerned with the creation and transmission of a moral foundation for the social lives of group members. Religiously styled discourse may valorize moral codes that challenge normative orthodoxies, and I term this type of discourse a religious antilanguage. By contrast with the antilanguages of crime, religious antilanguages are imbricated with religious or moral concepts and images. Like the argots used in criminal subcultures, the religious antilanguage is designed to create a counterreality that is also a countermorality, but it does so using a religious register. One might predict that when religious leaders introduce controversial social practices, they will redefine moral concepts by redefining words, including most notably meanings drawn from the religious register. In reworking moral concepts, then, the religious antilanguage is born.

Members of Chinese secret sworn brotherhoods have widely employed the world-creating potential of secret slang antilanguages. Studies of the Heaven and Earth Society, for example, often include extensive slang vocabularies. J. S. M. Ward and William G. Stirling claim that the complete vocabulary would fill a volume, but offer two-and-a-half pages of examples based on Stirling's long residence in Singapore as an official in the colonial Chinese Protectorate:

Triad Form	*Meaning*
The enemy	A Magistrate
A draught of wind	A spy, the police
There is wind	A stranger is here
To shoot partridges	Highway robbery
To eat ducks	To pirate a ship
To make a circuit	To plunder a village
To wash the body	To kill a man
To play theatricals	To hold a lodge
To be born	To enter a Lodge, be initiated[12]
The purse	A diploma
The clothes	Laws and statutes of the Society
The jacket	Books of the society
A hero	A Hung member
The son of a leper, or the son of wind	A non-member
Black dog	A pistol
Dog's bark	The report of a pistol

(Ward and Stirling 1977 [1925] Vol. I: 129–31)

These slang terms distinguish enemies from friends, and conceal acts of predation and violence under coded terms.

Frederic J. Masters provides the following sample from the nineteenth century San Francisco Triad, which suggests the euphemistic quality of this criminal
argot, in which an order to kill is expressed with an 'innocent sentence':

> Of the secret words used by the Society I can only select a few from the vocabulary given
> in the ritual. If a member is ordered to kill a person, he is told to "wash his body," the
> idea being that a baptism of blood can alone wash out the wrong done by an enemy to
> the society. A rifle is called a "big dog:" a revolver, a "puppy;" powder and bullet are
> called "dog feed;" and the order to fire is expressed by the innocent sentence, "let the
> dogs bark" (Masters 1892: 307).

This slang provided a means of concealment for groups that defined a strict
code of ethics and honor for insiders, but also condoned predation and violence
against outsiders. The group's leaders enforced a shared code of law, which
they called the group's 'clothes,' and enforcement typically included violent
action against enemies and wrongdoers. These secret signs expressed the group's
norms and promoted internal cohesion, since ideally, only insiders shared an
understanding of this language of concealment (see also Bok 1982; Luhrmann
1989).

As we have seen, Master Ooi's teachings also blended together religious argot
with a slang argot, using them both in slang expressions that inverted the values
of good and evil. The slang, emerging in dialog and ritual performance, has both
wit and compelling force, and is both inventive and expressive: the group and
its values are shaped as meanings are reshaped. This slang is not a transparent
statement of hostility to the government, nor is it an open revelation of group
values. The mask does not drop; rather, conventional symbols are used with
unconventional implications.

Let us examine the slang terms used in the course of the trance sessions I
have presented dialogically in these vignettes. Please refer to Table One, which
provides a list of the terms, and their translations as I infer them from the
interactions.

Broadly speaking, this particular Vagabond Buddha and his followers used
a slang antilanguage to redefine meanings for a group whose activities and
members the larger society labels as 'bad' (*phai^n*, *dai*). Possessed by a Buddha
who celebrates profane and impure values, the spirit medium prefers ghosts
to gods. In a language of symbols, he externalized the group's identification
with the dark or *yin* side of society, at the same time stigmatizing the group's
opponents as wicked.

But in a society in which much interpersonal social control takes place
through a rhetoric of praise and blame, people unambiguously describe youth-

TABLE 1

Slang terms antilanguage used by the Vagabond Buddha-in-his-medium

	Conventional meaning	Slang antilanguage meaning
To offend	The term usually describes an offense against ghosts or Datuk Kong spirits to which people ascribe misfortune	The Vagabond Buddha refers instead to conflict with the police and government
Buddha	A pure spiritual being detached from passion	The Vagabond Buddha (the 'Dirty Buddha') is described as an impure trickster
Immortal	A person who has achieved immortality through self-cultivation	Li Tieguai, one of the Eight Immortals, is called a "Lame Ghost"
Five Precepts	Guidelines for a moral, pure life	Guidelines for an impure, hedonistic life
Ghosts	Potentially dangerous spirits of the dead; 'seeing ghosts' is seen as unlucky, and collisions with ghosts are viewed as a source of misfortune	Local slang for gangsters and gamblers ("gambling ghost") and the Vagabond Buddha's preferred company: "I like ghosts, I don't like men."
Wind	Natural element that can penetrate the smallest crevice	Police, a slang term already widely used in the nineteenth-century Triad.
Thief-child	Thief	Detective or spy
Fierce people	Violent people, such as criminals	The government, police
Officials	Government (high-status people)	Government (a hostile opponent)
Poisonous things	Venomous snakes and insects	The group's enemies
Block with a black flag	Use of a black flag to prevent a spiritual collision between a possessed spirit medium and a spirit or demon.	Establish a protected relationship with an outsider
The Dao	Path; natural and moral order	The potential risks of participation in the group

ful gangsters as 'bad kids' (*phai^n gin-a*, *daihaizi*), and the act of becoming a criminal as 'doing bad' (*choephai^n*, *zuodai*). People often commented that contemporary gangs no longer listened to community elders as they once did, and that they did not follow the strict code of behavior to which members of the earlier sworn brotherhoods had adhered. Nonetheless, they recognize that this underworld has its own regulations, and that the penalty for breaking them is the threat of physical harm. Most assiduously avoid entanglements with them for fear of demands and reprisals.

Conclusion

Chinese spirit mediums inherit a complex religious idiom that often interprets moral meanings in binary terms: good and bad, pure and impure, spiritual and material, gods and ghosts. In performing the role of heroic gods or eloquent teachers in the microcosmic space of the temple, spirit mediums also sacralize, celebrate, and valorize their followers' activities (see also DeBernardi 1987; 1994a; 1994b). But Master Ooi, possessed by the gods, playfully reworked moral concepts and reversed meanings, using poetic tropes, historical allegories, irony, and metaphor to create a new world of meaning that exists in tension with commonsense understandings.

Master Ooi, possessed by the antinomian Vagabond Buddha, played with a logic of inversion to challenge conventional meanings, stigmatizing enemies (including agents of state control) as wicked things, at the same time that he elevated and sanctified the group's activities. The Vagabond Buddha's inverted moral world existed in tension with commonplace meanings of 'good' and 'bad,' however, which remained compelling. From Emile Durkheim's perspective, for example, language is a moral discourse, and a collective conscience that transcends and shapes the individual (Durkheim 1965 [1915]: 474–88). Because religious ideologies and the state's instruments of social control and coercion also support the commonplace meanings of good and bad, however, these meanings remain compelling in the face of competing definitions, which remain playful, parodic, and oppositional. Master Ooi, possessed by the Vagabond Buddha, may seek to create a new heaven on earth for his followers and disciples, but his antilanguage discourse remains vulnerable to the meanings set out in the binding, although temporarily reversible, social contract of language.

Conclusion

B Y N O W , I T I S a truism that the predictions of modernization theorists that global capitalist society would become rational and secularized have not been realized. For many in Penang, science may have raised doubts, but it has not yet banished belief in divination (and the principle of synchronicity on which it is based), geomancy, black magic, or spiritual collisions, and spirit mediums still hold a charismatic allure. I have argued in Chapter One that the symbolism and theodicy of Chinese popular religious culture is compatible with capitalist practice and that it provides an explanation for the circulation of wealth, luck, and misfortune. And although many people have challenged individual spirit mediums, accusing them of using the sanctifying cover of doing the god's salvation work to take advantage of those seeking help, they still expressed faith in the gods and confidence that some spirit mediums, at least, were genuine.

We might regard spirit mediums as antimodern in their adherence to Chinese tradition and their transmission of the icons and arcana of popular religious culture, but spirit mediumship has not been untouched by modernity. Indeed, spirit mediums are the petty capitalists of the Chinese religious tradition, individual entrepreneurs who learn their craft in apprenticeships with other mediums. Their performances involve knowledge of both the morality of popular religious culture – a morality formalized in the teachings of *Taishang's Treatise on Action and Retribution* but also known through proverb and common sense – and the physical disciplines of the self-mortifying practices of martial gods.

Although spirit mediumship in its diverse forms remains popular, many educated Chinese dismiss the trance performance as an ignorant, superstitious, peasant practice, a charge that some spirit mediums recognized as tantamount to an allegation of fraudulence and exploitation.[1] As one critic put it, Penang Chinese who were "modern-thinking" disliked the indigenous religions of China, with its emphasis on "mediums, magic, and mysticism" (Penang Taoist Centre 1986: 80; see also DeBernardi N.d.a). Many educated Penangites now prefer rationalized, global forms of religious expression, including modern forms of Buddhism or Daoism, the ritually ordered practices of moral uplifting associations, participation in Christian churches, or simply free thinking.

Spirit mediums continue to fascinate many Chinese. But however extraordinary their self-mortifying performances or how eloquent their teachings, undoubtedly the position of spirit mediums within Penang society remains ambivalent. The reasons for this marginality are many, but their authority has undoubtedly been undermined by modernist challenge to mystification, including both the mystification of the gift and the mystification of charismatic power. Even enthusiasts who have experienced deeply the magic of performance may feel doubt when faced with clumsy performances or questionable behavior.

Spirit Mediumship and the Mystification of the Gift

Spirit mediums deny that they perform their healing work for profit, but nonetheless they do expect an offering, which is a mystified payment in the form of a gift. As Pierre Bourdieu observes, the religious economy of the offering and the church volunteer is an antieconomic sub-universe, in which "exchange is transfigured into self-sacrifice to a sort of transcendental entity" (Bourdieu 1998 [1994]: 114). Similarly, at a spirit medium temple the offering of money is described as an offering to the god, and the client places it in a red packet left on the altar table rather than giving it directly to the god or a clerk. This red packet is like the ones elders give to juniors at New Year and wedding ceremonies, a symbol of the older generation's nurture and the younger generation's dependency.

Here, though, the red packet is offered to the gods and their human servants, the spirit medium and his helpers. Consequently, the economic relationship between the spirit medium and the client is euphemized as one of religious exchange. The economic truth of the relationship – the tacitly agreed-upon price – is literally hidden inside a decorative paper sleeve that does not name the donor, nor reveal its contents.[2] Moreover, if the cure is successful, clients should show their gratitude by making further gifts or contributions, including financial support for the temple's annual festival.[3]

Despite the claims that earning money is not their primary aim, small spirit medium temples compete for clients and devotees in an environment that is a thriving marketplace of spiritual cures. Some mediums undoubtedly are able

FIG. 41. Dragon incense at the Kong Hock Palace, Chinese New Year, George Town, 1999. Photo: Jean DeBernardi

to make a modest living from their practice, although community members criticize spirit mediums who have no other source of income. My landlady, for example, came home from the market one morning complaining that a spirit medium she knew had asked to borrow RM50 to put on a show for the gods. She refused, noting that if the gods were real, never mind, she would give RM100 if things were prosperous, but the medium gambled too much and he had two wives and no other work besides being a medium. Soon thereafter two of her young sons, who previously had been highly respectful of the man and his possessing deity, began to stage parodies of his trance performance in the kitchen. Despite their disillusion with this one spirit medium, they continued to visit and trust in others. Together we visited a festival at a small temple whose members claimed that someone to whom the god had given a winning lottery number had sponsored the expensive stage show of popular music. When the god fell into trance, my landlady joined the small crowd by the altar, craning her neck to read numbers that the god-in-his-medium scrawled for his worshippers.[4]

The scale and expense of temple festivals – in particular the quality of the theatrical performances – is a direct index of the success of the temple. Spirit mediums invariably claimed that they expended any surplus donations on the god's festival rather than on themselves. They and their committee members would mention that grateful clients who had struck the lottery or otherwise prospered with the god's help had sponsored days and nights of Chinese opera, costly Daoist rituals, and rows of enormous dragon incense. Some festival organizers proudly offered me a detailed accounting: it cost RM2,000 a day to hire a Teochiu opera troop from Thailand;[5] a puppet show performance, by contrast, was less than RM500; and two nights of Dondang Sayang at the Datuk Aunt's festival cost $240. The cost of a Daoist ritual performance depended on the number of ritual performers, but an average performance might cost as much as RM400–500; a whole roast pig added RM150 to the expense; camphor incense cost as much as RM50 a catty;[6] and everyone seemed to know the cost of a six-foot, eight-foot, ten-foot, or twelve-foot dragon joss stick.[7] Thus informed, any visitor may swiftly assess the amount of money expended on a festival event.

The size of the crowds drawn to these festival events is a further indication of the efficaciousness of the gods. As a temple souvenir pamphlet put it, "What more eloquent testimonial to the esteem in which he [the Shancai Boy, a Baby God] is held, than the mammoth gathering of devotees at all the functions and processions held on auspicious occasions in connection with the deity's birthdays" (Shancai Tong 1957). Moreover, most small temples also publicly display the names of grateful donors who repay the god for his or her help.

The amount of their donations, written on strips of paper suspended from long cords tied between two structures, provides a highly visible sign of the temple's popularity and success.

With these displays at the temple festival, spirit mediums translate economic capital into religious capital, and economic success into a reputation for spiritually efficacy. Temple committees may invest in a festival event precisely for this reason. As one committee member candidly pointed out to me, "To catch chickens you have to throw a bit of rice." But as Bourdieu points out, the denial of the economic aspect of the relationship between spirit medium and client can only succeed if the habitus of those involved conceals it through a process of shared misrecognition (Bourdieu 1998 [1994]: 121).

But in modern multicultural Penang, many doubt the spirit mediums' motives, and the mystification of the economic relationship sometimes fails. Precisely because so many people accuse them of cheating, many of the spirit mediums I interviewed spontaneously asserted that money was far from their minds and that the spirit used them in this way to 'save the world' (*kiuse, jiushi*). One spirit medium for the Third Prince added that although the gods were true, some people who claimed to be saviors cheated people of money, insisting on payment even from those who were too poor to pay. He and other spirit mediums observed that the god did not need money, and that it was humans who wanted it. Others stressed the charitable nature of their salvation practices:

Master Khoo, Choo Kong's medium: "This god will take money but there is no problem if people cannot pay. He cures people."
Master Lim: "I do not do this work for financial gain."
Master Ooi, the Vagabond Buddha's medium: "The medium is here to cure and help people. Money left over is given to charity...."
Mr. Khoo, medium for the Shancai Boy: To me, running a temple is not to make money out of it. The money I get is the small amount given as red packets during trancing services. This I use for the upkeep of our temple, buying oil and joss-sticks for offerings to our deities (Shancai Tong 1957).

But compare these altruistic statements with that of a retired spirit medium who regularly assisted a colleague whose temple had been donated by one of Penang's wealthiest businessmen:

The medium vows to not use this as a means to make money, he takes doing good as his purpose.... Money should be far from the medium's mind. Still, you can't blame the medium. A woman goes to Australia, Europe, America, for a cure with no luck, then comes to Taishang and gives four dollars. She sends servants for the charm and is cured, then is never seen again. It would only be fair for her to give a fee comparable to what she gave these foreign medical specialists who couldn't cure her.

I heard rumors that some spirit mediums had made financial claims on well-to-do clients, and I feared that one spirit medium would seek to claim a high payment from me after offering me private lessons on Daoism, which he taught me while possessed by his deity. Although most spirit mediums mediate the exchange between the gods and their devotees honorably, some do not, and many Penangites now fear to approach them.

The Mystification of Charismatic Power

The second mystification concerns the transformation that occurs when a human becomes a god in a social setting. In the sacred context of the temple, spirit mediums elevate themselves above their followers, taking on the status and prestige of their possessing deities. Spirit mediums often claim that the gods selected them to do their healing work; the entry of the deity into their bodies gives them extra-human powers to transcend their own suffering (as demonstrated in acts of self-mortification), and to ameliorate human suffering. They are textbook examples of charismatic religious practitioners: they are endowed with magical powers to heal and give prophecy and they cultivate their ability to go into trance, which is "the distinctive subjective condition that notably represents or mediates charisma, namely ecstasy" (Weber 1963 [1922]: 3). From a social science perspective, in performance a medium takes on the status of the god, magistrate, king, queen, or prince whose spirit possesses him or her – a status that partly resides in the power containers of the trance performance, including dazzling sacred clothes, imposing weapons, and seals modeled on those of the bureaucrats of the Chinese imperium.

Gary Seaman insightfully concludes that rather than focus on the psychological peculiarities of the trance performer, as many authors have done, or to analyze the social structures that produce shamanism as a social practice, we should examine the "roles, statuses, and behavioral sequences" enacted in the trance performance.[8] He concludes that the "idiom of authority which links the god, the shaman, and the supplicant" is able to domesticate outside authority by means of "the affective idioms of 'guestship' and 'fatherhood'" (Seaman 1981: 67), but that spirit mediums also enacted the role of the ideal ruler:

The functioning of the shamanistic cult in China allows personal, direct access to authority, and thus to the really virtuous ruler, the god who has the combined powers of administrative responsibility and policy making authority. Since the god is not to be suspected of the materialistic self-interest of this-worldly servants of central authority, the positive aspects of the ideology of the virtuous official can be realized (Seaman 1981: 72).

In addition to the role of virtuous ruler, many Penang spirit mediums considered it part of the role of the god to act as moral authority and arbiter, teaching people how to 'be human.' Master Poh and Master Lim, for example, both used story to explicate basic moral and cosmological concepts like filiality and the Dao (see Chapters Five and Six). By contrast, the lessons that I received from the antinomian Vagabond Buddha verged on a parody of these didactic styles (see Chapter Seven).

Many Penangites hover between belief and skepticism, but the most direct challenge to the spirit medium's charisma comes when spirit mediums exploit their clients or even commit criminal offenses while posing as gods. Recall the Datuk Aunt's comment that she feared Chinese male mediums: "They can fool you, they are more daring than women, and sometimes they are not honest." For this reason, she noted, many of her clients were women.

But when the Datuk Aunt was robbed of her exquisite ruby jewelry, she asked me to drive her to see a male spirit medium whom she frankly identified as a gangster and a heroin addict and whose modern house-temple had been purchased for him by a former prostitute. This spirit medium lamented to the Datuk Aunt that even his mother criticized him. To me, in English, he noted that his mother called him a 'black sheep.' When he showed me around his temple, he complained that the Chinese he healed were very ungrateful and would not recognize him when they ran into him outside, but his Indian clients would wave and call him 'Uncle' (*Laupeh, Laobo*). Although this spirit medium enjoyed the comforts of middle-class prosperity, including a newer house and a new car, he could not easily translate this prosperity into respectability and social honor.[9]

Spirit mediums sometimes openly located themselves along a cline of respectability. Take Taishang Laojun's spirit medium, a trained martial artist who also was regularly possessed by the God of War, who commented:

Most people are awake and active in the day. I am a man of the night. Taishang teaches that there is black and white, positive and negative. There is a dark spot in the moon. However perfect you are, there will be one weak point, and however bad you are, there is one bright light, one good point. There is always contrast, always comparison. Satan sits next to god.... These are symbols. There are two forces, man and woman, love and hatred.

In calling himself a 'man of the night' he appears to identify with his own dark side.

On another occasion, I asked him about the temple committee of the temple where I had first met him. He responded angrily that there had been difficulties with the head of the committee. Then, to my surprise, he discussed the break-up of his former temple committee:

But you know there were troubles with the old temple committee. . . . There is a danger that a medium might go mad. I was chosen as the new medium by the Master because I was more stable than the old medium. The old medium is now paralysed, and now I have problems walking, and have studied spiritual arts. . . . The old medium and I were on Penang Hill, and I went like this [he demonstrated a Buddhist mudra] on his head and he was paralysed. But he deserved it. He said that Daoism was higher than Buddhism, and that he could catch Guanyin [the Goddess of Mercy].

Here he attributed the misfortunes that befell the former spirit medium as being the consequences of the medium's irreverence toward Buddhism and the Goddess of Mercy rather than to his own actions, absolving himself of responsibility even though his story hints that he might in fact have fought with and harmed the older medium.

Similarly, when Master Ooi said that he preferred ghosts to people, taking on with relish the role of a dirty Buddha who drank Guinness Stout, gambled, and chased women, he hinted at his own affinity with Penang's hedonists, whom Hokkien slang describes as the Pleasure Immortal, the Gambling Ghost, and the Opium Immortal. Although hedonists may celebrate their pleasures, many Penangites describe them as 'bad.' As the Datuk Aunt complained to me, "In the old times, when a person suffered hardships, one day an immortal would come to save them. But now, we have the Wine Immortal, the Gambling Immortal, and the Gangster Immortal – they're all no good!"

When a spirit medium falls into trance, people attribute diagnoses, moral exhortations, and prescriptions not to the person of the spirit medium but to a god. In situations where the spirit medium speaks on behalf of a god who teaches a conventional ethical code, the performance of the rule further sacralizes it, investing the god's teachings with an emotional charge that would be lacking if someone simply read a list of moral conventions in a book. Although most spirit mediums do not exploit their spiritual authority, undoubtedly some have taken advantage of the symbolic capital they gain when they speak as gods to not only to sanctify activities that many Penangites (including other spirit mediums) deem to be hedonistic or 'bad,' but also to control and command others.

Mistress Tan, for example, was regularly possessed by a goddess who freely exercized her authority to command others (including other gods-in-their-mediums) when she possessed her medium. She observed of her possessing deity:

The Holy Mother wears yellow [the imperial color] because she is very pure (*chhengki, qingjie*). She is very high, she is the Lord of Heaven's woman. She is like a general. She fights with a sword, and controls (*koan, guan*) lower gods. She can take people, catch people, and do them in. She is like that. The Jade Emperor is something like her father. [She told someone else that the Holy Mother was the Jade Emperor's elder sister]. She is very big (*toa, da*). He loves the Holy Mother like a daughter. She has his flag, his command (*leng, ling*), thus she has the authority to act and then tell him. She has a bad temper....

Notable in this instance was the contrast between the high status and purity that Mistress Tan claimed for her possessing deity and the spirit medium's own ambiguous social position as the second wife – a mistress, really – to an older man whom people respectfully called the Master.

Hong Kong psychiatrist Pow Meng Yap (1969) asserts that Chinese become spirit mediums precisely because in the trance performance they are able to dramatize a "me-aspect" of the self. He concludes that the trance performance, as an enhancement of the ego, provides an ego outlet for persons who are blocked from normal self-assertion in everyday life. Indeed, for most spirit mediums the ability to claim high status and to command others does not persist when the trance performance is over.

The spirit medium acquires considerable social interactional power once the god has entered his body. When the Holy Mother, possessing Mistress Tan, criticized and scolded a temple caretaker for not having her favorite cooling tea ready, the caretaker did not dare argue, although she later complained bitterly to my landlady that no one had prepared her for the Holy Mother's request. When the Vagabond Buddha commanded a young man to undergo an ordeal by the sword, the young man did not dare resist. I, too, obeyed when he told me to express my respect for the god by bringing him an offering of Guinness Stout. One does not ignore the god-in-the-medium's commands lightly. Such divine leadership of charismatic sects can be a powerful albeit unstable means of exerting a compelling control over followers (see Spence 1996; Weller 1994b).

Recall Master Ooi's boast that he could hypnotize people and ask them to eat paper, apparently stripping away the misrecognition that attributed to the god the authority to prescribe ritual cures for his clients. And in a revealing court testimony, Adrian Lim (a spirit medium who was tried and convicted of the ritual murder of two children in the Singapore High Court in 1983) admitted that as part of his training to become a spirit medium he had studied strategies of "mind control." His wife remarked that when he was in trance, she "had to obey him all the time" (Singapore High Court 1983, D25:10). He defined himself as a god, and thus empowered labeled anyone who resisted his control as being possessed by evil spirits. (See also John 1992; Sit 1989a; 1989b.)

As Arthur Maurice Hocart astutely observed in his study of kingship, "It is a harmless doctrine that God is life and that the king is a repository of that life.

There are obvious dangers in a doctrine that God is infallibility and that the chief gunman is the mouthpiece of that infallibility" (Hocart 1970 [1936]: 101). The sacralization of authority in the trance performance usually is not problematic. The use of the sacred to sanctify violence or interpersonal exploitation is another matter, and raises issues of moral responsibility.

Adrian Lim engaged in sex magic designed to enhance the attractiveness of his female clients, who included prostitutes seeking magical means to ensure clients and also women who feared their husbands might be straying. Sex magic consisted, however, of sex with Lim's possessing deity. In the trance performance, moral responsibility becomes highly ambiguous. Did the god have sex with these women, or was Lim simply hoaxing them? For most Penangites, this kind of blatant violation of social mores would result in accusations of fraudulent behavior. For example, when my neighbors heard a rumor that police had arrested a Penang spirit medium for raping a young woman while claiming to be in trance, they were unanimous in their judgment that no god would behave in this way, and declared the spirit medium to be a fake.

And herein lies a paradox. Spirit mediums claim that they have effaced their personality in their surrender to the god. At the same time, the trance performance allows a deep connection with the past through a means by which the voices, movements, and identities of past heroes and teachers live again. Undoubtedly spirit mediums relinquish their individuality to adopt the speech patterns of the gods so that they may better enact the chronotope of an imagined pure Chinese-ness. As Mircea Eliade observes of shamans, they not only incarnate the sacred, but also "are lived" by the religious "form" that has chosen them (Eliade 1964 [1951]: 32).

But individual spirit mediums must have an affinity for the gods who possess them and sometimes they use this affinity to express their own identities: gods with extraordinary magical fighting skills like the Great Saint or Nazha commonly possess trained martial artists; philosopher gods like Taishang Laojun possess teachers who have a deep personal interest in Daoism and Buddhism; and trickster gods find soul-mates in the so-called bad kids of Penang's criminal underworld. The spirit medium, like someone speaking a language or improvising a piece of music or a theatrical role, is both a vehicle for shared structures of meaning and an agent in the construction and renewal of those structures in performance.

The trance performance of Chinese gods blends together the social and archetypal with the individual and idiosyncratic, and the vehicle for the sacred chronotope remains the teacher, martial artist, taxi driver, or beautician who becomes a god for a few minutes or hours. Their charisma as demon-expelling exorcists or teachers of moral values finally rests with the audience's willingness to believe. If the social alchemy of performance succeeds, then they accept that an ordinary person who might under other circumstances sell them a bowl of noodles is speaking and acting as a god, and they will ascribe all agency, responsibility, and knowledge to the god. Still, many Penangites hover between conviction that the trance performance is true – a conviction that is strongest while they are witnessing heaven on earth in the magic garden of ritual performance – and fear that the spirit medium might be a fake. But even as they express doubts, they tell a story of another spirit medium with prodigious powers whose temple is just down the road.

REFERENCE MATTER

Notes

Introduction

1. People were unsure of the character equivalent for *angkong*. One Hakka spirit medium claimed that *angkong* was a Penang word; a temple committee member described it as 'colloquial,' and claimed that the term *sin* (*shen*) was more standard. Based on his research in Taiwan, Stephan Feuchtwang, offers *wenggong,* which means an 'old or venerable lord,' as a plausible Mandarin equivalent (Feuchtwang 2001: 200), but the word *angkong* also refers to a doll, and *angkong-na* to a puppet, which suggests that the character might better be left unassigned.

2. I have borrowed this apt method of describing the possessed spirit medium as the 'deity' or 'god-in-the-medium' from Vivienne Wee, who writes about Hokkien Chinese spirit mediums in Singapore (2004).

3. Caroline Humphrey concludes that although many scholars describe the tripartite cosmos as one foundation of North Asian shamanism, among Daur Mongols, this structure arose only in particular narratives and was not employed in shamanic performances. On that basis, she questions Mircea Eliade's widely known characterization of shamanism in light of an ecstatic ascent to the sky (Humphrey 1996: 119–26). The tripartite cosmology is well established in Chinese religious practice, but Humphrey's insight also applies here, as alternative narratives are used to explain the relationship between the world of humans and the unseen world of spirits, as for example when the Datuk Aunt compared the world of humans and the world of ghosts to two sides of a sheet of paper, or when another spirit medium compared heaven and hell to two mountains coming down to a plain.

4. Indeed in Phuket, spirit mediums now take these practices to remarkable extremes, piercing their cheeks with heavy, high-seas fishing gear, patio umbrellas, a clock, a musket, a handsaw, or spears threaded on both sides of the medium's mouth with whole pineapples, a fruit whose name in Hokkien puns with the expression 'prosperity comes' (see illustrations in Cohen 2001).

5. As Paul Stoller observes of the Songhay of Nicer and Mali, in the bodies of their mediums their spirits become "replicas of ancestors which embody the past, make contact with the present and determine the future" (Stoller 1995: 43).

6. Some Penang spirit mediums were English educated and had European ancestry, but none whom I encountered ever were possessed by British spirits. And although the Japanese had occupied Penang during World War II and had tortured and killed Chinese – leaving rumors of anonymous mass graves on the island – Chinese did not routinely invite Japanese spirits to possess their spirit mediums. One friend did visit a spirit medium who became possessed by a Japanese spirit, but because no one could communicate with the spirit, he was chased away.

7. Studies of spirit mediumship and shamanism in Southeast Asia include Jane Atkinson's study of Wana shamanism (1989); Rosalind Morris's postmodernist study of Northern Thai spirit mediums (2000); Marina Roseman's work on the Temiar (2001); Mary Steedly's study of Karo spirit possession (1993); Stanley J. Tambiah's monograph on spirit cults in Northeastern Thailand (1970); and an edited collection of essays on shamanism and spirit mediumship in Borneo (Winzeler 1993a).

8. As William Shaw described it, "One superstition that the main racial communities inhabiting the Peninsular Malaysia hold in common is that ethereal or supernatural beings may enter a human body and by temporarily displacing and replacing his soul, or more probably his vital force (Mal.: *Semangat*), take possession of his physical being" (Shaw 1973: 71).

9. For a detailed study of *Taishang Ganying Pian* and its historical impact, see Catherine Bell (1996a; 1996b); see also DeBernardi (N.d.a).

10. Contemporary Austroasiatic languages include Mon-Khmer languages spoken in Vietnam, Cambodia, and by some *Orang Asli* populations of Malaysia; Mundaic languages spoken in north India, and Nicobarese in the Nicobar Islands in the Andaman Sea.

11. Bellwood concludes that Austronesian only differentiated into an ethnolinguistically distinct language family via migration to and beyond Taiwan (Bellwood 2004: 28).

12. See, for example, Terry Melton, Stephanie Clifford, Jeremy Martinson, Mark Batzer, and Mark Stoneking (1998). Although the use of genetic evidence promises to contribute greatly to our understanding of the prehistoric relationships of human populations, there is still much disagreement among scholars in this field.

13. These practices are not of course identical to Austronesian practices: Hokkien have a male Lord of Heaven and a goddess (Guanyin, albeit in a male transformation) governing the prisons of earth (as hell is known), but also venerate a Daoist goddess as the Queen of Heaven, and imagine many earth deities as male, although one spirit medium assured me that the local God of the Earth was under the control of Guanyin, the Goddess of Mercy. Nonetheless, we may recognize a high degree of congruency with the religious practices of contemporary Southeast Asian populations, including speakers of Austroasiatic and Austronesian languages who live throughout the region.

14. Anthropologist Piers Vitebsky (1997) similarly suggests that shamanic religion is strongest in hunting and gathering societies, where there is no competing priesthood,

and that agricultural societies often are inimical to shamans because they have institutionalized forms of religion.

15. Clive Kessler borrows the term 'scapeboat' from J. D. Gimlette's 1939 dictionary of Malay medicine (1939: 242, cited in Kessler 1977: 300).

16. The most famous example of this phenomenon is the Hauka movement in West Africa, whose African adepts were possessed by the spirits of Europeans. In trance, Hauka mediums wore military uniforms and mimed European military might; they consumed European food and drink, including cigarettes, alcohol, and meat prohibited by Islamic law. The mediums spoke Hausa with a pronounced accent, sometimes even switching to their European so-called mother tongue to better communicate (Krings 1999: 64; Stoller 1995: 44–45).

17. For diverse explorations of the dialectic between spirit mediums and modernity, see the essays in volumes edited by Heike Behrend and Ute Luig (1999) and Linda H. Connor and Geoffrey Samuel (2001).

18. Most studies of Mazu focus on her cult in specific locations, but see Johannes Widodo (2002) for a broader discussion of the role of Mazu temples in the region.

19. On the Kapitan system of governance under colonial rule in Malaya and the Straits Settlements, see C. S. Wong (1963); for Java, see Claudine Salmon and Denys Lombard (1980: lxii–lxiii).

20. Studies of Nonya-Baba culture include a study of the Malacca Baba by anthropologist Tan Chee Beng (1988); see also Cheo Kim Ban and Muriel Speeden (1988) and Felix Chia (1980).

21. For a detailed consideration of the wide range of religious institutions in traditional Chinese society, see C. K. Yang (1961).

22. Ong Seng Huat observes that in the past, the altar, community, and spirit medium worked together to ensure moral cohesion in Penang, but that these no longer work in concert (personal communication, 2004). Indeed, most spirit mediums are now individual entrepreneurs and have no connection to larger community organizations.

23. DD 38 Penang: Letters to the Governor May 1863-December 1863: 127 (NL604); see also DeBernardi (2002).

24. For a close consideration of the "structure of the conjuncture" as it played out in a number of societies, see Marshall Sahlins (1985, 1988, 1994).

25. For a more detailed discussion of Lim Boon Keng's life and impact, see DeBernardi (1995).

26. For further details on the impact of the Theosophical Enlightenment in Asia, see Joscelyn Godwin (1994: 327–8) and J. J. Clarke (1997: 89-91, 203).

27. In the 1980s the management renamed the temple the Penang Taoist Centre, and published two anniversary volumes, one in English (Penang Taoist Centre 1986), and the other in Mandarin (Penang Taoist Centre 1987). The English volume included a reprint of the 1914 scripture (Penang Taoist Centre 1986: 69–78).

28. As de Groot described it: "A temple-god of repute and popularity, a powerful protector of the parish, generally has a medium, into whom he preferably descends, in order to give through his mouth orders and good advice to his beloved people. In this way he may have ordered that this man shall appear in the procession. He then parades therein in a state of delirium which proves that the god is in him. He is naked to the

waist, his hair flowing down disheveled at his back. Long daggers stand implanted deep in his cheeks and upper arms, so that the blood drips out. With a double-edged sword he cleaves the air in his assaults on beings which nobody sees but he. At times he looks unconscious; then suddenly he hops, runs, spins round, and rolls from side to side, inflicting bloody wounds on his back with his sword, or with a ball studded with sharp iron points, which he bears by a cord. . . . " (de Groot 1964 [1892–1910] Vol. 6: 983).

29. Zhu Qiuhua describes contemporary forms of self-mortification by shamans (*tongzi*) in Jiangsu Province, an inland province adjacent to Fujian, which include standing on the blade of a hay-cutting knife while touring the village, striking the upper arm with a knife, and inserting a hot spade in the possessed shaman's mouth to drive away evil (Zhu 2002: 240).

30. Donald Sutton also notes that the self-mortifying practices of Taiwanese and Southern Fujianese spirit mediums are not found in other parts of China (Sutton 1990: 117).

31. David Freeman's account of the celebration of the Nine Emperor Gods festival near Kuala Lumpur describes the active participation of laypersons, whom the spirit medium led in fire-walking. The event, which was organized by Hokkien Chinese coolies, resembles many elements of the contemporary Nine Emperor Gods Festival, including the candidates' expression of their purity by wearing white, the hoisting of a red-painted mast with a green bamboo spar, the self-mortifying, exorcizing performance of a spirit medium, and a dramatic fire-walking at which a Chinese "fanatic" led 100 "candidates," all dressed in white, across hot coals at noon, together with a sedan chair carrying the spirit of the Ninth Emperor God (Freeman 1924: 75–76).

32. The missionaries commonly entered temples in order to proselytize, seeking crowds during festival and ritual events. In 1893, for example, missionary Alfred Green approached a trance performance in a small fishing village not far from the town of Taiping in order to find an audience for the gospel message. Engrossed in the trance event, they brushed Green and his companions off, "telling us they had no time, that next door was a better place, and so on." He added that in the day's itineration, they met Chinese who were "prepared to argue earnestly for the reality of these spirit possessions" (Green 1893: 213).

33. Although some consider the Shancai Boy to be Guanyin's disciple, others identify him as the companion and protector of the goddess Miao Shan, whom many Penangites equate with Guanyin. According to one version of his legend, Shancai was a young Buddhist priest who became a hermit after the death of his parents. Appointed Miao Shan's protector after she attained perfection, he flung himself off a precipice in an attempt to rescue her from robbers. He died in the attempt, but then was miraculously transformed so that he could fly through the air (Werner 1986 [1922]: 271–73). Miao Shan's story spread widely in China through a pious Buddhist literature that sought to instruct lay people in the ideals of Buddhist purity and bodily transcendence (see Dudbridge 1978.) Her story also is part of the lore of the Great Way of Former Heaven, a Buddhist sectarian group that in the nineteenth and the early twentieth centuries inspired some women in the Canton Delta to resist marriage and form collective vegetarian halls. Some of these women migrated to colonial Singapore and Penang to work, and there they formed vegetarian halls where they often took Guanyin – whom they merged with Miao

Shan – as one of their patron deities (See Topley 1978: 255). When, for example, the Datuk Aunt – the spirit medium whose teachings I present in Chapter Four – offered me a story about Guanyin, she retold instead the story of Miaoshan, identifying Guanyin's companion as Nazha, another 'Baby God' whose story is recounted in the *Canonization of Deities* (see Chapter Three).

34. The 1957 souvenir pamphlet prominently displayed a full-page ad for Singapore's Tiger Medical Hall and Tiger Remedies. Mrs. Aw donated funds to build a Phoenix Hall next to the temple, which suggests that the new temple also was a site for phoenix writing (*fuluan*), a form of spirit writing that this temple may have adopted when they began to worship the Mother of the Earth. For a translation of the *Earth Mother Scripture* (*Dimu Jing*), whose earliest known edition appeared in Shanghai in 1923, see Jordan and Overmyer (1986: 72–73).

35. Although promoting a Buddhist image, the Shancai Hall's annual festival days included events celebrating not only Buddhas and Bodhisattvas, but also a number of Daoist deities, including the birthdays of the Jade Emperor (1–9) and the Nine Emperor Gods (9–9).

36. As Daniel Overmyer had demonstrated, Chinese sectarian religious groups and the groups that Europeans termed secret societies, and which I call sworn brotherhoods, were distinct both in their ritual practices and their aspirations, although the latter often adopted religious symbols to fortify their political claims (Overmyer 1976: 193–204).

37. For further details on secret sworn brotherhoods in Malaysia, see Wilfred L. Blythe (1969), Jean DeBernardi (2004), and Mak Lau Fong (1981). Other works on the Triad include Barend ter Haar (1998), Dian Murray and Qin Baoqu (1994), David Ownby (1995, 1996), and David Ownby and Mary Somers Heidhues (1993).

Part I

1. Although *guan* literally means officer or official, when it appears in the names of deities Penangites tend to translate *guan* as "Lord."

2. Penangites call this a ceremony to 'open the eyes' (*khui bakchiu,kai muzhu*) or 'open the light' (*khui kui, kai guang*).

3. In Fujian, we find a similar practice of worshipping three divine kings (*ong ia, wangye*) who possess spirit mediums found in connection with worship of the Pure Water Patriarch, the god known in Penang as the Snake God (Dean 1993: 127). The three divine kings whose worship Dean describes for Fujian are called the Three Great Ones (*San Daren*), and have the surnames Zhu, Xing, and Li.

4. His name appeared to be written with the character Zhu, meaning crimson or vermillion; I did not get confirmation on this point, however, nor did I ask for the characters for the other two gods' names.

5. According to the reporter, he called the temple *Liongthian Keong Sam-ong Hu*, a name that I now guess to mean the Dragon Heaven Palace Three Kings Mansion (*Longtian Gong Sanwang Fu*).

6. Mrs. Huang believed the Dragon Great Official to be the popular deity known in Penang as the Founder God or Patriarch (*Cho·su Kong, Zushi Gong*), and more colloquially as the Snake God. His formal title is the Pure Water Patriarch (*Chheng Chui Cho·su*

Kong, Qingshui Zushi Gong), and he was said to be the deified spirit of Chen Puzu (Tan Pho· Chioh), an eleventh-century Chan Buddhist monk with extraordinary demon-expelling powers who for a time lived in the Qingshui grotto on Changyen mountain near Anxi (Wong 1967: 48–49; see also Dean 1993: 99–129; ter Haar 1990: 365–66). In Penang, his main temple in Sungai Nibong celebrated large-scale temple festivals on the sixth day of the first, sixth, and eleventh lunar months. The coincidence of dates – both temples celebrated a major festival on the sixth day of the sixth lunar month – suggests that she might have been correct, or that at the very least both deities shared similar attributes as healing deities. In the Chinese system of time reckoning, the sixth earthly branch is associated not with the dragon but with the snake. The dragon and the snake have similar attributes insofar as both are *yang* creatures with the power to produce clouds and mist, but the snake takes second place to the dragon.

7. These are two of the three so-called Baby Gods, child martial artists. People know the story of Nazha from reading a famous popular novel known as the *Canonization of Deities* (Low et. al. 1989; see also *Fengshen Yanyi* N.d.), which tells of his miraculous birth, and explains how he obtained his prodigious magical powers. I discuss this tale and the story of Monkey in Chapter Three.

8. Most of the gods who possess spirit mediums are well-known deities in the Chinese pantheon, and I remain puzzled as to which god this protective, martial deity might have been.

9. For example, a 1981 newspaper article reported that when the British army wished to destroy a Chinese temple at Bukit Terendak in Malacca in order to build a Church of Scotland in 1962, "To the disbelief of the army engineers, the demolition machines went out of action each time they approached the temple precincts," and a major involved in the project was seriously injured during a trip to Ipoh. Finally, a canteen owner advised them to discuss matters with the gods, which the "authorities" finally did through a spirit medium. After some negotiation, the gods agreed to move to an alternative home, and the British donated generously to the building fund (*The Star* 1981b). Meanwhile, stories abound in Malaysia of modern urban construction projects whose design was modified to accommodate existing small shrines.

10. Compare, for example, modern Shona spirit mediumship, whose gods are regarded as the protectors of a sacred ground and who served as the advisors and ritual specialists for Shona guerilla fighters (Lan 1985), and northwest Madagascar, where royal spirit mediums have become the guardians of sacred space (Sharp 1999).

11. This was especially true at the time of this festival event in 1979, when the Malaysian government still imposed restrictions on travel to China.

Chapter 1

1. See Rupert Hodder (1996) for a trenchant critique of these culturalist arguments.

2. Clarence Day's study of paper gods (1974 [1940]) neatly captures the materialist ethos of Chinese popular religious culture. In northern Zhejiang in the 1930s, worship focused on the protection of life and property, adjustment to the environment, peace and harmony in the home, prosperous livelihood, salvation from hell, and the attainment of virtue in heaven. Day describes a 'prosperous livelihood' as a "desideratum of supreme importance to the whole group as well as to the individual" (Day 1974 [1940]: 105). One

dimension of prosperity was agricultural success, and Zhejiang peasants offered worship to the God and Goddess of Fertility of the Fields, to the Five Sages of Domestic Animals, and the Star-God of the Corral. They worshiped the Melon Immortal for protection of their pumpkins and melons, and placed the flags of the Locust-Destroying General in their fields as insecticide (Day 1974 [1940]: 106–07). Zhejiang Chinese also prayed for wealth and success in capitalist ventures. As Day noted, "the securing of riches or fortune counted in terms of this world's goods is one of the aims of peasant religious practice" (Day 1974 [1940]: 113). He reported many wealth gods in the Zhejiang region, including "Call Riches," "Enter Wealth," "The Immortal Ruler of Favorable Markets," "As You Like It Mystic Altar," and "Lord of Fortune God of Wealth," which he equates with a god worshipped elsewhere, the "Giver of Joyful Opulence" (Day 1974 [1940]: 114–15).

3. According to Felix Chia, the Straits Chinese always placed images of these three gods representing Chinese 'great expectations' on their household altars, and they continue to be popular among Chinese in Penang and Singapore (Chia 1980: 88).

4. Alexeiev identifies this link between wealth and moral achievement as an important key to understanding the cult of the God of Wealth:

The coin in the foreground [of a picture of the God of Wealth] bears the following sentence which throws light upon the whole question of the cult of the God of Wealth: "Money can lead to godhead," i.e. can transform a man into a god. Thus, if a man use his money for the benefit of those who have none they will venerate him as a God of Wealth (Alexeiev 1989 [1928]: 19).

Although he proposes too direct a link between the charitable use of money and deification, nonetheless he has identified a crucial point, which is that wealth enables people to act charitably, which in turn wins them the praise (and perhaps even veneration) of others.

5. The morpheme *chu* also means 'to record,' and is used to describe the Birth-Recording Goddess (*Chuse^n Neoneo, Zhusheng Niangniang*), to whom women pray for fertility and childbirth, and whom some English-educated Chinese call the Goddess of Fate.

6. Many Daoist temples and monasteries set aside a separate shrine room for veneration of the Bushel Mother – the deification of the northern Pole Star, the still, creative center of the heavens – together with statues of sixty constitutive fate gods (*liushi jiazi benming shen*), each identified with a constellation, and each associated with one year in a sixty-year cycle. Each year in the sixty-year cycle is uniquely identified by a two-character name formed by combining a ten-year cycle of celestial stems and a twelve-year cycle of terrestrial branches, and each is further associated with a constellation. Every year a different constellation spirit governs the Ministry of Time, taking the title "Great Year" (*Taisui*), and every person born in a particular year falls under the influence of a constellation that is appointed to be the year's *Taisui* (Wu 2001: 72–75).

7. Weber was wrong when he conjectured that the notion of "religious sympathy" was poorly developed in China as a consequence of the fact that Chinese believed that "disease and misfortune are symptoms of divine wrath which the individual has brought upon himself" (Weber 1968 [1951]: 209–10; 233).

8. See also Majorie Topley 1974.

9. The child retains his or her surname and continues to live with its parents.

10. As C. K. Yang has pointed out (Yang 1968 [1964]: xxxix), Weber mistakenly thought that even Chinese folk belief lacked any notion of 'providence,' which he defined as "the concrete fate of the individual man," arguing that the notion only referred to "the harmony and the eventual destiny of the social collectivity per se..." (Weber 1968 [1951]: 207). By contrast, Yang convincingly argues that "the clearest expression of belief in the notion of fate among modern Confucians was their widespread practice of divination of all varieties," including the consultation of spirit mediums and the *Yijing* (Yang 1961: 259–60).

11. The title alludes to a story, but I have not been able to identify who 'Luokun' is or what story this might be.

12. A second fortune from the Snake Temple was more auspicious:

Dongyong Sells Himself (number forty-nine)
Serve both your parents with all your filial heart
You can model yourself on Imperial Heaven, ghosts and gods
If you trouble the gods, the mountains and rivers will listen attentively
The Dragon God can protect and assist the Lord's [your] body

This fortune suggests that moral behavior will result in the attention of the gods, and that the asker will have the protection of the Dragon God, a name some use for the Snake God. The explication added that business will be profitable; that if the asker seeks money he will find help; that he or she must request peace at their residence; and that a marriage will be harmonious. For a detailed consideration of the poetics of Taiwanese *chhiam* divination that also investigates notions of fate, see Donald Hatfield (2002).

13. In another context, however, I was told by Taishang's spirit medium that a paper representation of three colored rolls of cloth represented the three powers – Heaven, Earth, and Humans.

14. After all the committee members had finished the ceremony, the cloth was removed, and the priest aspersed water over the committee members, then removed his embroidered satin robes. A few minutes later, a young boy fell into trance, possessed by the Great Saint [Monkey God], and after a martial arts performance with a pole, he distributed the small pink cakes called "peaches," another symbol of long life, to the committee members. This might be a punning ritual action: the expression meaning "take peaches" (*siutho*) sounds very similar to the expression meaning "keep the dao" (*siuto·*).

15. At one temple dedicated to the Vagabond Buddha, worshippers sought to alter their luck (*kai-un, gaiyun*) by placing votive candles attached to the vital statistics of their name and birth horoscope in candelabra; on the god's birthday the temple was a blaze of light. At another temple celebrating Nazha's birthday, a possessed spirit medium led worshippers, some carrying replacement bodies, through two 'gates' (bamboo frameworks covered with paper) that represented the Northern and Southern Bushels, the constellations governing death and birth, as a ritualized prayer for longevity and peace.

16. A person might include a spirit medium and their possessing deity among their benefactors. For example, one of Master Lim's students was a stockbroker who called Master Lim his *guijin*, or benefactor, noting that he consulted with him before making investments.

17. Compare with the Confucian interpretation of the *Guandi* cult, which Prasenjit Duara argues has been 'superscribed' or "written over an older cult of the god of wealth" (Duara 1988: 146).

18. Ellen Oxfeld makes a similar point in her discussion of Chinese gambling in Calcutta. She observes that gambling may express "the contradictions inherent in their entrepreneurial ethos, an orientation which acknowledges both fate and skill as elements in business success, and which understands the roles of both prudence and risk taking. It is an outlook that gives status to those with the most wealth, but which thereby acknowledges the possibility of shake-ups in the status system when family fortunes change." She concludes that the ultimate goal is "to earn enough money to enjoy the luxuries of life, and to not worry about economizing" (Oxfeld 1993: 120).

19. Arthur Kleinman makes a similar point when he concludes that a spirit medium's diagnosis of a 'bad fate' absolved the unfortunate individual of personal responsibility for difficulties or failure, and that the ritual response helped to instill optimism (Kleinman 1980: 221, 235–38).

Chapter 2

1. In a detailed and richly illustrated study of the folk art of Korean shamanism, Alan Carter Covell concludes that both music and visual aids are crucial to the trance performance, and that an understanding of Korean shamanism as a religion requires close attention to both (Covell 1986: 16–17).

2. I borrow the felicitous term 'occult gossip' from Robert Hymes (2002).

3. J. J. M de Groot concludes that humans by their very nature are exorcists who can expel and destroy spirits because "a man's *yang* soul, called *hwun* [*hun*] or *shen*, must by its mere presence in his body endow him with exorcising capacities, especially if that soul is well developed and manifests itself by vitality, strength, courage, energy, intellect, and spiritual or even magical power, in short, by qualities comprised in the term ling (de Groot 1964 [1892–1910] Vol. 6: 1143). For this reason, according to de Groot, audacious, clever men are considered to have particular ability to expel demons, whereas those who lose their audacity or nerve also lose their spiritual (*shen*) substance, becoming vulnerable to malicious spirits (de Groot 1964 [1892–1910] Vol. 6: 1144–45).

4. Anthropologist Allan Elliott, who studied spirit mediums in Singapore in the 1950s, concluded that the term *shen* could not be translated into English, and chose to call Chinese popular religious culture "shenism" (Elliott 1955: 28).

5. In Taiwan, ghost shrines associated with the accidentally discovered bones of unknown persons are common. According to both Steven Harrell and Robert Weller, the devotees of these shrines often are socially marginal (including gamblers and the unemployed), but according to Weller they also include a cross-section of the population (Harrell 1974: 201; Weller 1994a; 1994b: 133).

6. Some temples organize special ceremonies to 'return thanks and gratitude' to the gods (*tapsia kamcheng, daxie ganqing*).

7. On the placation of ghosts in Taiwan, see also Robert Weller (1987, 1994a, 1994b) and Stevan Harrell (1974).

8. The Datuk Aunt noted that after the seventh day, the dead person went to the river to wash, and their fingernails fell out; only then did they realize that they were dead. The

ghostly demons, Cowhead and Horseface, give them wine to drink; they lose all memory of their previous life and enter hell, where they meet with their judge.

9. There are parallels between the nonreciprocal use of terms of address and the pronouns of power and solidarity that Roger Brown and A. Gilman (1960) and Paul Friedrich (1979 [1966]) have analyzed. On Chinese terms of address see Yuen Ren Chao (1976 [1956]).

10. Occasionally, actual age is not the criteria, but rather position in the generational structure. There are cases where a child must call a younger child 'uncle' because that child is a member of the next generation higher than himself, though in informal contexts adults did not insist on this.

11. Women who make formal speeches do not, however, use the equivalent "little sister," because it expresses an intimacy with sexual overtones.

12. Although this spirit medium was Cantonese, she offered consultations in Hokkien, and my research assistant and I also interviewed her in Hokkien.

13. Arthur Kleinman has provided a study of the Taiwanese health care system that includes consideration of the folk healing practices of spirit mediums. As a psychiatrist and medical anthropologist, Kleinman investigates the cultural categories and explanatory models that Taiwanese use, including categories like collision with ghosts (1980: 108–09, also see below) to discuss illness episodes. He concludes that Taiwanese, including spirit mediums, tend to somatize mental illness or emotional symptoms, experiencing anxiety or grief as physical pain, for example; he regards this approach to the diagnosis of mental illness as a culturally constituted coping mechanism. Kleinman provides, for example, the case of a lower-middle-class family whose members reported that they all experienced back pains after their young daughter-in-law's death in a motorcycle accident, which they feared might have been a suicide. The ghosts of suicides are vengeful, and the family was terrified that her spirit would attack them. Consequently, they consulted a spirit medium, who performed exorcistic rituals to drive away her ghost and reassured them. Kleinman noted that psychiatrists might view this as a case of group hysteria, and wondered whether the somatization would make it more difficult for family members to come to terms with their conflicted feelings, leading perhaps to depression in the future. Nonetheless, Kleinman concluded that in Taiwan somatized illness behavior is a crucial adaptive mechanism because mental illness is harshly stigmatized and psychotherapy is largely unavailable (1980: 157–58).

Like Kleinman, psychiatrist Teoh Jin-Inn concludes that the attribution of the client's problems to supernatural causation "provides a culturally-sanctioned externalization of his basic interpersonal and intrapsychic problems," one that is protective of family relationships. He observes that the spirit medium's diagnosis of supernatural causation is both more "concrete and compact" than the explanations that modern psychotherapists offer, and consequently more effective as a form of healing (Teoh 1973: 58).

14. A spirit medium who lived in a remote mountain temple noted that, "People ask the god for peace (*pengan, pingan*), luck at gambling, and good business. Sometimes women pray for a good husband. This god also can cure using green herbs gathered from the hills...." At another temple, the spirit medium/god dispensed green charms that were to be burned and applied externally in a green herbal oil whose secret formula was written by the god.

15. Planchette divination (*fuji*), or phoenix writing (*fuluan*), has been widely practiced in China, Taiwan, and Southeast Asia. For a detailed historical study of a planchette divination cult and its texts, see Terry F. Kleeman (1994). Contemporary studies of planchette divination in Taiwan include Philip Clart (1996), David Jordan and Daniel Overmyer (1986), and in Malaysia Soo Khin Wah (1997) and Tan Chee Beng (1985).

16. As one research assistant explained it, black is bad luck (*soe, shuai*), and Malaysian Chinese also associate it with mourning. If a person wears black they cannot celebrate the New Year festival, or attend a wedding feast, or visit a sick person because it is an avoidance (Malay: *pantang*) color. If someone does visit the sick, they might suffer a spiritual collision (*tioh chhiong, de chong*), or bad luck would come. He added that black-faced idols were ghosts. The practice of making black-faced idols may have had its origin in the veneration of mummified corpses of monks, priests, and other individuals in Fujian (ter Haar 1990: 365; also see Baity 1975).

17. Some authors translate the terms for the so-called spiritual illness that mediums are asked to cure 'spirit possession.' This translation of the Hokkien *hoantioh* or *chhiongtiok* is imprecise, and implies a more dramatic phenomenon than is normally found. Elaborate exorcisms such as those described by Gananath Obeyesekere (1977, 1981) and others for Sri Lanka do not appear to occur.

18. Max Weber correctly observed that in Mandarin, "I have sinned" corresponded to "I beg your pardon" in violating a convention, and that magical infringements were thus quite like lapses of etiquette (Weber 1968 [1951]: 229).

19. I did not attempt to gather information on the herbs dispensed, nor am I aware of any research on this topic, which would be worthwhile to study in more detail.

20. Although the name *chuse* indicates that the powder used to make the ink is cinnabar, I do not know if this name accurately identifies the ink's chief ingredient or refers only to its color.

21. Some also recommended wearing the ashes of the testicles of a totally black dog as protection against black magic.

22. A Taiwanese friend claimed: "Spirit mediums can raise ghosts, and the spirits will do things for the mediums. So, the medium will take a handful of beans, chant, and throw them, and they become men and can work...." The Datuk Aunt also recounted lurid stories of people who raised the spirits of children whose bodies they buried at night, who then (vampire-like) flew at night sucking blood.

23. People also believed that discontented builders sometimes used black paper charms to disrupt a household. A Taiwanese friend living in Penang noted:

"When you put in the main rafter of a house, you must give a 'red packet' (gift of money) to the contractor, and also feast him. Otherwise the contractor will put garlic and mucus in the rafters, and in 100 days there will be a White-Haired Ghost. Or else he can write a black charm paper, and then the house will not be peaceful. If this happens you must invite Taoist priests to cancel the spell."

As historian Philip Kuhn documents, a popular Qing dynasty carpentry manual included "rules for proper ritual construction" (which was considered necessary to ensure the prosperity of those living in the house), but also "baleful charms for builders to hide atop rafters or under floors." The manual also recommended specific countermagic, however – remedies that would send the harm back to the would-be sorcerer (Kuhn 1990: 104–05). In Penang, people sometimes employ Daoist priests or spirit mediums to exorcize the house, and they sometimes use the Eight-Trigrams bushel basket, a ritual object that represents an ordered cosmos.

24. As an additional example, take *The Journey to the North*, a popular novel that Master Ong translated into English and made available in his temple. The authors follow the hero, the Emperor of the Dark Heavens, through successive rebirths as he seeks to perfect himself and achieve the *Dao* (*tekto, dedao*). In one rebirth, the Emperor of the Dark Heavens confronts two evil spirits, the turtle and the snake. These are transformations of his own stomach and intestines, which his heavenly mentor removed while he slept, and represent his own passions [Seaman 1987: 2]). After many battles, the hero triumphs, and the turtle and snake surrender: "The two evils knelt down and said that they were willing to follow Chor Soo" (*Park Yew Kee* 1974: 32).

Chapter 3

1. The practice of spirit mediumship in Taiwan and southern Fujian closely resembles the practices of spirit mediums in Malaysia. For discussions of Chinese spirit mediums in Taiwan, see David K. Jordan (1972); Jordan Paper (1995; 1996); Arthur Kleinman (1980); Peter Nickerson (2001); Gary Seaman (1978); Donald Sutton (1990, 2003); Alison Marshall (2004c); and Margery Wolf (1992).

2. For a detailed study of the healing diagnoses of Taiwanese spirit medium, evaluated from the perspective of medical anthropology, see Kleinman (1980: 210–43; 311–74).

3. Maurice Freedman and Marjorie Topley note, for example, that spirit mediums normally are occupied with personal and private matters and regard it as uncommon for them to "produce divine utterances of a broad moral significance" (Freedman and Topley 1979 [1961]: 184).

4. See, for example, Erika Bourguignon's work on spirit possession (1973, 1976), Vincent Crapanzano and Vivian Garrison's edited volume, *Case Studies in Spirit Possession* (1977), Colleen Ward (1989), and Ruth-Inge Heinze (1997).

5. Contemporary Penang Hokkien speakers use the term *tong* in compounds that describe spirit mediums who, like shamans, seek to control the spirit world to help humans, but whose spirits do not make the journeys to Heaven and the underworld that scholars like Mircea Eliade regard as the chief characteric of shamanic performance.

6. Similarly, the classical Chinese name for spirit medium, *wu*, is homophonous with, and may be related to, the Chinese word meaning 'to dance, jump, or posture' (Needham 1956: 134, cited in Seaman 1994: 229). For a detailed consideration of the etymology of the term *shaman*, see Seaman (1994: 227–29). The author of one Hokkien dictionary translates *thiau tong* as a verb meaning "to dance in religious ecstacy" (Embree 1973: 284).

7. For a dialogic account of the circumstances of this challenge, see DeBernardi (1994b).

8. On the ritual performances of the imperial cult, see Stephen Bokenkamp (1996), Edouard Chavannes (1910), and Angela Zito (1997). For a detailed consideration of possible historical relationships between shamanism and kingship see Alison Marshall (2004a).

9. Bernard Faure traces the historical process by which Bodhidharma came to be claimed as the patriarch of the Shaolin monastery and posthumously designated the founder of Shaolin temple boxing (Faure 1993: 133).

10. In Penang popular sources, the authors describe Lohans as bandits who met a monk, were reformed, and became Buddhist saviors (Poh 1971: 27; P'ng and Draeger 1979: 82). The 'Monkey' is of course the Monkey God, a formidable martial artist, and Erh-lang [Erlang] is an exorcising deity who was the chief possessing deity for Master Poh, whose teachings I discuss in Chapter 5. The authors also list the five branches of Southern Shaolin but do not explicate them in depth, although four appear to involve demonic guardian spirits (P'ng and Draeger 1979: 20).

11. Observers consistently describe the god's language elsewhere in the Southern Min cultural world as consisting of shrill incoherent sounds, meaningless without the assistance of the god's interpreter. Consequently, it seems likely that the literary speech register spoken by some Penang trance performers is more comprehensible than that spoken by spirit mediums elsewhere, perhaps because of their didactic role.

12. My Mandarin teacher employed a worker in the ironworks factory she managed who had studied to become a spirit medium, but then given it up. A Christian herself, she asked him if he thought it was true that the god spoke through him. He replied that he had just done what the master had told him to do. She took this as evidence that the whole business was fraudulent and worthless. Later, on seeing some photographs I had taken of a spirit medium possessed by Taishang Laojun, she scornfully produced this proverb: "Dress up as a god to play the ghost."

13. Another complex and fascinating case is that of the Taiping Rebellion, whose leaders developed a sectarian movement that syncretized Christianity and spirit possession. Jonathan Spence (1996) and Robert Weller (1994b) have insightfully explored the charismatic foundations of this sectarian movement.

14. Robert Ruhlman observed, for example, that: "There is no single and clear-cut answer to whether popular imagination conceived its heroes as gods, genii, or just superior men. The use of the word 'divine' (shen) in fiction is suggestive; Wu Sung [Wu Song] lightly tosses about a stone pedestal, and enthusiastic onlookers cheer, 'This is no common man! Truly he is a god!' (or, 'divine man!' *T'ien shen, shen-jen*). But obviously this record-smashing champion is considered part of the human race" (Ruhlman 1960: 153).

15. Stephen Sangren explores the story of Nazha, focusing on the way that his story, along with the stories of Mulian and Miaoshan, highlight particular intergenerational family relationships: father-son, mother-son, and father-daughter (Sangren 1996). Avron Boretz suggests that with characters like Nazha, "There is an intersubjective association of paternal power with the power of political and social elites and of the repressed desire for rebellion with the 'Oedipal' rebellion represented in the Nazha myth – particularly by the subjugated classes" (Boretz 1995: 107).

16. This summary is based on my own translation of the text. For English translations, see C. C. Low's 1989 bilingual comic book edition (Low et al. 1989: 133–92) and Edward T. C. Werner's brief summary (Werner 1986 [1922]: 305–19).

17. For a consideration of the origins of Sun Wukong that investigates the monkey lore associated with a Buddhist monastery in the Hangchow area, see Meir Shahar (1992).

18. See, for example, James Watson (1985) and Prasenjit Duara (1988).

19. I based this summary on Arthur Waley's entertaining translation of the *Journey to the West* (Waley 1980 [1943]).

20. In his detailed study of Jigong, Meir Shahar explores the development of fictional accounts of the 'mad monk' Jigong and the influence of these narratives on the growing popularity of this deity in China and Taiwan. As in Malaysia, Jigong commonly possesses spirit mediums or communicates through spirit writing with his followers (see Shahar 1998: 176–98).

21. I base this summary on my own translation of the version of Jigong's study that I obtained in Penang (*Jigong Quanzhuan* N.d.).

22. For a discussion of this text, whose title he translates as *Journey to Purgatory*, see Meir Shahar (1998: 190–95).

23. It appeared that they had compiled and published this book themselves, but aside from the printer's address, no publication information appears in the book to confirm this.

24. The World Red Swastika Society Prospectus reports that the group's primary spiritual practices were quiet prayer, collective scripture study (of sacred writings that will vary with the religion of members), relief work, and spirit writing (Wang 1949: 17–18).

25. The identification of General Montgomery as one of their saints may be a modification of their teachings to suit local taste: Gary Seaman notes that in Los Angeles, this group names General MacArthur as the sainted World War II general (personal communication).

26. In Hokkien, this proverb is *Jit iu^n bi chhi pah iu^n lang* (*yiyang mi si baiyang ren*).

Part II

1. See also Kenneth Dean 1993: 181–82. For a critical discussion of debates regarding the relationship between popular religious movements and more specialized forms of Daoism, see Paul Katz (1995: 36–38; 172–74). In relationship to the practice of spirit mediumship in Penang, Schipper's formulation overstates the division between ritual masters and spirit mediums.

2. For a discussion of moral mediums, see Philip Clart (2003).

Chapter 4

1. Because the Malay derivation for this term is transparent and meaningful to Hokkien speakers, I use the standard Malay term *datuk* rather than its Hokkien pronunciation *natu* or *latu* to refer to the Datuk Aunt and to datuk spirits.

2. To give a few examples, the Bugis in south Sulawesi sometimes pray at *keramat* shrines for healing, fertility, success, and money (Pelras 2002); the Gumai of south Sumatra, when faced with difficulties, may fast and meditate on an ancestor's tomb and ask for advice in dreams (Sakai 2002); Javanese by the thousands make pilgrimages to famous sacred sites (Chambert-Loir 2002).

3. Although the Datuk Aunt's teachings about ghosts and divination practices might not have drawn deeply on China's literary tradition, nonetheless that tradition is rich in stories of gods and ghosts. De Groot observed, "Where belief in spectres and spectrophoby

so thoroughly dominate thought and life, demon lore is bound to attain its highest development. Literature in China abounds with spectre tales,—no stories in Chinese eyes, but undeniable truth" (de Groot 1912: 9).

4. The Datuk Aunt explained to us that Malays did not eat pork because their ancestors were pigs, explaining the prohibition as a form of totemic taboo rather than as Islamic law.

5. For example, one man present at the group interview that I describe in the Introduction to Part One recalled that some years earlier he had fallen seriously ill. He went into the hospital, but the doctors could find no cause for his illness. One of the nurses suggested that he consult a spirit medium, who advised him that he had offended a Datuk Kong. He realized that he probably had offended the spirit by throwing cigarette butts out of his bathroom window in the direction of a tree, and recalled that after he replaced this thoughtless act with acts of ritual respect, he recovered.

6. In the Bulusu practice of spirit mediumship in Borneo, the offerings made to the spirits are strikingly similar to those that Penangites offer to Datuk spirits, including rice prepared with turmeric, and betel-nut chewing supplies (Appell and Appell 1993: 76–77).

7. At the festival event, she also was possessed by Datuk Bisu, a deaf Datuk spirit.

8. This story resembles one told of Zhang Daoling, the founder of the Celestial Master sect of Daoism, a famous exorcist who used his magic to decapitate eighteen hidden musicians when the Emperor tested him.

9. The Inconstant Uncle is widely worshipped in Hokkien communities, often in conjunction with a short god who is regarded as his partner or younger brother. The identification of the taller god as a Wealth God is not universal, and is not found, for example, in Taiwan (personal communication, Donald Sutton).

10. A few months later a gang robbed her of his gold and ruby jewelry, and she asked me to drive her to see another spirit medium possessed by the Inconstant Uncle so that she could ask for his help in retrieving her jewelry (see DeBernardi 1994b).

11. Compare the Datuk Aunt's practice of attaching stories with morals to sites on the landscape to the Apache practice of associating the names of places on the landscape with didactic stories, as reported by Keith Basso (Basso 1984, 1990).

12. *Koan* (*guan*), which means 'control' is the same word used to describe calling the god to possess a spirit medium.

13. Although Chaozhou is closely related to Hokkien, the meaning of this chant was obscure to my research assistant. Kim Ban Cheo and Muriel Speeden also report this practice, noting in addition that, "The number of times the ladle knocks against the basket indicates the numbers given" (Cheo and Speeden 1988: 76).

Chapter 5

1. Some English-speaking Penangites called this deity the 'Goat God,' based on a false etymology for his surname Iu[n] – which means 'aspen' or 'poplar,' which are trees not found in Malaysia, but it is also homophonous with 'goat.'

2. Today, Chinese government policy continues to restrict 'feudal and superstitious activities' and condemns activities such as using exorcism to cure illness and 'pretending to be gods and ghosts' (Marshall 2004b: 718–19).

3. Another spirit medium noted that Master Poh once had been famous, but that when his sister had needed money, she had come to him for assistance instead of going to her brother, implying that he would not have had the means to help her.

4. Martial artists believe that his teachings, including physical exercises, form the foundation for the Shaolin fighting arts (see, for example, P'ng and Draeger 1979).

5. Master Poh's 'deep Hokkien' was difficult to follow; consequently Eng Hok, the student helping me, offered invaluable assistance by asking most of the questions at the first interview. I waited until I had transcribed the first taped session to return to interview him a second time, and he clarified some points for me at that second interview. The second lecture repeats many of the points made in the first lecture almost word for word, but his expositions on certain (but not all) topics were fuller.

In earlier publications in which I present Master Poh's teachings, I combined the two interviews into a composite, adding new information from the second session into the first interview (see DeBernardi 1996; 2002). In this translation, I have made several corrections to the earlier one, but some terms remain obscure to me. Master Poh was China-born, and his 'deep Hokkien" was difficult even for my research assistants to understand, even though one was a fluent speaker of Hokkien with an excellent grasp of literary Hokkien. I have indicated with ellipses or footnotes places in the text where I was unable to translate with certainty.

6. He used the term *hongkau* (*fengjiao*), which my research assistants agreed meant 'Christianity.' This term means 'to join a church,' but also 'to receive instruction,' and it seems more likely that he referred to Confucianism. Although I can only speculate that this is the case, I am opting for that translation here.

7. I am unable to propose Mandarin equivalents for these terms.

8. Master Poh's account of Bodhidharma diverges from the standard biographical legend, which describes his form of practice not as "hanging on the wall" but as "wall meditation" (Faure 1986: 188).

Chapter 6

1. For a discussion of cosmopolitanism, see Ulf Hannerz (1990; 1992b).

2. The authors Master Lim recommended to me were Paul Grunton, a journalist who went to India intending to expose the Maharishi as a fraud but ended up a convert, and Dr. Alexander Cannon, who entered a Buddhist monastery in Tibet.

3. When I showed Richard Wilhelm's translation of *The Secret of the Golden Flower* (1962 [1931]) to Master Lim, he claimed to recognize the text, and expressed surprise and disapproval that it had been published. According to Wilhelm, who relies on "oral tradition" for these details, the text was the product of an eighth-century sect known as the Religion of the Golden Elixir of Life, which was allegedly founded by Lü Dongbin. Lü Dongbin later was absorbed into the Eight Immortals, and was Master Lim's 'ancestral patriarch,' and also one of his possessing deities (Wilhelm 1962 [1931]: 5).

4. Theravada Buddhism also was taught at Penang's Mahindarama Temple, a Sinhalese Buddhist temple founded in 1918 that was active in dharma teaching and established a Buddhist Sunday School for children. Buddhist proselytizing is not, of course, a modern phenomenon (see, for example, Kent 1982), although it did take new forms influenced by Christian evangelical practices.

5. The World Fellowship of Buddhists, an international organization formed in Sri Lanka in 1950 with representatives from twenty-seven countries in Asia, Europe, and North America, has been a powerful force for the unification of diverse communities of Buddhism, including Theravada, Mahayana, and Vajrayana traditions.

6. Another spirit medium told me that Master Lim's father was the Daoist immortal Lü Dongbin.

7. Shakyamuni and Amitabha Buddha, but not Maitreya, were represented by images in this temple, but when I asked Master Lim about Maitreya he emphatically replied, "The stories are nonsense, there are no names, all names are false."

8. For a historical consideration of the cult of Lü Dongbin that explores varied representations of this immortal, see Paul Katz (1996).

9. In my citations of the *Daodejing*, I am using both my notes on Master Lim's translation and D. C. Lau's translation (1963). I identify Lau's translation with a citation, and Lim's with brackets.

10. Master Lim translated the Hokkien term *lang*, a nongendered term that means 'human, person' with the English generic 'man.' Although I would prefer to use the nongendered translation, in translating his teachings from Hokkien into English in this chapter I have usually followed his practice in order to be consistent with his personal style.

11. Scholars date the compilation of the *Daodejing* earlier than this, to the fourth century BC (Lao Tzu 1963:12–13), and estimate that the *Yijing* was put together in the ninth century BC (Lynn 1994:1)

12. He also included a much fuller version of this story in his autobiography, but here I give the story as he retold it to me.

13. We find traces of Master Lim's influence in the publications of Penang's Taishang Laojun temple, which is also known as the Penang Taoist Centre (1986), and those of a wealthy and successful moral uplifting society (Che Hoon Khor Moral Uplifting Society 2001). Like reformed Buddhists and Master Lim, the authors of these publications (two of whom were his students) propose a new form of Daoist practice that we might describe as modernist Daoism (see DeBernardi N.d.a).

Chapter 7

1. According to Master Ooi, these spirits were Datuk Haji, Datuk Ali, Datuk Merah, Datuk Kuning, Datuk Hitam, Datuk Hijau, and Datuk Rimau [Harimau]. Thus these seven included the Red, Yellow, Black, and Green Datuk spirits, all spirits of nature, together with the Tiger spirit, and two deified humans, Datuk Haji and Datuk Ali.

2. The character for *lun (ren)* is a graphic metaphor that shows the heart radical beneath the knife radical.

3. A ritual was performed in the Heaven and Earth Society's initiation ceremony in which the group's 'generals' gave candidates a "slight wound on the chest" with the 'swords of justice and sincerity' (Ward and Stirling 1977 [1925] Vol. I: 57).

4. *Er Lang* means 'Second Man' or 'Second Son,' and the first part of his other name, *Yang Jian*, means 'Aspen.'

5. A Penang author who writes about the Shaolin martial arts tradition identified Lohans as deities who possess martial artists (P'ng and Draeger), which may represent an extension of their role as protectors of Buddhist law.

6. These numbers represent the thirty-six (4 x 9) spirits that rule the zodiacal divisions of heaven, and seventy-two (8 × 9) guardian spirits of the earth (Schlegel 1991 [1866]: xxviii; Shaw 1973: 107). The number 108 also refers to the total number of constellations (Schipper 1993 [1982]: 45).

7. According to Meir Shahar, historically the Buddhist laity widely considered an eccentric Buddhist figure, the 'Cloth-Bag Monk' (*Budai heshang*), to be an incarnation of Maitreya, but Shahar does not note a similar equation between Jigong and Maitreya (Shahar 1998: 218). Guillaume Dunstheimer observes, however, that the Boxers considered Jigong, who was the patriarch of numerous heterodox sects, to be a reincarnation of Maitreya (Dunstheimer 1972: 24–25).

8. Tiger General' (*hujiang*) is the slang term used to refer to the fighters and protectors for contemporary secret societies. See also Mak Lau Fong (1981: 69, 77).

9. The Hokkien for these terms is: the Pleasure Immortal (*thiongsian, changxian*); the Gambling Ghost (*puahkiau kui, dubo gui*); and the Opium Immortal (*a-phian sian, yapian xian*).

10. More intriguing is the stamped copy of the temple seal, which includes the names of five gods that the medium's assistant also wrote out in modern characters for me: the Old Ancestor of the Vast Creation (*Hongjun Laozu*) took first position; followed by the Very High Old Lord (*Taishang Laojun*, the deified spirit of Laozi); the Influence-Heaven Sect Founder (*Tongtian Jiaozhu*); the Primal Heavenly Lord (*Yuanshi Tianjun*); and the Five Thunder Patriarch-Founder (*Wulei Zushi*). Sinologist Wolfgang Franke identifies the first four of these gods as the legendary first ancestor of Daoism and his three disciples, the Three Pure Ones (*Sanqing* [Franke 1989: 408]). But this five-fold association of gods appears to associate the temple with the Kunlun style of martial arts, named for Mount Kunlun, which Daoists regard as the world mountain connecting Heaven and Earth and the residence of the Queen Mother of the West, her husband, and the immortals. According to their founding legend (which might be a modern invention), the Taoist ancestor, Hongjun taught three disciples: Laozi, Yuanshi, and Tongtian. Tongtian became a powerful Daoist patriarch, and the Kunlun school claims him as an ancestor. He also is a character in the *Canonization of Deities*.

11. In a 1941 study, *Triad and Tabut: A Survey of the Origin and Diffusion of Chinese and Mohamedan Secret Societies in the Malay Peninsula, A.D. 1800–1933*, an encyclopedic study of Chinese secret societies in Malaya that the colonial government published for internal distribution in 1941, Mervyn Llewelyn Wynne sought to develop a 'subjective' approach that would allow him to comprehend the discourse and practice of the secret sworn brotherhoods,. Drawing on the writings of Arthur Maurice Hocart and Max Muller, Wynne explored the shared dualistic symbolism of the diverse religious traditions originating in the Middle East, noting that the "ancient underlying concept appears to develop from the fact of the two principles in nature, male and female, light and darkness, etc." (Wynne 1957 [1941]: xxxiv). But dualism, he concluded, divided religion "into two halves or sides, the exoteric and esoteric," which he contrasted as a relationship of the "upright to the debased" (Wynne 1957 [1941]: xxxv). Thus according to Wynne, the

criminal secret societies used a shared dualistic symbolism to identify themselves with occult forces, much as Satanists and some Kali worshippers do. The symbolic dimensions of worship of the left were, he claimed, universal: "The association of the colour black with night and the Yin principle of the Chinese: the left side in dualism, the things of darkness, evil and death is constant . . . " (Wynne 1957 [1941]: liv). Although this dualistic language of good and evil may strike us as unsophisticated, nonetheless Wynne took an important step in recognizing that ritual practice was a means to form a diversity of associations with diverse social ends. The work has been reprinted as volume six of Kingsley Bolton and Christopher Hutton's edited collection of Western writings on Triad societies (2000).

12. In a contemporary analysis of Triad slang in the Hong Kong media, Bolton and Hutton report that in contemporary Hong Kong Triad slang, initiation is not equated with birth but with death, thus the question, "Have you died yet?" means "Have you been initiated?" (Bolton and Hutton 1995: 161).

Conclusion

1. As Donald Sutton has observed, "Opponents of spirit mediums deny their good faith; they regard possession and feats in the god's name as disorderly dancing and fakery, and connection with the community of worshippers as selfish and exploitative" (Sutton 2000: 3). He concludes that in late imperial China, spirit medium survived due to their "usefulness and persuasiveness among the common people" despite the hostility of the Chinese literati (Sutton 2000: 36).

2. In Thailand, spirit mediums also invite donations in envelopes. The mediums send invitations to their Praise Ceremonies printed on empty envelopes that are similar to those used for weddings and funerals. They expect that participants will place them on the spirit's dish filled with offerings (Morris 2000: 168–69).

3. William G. Stirling also mentions that in 1924 a gift of money was expected of patients who are cured. In addition, patients paid a musician to escort back to the temple the god image that has been left on the home's family altar and they were expected to make a gift of wooden scrolls praising the god (Stirling 1924: 46).

4. For a more detailed discussion of this temple, see DeBernardi 1994b.

5. The figures given here are based on what organizers gave me in the early 1980s; in 2003, a night of Chinese opera performed by a well-known troupe from Singapore was only slightly more at RM2,500 per night (Dielenberg 2003).

6. A catty weighs approximately one-and-a-third pounds.

7. Some also mentioned that the government required a deposit of RM1000 before issuing a permit to hold a stage show.

8. Malaysian psychotherapist Teoh Jin-Inn also explores spirit mediums' performance of roles and statuses, outlining six prominent roles taken by spirit mediums, including: (1) the *succourant* role, in which the spirit medium offers help or relief to his clients to ameliorate their suffering; (2) the *reciprocal* role, in which the client bestows gratitude and gifts on the spirit; (3) the *dominant disciplinarian* role, in which the spirit medium may verbally and even physically assault the client, berating them for their lack of discipline and sincerity; (4) the *retaliatory* role, in which the spirit expresses

his malevolent anger and grudge, seeking an apology from the client; (5) the *status-demonstrative* role, in which the spirit medium seeks to enhance his prestige to increase his credibility with clients; and (6) the *informant* role, in which the spirit provides a diagnosis (Teoh 1973: 57–58).

9. One friend noted that wealthy Penangites claimed face in the community by making public contributions to community causes at banquets, including those that accompanied major temple festivals, but that police closely tracked these donations. She guessed that this prevented individuals who had made money on the black market from making public donations, thereby also preventing them from translating money into social capital.

Bibliography

Aasen, Clarence. 2004. "Material and Social Indicators of Incipient Globalisation: Southeast Asian Chinese Settlements, Architecture and Artefacts, 1500–1930." Paper presented at the 5th Conference of the International Society for the Study of Chinese Overseas, Denmark. http://www.nias.ku.dk/issco5/documents/AasenClarence.doc.

Ahern, Emily Martin. 1981. *Chinese Ritual and Politics.* Cambridge: Cambridge University Press.

Alexeiev, Basil M. 1989 [1928]. *Chinese Gods of Wealth.* Singapore: Graham Brash.

Anon. 2001. "Early Chinese in Bali," Denpasar, 12 January 2001. http://www.balitouring.com/bali_articles/earlychinese.htm.

Appell, Laura W. R., and George Appell. 1993. "To Do Battle with the Spirits: Bulusu Spirit Mediums." In *The Seen and the Unseen: Shaman, Priest, and Spirit Medium: Religious Specialists, Tradition and Innovation in Borneo*, edited by Robert L. Winzeler, 55–99. Williamsburg, VA: Borneo Research Council.

Arnold, Sir Edwin. 1995 [1879]. *Light of Asia.* New Delhi: Navrang.

Ashdown, W. D. 1894. "A Demon From the Sea." Letter to *Echoes of Service* from Tongkah, 30 October 1894. *Echoes of Service* 301 (Jan. 1894): 20–21.

Atkinson, Jane Monnig. 1989. *The Art and Politics of Wana Shamanship.* Berkeley: University of California Press.

Baity, Philip Chesley. 1975. *Religion in a Chinese Town.* Taipei: The Chinese Association for Folklore.

Bakhtin, Mikhail. 1981a. "Forms of Time and of the Chronotope in the Novel." In *The Dialogic Imagination: Four Essays by M. M. Bakhtin*, edited by Michael Holquist, translated by C. Emerson and Michael Holquist, 84–258. Austin: University of Texas Press.

————. 1981b. "Discourse in the Novel." In *The Dialogic Imagination: Four Essays by M. M. Bakhtin*, edited by Michael Holquist, and translated by C. Emerson and Michael Holquist, 259–422. Austin: University of Texas Press.

Barrett, Robert J. 1993. "Performance, Effectiveness, and the Iban Manang." In *The Seen and the Unseen: Shaman, Priest, and Spirit Medium: Religious Specialists, Tradition and Innovation in Borneo*, edited by Robert L. Winzeler, 235–79. Williamsburg, VA: Borneo Research Council.

Basso, Keith. 1984. " 'Stalking with Stories': Names, Places, and Moral Narratives among the Western Apache." In *Text, Play, and Story: The Construction and Reconstruction of Self and Society*, edited by E. M. Bruner, 19–55. Prospect Heights, IL: Waveland Press.

———. 1990. *Western Apache Language and Culture: Essays in Linguistic Anthropology*. Tucson: University of Arizona Press.

Behrend, Heike, and Ute Luig, editors. 1999. *Spirit Possession, Modernity and Power in Africa*. Madison: University of Wisconsin Press.

Bell, Catherine. 1996a. " 'A Precious Raft to Save the World': The Interaction of Scriptural Traditions and Printing in a Chinese Morality Book." *Late Imperial China* 17(1): 158–200.

———. 1996b. "Stories from an Illustrated Explanation of the Tract of the Most Exalted on Action and Response." In *Religions of China in Practice*, edited by Donald S. Lopez, Jr., 437–45. Princeton: Princeton University Press.

Bellwood, Peter. 1997 [1985]. Prehistory of the Indo-Malaysian Archipelago, revised edition. Honolulu: University of Hawaii Press.

———. 2004. "The Origins and Dispersals of Agricultural Communities in Southeast Asia." *Southeast Asia: From Prehistory to History*, edited by Ian Glover and Peter Bellwood, 21–40. London and New York: RoutledgeCurzon.

Bellwood, Peter, and Ian Glover. 2004. "Southeast Asia: Foundations for an Archaeological History." *Southeast Asia: From Prehistory to History*, edited by Ian Glover and Peter Bellwood, 4–20. London and New York: RoutledgeCurzon.

Blythe, Wilfred L. 1969. *The Impact of Chinese Secret Societies in Malaya: A Historical Study*. Kuala Lumpur: Oxford University Press.

Bok, Sissela. 1982. *Secrets: On the Ethics of Concealment and Revelation*. New York: Pantheon Books.

Bokenkamp, Stephen. 1996. "Record of the Feng and Shan Sacrifices." In *Religions of China in Practice*, edited by Donald S. Lopez, Jr., 251–60. Princeton: Princeton University Press.

Bolton, Kingsley, and Christopher Hutton. 1995. "Bad Language and Banned Language: Triad Societies, the Censorship of the Cantonese Vernacular and Colonial Language Policy in Hong Kong." *Language in Society* 24 (1995): 159–86.

———, editors. 2000. *Triad Societies: Western Accounts of the History, Sociology, and Linguistics of Chinese Secret Societies*. London: Routledge.

Boretz, Avron A. 1995. "Martial Gods and Magic Swords: Identity, Myth, and Violence in Chinese Popular Religious Culture." *Journal of Popular Culture* 29(1): 93–109.

Bourdieu, Pierre. 1990 [1980]. *The Logic of Practice*, translated by Richard Nice. Stanford: Stanford University Press.

———. 1998 [1994]. "The Economy of Symbolic Goods." In *Practical Reason*, 92–123. Stanford: Stanford University Press.

Bourguignon, Erika. 1973. *Religion, Altered States of Consciousness and Social Change*. Columbus: Ohio State University Press.

———. 1976. *Possession*. San Francisco: Chandler & Sharp.

Brown, Callum. 2001. *The Death of Christian Britain: Understanding Secularization 1800–2000*. London: Routledge.

Brown, Roger, and A. Gilman. 1960. "The Pronouns of Power and Solidarity." In *Style in Language,* edited by Thomas A. Sebeok, 253–76. Cambridge, MA: The M.I.T. Press.

Buddhist Missionary Society. N.d. *Buddhist Publications.* Kuala Lumpur.

Carstens, Sharon. 1983. "Pulai Hakka Chinese Malaysians: A Labyrinth of Cultural Identities." In *The Chinese of Southeast Asia.* Vol. 2, *Identity, Culture, and Politics,* edited by Linda Y. C. Lim and L.A. Peter Gosling, 79–98. Singapore: Maruzan Asia.

————. 1988. "From Myth to History: Yap Ah Loy and the Heroic Past of Chinese Malaysians." *Journal of Southeast Asian Studies* 19(2): 185–208.

Cause and Effect Sutra. 1980. Penang. Also available as an e-book; see http://www.gracioushearts.com/ebooks/san-shi-yin-guo/

Cedzich, Ursula-Angelika. 1995. *The Cult of the Wu-t'ung/Wu-hsien in History and Fiction: The Religious Roots of the* Journey to the South. In *Ritual and Scripture in Chinese Popular Religion: Five Studies,* edited by David Johnson, 137–218. Berkeley: Institute of East Asian Studies.

Chambert-Loir, Henri. 2002. "Saints and Ancestors: The Cult of Muslim Saints in Java." In *The Potent Dead: Ancestors, Saints, and Heroes in Contemporary Indonesia,* edited by Henri Chambert-Loir and Anthony Reid, 132–40. Honolulu: Asian Studies Association of Australia, Allen & Unwin, and University of Hawaii Press.

Chambert-Loir, Henri, and Anthony Reid, editors. 2002. *The Potent Dead: Ancestors, Saints, and Heroes in Contemporary Indonesia.* Honolulu: Asian Studies Association of Australia, Allen & Unwin, and University of Hawaii Press.

Chan Kok Sing, illustrator. 1996. *The Eight Immortals.* Singapore: Asiapac.

Chan, Kwok Bun, and Claire Chiang. 1994. *Stepping Out: The Making of Chinese Entrepreneurs.* Singapore: Prentice Hall International.

Chan, Margaret. 2006. *Ritual is Theatre, Theatre is Ritual: Tang-ki Spirit Medium Worship.* Singapore: SNP International Publishing and Wee Kim Wee Centre, Singapore Management University.

Chao, Yuen Ren. 1976 [1956]. "Chinese Terms of Address." In *Aspects of Chinese Sociolinguistics: Essays by Yuen Ren Chao,* selected and introduced by Anwar S. Dil, 309–42. Stanford: Stanford University Press.

Chavannes, Edouard. 1910. *Le T'ai Chan: Essai de monographie d'un culte Chinois.* Paris: Ernest Lerous.

Che Hoon Khor Moral Uplifting Society (檳城德教會紫雲閣) 2001. 檳城德教會紫雲閣創閣 47周年 新閣成紀念特刊 (*Penang Island Moral Uplifting Society Purple Cloud Council 47th Anniversary of Creation of the Council Commemorative Publication*). Penang.

Cheo, Kim Ban, and Muriel Speeden. 1988. *Baba Folk Beliefs and Superstitions.* Singapore: Landmark Books.

Cheu Hock Tong. 1988. *The Nine Emperor Gods: A Study of Spirit Mediums.* Singapore: Times Books International.

Chia, Felix. 1980. *The Babas.* Singapore: Times Books International.

Chiang Ker Chiu. N.d. *A Practical English-Hokkien Dictionary.* Singapore: Chin Fen.

Chun Yi Jing (Choon Yik Kheng) 春一敬. 1914. *Taishang Laozu Daojing: Taishang Daode Wuqian Zhenyan* 太上老組道經: 太上道德五千真言 (*Old Ancestor Taishang's Daoist Scripture: Taishang's Ethics 5,000 Characters of True Words*). Penang: Taishang Miao.

Clarke, J. J. 1997. *Oriental Enlightenment: The Encounter Between Asian and Western Thought.* London: Routledge.

Clart, Philip Arthur. 1996. *The Ritual Context of Morality Books: A Case-Study of a Taiwanese Spirit-Writing Cult*. Ph.D. Thesis, University of British Columbia.

———. 2003. "Moral Mediums: Spirit-Writing and the Cultural Construction of Chinese Spirit-Mediumship." *Folklore Studies Association of Canada* 25(1):153–89.

Cohen, Eric. 2001. *The Chinese Vegetarian Festival in Phuket: Religion, Ethnicity and Tourism on a Southern Thai Island*. Bangkok: White Lotus.

Connor, Linda H., and Geoffrey Samuel. 2001. *Healing Powers and Modernity: Traditional Medicine, Shamanism, and Science in Asian Societies*. Westport, CT: Bergin & Garvey.

Coope, A. E. 1976. *A Malay-English Dictionary*. Kuala Lumpur: Macmillan Malaysia.

Covell, Alan Carter. 1986. *Folk Art and Magic: Shamanism in Korea*. Seoul, Korea: Hollym Corporation.

Crapanzano, Vincent, and Vivian Garrison, editors. 1977. *Case Studies in Spirit Possession*. New York: John Wiley & Sons.

Csordas, Thomas J. 1994. *The Sacred Self: A Cultural Phenomenology of Charismatic Healing*. Berkeley: University of California Press.

Day, Clarence Burton. 1974 [1940]. *Chinese Peasant Cults, Being a Study of Chinese Paper Gods*. Taipei: Ch'eng Wen.

Dean, Kenneth. 1993. *Taoist Ritual and Popular Cults of Southeast China*. Princeton: Princeton University Press.

———. 2003. "Local Communal Religion in Contemporary South-east China." In *Religion in China Today*, edited by Daniel L. Overmyer, 32–52. *China Quarterly* Special Issues: New Series, No. 3. Cambridge: Cambridge University Press.

DeBernardi, Jean. 1985. "Seng Ma" in *Reflections: The Anthropological Muse*, edited by Ian Prattis, 157–58. Washington: American Anthropological Association.

———. 1986. *Heaven, Earth, and Man: A Study of Chinese Spirit Mediums*. Ph.D. Dissertation, Department of Anthropology, University of Chicago.

———. 1987. "The God of War and the Vagabond Buddha." *Modern China* 13(3):310–33.

———. 1991. "Linguistic Nationalism: The Case of Southern Min." *Sino-Platonic Papers* 25, edited by Victor Mair. Department of Oriental Studies, University of Pennsylvania.

———. 1992. "Space and Time in Chinese Religious Culture." *History of Religions* 31(3):247–68.

———. 1994a. "Historical Allusion and the Defense of Identity: Malaysian Chinese Popular Religion." In *Asian Visions of Authority: Religion and the Modern States of East and Southeast Asia*, edited by Charles F. Keyes, Laurel Kendall, and Helen Hardacre, 117–139. Honolulu: University of Hawaii Press.

———. 1994b. "Tasting the Water." In *The Dialogic Emergence of Culture*, edited by Dennis Tedlock and Bruce Mannheim, 234–59. Urbana: University of Illinois Press.

———. 1995. "Lim Boon Keng and the Invention of Cosmopolitanism." In *Managing Change in Southeast Asia: Local Identities, Global Connections* (CCSEAS 21), edited by Jean DeBernardi, Gregory Forth, and Sandra Niessen, 173–87. Edmonton: Canadian Council for Southeast Asian Studies.

———. 1996. "Teachings of a Spirit Medium." In *Religions of China in Practice*, edited by Donald S. Lopez, Jr., 229–38. Princeton: Princeton University Press. Reprinted in *Religions of Asia in Practice: An Anthology*, edited by Donald S. Lopez, Jr., 366–75. Princeton: Princeton University Press, 2002.

———. 2004. *Rites of Belonging: Memory, Modernity and Identity in a Malaysian Chinese Community*. Stanford: Stanford University Press.

———. N.d.a. "Ascend to Heaven and Stand on a Cloud": Daoist Teaching and Practice at Penang's Taishang Laojun Temple." Forthcoming in *The People and the Dao: New Studies of Chinese Religions in Honour of Prof. Daniel L. Overmyer*, edited by Philip Clart and Paul Crowe. Sankt Augustin: Institut Monumenta Serica.

———. N.d.b. *'If the Lord Be Not Come': The Brethren Movement in Singapore and Penang, Malaysia, 1860–2000*. Unpublished manuscript.

Dennys, N. B. 1876. *The Folklore of China and Its Affinities with that of the Aryan and Semitic Races*. London: Trubner.

Dhammananda, K. Sri. 1976. *Day-to-Day Buddhist Practices*. Second edition. Kuala Lumpur: Buddhist Missionary Society.

———. 1977. *Buddhism and Duties of a Lay Buddhist*. Kuala Lumpur: Buddhist Missionary Society.

———. N.d.a. Sri Lanka's Contribution to Buddhism. Kuala Lumpur: Buddhist Missionary Society. http://www.ksridhammananda.com. Website maintained by the Sasana Abhiwurdhi Wardhana Society.

———. N.d.b. *Why Religion?* Kuala Lumpur: Buddhist Missionary Society.

———. N.d.c. *You Are Responsible*. Kuala Lumpur: Buddhist Missionary Society.

Dielenberg, Priscilla. 2003. "Divine Guests are Here." *The Star*. 20 August 2003. http://penang.thestar.com.my/content/focus/2003/8/20/6082623.asp

Diyu Youji 地獄遊記 (*Journey to Purgatory*). 1978. Taizhong: Shengxian Tang.

Duara, Prasenjit. 1988. *Culture, Power, and the State: Rural North China, 1900–1942*. Stanford: Stanford University Press.

Dudbridge, Glen. 1978. *The Legend of Miao-shan*. Published for Oxford University by London: Ithaca Press.

Dunstheimer, Guillaume. 1972. "Some Religious Aspects of Secret Societies." In *Popular Movements and Secret Societies in China, 1840–1950*, 23–28. Stanford: Stanford University Press.

Durkheim, Emile. 1965 [1915]. *The Elementary Forms of the Religious Life*. Translated by Joseph Ward Swain. New York: Free Press.

Eliade, Mircea. 1964 [1951]. *Shamanism: Archaic Techniques of Ecstasy*. Translated by Willard R. Trask. Princeton: Princeton University Press.

Elliott, Alan J. A. 1955. *Chinese Spirit-Medium Cults in Singapore*. Taipei: Southern Materials Center.

Embree, Bernard L. M. 1973. *A Dictionary of Southern Min*. Hong Kong: Hong Kong Language Institute.

Emerson, Ralph Waldo. N.d. "Experience." *Emerson's Essays and Representative Men*, 244–71. London: Collins.

Esherick, Joseph W. 1987. *The Origins of the Boxer Uprising*. Berkeley: University of California Press.

Evans-Pritchard, E. E. 1937. *Witchcraft, Oracles, and Magic Among the Azande*. Oxford: Clarendon.

Faure, Bernard. 1986. "Bodhidharma as Textual and Religious Paradigm." *History of Religions* 25(3): 187–98.

———. 1987. "Space and Place in Chinese Religious Traditions." *History of Religions* 26(4): 337–56.

———. 1993. *Chan Insights and Oversights: An Epistemological Critique of the Chan Tradition.* Princeton: Princeton University Press.

Fengshen Yanyi 封神演義 (*Canonization of Deities/Romance of the Investiture of the Gods*). N.d. Singapore: Xingzhou Shijie.

Feuchtwang, Stephan. 2001. *Popular Religion in China: The Imperial Metaphor.* Richmond, Surrey: Curzon.

———. 2004. "Curves and the Urbanisation of Meifa Village." In *Making Place: State Projects, Globalisation and Local Responses in China*, edited by Stephan Feuchtwang, 163–79. London: UCL Press.

Franke, Wolfgang. 1989. "Chinese Religion in Southeast Asia with Particular Consideration of Medan, North Sumatra." In *Sino-Malaysiana: Selected Papers on Ming and Qing History and on the Overseas Chinese in Southeast Asia, 1942–1988*, 401–20. Singapore: South Seas Society.

Freedman, Maurice. 1979 [1959]. "The Handling of Money." In *The Study of Chinese Society: Essays by Maurice Freedman*, selected and introduced by G. William Skinner, 22–26. Stanford: Stanford University Press.

Freedman, Maurice, and Marjorie Topley. 1979 [1961]. "Religion and Social Realignment Among the Chinese in Singapore." In *The Study of Chinese Society: Essays by Maurice Freedman*, selected and introduced by G. William Skinner, 161–85. Stanford: Stanford University Press.

Freeman, David. 1924. "Fire-Walking at Ampang, Selangor." *Journal of the Malayan Branch of the Royal Asiatic Society* 2: 74–76.

Friedrich, Paul. 1979 [1966]. "Structural Implications of Russian Pronominal Usage." In *Language, Context, and the Imagination*, edited by Anwar S. Dil, 63–125. Stanford: Stanford University Press.

Geertz, Clifford. 1973. "Religion as a Cultural System." In *The Interpretation of Cultures*, 87–125. New York: Basic Books.

———. 1976 [1960]. *The Religion of Java.* Chicago: University of Chicago Press.

———. 1980. *Negara: The Theatre State in Nineteenth-Century Bali.* Princeton: Princeton University Press.

———. 1983. "Centers, Kings, and Charisma: Reflections on the Symbolics of Power." In *Local Knowledge: Further Essays in Interpretive Anthropology*, 121–46. New York: Basic Books.

Glover, Ian, and Peter Bellwood, editors. 2004. *Southeast Asia: From Prehistory to History.* London and New York: RoutledgeCurzon.

Godwin, Joscelyn. 1994. *The Theosophical Enlightenment.* Albany: State University of New York Press.

Goh, Katherine Pei Ki, compiler. 1996. *Legends of Ji Gong: Reincarnation of an Arhat (Jigong quanji)*, illustrated by Chan Kok Sing and translated by Wu Jingyu. Singapore: Asiapac.

Golomb, Louis. 1978. *Brokers of Morality: Thai Ethnic Adaptation in a Rural Malaysian Setting.* Honolulu: University Press of Hawaii.

Green, Alfred E. 1893. "Letter to *Echoes of Service* from Thaipeng [Taiping], 25 July 1893." *Echoes of Service* 294 (Sept. Pt. II 1893): 212–13.

————. 1899. "Letter to *Echoes of Service* from Kuala Lumpur, 25 September 1899." *Echoes of Service* 442 (Nov. Pt. II 1899): 345–46.

de Groot, Jan Jakob Maria. 1912. *The Religion of the Chinese*. New York: Macmillan.

————. 1963 [1903–4]. *Sectarianism and Religious Persecution in China*, 2 vols. Amsterdam: Johannes Muller [Reprint: Literature House (Taipei, 1963), 1 vol.]

————. 1964 [1892–1910]. *The Religious System of China*. Leiden: E. J. Brill. [Reprint: Literature House (Taipei, 1964), 6 vols.].

Guanyin Pusa Lingqian Jieshuo 觀音菩薩靈簽解說 (*Guanyin Pusa's Numinous Divination Slips Explained*). N.d. Penang: Hock Huat.

Haar, Barend J. ter. 1990. "The Genesis and Spread of Temple Cults in Fukien." In *Development and Decline of Fukien Province in the 17th and 18th Centuries*, edited by E. B. Vermeer, 349–396. Leiden: E. J. Brill.

————. 1998. *Ritual and Mythology of the Chinese Triads: Creating an Identity*. Leiden: Brill.

Halliday, Michael Alexander Kirkwood. 1978. "Antilanguages," In *Language as Social Semiotic: The Social Interpretation of Language and Meaning*, 164–82. Baltimore, MD: University Park Press.

Hannerz, Ulf. 1990. "Cosmopolitans and Locals in World Culture." *Theory, Culture, and Society: Explorations in Critical Social Science. Special Issue on Global Culture* 7(2–3): 237–51.

————. 1992a. "The Global Ecumene as a Network of Networks." In *Conceptualizing Anthropology*, edited by Adam Kuper, 34–56. London and New York: Routledge.

————. 1992b. *Cultural Complexity: Studies in the Social Organization of Meaning*. New York: Columbia University Press.

Harrell, C. Stevan. 1974. "When a Ghost Becomes a God." In *Religion and Ritual in Chinese Society*, edited by Arthur P. Wolf, 193–206. Stanford: Stanford University Press.

Hatfield, Donald J. 2002. "Fate in the Narrativity and Experience of Selfhood, a Case from Taiwanese Chhiam Divination." *American Ethnologist* 29(1): 857–77.

Heinze, Ruth-Inge. 1997. *Trance and Healing in Southeast Asia Today*. Bangkok: White Lotus.

Higham, Charles. 2004. "Mainland Southeast Asia from the Neolithic to the Iron Age." In *Southeast Asia: From Prehistory to History*, edited by Ian Glover and Peter Bellwood, 41–67. London and New York: RoutledgeCurzon.

Hocart, Arthur Maurice. 1970 [1936]. *Kings and Councillors: An Essay in the Comparative Anatomy of Human Society*, edited and with an introduction by Rodney Needham. Chicago: University of Chicago Press.

Hodder, Rupert. 1996. *Merchant Princes of the East: Cultural Delusions, Economic Success and the Overseas Chinese in Southeast Asia*. Chichester: John Wiley and Sons.

Humphrey, Caroline, with Urgunge Onon. 1996. *Shamans and Elders: Experience, Knowledge, and Power among the Daur Mongols*. Oxford: Clarendon.

Hymes, Robert. 2002. *Way and Byway: Taoism, Local Religion, and Models of Divinity in Sung and Modern China*. Berkeley: University of California Press.

I Ching or *Book of Changes*. 1950. Translated by Richard Wilhelm, rendered into English by Cary F. Baynes. Bollingen Series XIX. Princeton: Princeton University Press.

Jesperson, Otto. 1946. *Mankind, Nation and Individual from a Linguistic Point of View*. London: George Allen and Unwin.

Jigong Quanzhuan 濟公全傳 (*Jigong's Complete Biography*). N.d. Hong Kong: Xinsheng.

John, Alan. 1992. *Unholy Trinity: The Adrian Lim 'Ritual' Child Killings*. Singapore: Times Books International.

Jordan, David. 1972. *Gods, Ghosts, and Ancestors: The Folk Religion of a Taiwanese Village*. Berkeley: University of California Press.

Jordan, David K., and Daniel L. Overmyer. 1986. *The Flying Phoenix: Aspects of Chinese Sectarianism in Taiwan*. Princeton: Princeton University Press.

Jung, C. G. 1950. "Foreword." *The I Ching or Book of Changes*, the Richard Wilhelm translation rendered into English by Cary F. Baynes. New York: Bollingen Foundation. Published by Princeton University Press.

———. 1960. "Synchronicity: An Acausal Connecting Principle." *The Collected Words of C. G. Jung* Volume 8, translated by R. F. C. Hull. Bollingen Series XX, 419–531. Princeton: Princeton University Press.

Kapferer, Bruce. 1983. *A Celebration of Demons: Exorcism and the Aesthetics of Healing in Sri Lanka*. Bloomington: Indiana University Press.

Katz, Paul R. 1992. "Changes in Wang-Yeh Beliefs in Postwar Taiwan: A Case Study of Two Wang-Yeh Temples." *Journal of Chinese Religions* 20: 203–14.

———. 1995. *Demon Hordes and Burning Boats: The Cult of Marshal Wen in Late Imperial Chekiang*. Albany: State University of New York Press.

———. 1996. "Enlightened Alchemist or Immoral Immortal? The Growth of Lü Dongbin's Cult in Late Imperial China." In *Unruly Gods: Divinity and Society in China*, edited by Meir Shahar and Robert P. Weller, 70–104. Honolulu: University of Hawaii Press.

Kent, Stephen A. 1982. "A Sectarian Interpretation of the Rise of Mahayana." *Religion* 12: 311–32.

Kessler, Clive S. 1977. "Conflict and Sovereignty in Kelantanese Malay Spirit Seances." In *Case Studies in Spirit Possession*, edited by Vincent Crapanzano and Vivian Garrison, 295–331. New York: John Wiley & Sons.

Khoo Su Nin. 1993. *Streets of George Town, Penang: An Illustrated Guide to Penang's City Streets and Historic Attractions*. Penang: Janus.

King, Ambrose Y. C. 1996. *Confucian Traditions in East Asian Modernity: Moral Education and Economic Culture in Japan and the Four Mini-Dragons*. Cambridge: Harvard University Press.

Kleeman, Terry F. 1994. *A God's Own Tale: The Book of Transformations of Wenchang, the Divine Lord of Zitong*. Albany: State University of New York Press.

Kleinman, Arthur. 1980. *Patients and Healers in the Context of Culture: An Exploration of the Borderland between Anthropology, Medicine, and Psychiatry*. Berkeley: University of California Press.

Koh Kok Kiang, translator. 1996. *The Eight Immortals*, illustrated by Chan Kok Sing. Singapore: Asiapac.

Krings, Matthias. 1999. "On History and Language of the 'European' *Bori* Spirits of *Kano, Nigeria*." In *Spirit Possession, Modernity and Power in Africa*, edited by Heike Behrend and Ute Luig, 53–67. Madison: University of Wisconsin Press.

Kuhn, Philip. 1990. *Soulstealers: The Chinese Sorcery Scare of 1768*. Cambridge: Harvard University Press.

Kuo, Eddie. 1996. "Confucianism as Political Discourse in Singapore: The Case of an Incomplete Revitalization Movement." In *Confucian Traditions in East Asian Modernity: Moral Education and Economic Culture in Japan and the Four Mini-Dragons*, edited by Eddie Kuo, 294–309. Cambridge: Harvard University Press.

Lambek, Michael. 1989. "From Disease to Discourse: Remarks on the Conceptualization of Trance and Spirit Possession." In *Altered States of Consciousness and Mental Health: A Cross-Cultural Perspective*, edited by Colleen Ward, 36–61. Newbury Park: Sage.

Lan, David. 1985. *Guns and Rain: Guerillas and Spirit Mediums in Zimbabwe*. Berkeley: University of California Press.

Langlands, Mary B. 1894. "Letter to *Echoes of Service*, 13 July 1894." *Echoes of Service* 319 (Oct. Pt. I 1894): 232–33.

Lao Tzu. 1963. *Tao te Ching*, translated and with an Introduction by D. C. Lau. London: Penguin Classics.

Lee, Raymond L. M. 1989. "Self-Presentation in Malaysian Spirit Seances: A Dramaturgical Perspective on Altered States of Consciousness in Healing Ceremonies." In *Altered States of Consciousness and Mental Health: A Cross-Cultural Perspective*, edited by Colleen Ward, 251–66. Newbury Park: Sage.

Lee, Russell, & team of ghost writers. 1995 [1989]. *The Almost Complete Collection of True Singapore Ghosts Stories* Volume 1. Singapore: Angsana.

Lévy, Sylvain and Edouard Chavannes. 1916. "Les seize Arhats protecteurs de la loi." *Journal Asiatiques* 2: 204–75.

Lewis, I. M. 1971. *Ecstatic Religion: An Anthropological Study of Spirit Possession and Shamanism*. Harmondsworth: Penguin.

Lien, Chinfa. 1995. "Language Adaptation in Taoist Liturgical Texts." In *Ritual and Scripture in Chinese Popular Religion: Five Studies*, edited by David Johnson, 219–46. Berkeley: Institute of East Asian Studies.

Lim Boon Keng. 1905. "The Confucian Cult." *Straits Chinese Magazine* 8(2): 73–78.

Lim Peng Eok. N.d. *Out of the Thought*. Kuala Lumpur: Printcraft.

———. 1969. Unpublished manuscript. Penang.

Lim Teong Aik., N.d. "Wesak Day Public Holiday." Malaysia Buddhist Association website. http://www.malaysianbuddhistassociation.org.my/majoreventsmain/Wesakholiday.htm

Liu, James J. Y. 1967. *The Chinese Knight Errant*. Chicago: University of Chicago Press.

Lopez, Donald S., Jr., editor. 1996. *Religions of China in Practice*. Princeton: Princeton University Press.

———. 2002. *Religions of Asia in Practice: An Anthology*. Princeton: Princeton University Press.

Low, C. C. et al., translators and editors. 1989. *Canonization of Deities*. Singapore: Canfonian.

Low, Lt.-Colonel James 1972 [1836]. *The British Settlement of Penang: A Dissertation on the Soil and Agriculture of the British Settlement of Penang or Prince of Wales Island in the Straits of Malacca, Including Province Wellesley on the Malayan Peninsula, with Brief*

References to the Settlements of Singapore and Malacca. Singapore: Oxford University Press.

Low Jui Liat. 1979. "Shrine to Go: Will Evil Befall Poser." *The Star.* July 10, 1979.

Luhrmann, Tanya M. 1989. "The Magic of Secrecy." *Ethos* 17(2): 131–65.

Luper, Steven. 1996. *Invulnerability: On Securing Happiness.* Chicago: Open Court.

Mak Lau Fong. 1981. *The Sociology of Secret Societies: A Study of Chinese Secret Societies in Singapore and Peninsular Malaysia.* Kuala Lumpur: Oxford University Press.

Malinowski, Bronislaw. 1948. *Magic, Science and Religion and Other Essays.* New York: Doubleday.

Marshall, Alison. 2004a. "Chinese Shamanism, Classical." In *Shamanism: An Encyclopedia of World Beliefs, Practices, and Culture,* edited by Mariko Namba Walter and Evan Jane Neumann Fridman, 709–13. Santa Barbara: ABC-CLIO.

———. 2004b. "Chinese Shamanism, Contemporary." In *Shamanism: An Encyclopedia of World Beliefs, Practices, and Culture,* edited by Mariko Namba Walter and Evan Jane Neumann Fridman, 713–21. Santa Barbara: ABC-CLIO.

———. 2004c. "Taiwanese Shamanic Performance and Dance." In *Shamanism: An Encyclopedia of World Beliefs, Practices, and Culture,* edited by Mariko Namba Walter and Evan Jane Neumann Fridman, 736–39. Santa Barbara: ABC-CLIO.

Mann, Thomas. 1947 [1936]. "Freud and the Future." In *Essays of Three Decades,* 411–28. New York: Alfred A. Knopf.

Masters, Frederic H. 1892. "Among the Highbinders: An Account of Chinese Secret Societies." *Chinese Recorder and Missionary Journal* 23(6): 268–315.

Maurer, D. W. 1964 [1955]. *Whiz Mob: A Correlation of the Technical Argot of Pickpockets with Their Behavioral Pattern.* New Haven: College and University Press.

Mauss, Marcel. 1972 [1950]. *A General Theory of Magic,* translated from the French by Robert Brain. New York: W. W. Norton.

McClenon, James. 2002. *Wondrous Healing: Shamanism, Human Evolution, and the Origin of Religion.* DeKalb: Northern Illinois University Press.

Melton, Terry, Stephanie Clifford, Jeremy Martinson, Mark Baltzer, and Mark Stoneking. 1998. "Genetic Evidence for the Proto-Austronesian Homeland in Asia: mtDNA and Nuclear DNA variation in Taiwanese Aboriginal Tribes." *American Journal of Human Genetics* 63: 1807–23.

Morris, Rosalind. 2000. *In the Place of Origins: Modernity and Its Mediums in Northern Thailand.* Durham: Duke University Press.

Murray, Dian H, in collaboration with Qin Baoqu. 1994. *The Origins of Tiandihui: The Chinese Triads in Legend and History,* 177–89. Stanford: Stanford University Press.

Needham, Joseph. 1956. *Science and Civilization in China,* Vol. 2. Cambridge: Cambridge University Press.

Nickerson, Peter. 2001. "A Poetics and Politics of Possession: Taiwanese Spirit-Medium Cults and Autonomous Popular Cultural Space." *Positions* 9(1): 187–217.

Norman, Jerry. 1988. *Chinese.* Cambridge: Cambridge University Press.

Nussbaum, Martha. 1986. *The Fragility of Goodness: Luck and Ethics in Greek Tragedy and Philosophy.* Cambridge: Cambridge University Press.

Obeyesekere, Gananath. 1977. "Psychocultural Exegesis of a Case of Spirit Possession in Sri Lanka." In *Case Studies in Spirit Possession*, edited by Vincent Crapanzano and Vivian Garrison, 235–94. New York: Wiley and Sons.

———. 1981. *Medusa's Hair: An Essay in Personal Symbols and Religious Experience*. Chicago: University of Chicago Press.

Ong Ju Lynn. 2002. "Nayaka Thera Who Cared for All." *Daily News* 6 March 2002. http://ww.dailynews.lk/2002/03/06/fea50.html.

Overmyer, Daniel L. 1976. *Folk Buddhist Religion: Dissenting Sects in Late Traditional China*. Cambridge: Harvard University Press.

Owen, Stephen. 1986. *Remembrances: The Experience of the Past in Classical Chinese Literature*. Cambridge, MA: Harvard University Press.

Ownby, David. 1995. "The Heaven and Earth Society as Popular Religion." *The Journal of Asian Studies* 54(4):1023–1046.

———. 1996. *Brotherhood and Secret Societies in Early and Mid-Qing China*. Stanford: Stanford University Press.

Ownby, David, and Mary Somers Heidhues, editors. 1993. *Secret Societies Reconsidered*. Armonk, NY: M.E. Sharpe.

Oxfeld, Ellen. 1993. *Blood, Sweat, and Mahjong: Family and Enterprise in an Overseas Chinese Community*. Ithaca: Cornell University Press.

Paper, Jordan. 1995. *The Spirits are Drunk: Comparative Approaches to Chinese Religion*. Albany: State University of New York Press.

———. 1996. "Mediums and Modernity: The Institutionalization of Ecstatic Religious Functionaries in Taiwan." *Journal of Chinese Religions* 24: 105–30.

Park Yew Kee: A Translation [*Beiyouji* 北游記]. 1974. Penang: Nanyang.

Pelras, Christian. 2002. "Ancestor's Blood: Genealogical Memory, Genealogical Amnesia and Hierarchy among the Bugis." In *The Potent Dead: Ancestors, Saints, and Heroes in Contemporary Indonesia*, edited by Henri Chambert-Loir and Anthony Reid, 117–31. Honolulu: Asian Studies Association of Australia, Allen & Unwin, and University of Hawaii Press.

Penang Taoist Centre. 1986. *Timeless Wisdom for Today*. Penang.

Penang Taoist Center 道家中心. 1987. *Daozhi Bianhuo* 道之辨惑 (Daoist Perplexities). Penang.

P'ng Chye Khim, and Donn F. Draeger. 1979. *Shaolin: An Introduction to Lohan Fighting Techniques*. Rutland, VT: Charles E. Tuttle.

Poh, T. 1971. *T. Poh's Guidebook to the Temple of Paradise*. Penang: Forda.

———. 1973. *Gods and Deities in Popular Chinese Worship*. Penang.

———. 1978. *Chinese Temples in Penang*. Penang: Forda.

Purcell, Victor W. W. S. 1967 [1948]. *The Chinese in Malaya*. Kuala Lumpur: Oxford University Press.

Qianzi Wentu Jieshu 千字文圖解書 (*The Thousand Character Text and Picture Explanation Book*). 1980. Penang.

Redding, S. Gordon. 1996. "Societal Transformation and the Contribution of Authority Relations and Cooperation Norms in Overseas Chinese Business." In *Confucian Traditions in East Asian Modernity: Moral Education and Economic Culture in Japan and the Four Mini-Dragons*, edited by Eddie Kuo, 310–27. Cambridge: Harvard University Press.

Reid, Anthony. 1996. "Flows and Seepages in the Long-Term Chinese Interaction with Southeast Asia." In *Soujourners and Settlers: Histories of Southeast Asia and the Chinese*, edited by Anthony Reid, 15–49. St. Leonards: Allen and Unwin and the Asian Studies Association of Australia.

Roseman, Marina. 2001. "Engaging the Spirits of Modernity: The Temiars." In *Healing Powers and Modernity: Traditional Medicine, Shamanism, and Science in Asian Societies*, edited by Linda H. Connor and Geoffrey Samuel, 109–29. Westport, CT: Bergin & Garvey.

Ruhlman, Robert. 1960. "Traditional Heroes in Chinese Popular Fiction." In *The Confucian Persuasion*, edited by Arthur F. Wright, 141–76. Stanford: Stanford University Press.

Sahlins, Marshall. 1985. *Islands of History*. Chicago: University of Chicago Press.

———. 1988. "Cosmologies of Capitalism: The Trans-Pacific Sector of 'The World System.'" *Proceedings of the British Academy* 74: 1–51.

———. 1994. "Goodbye to Tristes Tropes: Ethnography in the Context of Modern World History." In *Assessing Cultural Anthropology*, edited by Robert Borofsky, 377–94. New York: McGraw-Hill.

Sakai, Minako. 2002. "Modernizing Sacred Sites in South Sumatra: Islamicization of Gumai Ancestral Places." In *The Potent Dead: Ancestors, Saints, and Heroes in Contemporary Indonesia*, edited by Henri Chambert-Loir and Anthony Reid, 103–16. Honolulu: Asian Studies Association of Australia, Allen & Unwin, and University of Hawaii Press.

Salmon, Claudine. 1991. "Cults Peculiar to the Chinese of Java." *Yazhou wenhua* 亞洲文化 *Asian Culture* 15: 7–23 (June 1991). Singapore.

Salmon, Claudine, and Denys Lombard. 1980. *Les Chinois de Jakarta: temples et vie collective. The Chinese of Jakarta: Temples and Communal Life.* Second edition. Association Archipel, published through Ann Arbor: University Microfilms International.

Sangren, P. Steven. 1984. "Great Tradition and Little Traditions Reconsidered: The Question of Cultural Integration in China." *Journal of Chinese Studies* 1: 1–24.

———. 1987. *History and Magical Power in a Chinese Community*. Stanford: Stanford University Press.

———. 1996. "Myths, Gods, and Family Relations." In *Unruly Gods: Divinity and Society in China*, edited by Meir Shahar and Robert P. Weller, 150–83. Honolulu: University of Hawaii Press.

Sapir, Edward. 1949 [1927]. "Speech as a Personality Trait." In *Selected Writings of Edward Sapir*, 533–43. Berkeley: University of California Press.

Sasana Abhiwurdhi Wardhana Society. 2002. http://www.ksridhammananda.com.

Schipper, Kristofer. 1993 [1982]. *The Taoist Body*, translated by Karen C. Duval. Berkeley: University of California Press.

Schlegel, Gustave. 1991 [1866]. *Thian Ti Hwui The Hung-League or Heaven-Earth-League: A Secret Society with the Chinese in China and India*. Reprinted in 1991. Thornhill, Dumfriesshire: Tynron.

Schwartz, Benjamin. 1998 [1975]. Excerpt from "Transcendence in Ancient China." *Daedalus* 127(3): 190.

Seaman, Gary. 1978. *Temple Organization in a Chinese Village*. Taipei: Asian Folklore and Social Life Monographs.

————. 1981. "In the Presence of Authority: Hierarchical Roles in Chinese Spirit Medium Cults." In *Normal and Abnormal Behavior in Chinese Culture*, edited by Arthur Kleinman and Tsung-yi Lin, 61–74. Dordrecht, Holland: D. Reidel Publishing Company.

————. 1987. *Journey to the North: An Ethnohistorical Analysis and Annotated Translation of the Chinese Folk Novel Pei-yu Chi*. Berkeley: University of California Press.

————. 1994. "The Dark Emperor: Central Asian Origins in Chinese Shamanism." In *Ancient Traditions: Shamanism in Central Asia and the Americas*, edited by Gary Seaman and Jane S. Day, 227–43. Niwat, Colorado: University Press of Colorado.

Shahar, Meir. 1992. "The Lingyin Si Monkey Disciples and the Origins of Sun Wukong." *Harvard Journal of Asiatic Studies* 52(1): 193–224.

————. 1996. "Vernacular Fiction and the Transmission of God's Cults in Late Imperial China." In *Unruly Gods: Divinity and Society in China*, edited by Robert Weller and Meir Shahar, 184–211. Honolulu: University of Hawaii Press.

————. 1998. *Crazy Ji: Chinese Religion and Popular Literature*. Cambridge: Harvard University Press.

Shahar, Meir, and Robert Weller, editors. 1996. *Unruly Gods: Divinity and Society in China*. Honolulu: University of Hawaii Press.

Shancai Tong (Sian Shye Tong) 善才堂. 1952. Penang Procession Souvenir in Honour of Sian Chye Tong Choo and Tay Boh Neo Neo. 4 December 1952 [18th day of the 10th lunar month]. Penang: Sun Sun.

————. 1957. *Sian Chye Tong Souvenir. 27th Anniversary in commemoration of the Birthday of Sian Chye Phor Sat (Baby God)*. 22 February 1957. Penang: Criterion. Unpaginated.

Sharp, Lesley A. 1999. "The Power of Possession in Northwest Madagascar: Contesting Colonial and National Hegemonies." In *Spirit Possession, Modernity and Power in Africa*, edited by Heike Behrend and Ute Luig, 3–19. Madison: University of Wisconsin Press.

Shaw, William. 1973. "Aspects of Spirit-Mediumship in Peninsular Malaysia." *Federation Museums Journal* 18 (New Series): 71–176. Kuala Lumpur: Museums Department, States of Malaya.

Shi Nai'an and Luo Guanzhong. 1981. *Outlaws of the Marsh*, translated by Sidney Shapiro. Bloomington: Indiana University Press in association with Foreign Languages Press, Beijing.

Shiquan Jiuku Pian (The Perfect Book to Save the Afflicted) 十全救苦篇. 1980. Penang: Sim.

Simmel, Georg. 1978 [1907]. *The Philosophy of Money*, translated by Tom Bottomore and David Frisby. Boston: Routledge and Kegan Paul.

Singapore High Court. 1983. Transcripts, trial of Adrian Lim, Catherine Tan Mui Choo, and Hoe Kah Hong.

Sit Yin Fong. 1989a. *I Confess*. Singapore: Heinemann Asia.

————. 1989b. *Was Adrian Lim Mad?* Singapore: Heinemann Asia.

Skinner, G. William. 1996. "Creolized Chinese Societies in Southeast Asia." In *Sojourners and Settlers: Histories of Southeast Asia and the Chinese*, edited by Anthony Reid, 51–93. St. Leonards: Allen and Unwin and the Asian Studies Association of Australia.

Smith, Richard J. 1993. *Fortune Tellers and Philosophers: Divination in Traditional Chinese Society*. Boulder: Westview Press.

Soo Khin Wah. 1997. "A Study of the Yiguan Dao (Unity Sect) and Its Development in Peninsular Malaysia." Ph.D. dissertation, Department of Asian Studies, University of British Columbia.

Spence, Jonathan D. 1996. *God's Chinese Son: The Taiping Kingdom of Hong Xiuquan*. New York: W. W. Norton & Company.

Spiro, Melford E. 1970. *Buddhism and Society: A Great Tradition and Its Vicissitudes*. New York: Harper and Row.

Star, The. 1981a. "The Legendary Well of Sam Poh Kong." June 10, 1981: 23.

———. 1981b. "A Chinese Temple Built by the British." June 10, 1981: 20.

Steedly, Mary Margaret. 1993. *Hanging without a Rope: Narrative Experience in Colonial and Postcolonial Karoland*. Princeton: Princeton University Press.

Stein, Rolf. 1991 [1981]. "The Guardian of the Gate: An Example of Buddhist Mythology, from India to Japan." In *Asian Mythologies*, compiled by Yves Bonnefoy, translated under the direction of Wendy Doniger, 122–36. Chicago: University of Chicago Press.

Stirling, William G. 1924. "Chinese Exorcists." *Journal of the Malayan Branch of the Royal Asiatic Society* 2: 41–47.

Stoller, Paul. 1995. *Embodying Colonial Memories: Spirit Possession, Power, and the Hauka in West Africa*. New York: Routledge.

Straits Echo and Times of Malaya. 1956. "Opening of New Chinese Temple." 3 April 1956. Reprinted in *Sian Chye Tong [Shancai Tong] Souvenir*. Penang: Criterion. Unpaginated.

Strickmann, Michel. 2002. *Chinese Magical Medicine*, edited by Bernard Faure. Stanford: Stanford University Press.

Stutley, Margaret. 2003. *Shamanism: An Introduction*. London and New York: Routledge.

Suryadinata, Leo, editor. 2005. *Admiral Zheng He and Southeast Asia*. Singapore: International Zheng He Society and the Institute of Southeast Asian Studies.

Sutton, Donald. 1990. "Rituals of Self-Mortification: Taiwanese Spirit Mediums in Comparative Perspective." *Journal of Ritual Studies* 4(1): 99–125.

———. 2000. "From Credulity to Scorn: Confucians Confront Spirit Mediums in Late Imperial China." *Late Imperial China* 21(2): 1–39.

———. 2003. *Steps of Perfection: Exorcistic Performers and Chinese Religion in Twentieth-Century Taiwan*. Cambridge, MA: Harvard University Asia Center and Harvard University Press.

Taishang Ganying Pian 太上感應篇 (Taishang's Treatise on Action and Retribution). N.d. Beihai.

Tambiah, Stanley J. 1970. *Buddhism and the Spirit Cults in North-east Thailand*. Cambridge: Cambridge University Press.

———. 1984. "The Objectification of Charisma and the Fetishism of Objects," In *The Buddhist Saints of the Forest and the Cult of Amulets: A Study in Charisma, Hagiography, Sectarianism, and Millennial Buddhism*, 335–47. Cambridge: Cambridge University Press.

———. 1985. "The Galactic Polity." In *Culture, Thought, and Social Action: An Anthropological Perspective*, 254–86. Cambridge: Harvard University Press.

Tan Chee Beng. 1985. *The Development and Distribution of Dejiao Associations in Malaysia and Singapore: A Study on a Chinese Religious Organization*. ISEAS Occasional Paper No. 79. Singapore: Institute of Southeast Asian Studies.

———. 1988. *The Baba of Melaka: Culture and Identity of a Chinese Peranakan Community in Malaysia*. Petaling Jaya: Pelanduk.

Tan Cheng Lock. 1949. "Cheng Hoon Teng Temple." Reprinted from *Straits Times*, 31 August 1949.

Teoh Jin-Inn. 1973. "Chinese Spirit-mediumship: Its Socio-cultural Interpretation and Psychotherapeutic Aspects." *Singapore Medical Journal* 14(1): 55–61.

Topley, Marjorie. 1956. "Review of Chinese Spirit-Medium Cults in Singapore, by Alan J. A. Elliott." *Journal of the Malayan Branch of the Royal Asiatic Society* 29 (1): 214–19.

———. 1963. "The Great Way of Former Heaven: A Group of Chinese Secret Religious Sects." *Bulletin of the School of Oriental and African Studies* 26: 362–92.

———. 1974. "Cosmic Antagonisms: A Mother-Child Syndrome." In *Religion and Ritual in Chinese Society*, edited by Arthur P. Wolf, 233–49. Stanford: Stanford University Press.

———. 1978. "Marriage Resistance in Rural Kwangtung." In *Studies in Chinese Society*, edited by Arthur Wolf, 247–68. Stanford: Stanford University Press.

Tu Wei-ming, editor. 1996. *Confucian Traditions in East Asian Modernity: Moral Education and Economic Culture in Japan and the Four Mini-Dragons*. Cambridge: Harvard University Press.

Vaughan, Jonas Daniel. 1854. "Notes on the Chinese of Pinang." *Journal of the Indian Archipelago* 8: 1–27.

———. 1879 [1971]. *The Manners and Customs of the Chinese of the Straits Settlements*. Kuala Lumpur: Oxford University Press.

Vitebsky, Piers. 1997. "What Is a Shaman?" *Natural History* March 1997 Vol. 106(2): 34–35.

Waley, Arthur, translator. 1980 [1943]. *Monkey*. Translation of Wu Cheng-en's 吳承恩 *Xiyouji* 西游記 (*Journey to the West*). New York: Grove.

Walter, Mariko Namba, and Eva Jane Neumann Fridman, editors. 2004. *Shamanism: An Encyclopedia of World Beliefs, Practices, and Culture*, 2 vols. Santa Barbara: ABC-CLIO.

Wanshou Wuliang 萬壽無疆 (Limitless Longevity). 1981. Handwritten invocation.

Wang Chenfa (Ong Seng Huat) 王琛發. 1999. *Guangfu Gong Lishi yu Chuanqi* 廣福宮歷史與傳奇 (*History and Miraculous Stories of Guangfu Gong*). Penang: Binchengzhou Zhengfu Huaren Zongjiao (Shehui Shiwu) Lishihui he Binlangyu Guangfu Gong Xinlibu.

Wang, C. T. 1949. "Origin and Progress of the World Red Swastika Society." In *The World Red Swastika Prospectus*, 12–19. Singapore: Khai Wah.

Ward, Colleen, editor. 1989. *Altered States of Consciousness and Mental Health: A Cross-cultural Perspective*. Newbury Park: Sage.

Ward, John Sebastian Marlo, and William G. Stirling. 1977 [1925]. *The Hung Society, or the Society of Heaven and Earth*. Vol. 1. Taipei: Southern Materials Center.

Watson, James L. 1985. "Standardizing the Gods: The Promotion of T'ien Hou ("Empress of Heaven") Along the South China Coast, 960–1960." In *Popular Culture in Late Imperial China*, edited by David Johnson, Andrew J. Nathan, and Evelyn S. Rawski, 292–324. Berkeley: University of California Press.

Weber, Max. 1946a [1906]. "The Protestant Sects and the Spirit of Capitalism." In *From Max Weber: Essays in Sociology*, translated, edited, and with an introduction by H. H. Gerth and C. Wright Mills, 302–22. New York: Oxford University Press.

———. 1946b. "Class, Status, Power." *From Max Weber: Essays in Sociology*, translated, edited, and with an introduction by H. H. Gerth and C. Wright Mills, 180–95. New York: Oxford University Press.

———. 1958 [1920]. *The Protestant Ethic and the Spirit of Capitalism: The Relationships Between Religion and the Economic and Social Life in Modern Culture*, translated by Talcott Parsons. New York: Charles Scribner's Sons.

———. 1963 [1922]. *The Sociology of Religion*, translated by Ephraim Fischoff, with an introduction by Talcott Parsons. London: Methuen.

———. 1968 [1951]. *The Religion of China*, translated from the German and edited by Hans H. Gerth, with an Introduction by C. K. Yang. New York: Free Press.

Wee, Vivienne. 2004. "Spirit Mediumship (Singapore)." In *Shamanism: An Encyclopedia of World Beliefs, Practices, and Culture*, edited by Mariko Namba Walter and Evan Jane Neumann Fridman, 732–36. Santa Barbara: ABC-CLIO.

Weller, Robert P. 1987. *Unities and Diversities in Chinese Religion*. Seattle: University of Washington Press.

———. 1994a. "Capitalism, Community, and the Rise of Amoral Cults in Taiwan." In *Asian Visions of Authority: Religion and the Modern States of East and Southeast Asia*, edited by Charles F. Keyes, Laurel Kendall, and Helen Hardacre, 141–64. Honolulu: University of Hawaii Press.

———. 1994b. *Resistance, Chaos and Control in China: Taiping Rebels, Taiwanese Ghosts and Tiananmen*. Seattle: University of Washington Press.

Werner, E. T. C. 1986 [1922]. *Myths and Legends of China*. London: George Harrap & Co.

Widodo, Johannes. 2002. "Fragments of History – Links and Corridors in Early Southeast Asia. *ASEAN Journal on Hospitality and Tourism* 1(1): 35–44.

———. 2003. "Admiral Zheng He and Pre-Colonial Coastal Urban Development in Southeast Asia." http://www.geocities.com/johannes_widodo/Zhenghe.htm?200526.

———. 2004. *The Boat and the City: Chinese Diaspora and the Architecture of Southeast Asian Coastal Cities*. Singapore: Marshall Cavendish.

Wilhelm, Richard, translator. 1962 [1931]. *Secret of the Golden Flower* [*Taiyi Jinhoa Zongzhi*]. Translated and explained by Richard Wilhelm with a Foreword and Commentary by C. G. Jung, and translated into English by Cary F. Baynes. New York: Harvest/Harcourt Brace Jovanovich.

Williams, Bernard. 1981. *Moral Luck*. Cambridge: Cambridge University Press.

Winstedt, R. O. 1977 [1924]. "Karamat: Sacred Places and Persons in Malaya." In *A Centenary Volume, 1877–1977. Malayan Branch of the Royal Asiatic Society Reprint Number Four*, 48–63. Singapore: Times.

Winzeler, Robert L., editor. 1993a. *The Seen and the Unseen: Shaman, Priest, and Spirit Medium: Religious Specialists, Tradition and Innovation in Borneo*. Williamsburg, VA: Borneo Research Council.

———. 1993b. "Introduction." In *The Seen and the Unseen: Shaman, Priest, and Spirit Medium: Religious Specialists, Tradition and Innovation in Borneo*, edited by Robert L. Winzeler, xi–xxxiii. Williamsburg, VA: Borneo Research Council.

————. 2004a. "Overview: Southeast Asia." In *Shamanism: An Encyclopedia of World Beliefs, Practices, and Culture*, edited by Mariko Namba Walter and Evan Jane Neumann Fridman, 799–801. Santa Barbara: ABC-CLIO.

————. 2004b. "Southeast Asian Shamanism." In *Shamanism: An Encyclopedia of World Beliefs, Practices, and Culture*, edited by Mariko Namba Walter and Evan Jane Neumann Fridman, 834–42. Santa Barbara: ABC-CLIO.

Wolf, Arthur. 1974. "Gods, Ghosts, and Ancestors." In *Religion and Ritual in Chinese Society*, edited by Arthur P. Wolf, 131–82. Stanford: Stanford University Press.

Wolf, Margery. 1992. *A Thrice-Told Tale: Feminism, Postmodernism, and Ethnographic Responsibility*. Stanford: Stanford University Press.

Wong, Choon San. 1963. *A Gallery of Chinese Kapitans*. Singapore: Dewan Bahasa Dan Kebudayaan Kebangsaan/Ministry of Culture.

————. 1967. *A Cycle of Chinese Festivities*. Singapore: Malaysia Publishing House Limited.

World Red Swastika Prospectus. 1949. Singapore: Khai Wah.

Wu Chengzhen 吳誠真. 2001. "Doumu Yuanjun" 斗姥元君 (Grandmother Bushel the First Ruler). In *Chang Chun Guan* 長春觀 (*Eternal Spring Monastery*), 68–73. Wuhan: Chang Chun Guan.

Wynne, Mervyn Llewelyn. 1957 [1941]. *Triad and Tabut: A Survey of the Origin and Diffusion of Chinese and Mohamedan Secret Societies in the Malay Peninsula, A.D. 1800–1933*. Singapore: Government Printing Office. [Released in 1957 with an introduction by Wilfred L. Blythe].

Xiamen Daxue Zhongguo Yuyan Wenxue Yanjiusuo Hanyu Fangyan Yanjiushi Zhubian 廈門大學中國語言文學研究所漢語方言研究室主編 (Chief Editor: Xiamen University Chinese Language and Literature Research Institute, Chinese Topolect Study Unit). 1982. *Putong Hua Minnan Fangyan Cidian* 普通話閩南方言辭典 (*Standard Chinese-Minnan Topolect Dictionary*). Hong Kong: Joint Publishing.

Yang, C. K. 1961. *Religion in Chinese Society: The First Comprehensive Sociological Analysis of Chinese Religious Behavior*. Berkeley: University of California Press.

————. 1968 [1964]. "Introduction." In *The Religion of China*, translated by Hans H. Gerth, xiii–xliii. New York: Free Press.

Yap, Pow Meng. 1969. "The Culture-Bound Reactive Syndromes," in *Mental Health Research in Asia and the Pacific*, edited by W. Caudill and Tsung-yi Lin, 33–53. Honolulu: East-West Center.

Yu, Anthony, translator and editor. 1977–1983. *The Journey to the West*. 4 vols. Translation of Wu Cheng-en's 吳承恩 *Xiyouji* 西游記 (*Journey to the West*). Chicago: University of Chicago Press.

Zhu Qiuhua. 2002. "Achievements in the Study of the Tongzi Ritual in Jiangsu." In *Ethnography in China Today: A Critical Assessment of Methods and Results*, edited by Daniel L. Overmyer, with the assistance of Shin-Yi Chao, 231–41. Taipei: Yuan-Liou Publishing Co.

Zito, Angela. 1997. *Of Body & Brush: Grand Sacrifice as Text/Performance in Eighteenth-Century China*. Chicago: University of Chicago Press.

Chinese Glossary

Mandarin romanization followed by Hokkien equivalent in parentheses, English translation, and Chinese characters. Some Hokkien terms lack conventionally agreed upon character equivalents, and I have italicized these terms. In the case of punning homophones I give characters for both terms.

A Bo (Ah Pek) *father's elder brother; uncle (term of address)* 阿伯
andua *slang for 'boss'* [Southern Min]
angkong *gods* [Southern Min]
Baimao Xian (Pehmo· Sian) *White-Haired Immortal* 白毛仙
bai (pai) *pray* 拜
bai Fo (pai Hut) *worship Buddha* 拜佛
bai jiao jing (pai kio kia^n) *praying to call the fear [to go away]* 拜叫驚
baishen (paisin) *worship gods* 拜神
baohu (poho·) *protect* 保護
baojian (pokiam) *precious sword* 寶劍
Baoyue Gong (Pogeh Kiong) *Jewel Moon Palace* 寶月宮
baoshen fu (po·sin hu) *body-protection charm* 保身符
Baosheng Dadi *Life-Protecting God* 保生大帝
Beiji Xianzu (Pakkek Siancho·) *North Pole Immortal Ancestor, the Lord of the Dark Heavens* 北極仙祖
Beiyouji (Pak Iu Ki [Park Yew Kee]) *Journey to the North* 北游紀
benming *constitutive fate* 本命
Bojiao Gui (Paikha Kui) *Lame Ghost* 跛腳鬼
bujinzhong (bochintiong) *unfaithful* 不盡忠
buyi (boeki) *unjust* 不義
bu bei (poah poe) *throw the divining crescents* 卜貝
bu yun (po· un) *mend luck* 補運

budai heshang *Cloth-bag Monk, an eccentric Buddhist figure* 布袋和尚

Caishen (Chaisin) *Wealth God* 財神

caigu (chhaiko·) *vegetarian nun* 菜姑

cha yundao (chha unto) *check luck* 查運道

changxian (thiongsian) *pleasure immortal, hedonist* 暢仙

chaoluan (chhaloan) *disturb* 吵亂

Chen Puzu (Tan Pho· Chioh) *Buddhist monk deified as the Clear Water Patri-arch* 陳普足

chi fu (chiah hok) *eating luck* 吃福

chi heigou (chiah o·kau) *eat black dog, slang for 'drink Guinness Stout'* 吃黑狗

chi laolao (chiah laulau) *'eat' until old – enjoy a long life* 吃老老

chi pingan (chiah pengan) *'eat' peace* 吃平安

chi qingqing, lai pingping (chiah chhengchheng, lai pengpeng) *eat pure [foods], and peace will come* 吃清清，來平平

chi yisi (chiah isu) *eat meaning* 吃意思

chong (chhiong) *collide* 沖

chongde (chhiongtioh) *spiritual collision* 沖得

chongbai (chongpai) *to worship* 崇拜

Chu Shen (Chau Kun or Chau Kun Kong) *Kitchen God* 廚神

chuan guoshui wuhen le (chun koechui bohun liao) *the boat crosses the water leaving no trace* 船過水無痕

chhinchhai *easy-going, casual* [Southern Min]

Cihui Tang *Compassion Society* 慈惠堂

ciqiu (chhikiu) *ball of thorns* 刺球

da (tap) *repay* 答

daxie ganqing (tapsia kamcheng) *return thanks and gratitude* 答謝感情

da (toa) *large or high status* 大

Dabo Gong (Toa Peh [Tua Pek] Kong) *God of Prosperity, literally Great Uncle God* 大伯公

Dadiye (Taite-ia) *Great Emperor God, a common name for Baosheng Dadi* 大帝爺

dashen (toasin) *'big' god, a god with high status* 大神

dai haizi (phai^n gin-a) *'bad kids,' slang for gangsters* 歹孩子

dai ming (phai^n mia) *bad fate, bad life* 歹命

dai xin (phai^n sim) *bad-hearted, immoral* 歹心

dai yun (phai^n un) *bad luck* 歹運

dan (ta^n) *gall, courage* 膽

daojiao (tokio) *knife sedan chair* 刀轎

daoyi (to-i) *knife chair* 刀椅

daode (totek) *morals* 道德

Daodejing (Totekkeng) *Daodejing* 道德經

Daoji *name for the Vagabond Buddha* 道濟

daoli (toli) *Daoist term meaning organizing patterns of the Way* 道理

Dede She (Tektek Sia) *Virtue Society, term that the Heavenly Dao Association used to refer to itself* 德德社

dejiao hua (tekkau ui) *moral uplifting picture, used to describe the reverse swastika on which are superimposed pictures of five founders of world religions* 德教畫

dejiao hui (tekkau hoe) *moral uplifting association (modern syncretic religious associations)* 德教會

dexing (tekheng) *virtuous conduct* 德行

de chong (tioh chhiong) *suffer a spiritual collision* 得沖

de fan (tioh hoan) *'get an offense,' offend a spirit and become afflicted* 得犯

de lasam (tioh lasam) *get 'dirt,' encounter a ghost* 得 lasam

de qingjing (tioh chhe^{n}kia^n) *take a 'green' fear* 得青驚

Dimu Niangniang (Tebu Neoneo) *Earth Mother* 地母娘娘

Dimujing (Tebukeng) *Earth Mother Scripture* 地母經

diyu (tegek) *the prisons of earth, hell* 地獄

Dongfang Er Yuanshi *Eastern Quarter Second Leader, title for Er Lang [Yang Jian]* 東方二元師

dubo gui (puahkiau kui) *gambling ghost* 賭博鬼

duangong *magical experts and diviners, described as shamans* 端公

Er Lang *Second Man or Second Son, another name for Yang Jian* 二郎

fagao (hoat koe) *rising cakes* 發糕

fa (hoat) *law; magical power* 法

fande (hoantioh) *disturb [a ghost]* 犯得

fande Datuk Gongde dongxi (hoantioh Natu Konge migia) *offend Datuk Gong things* 犯得 Datuk 公的東西

fande Wuchang Bo (hoantioh Po·tiao Peh) *offend the Inconstant Uncle* 犯得無常伯

fangchai (phangchha) *camphor wood, used as incense for Malay spirits* 芳柴

feng (hong) *canonization, investiture with a title* 封

feng (hong) *wind; slang for police* 風

fengshui (hongchui) *geomancy, literally 'wind and water'* 風水

fengjiao (hongkao) *instructed, join a Church; Confucianism?* 奉教

Fo (Hut) *Buddha* 佛

Fozu (Hutcho·) *Buddhist ancestor* 佛祖

fuji *planchette writing, a form of divination* 扶乩

fuluan *phoenix writing, a form of divination* 扶鸞

fu (hu) *charm, talisman* 符

fu (hok) *happiness, good fortune* 福

fulu (hoklok) *happiness* 福祿

fulushou (hokloksiu) *star gods representing prosperity, status, and longevity* 福祿壽

fuqi (hokkhi) *good fortune, blessings* 福氣

Fuxing Gong (Hok Heng Keong) *Prosperity Palace, name for the Snake Temple* 福興宮

fushi (hoksai) *serve, worship* 服侍

gai nide daiyun (kai lu-e phaiⁿun) *change your bad luck* 改你的歹運

gaiyun (kai-un) *use ritual to alter one's luck* 改運

gai (kham) *cover* 蓋

gan (koaⁿ) *chase away, expel* 趕

ganqing (kamcheng) *gratitude, attachment* 感情

gao (koan) and di (ke) *high and low* 高 and 低

geming (kekbeng) *revolution* 革命

gei mianzi (ho·bin) *give face* 給面

gei ta chifu, gei ta hui tinghua (ho·i chiah hu, ho·i ehiao tia wa) *Give him a charm to eat, to that he know how to listen (become obedient)* 給他吃符, 給他會聽話

gongfu (konghu) *gongfu, martial arts* 功夫

gu (ko·) *look after, care for* 顧

Guangong (Koan [Kuan] Kong) *Lord Guan, the God of War* 關公

guan (koan) *control* 管

Guanyin (Koan [Kuan] Im) *Goddess of Mercy* 觀音

Guangfu Gong (Kong Hock Kiong) *the Kong Hock Palace, Penang's Guanyin Temple* 廣福宮

Guangze Zunwang (Kongtek Chunong) *Vast Favor Venerable King* 廣澤尊王

guibin (kuipin) *honored guest, VIP* 貴賓

guiren (kuijin) *benefactors* 貴人

gui (kui) *ghost* 鬼

guo yun (ge-un) *pass over [a period of bad] luck* 過運

guo daiyun (ke pai-un) *cross over a period of bad luck* 過歹運

guo xuehai (ke huih-hai) *cross over the sea of blood – be born* 過血海

haoxin (hosim) *good heart* 好心

hehe (hapho) *harmonious* 和合

heigou (o·kau) *black dog* 黑狗

hei shehui (o· siahui) *black society* 黑社會

hongbao (angbao) *red packet containing a gift of money* 紅包

hongshi (angsu) *'red event,' a wedding* 紅事

Hongjun Laozu *Vast Creation Venerable Ancestor* 鴻鈞老祖

Hongmen *Vast Gate, a name for the Heaven and Earth Society* 洪門

Hu Ye (Ho· Ia) *Tiger God* 虎爺

Hua Guang Dadi (Hoa Kng Taite) *Fire God, associated with the south* 華光大帝

huoshan (hesuaⁿ) *'fire mountain,' a volcano* 火山

hun (hun) *soul* 魂

ji (ki) *to divine* 乩

jitong (kitong) *spirit medium, divining shaman* 乩佟, more commonly written as 乩童

jitong de shifu (kitang e suhu) *the master of the mediums* 乩佟[乩童]的師傅

Jigong (Che Kong) *Saving Buddha, Vagabond Buddha* 濟公

Jigong Huofo *Jigong the Living Buddha* 濟公活佛

jianku (kankho·) *suffering, misery* 艱苦

jianshi (chhiamsi) *oracle acquired by throwing numbered sticks* 簡詩

Jiande Tang (Kian [Kien] Tek Tng) *Kian Tek Society* 建得堂

jiang daoli (kong doli) *discussing daoli* 講道理

jiang sanguo (kong samkok) *story-telling, literally 'speak' the Three King-doms* 講三國

jiangjun tou (chiongkun thao) *generals' heads, set of five daggers* 將軍頭

jiebai (kiatpai) *sworn brother or sister* 結拜

Jingu (Kimko) *Golden Aunt* 金姑

jingui (jipkui) *ghost enters, possession by a spirit* 進鬼

Jiu Wangye (Kao Ongia) *Nine Emperor Gods* 九王爺

jiuliu (kiuliu) *nine streams* 九流

jiushi (kiuse) *save the world* 救世

jiugong (kukong) *great uncle; mother's mother's brother* 舅公

kai kou *open the mouth* 開口

kai guang (khui kui) *perform a ritual to bring consciousness into an image* 開光

kai muzhu (khui bakchiu) *'open the eyes,' bring consciousness into an image* 開目珠

kanpo (khoaphoa) *see through [life's vanities]* 看破

kongtau *black magic* [Southern Min]

koujun (ko·kun) *offerings to the gods' troops* 扣軍

kuan (khoan) *manner* 款

kun *earth* 坤

Laobo (Laupeh) *Uncle, term of address* 老伯

lasam *dirty, ghosts, applied to polluting body fluids such as menstrual blood* [Southern Min]

lasam Fo (lasam Hut) *dirty Buddha, nickname for the Vagabond Buddha* lasam 佛

li (li) *principle* 理

Li, Lian, Xiao, Liu, Zhang *Five surnames on the flags of the center (yellow), north (black), south (red), west (white), and east (green)* 李, 連, 蕭, 劉, 張

Li Nazha (Lo·chhia) *name for a child deity* 李哪吒

Li Tieguai (Li Tok Kuai) *Li Iron Crutch, one of the Eight Immortals* 李鐵拐

li (lat) *strength* 力

ling or lingyan (sia) *spiritousness, spiritual efficacy* 靈 or 靈驗

lingfu (lenghu) *spiritually efficacious charm* 靈符

linghun (lenghun) *soul* 靈魂

ling (leng) *command or decree* 令

liushi jiazi benming shen *sixty-year cycle constitutive fate gods* 六十甲子本命神

loye guigen *falling leaves return to the root* 落葉歸根

Long Daguan *Dragon Great Official* 龍大官

Longtian Gong Sanwang Fu (Liongthian Keong Sam-ong Hu) *Dragon Heaven Palace Three King Mansion* 龍天宮三王府

luzhu (lo·chu) *keeper of the incense urn, the head of the temple committee* 爐主

lu (lok) *official status* 祿

Lü Dongbin 呂洞賓

luan (loan) *chaotic, disordered* 亂

luanlai (loanli) *immorality* 亂來

lue (liah) *sieze, capture* 掠

Mazu Po (Ma Cho Po·) *Queen of Heaven* 媽祖婆

Mao Shan (Mau San) *Mount Mao; in Penang, the name for a type of magician* 茅山

men shen (muisin) *door god* 門神

meng Fo (beng Put) *oath Buddha* 盟佛

meng xiongdi (beng hia^{n}ti) *sworn brothers* 盟兄弟

mishai shen (bithai sin) *rice sieve deity* 米篩神

mian (bin) *face* 面

miangui (miku) *bread tortoise, a small round bread dyed pink* 麵龜

ming (miasia^n) *reputation* 名

ming (mia) *fate* 命

mingyun (mia-un) *fate* 命運

moguai (mo·koai) *'black force,' literally 'demons and monsters'* 魔怪

Natu or *Natu* Kong (*Datuk* or *Datuk* Gong) Datuk *spirit, local animist spirits and spirits of community founders Datuk* 公

Nazha (Lo·chhia) *name for a child deity* 哪吒

Nanhai Fozu (Lamhai Hutcho·) *South Sea Buddhist Ancestor, Guanyin* 南海佛祖

nianjing (liamkeng) *chant sutras* 念經

nianzhou (liamchiu) *chant incantations to invite the gods* 念咒

pantang *taboo* [Malay]

pei (poe) *association* 陪

pingan (pengan) *peace* 平安

pingan facai (pengan hoatchai) *[have] peace and prosperity* 平安發財

po (pek) *yin, or animal soul* 魄

Pusa (Pho·sat) *Bodhisattva* 菩薩

Qitian Dasheng *Great Saint Equal to Heaven* 齊天大聖

qizan *start praising* 起贊

qi (khoe) *fictive adoption* 契

qi (khi) *air, breath, life-giving principle* 氣

qianmu (khanbong) *'lead by the hand to the grave,' to communicate with dead relatives through a spirit medium* 牽墓

qian (chian) *migrate, as of souls* 遷

qian *heaven* 乾

qiankun quan *Circle of Heaven and Earth* 乾坤圈

qingjie (chiengki) *pure, clean* 清潔

Qingshui Zushi Gong (Chheng Chui Cho·su Kong) *Pure/Clear Water Patriarch*
清水祖師公

qing shenqu (khin sinku) *light body, said of a spirit medium* 輕身軀

qing buzui (sia pochoe) *apologize, literally 'ask no sin'* 請不罪

Qingshen Zhou *Incantation to Invite the God* 請神咒

quanshan (khoansian) *exhort people to do good, preach morality* 勸善

Quan Zhongli *one of the Eight Immortals* 權種離

qundu (kundo·) *literally, 'skirt and stomach[er], the martial spirit medium's set
of clothes* 裙肚

renau (laujoah) *festival, literally 'hot and exciting'* 熱鬧

ren (lang) *person* 人

renli (lang-e li) *human principles* 人理

ren (lun) *endure, bear in silence* 忍

ruyi (lu-i) *scepter* 如意

ru jinhua (jip kimhoa) *enter the golden flower* 入金花

Sanbao (Sam Po) *Three Treasures, referring to Buddha, his teachings (dharma),
and the monks (sangha); a name for the deified spirit of Admiral Zheng He* 三寶

San Daren *Three Great Ones, three divine kings* 三大人

Sanjiao (Samkau) *the Three Religions/Doctrines* 三教

samseng *slang term meaning gangster* [Southern Min, possibly borrowed from
Cantonese]

San Taizi (Sam Thaichu) Third Prince 三太子

shamen *shaman* 沙門

shan (sam) *name given to various species of pine and fir* 杉

Shanding Dimu Miao *Mountain-top Earth Mother Temple* 山頂地母廟

shanshu *morality book* 善書

Shancai Tongzi (Sian Chye Tong Choo) *Virtuous Boy* 善才童子

shang (siong) *above, superior* 上

shangsheng (tengseng) *rise above, ascend* 上升

shen (chhim) *deep* 深

shen Fujian hua (chhim Hokkien oe) *deep or literary register of Southern
Min* 深福建話

shen (sin) *saint, deity* 神

shenbian (sinpi^n) *god's whip* 神鞭

shenda *god fighting* 神打

shentong (sinthong) *magical power* 神通

shentong (sintong) *spirit medium, literally 'divine youth'* 神童

shenwu *another name for spirit medium* 神巫

Sheng Bou (Seng Ma) *Holy Mother* 聖母

Shengwang (Seng Ong) *Holy King* 聖王

shengren (sengjin) *holy person, a saint* 聖人

shengshe (sengchoa) *'holy snake,' the snake-handled whip* 聖蛇

shengsuo (sengsut) *holy weapon* 聖索

Shigong (Saikong) *Daoist priest* 師公

shipo *female ritual practitioner, spirit medium* 師婆

shisheng (suseng) *gentry, gentleman-scholar* 士生

shou (siu) *long life* 壽

shoufeng (siuhong) *keep the wind, the Vagabond Buddha's 'name,' and slang for 'bookie'* 收風

shuai (soe) *extreme misfortune, decline* 衰

shun (sun) *follow* 順

shun bei (siu^n poe) *positive answer obtained by divination* 順貝

sixiang *mentality* 思想

Song Huzhi Li *exalted [Mount Song] invocation ritual* 嵩呼之禮

Ta Tianwang (Thah Thian-ong) *Pagoda Heavenly King* 塔天王

Taiji (thaikek) *Great Ultimate* 太極

Taishang Laojun (Thai Siong Lokun) *Very High Old Lord, name for Laozi* 太上老君

Taisheng Ye (Thai Seng Ia) *Great Saint* 太聖爺

Taisui *'Great Year,' head of the Ministry of Time* 太歲

Taizi Ye (Thaichu Ia) *Sir Crown Prince, a polite term of address for the Baby God, Shancai Tong* 太子爺

to (thoat) *escape* 脫

toukong (thaukhang) *empty head, a type of mediation practice* 頭空

tishen (thoesin) *replacement body* 替身

tieding yi (thihteng i) *iron-nail chair* 鐵釘椅

Tiandao Hui *Heavenly Dao Association* 天道會

tianfa (thi^n-e hoat) *heavenly law* 天法

Tiangong Tan (Thi^n kong Toa^n [Thnee Kong Thnua]) *Lord of Heaven Altar* 天宮壇

Tianhou (Thiansiong Sengbu) *Queen of Heaven* 天后(天上聖母)

tianli (thi^{n}e li) *the principle of heaven* 天理

Tiandi Hui *Heaven and Earth Society* 天地會

tiaotong (thiautong) *dance in trance* 跳佟; more commonly written as 跳童

tim Hu Ye, chi changming (*tim* Ho· Ia, ciah dngmia) *throw to the tiger god, 'eat' a long life* 虎爺 爺, 吃長命

Tongtian Jiaozhu *Influence-Heaven Sect Founder* 通天教主

tong *child, virgin* 童

tongzi *spirit medium* 童子

Tudi Gong (Tho·te Kong) *Lord of the Earth* 土地公

tuitong (thetang) *'withdraw,' fall out of trance* 退童

wanzi *Buddhist reverse swastika* 卍字

wangchuan (wangkang) *king's boat* 王船

Wangmu Niangniang (*Wangbu Niuniu*) 王母娘娘

wangye (ongia) *divine king* 王爺

wangen beiyi (pong-un boki) *ungrateful* 忘恩背義 [standard form: *wangen fuyi* 忘恩負義]

wenggong (angkong) *old or venerable lord, referring to deities* 翁公

wu *spirit medium, witch (literary Chinese)* 巫

wushi *spirit medium* 巫師

Wuchangbo (Botia^n Peh) *Inconstant Uncle* 無常伯

Wuji *Ultimate of Non-Being* 無極

Wuji Tianshu (*Bochi-e Thiansu*) *Non-Ultimate Heavenly Book* 無極天書

wuwei *non-striving* 無爲

wuyi (butgi) *unrighteous* 無義

wuxiao (but-hau) *unfilial* 無孝

wuzhong (buttiong) *disloyal* 無忠

wuzhong, wuyi (butdiong, butgi) *disloyalty and unjustness* 無忠，無義

Wulei Gong *Five Thunder Gods* 五雷公

Wulei Zushi *Five Thunder Patriarch-founder* 五雷祖師

xigua (sikoe) *watermelon,* 西瓜; *Hokkien* si *puns with* ci (si) *to dismiss or resign* 辭

Xitian (Sethian) *Western Heaven, Amitabha's Western Paradise* 西天

xia *chivalrous swordsman* 俠

xia (e) *below, inferior* 下

Xiansheng (Sinse^n) *Master* 先生

Xiantian Dadao *Great Way of Former Heaven* 先天大道

xian (sian) *immortal* 仙

Xiansi Shiye Miao (Sin Sze Si Ya) *Immortal Si and Lord Master Temple* 仙四師爺廟

xianzu (siancho·) *immortal ancestor* 仙祖

xian (ham) *power, force, awe; literally, a horse's bit* 銜

xiao (se) *small, lower status* 小

xiaodi (siuti) *younger brother(s)* 小弟

xiaoren (siaujin) *literally, 'small people,' enemies or detractors* 小人

xiao (hau) *filiality* 孝

xiao bei (chhio poe) *'laughing' answer given by divination blocks* 笑貝

xin buhui luan, shenqu you li (sim peiloan, sinkhu u lat) *[her] heart won't be troubled, [her] body will be strong* 心不會亂身軀有力

xin luan (sim loan) *heart troubled* 心亂

xinhun (simhun) *heart-soul* 心魂

xiudao (siuto) *keep the Dao* 修道

xiuxing (siuheng) *self-cultivation* 修行

xiuzheng (siucheng) *keep correctness, orthodoxy* 修正

xiudu (siuto·) *embroidered stomach[er]* 繡肚

Xuantian Shangdi *The Emperor of the Dark Heavens* 玄天上帝

xuedao (hakto) *mastering the dao* 學道

yapian xian (a-phian sian) *Opium Immortal* 鴉片仙

yang (iong) *male principle* 陽

Yang Jian (Iuⁿ Chen) *name of a three-eyed Chinese martial deity* 楊戩

Yi Guan Dao *Religion of One Unity* 一貫道

yiyang mi si baiyang ren (jit iuⁿ bi chhi pah iuⁿ lang) *The same rice nourishes one hundred types of person* 一樣米飼百樣人

Yijing (Iⁿ Keng) The Book of Changes 易經

yi (gi) *righteousness* 義

Yixing (Gi [Ghee] Hin) *Justice and Happiness [Society]* 義興

yin (im) *female principle* 陰

yin bei (im poe) *negative answer, given by block divination* 陰貝

yinhun (imhun) *yin soul* 陰魂

yinjian (imkan) *Hades, literally the 'yin space'* 陰間

youqiu biying (u-kiu pit-eng) *if you ask there will be a reply* 有求必應

yude (tutioh) *encounter, meet* 遇得

yuanfen (ianhun) *affinity* 緣分

Yuanshi Tianjun *The Primal Heavenly Lord* 元始天尊

yun (un) *luck* 運

yun an (un am) *luck dark* 運暗

yun buhao (un boho) *luck not good* 運不好

yun di (un ke) *low luck* 運低

yunqi (unkhi) *luck* 運氣

zhasin (keksim) *sorrowful* 扎心

Zhang Xianshi (Tiaoⁿ Sensu) *Immortal Master Chang* 張仙士

zhen *true* 真

Zhen Tiandao *True Heavenly Dao* 真天道

Zhenwu *The Perfected Warrior, a name for the Emperor of the Dark Heavens* 真武

zheng (cheng) *upright* 正

zhengjing (chengkeng) *honest, respectable* 正經

zhong (tiong) *middle, central* 中

Zhong Da (Tiong Toa) *Central Great One, Master Ooi's name for Nazha* 中大

Zhongtan Yuanshuai *Commander of the Central Altar (Nazha's title)* 中壇元帥

Zhongyang Yuanshuai *Central Commander-in-Chief (Nazha's title)* 中央元帥

zhou (chiu) *incantation* 咒

Zhu Wangye (Chu Ongia) *Crimson Divine King* 朱王爺

zhusha (chuse) *cinnabar, powder used to prepare red ink used by spirit mediums* 朱砂

zhushui (chusui) *vermillion ink* 朱水

Zhuxiang Ci *Greeting Incense Song* 祝香辭

zhuding (chutiaⁿ) *determined (by fate, heaven)* 註定

Zhusheng Niangniang (Chuse[n] Neoneo) *Goddess who Registers Birth* 註生娘娘
zhuangyi (chingay) *float procession* 妝藝
zu (cho·) *founder, ancestor* 祖
Zushi (Cho·su) *founder, patriarch* 祖師
Zushi Gong (Cho·su Kong) *Founder God* 祖師公
zuochan (chesian) *to meditate* 坐禪
zuodai (choephai[n]) *do bad, become involved in illegal activities* 做歹
zuo daode (choe totek) *seek moral perfection* 做道德
zuohao (choeho) *do good* 做好
zuoren (choelang) *be human* 做人

Index